WHY THE BIBLE BEGAN

Why did no other ancient society produce something like the Bible? That a tiny, out of the way community could have created a literary corpus so determinative for peoples across the globe seems improbable.

For Jacob Wright, the Bible is not only a testimony of survival, but also an unparalleled achievement in human history. Forged after Babylon's devastation of Jerusalem, it makes not victory but total humiliation the foundation of a new idea of belonging. Lamenting the destruction of their homeland, scribes who composed the Bible imagined a promise-filled past while reflecting deeply on abject failure. More than just religious scripture, the Bible began as a trailblazing blueprint for a new form of political community. Its response to catastrophe offers a powerful message of hope and restoration that is unique in the Ancient Near Eastern and Greco-Roman worlds.

Wright's Bible is thus a social, political, and even economic roadmap – one that enabled a small and obscure community located on the periphery of leading civilizations and empires not just to come back from the brink, but ultimately to shape the world's destiny. The Bible speaks ultimately of being a united yet diverse people, and its pages present a manual of pragmatic survival strategies for communities confronting societal collapse.

Jacob L. Wright is a professor of Hebrew Bible at the Candler School of Theology, Emory University. His first book, *Rebuilding Identity: The Nehemiah Memoir and Its Earliest Readers* (de Gruyter, 2004), won the 2008 Templeton Prize for a first book in the field of religion. He is also the author of *David, King of Israel, and Caleb in Biblical Memory* (Cambridge University Press, 2014), which won the Nancy Lapp Popular Book Award from the American Schools of Oriental Research, and most recently, *War, Memory, and National Identity in the Hebrew Bible* (Cambridge University Press, 2020).

WHY THE BIBLE BEGAN

An Alternative History of Scripture and Its Origins

Jacob L. Wright

Shaftesbury Road, Cambridge CB2 8EA, United Kingdom

One Liberty Plaza, 20th Floor, New York, NY 10006, USA

477 Williamstown Road, Port Melbourne, VIC 3207, Australia

314–321, 3rd Floor, Plot 3, Splendor Forum, Jasola District Centre, New Delhi – 110025, India

103 Penang Road, #05–06/07, Visioncrest Commercial, Singapore 238467

Cambridge University Press is part of Cambridge University Press & Assessment, a department of the University of Cambridge.

We share the University's mission to contribute to society through the pursuit of education, learning and research at the highest international levels of excellence.

www.cambridge.org
Information on this title: www.cambridge.org/9781108490931

DOI: 10.1017/9781108859240

First published 2023

Printed in the United Kingdom by TJ Books Limited, Padstow Cornwall

A catalogue record for this publication is available from the British Library

Library of Congress Cataloging-in-Publication Data
Names: Wright, Jacob L., author.
Title: Why the Bible began : an alternative history of scripture and its origins / Jacob L. Wright, Emory University.
Description: First edition. | Cambridge, United Kingdom ; New York, NY, USA : Cambridge University Press, [2023] | Includes bibliographical references and index.
Identifiers: LCCN 2022056302 (print) | LCCN 2022056303 (ebook) | ISBN 9781108490931 (hardback) | ISBN 9781108796682 (paperback) | ISBN 9781108859240 (epub)
Subjects: LCSH: Bible–History. | Jews–History–To 70 A.D.
Classification: LCC BS447 .W75 2023 (print) | LCC BS447 (ebook) | DDC 220.9–dc23/eng/20230418
LC record available at https://lccn.loc.gov/2022056302
LC ebook record available at https://lccn.loc.gov/2022056303

ISBN 978-1-108-49093-1 Hardback

In memory of my mother, whose untimely death ten years ago left an unfillable void.

Die großen Worte aus den Zeiten, da
Geschehn noch sichtbar war, sind nicht für uns.
Wer spricht von Siegen? Überstehn ist alles.
– Rainer Maria Rilke, *Requiem,* 1908

Contents

Figures

Maps

Acknowledgments

My objective in writing this book has been to demonstrate that the Bible's achievements as an innovative and ambitious "project of peoplehood" go unappreciated when readers reduce it to a moral guide (even for those who deem it a reliable one). I have many to thank for encouraging me to start the project and supporting me along the way. They include great mentors and colleagues such as Profs. Carol Newsom and Marc Brettler, and extraordinary students at the Candler School of Theology and Emory University. From the inception to the completion, the project owes much to the vision and wisdom of the indefatigable Beatrice Rehl of Cambridge University Press. Vinithan Sedumadhavan and his team, as well as Kaye Barbaro, provided excellent editorial oversight. The feedback from unnamed peer reviewers proved to be unusually rich and helpful. Likewise, the writings of Prof. Mark Brett have been productive stimulants for my thinking over the years. *Shukran* to "Abraham Kahn Amon," Thing Thing Lee, and Leslie Flores for their help in improving many chapters. Countless conversations with members from our Coursera course (www.coursera.org/learn/bible-history) have greatly enriched this work, and I look forward to learning from these new friends and acquaintances in the years ahead. Finally, it is a particular honor to acknowledge the contributions of Prof. Tamara Cohn Eskenazi, whose courage and "stubborn hope" stand out in our cynical age. Few scholars can read biblical texts as brilliantly as Prof. Eskenazi, and much of what is found on the following pages is indebted directly to conversations with her and her work.

Prologue

After a long and brutal siege, Babylon's armies finally conquered Jerusalem in the summer of 586 BCE – some 2,600 years ago. The famine had become unbearable for the city's inhabitants, and when Judah's king attempted to escape, enemy forces seized and sent him to Babylon bound in bronze fetters. Having already devastated the countryside, they proceeded to plunder the palace, torch the temple, and demolish many private homes. Much of the population had died from starvation and disease, while many others had fled to neighboring lands. Among the few who remained, the Babylonians exiled the elites, while executing those who organized the resistance to their rule.

To all appearances this was the end of a people who had flourished for many centuries. And it should have been the end: after imperial forces ravaged the region, Judah was destined to perish, along with the many other kingdoms that surrounded it.

But something surprising happened. Instead of vanishing from history, the vanquished gradually returned to their homeland, and under conditions of foreign rule, reconstituted their collective life. Without a king of their own, they built a new temple, even if it was not as grand as the one before. They also repaired Jerusalem's ramparts, restoring some semblance of their pride.

Their society was not what it once was. Without much of an infrastructure, and with a meager population, there was only so much they could achieve. Their resilience was nevertheless remarkable.

Yet what makes this historical moment truly momentous is what some in their midst achieved. Beset with many obstacles, and living in subsistence conditions, circles of scribes came together and created the most influential corpus of literature the world has ever known. Over the past two millennia, these writings have had an immeasurable impact in the realm of not only religion and theology but also politics, directly informing the way many communities across the globe think of themselves as "peoples" and "nations."

After being razed to the ground, Jerusalem joined a long line of conquered capitals. While some recovered from the destruction, many did not. But as far as we can tell, none responded by fashioning the kind of elaborate and enduring monument to *their own* downfall that Jews call the "Tanakh," Christians the "Old Testament," and academics the "Hebrew Bible."[1]

Most defeated populations viewed their subjugation as a source of shame; they consigned it to oblivion, opting instead to extol the golden ages of the past. In the biblical corpus, however, defeat's presence is all pervasive. The generations of anonymous scribes who curated these writings reflected, in various and sundry ways, upon their people's collective failures, gathering the fragments of their diverse pasts and weaving them into a sweeping story of one people. In this epic narrative, they embedded ideals and aspirations that could bring together rival groups and form from them vibrant, enduring communities. They also collected prophecies, songs, laments, and wisdom for the edification and instruction of all their members.

The thread that ties together this body of writings is a question that was trailblazing at the time: What does it mean to be a people? Not a kingdom, city, clan, empire, or ethnicity, but a people. In other words, a national community that embraces many different cities, clans, ethnicities, and so on, and that may have kingdoms in their collective past, but that now – thanks to a new self-understanding, survival strategies, and institutions – does not depend on territorial sovereignty or statehood.

Focused on this foundational question, the library of books that we know as the Bible stands apart from other ancient writings, and we are hard pressed to find anything similar even from later times. Moreover, in contrast to the archives that archeologists discover throughout ancient

[1] In what follows, I will usually refer to this corpus of writings simply as "the Bible." The best English rendering of this corpus is Robert Alter's three-volume *The Hebrew Bible: A Translation with Commentary*.

West Asia and North Africa, the biblical collection was transmitted from generation to generation for the past 2,500 years.

The Bible's extraordinary character and long history of transmission beg basic questions: To what end was this corpus created? And why does it have its origins in a remote region of the ancient world, rather than at the centers of civilization? After all, these world powers not only did much to develop systems of writing and techniques of text production, but also boasted a military superiority and administrative expertise that enabled them to establish world empires. How is it, then, that the literary legacies of these leading civilizations were completely forgotten, while a body of writings from a conquered and colonized community survived?

When I pose these questions in churches and synagogues, the response I most frequently receive is: "The Bible exists because God wanted to reveal divine truth to us." My aim is not to challenge this conviction. But just as a wildlife biologist would not be satisfied with the response, "the leopard has spots because God wanted it that way," so as a historian, I want to know the more immediate reasons why the Bible was written at this particular time and place.

When I ask these same questions in non-confessional and secular settings, many assume that 1) the Bible originated as religious scripture and 2) most ancient religions required scriptures. Both assumptions are demonstrably false. Much of the Hebrew Bible has very little to do with religion or theology, and ancient religions managed very well without holy writ. Priests and temple musicians may have occasionally consulted manuals and compendia, yet a sacred text was rarely central to their rites and rituals. Thus, the New Testament scholar Bart Ehrman observes:

> For modern people intimately familiar with any of the major contemporary Western religions (Judaism, Christianity, Islam), it may be hard to imagine, but books played virtually no role in the polytheistic religions of the ancient Western world. These religions were almost exclusively concerned with honoring the gods through ritual acts of sacrifice. There were no doctrines to be learned, as explained in books, and almost no ethical principles to be followed, as laid out in books.[2]

[2] Ehrman, *Misquoting Jesus*, 2005, p. 19.

Ehrman points out that Christianity and Islam would not be "religions of the book" were it not for the Hebrew Bible. In view of the revolutionary changes that this corpus introduced to the practice of religion, the mystery of its why and wherefore becomes all the more crucial for us to explore.

Even if one is convinced that the biblical corpus was intended from the beginning to serve as sacred scripture for a religious community, there can be no denying a basic fact: no one produced something like it. Neither small kingdoms nor superpowers that conquered those kingdoms devoted their energies to composing a body of literature that asks what it means to be a people without a palace. The existence of the Bible, therefore, cannot to be taken for granted. It is a big riddle, and one that scholars have been reluctant to tackle.

I must confess that the Bible is not always to my liking. It is difficult to countenance a collection of writings that, in one of its laws, mandates capital punishment for a rebellious child (Deuteronomy 21:18–21). Even so, I cannot help but appreciate the thoroughgoing manner with which biblical authors responded to defeat and destruction by advancing a demotic agenda that gives power to the people.

These authors were professional scribes, and having devoted their lives to texts, they were convinced that a rich and often contradictory corpus of writings – which includes stories and songs, wisdom and laws – could attract a readership beyond their scribal circles. Experience and intuition told them that writing technologies had a yet unimagined political potential. Although they may not (always) have been conscious of what they were doing, their collaborative efforts produced a new, and enduring, form of community.

Without a doubt, this body of writings belongs to humanity's greatest achievements. In comparison to imposing cities and temples that celebrate military might, the Bible constitutes a "movable monument," one that foregrounds political failure and military defeat while simultaneously celebrating the lives of common folk and their families. Whereas cities and temples eventually disintegrated in the sands of time (if they were not first demolished by their enemies), this literary monument became the cornerstone for world religions and political communities that still shape the course of history. In responding to catastrophe and rupture, its architects brought to light a new wisdom: the notion that a people is greater than the kings who govern it, and that a nation will survive conquest when all of its members can claim a piece of the pie and therefore have a reason to take an active part in its collective life.

Sixteen-hundred years before Edward Gibbon published *The Decline and Fall of the Roman Empire*, the Syrian satirist Lucian was already contemplating the extinction of ancient civilizations. Referring to what was once the world's largest city, he wrote in the second century CE: "Nineveh has already perished, and not a trace of it now remains. As for Babylon, the city of the magnificent towers and the great circuit-wall, soon it too will be like Nineveh, and men will look for it in vain."[3]

Kingdoms and empires come and go, yet some communities have managed to survive. Their stories demand our attention just as much as, if not more than, the military powers that have long preoccupied Western historians. This book explores how one ancient community, in the aftermath of defeat and devastation, reinvented itself, and in the process, discovered many survival strategies that we take for granted today – and many more that we have yet to learn.

FURTHER READING

Alter, Robert, *The Hebrew Bible: A Translation with Commentary*, W.W. Norton, 2018.

Cooper, Paul M.M., *fallofcivilizationspodcast.com*

Ehrman, Bart, *Misquoting Jesus: The Story behind Who Changed the Bible and Why*, Harper Collins, 2005.

Finegan, Jack, *The Archaeology of the New Testament: The Mediterranean World of the Early Christian Apostles*, Taylor & Francis, 2019.

Gibbon, Edward, *The History of the Decline and Fall of the Roman Empire*, Strahan & Cadell, 1776–1789.

Podany, Amanda, *Weavers, Scribes, and Kings: A New History of the Ancient Near East*, Oxford University Press, 2022.

[3] Lucian's *Charon* 23 quoted from Jack Finegan, *The Archaeology of the New Testament*, p. 21, with further references to Strabo and Pliny.

Introduction

IMPERIALISM AND THE "DISOVERY OF THE ORIENT"

Interpretation of the Bible has continued, without interruption, for more than two millennia, yet our understanding of its origins and teachings has dramatically expanded in recent times thanks to remarkable discoveries. Over the past century, methods of archeological research have reached impressive levels of sophistication, and excavation teams working at scores of sites throughout the Middle East continue to unearth all kinds of evidence for the communities that produced the Bible – their ways of life, their mechanisms for coping with crises, and the historical events that shaped their destinies.

Western interest in Eastern antiquity originally had very little to do with the Bible and a lot to do with imperial politics. In 1798, a French general named Napoleon Bonaparte and his "Army of the Orient" set sail for Egypt. With the goal of annexing the country and establishing a French presence in the region, Napoleon brought with him 167 scientists and scholars of all sorts and stripes. They mapped and sketched all they saw. They also collected and deported many objects back to Europe, and these artifacts of ancient empires had strategic, symbolic significance for Napoleon when he, in 1804, donned the mantle of "Emperor of the French."

The most important object deported from Egypt was an otherwise unremarkable stele inscribed with a decree from Ptolemy V in 196 BCE; today we know it as the "Rosetta Stone." The imperial powers of Europe fought over rights to this text because it held a key that unlocked ancient secrets: The inscription is rendered not only in Greek, but also in Demotic script and Egyptian hieroglyphs, and therefore scholars could use this "trilingual" to decipher the language of the dynasties that had ruled Egypt for millennia. Thanks to the Rosetta Stone, and the painstaking efforts of philologists, we can read the many writings that line the walls of Egyptian temples and palaces, as well as the precious caches of ancient papyri preserved by the arid North African climate.

Napoleon's voyages throughout the Middle East ignited Europe's imagination for years to come. Among the many colorful personalities of the following generation was an ambitious Englishman named Austen Henry Layard (1817–1894). Born in Paris, Layard grew up in Italy and began his travels in West Asia by the age of twenty-two. His original intention was to travel overland to Sri Lanka, but he eventually ended up in Mosul near the ancient site of Kuyunjik. Others had already been excavating at this site before his arrival, and as their finds were beginning to attract public attention, Layard was eager to stake a claim and make a name for himself. Beginning in 1845, he dug at both this site and nearby Nimrud, and within just two years, he managed to make astonishing progress. Not least he was able to identity Kuyunjik as the city of Nineveh, the capital of the formidable Assyrian Empire that conquered the kingdom of Israel in 722 BCE.

When Layard returned to England a couple years later, he promptly published a two-volume, highly romanticized, account of his voyages and discoveries (*Nineveh and Its Remains*, 1848–1849), which made him a household name. As one of the finest exemplars of English travel literature, the work begins:

> A deep mystery hangs over Assyria, Babylonia, and Chaldea. With these names are linked great nations and great cities dimly shadowed forth in history; mighty ruins, in the midst of deserts, defying, by their very desolation and lack of definite form, the description of the traveler; the remnants of mighty races still roving over the land; the fulfilling and fulfillment of prophecies; the plains to which the Jew and the Gentile alike look as the cradle of their race. After a journey in Syria, the thoughts naturally turn eastward; and without treading on the remains of Nineveh and Babylon our pilgrimage is incomplete.

Figure 0.1 Artist's impression of a hall in an Assyrian palace from *The Monuments of Nineveh by Sir Austen Henry Layard*, 1853.

With a pronounced penchant for self-promotion, and thanks to his own superb sketches of the finds that he published in a spectacular folio volume (*The Monuments of Nineveh – From Drawings Made on the Spot*, 1849), Layard was able to return to the region as an attaché of the British embassy. His excavations at Nineveh during this second excursion laid bare the remains of monumental palaces whose gates were guarded by massive sphinxes and whose walls were lined with stunning reliefs featuring a wide spectrum of scenes (Figure 0.1). Some depict lion hunting, others portray siege and deportation, but all celebrate the might of the great Assyrian Empire.

Layard shipped off the most impressive reliefs and statues to London. The British Museum displayed these exiled artifacts not only for the personal enjoyment of the thousands who visited the exhibits each week, but also for the political message they communicated to France and other colonialist competitors: Queen Victoria and the British Empire had discovered, and now possessed, the remains of what her historians billed as "the world's first empire." The sensational tidings took England by storm, and many eagerly awaited the daily reports, along with the drawings of the phenomenal finds, that appeared in newspapers (Figure 0.2).

184 THE ILLUSTRATED LONDON NEWS. [Feb. 28, 1852.

RECEPTION OF NINEVEH SCULPTURES AT THE BRITISH MUSEUM.

RECEPTION OF NINEVEH SCULPTURES AT THE BRITISH MUSEUM.

Amongst the recent arrivals from Nimroud, the most striking and important is a colossal Lion, the weight of which is upwards of ten tons.

PARIS FASHIONS FOR MARCH.

Commencer à commencement, it is a matter of difficulty to recommend this month as morning toilet, all the attention being centred on ball-dresses. The Carnival absorbs public attention, and dancing reigns

the second of net had teeth, edged with rings, linked one with the other; they were alternately of gold and white silk, that of the middle larger than the others, which diminished as they reached the upper part of the tooth. The Louis XV. body was trimmed in the same manner with blond, retained by rings of gold and silk. The head-dress was composed of bunches of gold ribbon and gold grapes.

Figure 0.2 Engraving from *Illustrated London News*, Feb. 28, 1852, showing a recent arrival from ancient Nineveh at the British Museum.

IMPERIAL ARCHIVES

In the long run, what turned out to be much more important than these magnificent monuments were piles of clay tablets that Layard's supervisor, Toma Shishman, unearthed in 1849. While Layard was away on business for a few days, Shishman and his crew continued excavating the palace of the Assyrian king Sennacherib (705–681 BCE) – the same ruler who besieged Jerusalem in a dramatic episode that figures prominently in the biblical narrative. As they proceeded through subterraneous passageways, they entered chambers whose floors were covered, over a foot-deep, with clay tablets, which bore neatly inscribed cuneiform writing.[1]

Layard's expedition had landed in what was once the state archive of the Assyrian Empire (Map 0.1). Although they had no doubt of the discovery's significance, little could they imagine just how important it was.

[1] Cuneiform refers to the "wedge-shaped" scripts in which many ancient West Asian texts were written. See Chapter 4 for more on their complexity and their relationship to Egyptian "hieroglyphs."

Map 0.1 The Assyrian Empire, *c.*700 BCE.
Map created by Gerry Krieg (kriegmapping.com).

Eager to capitalize on his fame, Layard returned to England soon thereafter to pursue a career as a politician. However, his lifelong friend – an oft-forgotten Assyrian-Christian named Hormuzd Rassam, who grew up just across the river in Mosul – would continue to excavate at Nineveh. Several years later, Rassam and his team found another archive, this one from Sennacherib's grandson Ashurbanipal (668–627 BCE).

Both archives came to be known as "The Royal Library of Ashurbanipal." Their 30,000 volumes, which are still being studied today, bear testimony to the erudition that Assyrian kings fostered by collecting both ancient writings and brilliant scholars to copy and study them. These collections have thoroughly reshaped our understanding of the world's oldest civilizations. Not only do they provide historical evidence for influential kingdoms that existed for millennia before Sennacherib and Ashurbanipal, but they also bear witness to a long tradition of innovative research in astronomy, medicine, and mathematics.[2]

This ancient "library" was not open to the public. Only a select few from the court were granted access, and they were required to swear allegiance to the throne. Closely related to its limited access is the cause of its destruction and rediscovery. As invading armies razed the capital to the ground in 612 BCE, they torched the palaces, and the blazing heat from the fires fossilized the clay tablets, baking them hard as bricks. Had it not been for these conflagrations, the texts would have disintegrated in the rubble long ago, and we would never have been able to recover them in modern times.

PARALLELS AND PARTICULARITY

Over the course of the nineteenth century, archeologists continued to discover other archives, while philologists decoded the demanding Assyrian and Babylonian languages in which their texts were written. As they began to make sense of their contents, they noticed many striking parallels to biblical writings.

The most famous of these discoveries was made in 1872 by a young man named George Smith. Born to a working-class family in Victorian England, Smith had a limited education and worked as an engraver. However, the finds from Nineveh were in the headlines when he was a teenager, and they captivated his imagination. Every spare moment he would spend reading and learning in the British Museum, and within just a few years, he became an expert – a truly incredible feat considering the complexity of the languages. Unsurprisingly, he caught the attention of a leading Assyriologist and eventually landed a position in the museum as a senior assistant.

While working through tablets that Rassam had found in the Ashurbanipal Library, Smith started noticing astonishing points of

[2] According to modern myth, many of the most important works from antiquity were lost when the Library of Alexandria was destroyed in a tragic conflagration. However, the library suffered from centuries of decline and any fires that the library endured were minimal. In contrast to that myth, the historic destruction of the Ashurbanipal Library had a real and profound impact on the future, with its extraordinary erudition lost to posterity.

overlap between one text and the biblical flood story. The parallels were indeed so stunning that in his excitement, he reportedly ran around the room, shouting in delight and shedding his clothes. A couple weeks later he brought his findings before the Society of Biblical Archaeology in the presence of the British prime minister.

The text turned out to be part of the now well-known Epic of Gilgamesh, which in its eleventh tablet tells of a cosmic flood that bears an uncanny resemblance to the biblical deluge in Genesis. The public interest in Smith's discovery was immense, and soon thereafter he left for Nineveh with funding from the *Daily Telegraph.* His mission was impossible: to find other parts of the flood story. Astoundingly, however, he succeeded. Within the shortest time, he managed to unearth not only more (and older) fragments of the flood story, but also ancient texts with remarkable parallels to biblical writings.

In his *Assyrian Discoveries* from 1875, Smith summarized his sensational success with surprising sobriety:

> The light already thrown by the Assyrian inscriptions on Biblical history forms one of the most interesting features in cuneiform inquiry, and there can be no question that further researches will settle many of the questions still in doubt, and give us new information in this field, of an important character.[3]

Soon thereafter Smith published *The Chaldean Account of Genesis* (1876), a book that invites its readers to compare, side-by-side, biblical and Babylonian texts. It was this work that, more than any other from the burgeoning field of "Assyriology," rocked the world of Christians and Jews.[4]

In 1902 the Assyriologist Friedrich Delitzsch (whose brother had translated Smith's book into German) gave a lecture in the presence of the German emperor Willhelm II, arguing that the Jewish religion, and the Old Testament upon which it is founded, derives from Babylonian roots. A year later he lectured again, causing a stir with his claim that Babylonian-Assyrian civilization was culturally, morally, and religiously

[3] Smith, *Assyrian Discoveries*, pp. 448–449.

[4] It was also this work that, some 125 years later, caught my attention as a teenager, who, similar to Smith, was working full time and studying at a city college; in fact, it prompted me to change my major from medicine to history and, casting caution to the wind, embark on a career in the humanities.

superior to Judaism and the Old Testament. Delitzsch maintained that both are little more than a pathetic pastiche of Babylonian-Assyrian ideas, and later he made a plea for expunging the Old Testament from Christian liturgy and theology.

Today Assyriologists continue to mine the Ashurbanipal Library and other archives for precious data pertaining to ancient Near Eastern empires and the populations they conquered. Questions about the influence of these cultures on the Bible's formation – and by extension, about the uniqueness of its thought and theology – continue to play a central role in research. Strangely, however, the most obvious facets of the Bible's distinctiveness have yet to be seriously appreciated:

1. Why did no one attempt to rescue precious works from the Ashurbanipal Library when enemies stormed the city in 612 BCE?
2. Why did we have to wait thousands of years for Layard, Rassam, and others to discover the fossilized literary remains of the formidable empire that conquered Israel and destroyed much of Judah?
3. Why, during all those years, have biblical writings enjoyed an ongoing reception among diverse communities of readers?

We might assume that the Bible's preservation is simply a result of Christianity's ascendancy. However, Christianity began as a sect that emerged from a new interpretation of the Jewish Scriptures. Were power the determining factor, we would have difficulty explaining why such a tiny population as the Jews, despite facing persistent Christian persecution, have survived for millennia, along with their myriad tomes of texts that interpret the Bible.

The question I am posing here is not about Christian triumph or Jewish survival, but about the biblical writings themselves. Had they not been handed down from generation to generation for 2,500 years, and had modern archeologists discovered them in their excavations of ancient sites, they would still be distinctive.

The texts we recovered from ancient West Asia and North Africa are, with few exceptions, palace and temple productions. While the biblical corpus contains many parallels to these excavated texts, what distinguishes it is how they have been reframed and reformulated to address the concerns of a new kind of political community.

Indeed, biblical writings represent one of the earliest and most elaborate projects of peoplehood. Working after the defeat of their kingdoms, their authors expanded inherited traditions with wider, and often competing, perspectives as they sought to consolidate what may be properly called a *nation*.

The question then is: Why? Why do we have a Bible. And why did it originate among a marginal population rather than at the center of ancient civilizations?

Many books on the Bible seek to answer the other "Four Ws" that guide the work of historians – the *Who*, the *What*, the *When*, and the *Where*? Thus, one of the best-selling works of all time in biblical studies addresses the question *Who Wrote the Bible?* Other works, whether they are written for popular or academic audiences, focus on the Bible's historicity, the moral dilemmas and ethical issues it poses for modern readers, the literary qualities of its various genres, the lives and afterlives of individual figures from its narratives, or particular themes and teachings (very often of a theological nature).

These are all undeniably important subjects, and they deserve serious attention. Yet after we have addressed the *Who*, the *What*, the *When*, and the *Where*, we are still left with the *Why*. This is perhaps the most intriguing problem, and it is certainly the most difficult one.

THE BIRTH OF RELIGION

"Why, beginning from approximately the same starting point, did Israelite history end at a very different place from, say, their Moabite neighbors?" These are the words of Julius Wellhausen (1844–1918), one of the most incisive and influential biblical scholars to have ever lived. He is also one of the few to have appreciated the significance of the *why*-question.

Wellhausen thought the question, or "riddle," was ultimately unanswerable; nevertheless, he deemed it possible to describe, "in spirit and in truth," a series of transitions "from paganism to rational worship." The German scholar began by demonstrating that ancient Israel was essentially the same as its neighbors, in both its political constitution and its religious practices. What created the conditions for the Bible and its distinctive perspectives was the rise of a new superpower: the Assyrians.

Before this empire arrived on the scene, ancient Palestine had witnessed a host of petty kingdoms fighting and making peace with one another, but otherwise paying no heed to anything beyond their horizon. Yet now Assyria's unprecedented military might and global ambitions forced these kingdoms to come to terms with the alarming prospect that their days were numbered:

> [The Assyrians] destroyed peoples as if they were nests, and as one gathers eggs, they collected the treasures of the world. No flapping of the wings, no opening of the beak or chirping helped. They crushed the national individualities of antiquity, they tore down the fences in which these nations nourished their customs and beliefs. They commenced the work which was carried on by the Babylonians, Persians, and Greeks, and completed by the Romans. They introduced into the history of nations a new factor, that of the world empire or, more generally, the world.[5]

Why then did Israel survive? Wellhausen assigned credit first and foremost to prophets such as Amos and Hosea. These prescient and original thinkers responded to the imperial onslaught by declaring that Yhwh had determined to make an end of his people, and that Assyria was the divine instrument of judgment.[6] By separating Yhwh from the nation, and by allowing Yhwh to "triumph over Israel through Assyria," they allowed the nation to be destroyed and rescued religion. The foreign empire had purged Israel of their national identity and created "an unpolitical and artificial construct" called Judaism:

> Through its destruction at the hands of the Assyrians and Babylonians, the nation became essentially a religious community held together by the cult. The precondition for this religious community was foreign control, which forced Jews from the political sphere into the spiritual.[7]

[5] Wellhausen, *Israelitische und jüdische Geschichte*, p. 114. All translations of Wellhausen's writings are my own. For a fuller discussion of these passages, see Wright, *War, Memory, and National Identity*, pp. 1–10 and 248–250.

[6] Yhwh is the name of the national deity in the Bible; it is pronounced "Yahweh" but usually translated in English Bible versions as "LORD" or "Jehovah."

[7] Wellhausen, *Israelitische und jüdische Geschichte*, p. 22.

In a world ruled by empires, Wellhausen insisted, there could be no nations, only religions. Even so, the religion of the Bible was not what it once was; it had evolved from "its original and natural role" that it had long played during the period of statehood. The symbiosis of the national and the spiritual ceased, and in the process, religious life assumed a rational, legalistic, monotone character.

In espousing these views, Wellhausen was taking aim at the Christian church much more than at Judaism. Living after the Napoleonic and the Franco-Prussian Wars that catalyzed Germany's national unification, he harbored a deep antipathy for multinational empires and the ("rational") religions they created. Christians, he believed, should possess a "natural fatherland in the nation." The Church still had a role to play, namely to prepare "an inner unity of practical conviction" and awaken "a sentiment, first in small circles, that we belong to each other." Early in his career, Wellhausen decided that he, in good conscience, could no longer prepare pastors for ministry and left the theological faculty.

PEOPLES AND NATIONS

Biblical scholars today work in Wellhausen's wake. In England and America, his dating of the Bible's sources aroused vociferous reactions from both clergy and scholars, and they continue to do so in some circles. Yet many embrace, often unknowingly, his claim that defeat brought an end to the national community and replaced it with a religion.

Colleagues in my field commonly refer to the community envisioned in the Bible as "Yahwists" and speak of the Bible as the scriptures of a religion called "Yahwism." This understanding is informed not only by Wellhausen but also by a longstanding Christian confessional approach, one that (often unconsciously) uses the category of religion to establish continuity between the national-political community of the Hebrew Bible and the transnational faith-community of the New Testament.

While Wellhausen did much to advance our understanding of the Bible and its origins, he was deeply misguided, I maintain, when it came to interpreting his findings. Rather than stripping Israel of its political character and reducing it to a religious sect, the biblical authors were creating the first nation. They responded to military defeat by demonstrating that their vanquished communities could, even without a king, still be a diverse and dispersed, yet unified, people.

The biblical writings articulated a new model of political community, one that we will call "peoplehood." As these writings came to be circulated across the globe, the model was repeatedly adopted and adapted in projects of national unification, with populations coming together as peoples to counter Europe's imperialist expansion.

What we witness in the Bible, then, is the genesis of a nation, not its death and replacement by religion. Of course, rituals and religious activities play an important part in this project of peoplehood, but in reducing the complexity of the biblical corpus to the realm of the spiritual, scholars have disregarded its most distinctive and important political innovations.

In this book, I claim that the Hebrew Bible represents the first attempt in world history to construct what we may properly call a "national identity." Many historians insist that the nation is a product of modernity, but I find their arguments to be (often severely) myopic.

A state may be defined as a polity with institutions of government and a territory that can be conquered and destroyed. Nation, by contrast, is a political community held together by shared memories and a will to act in solidarity. It is fundamentally a work of the collective imagination – a state of mind.

A nation may lay claim to a homeland, but it does not have to occupy it. Its corporate identity may have originated in the context of a unified state, but it does not currently have to possess statehood (a "stateless nation"). In fact, a national consciousness may emerge among its members after the demise of statehood or among populations of neighboring states who consider themselves to be "one people."

I use the term nation in the sense of a (diverse) political community whose members share a culture and a collective consciousness. In some cases, such as in that of biblical "Israel," they may also self-identify by a collective proper name, cultivate memories of an ancestral land, abide by established legal traditions, expect solidarity and loyalty, follow a communal calendar, celebrate public festivals, create (competing) narratives of their collective past, immerse themselves in a literary canon, and so on.

Many biblical scholars prefer to use the term "ethnic," rather than "national," when describing the corporate identity of the people of Israel on display in biblical texts. I find this usage confusing inasmuch as a nation may, and often does, include multiple ethnicities. Thus, for ancient Israel, the Transjordanian communities were ethnically distinct from communities in the Negev or in the central hill country (see Map 4.1 on page 62).

Ethnicities are tangible, often involving distinct dress, diet, dialect, endogamous marriage, and so on. Nations, in contrast, are abstract and volitional. They depend on an *esprit de corps* and a collective consciousness among their members, even if that consciousness is often feeble and fails to mobilize (coherent) collective action. As mental constructs, nations need narratives, and in this respect, the Bible offers us a powerful case study.

STRUCTURE OF THE BOOK

In what follows we explore the Bible's origins and purpose – as well as its capacity to endure – by means of a fourfold exposition.

Our story begins with a survey of the world in which the earliest biblical writings emerged. A wealth of archaeological discoveries now challenges earlier theories while also helping us appreciate the creative contributions of the biblical authors. In Part I, we will trace, simultaneously, two separate narratives: the biblical *story* beginning with Abraham and Sarah, and the *history* of a strip of land that connected the world's oldest centers of civilization. As we learn about the dramatic rise and fall of two neighboring kingdoms (Israel in the North and Judah in the South), we will see that the biblical narrative and historical data often agree. But in many cases, the archeological record tells a very different story, and in examining where it diverges from the biblical narrative, we will begin to understand what the motivated the earliest biblical writers.

Part II starts with the survivors from the Southern kingdom of Judah as they struggled to express their outrage over the suffering and humiliation that foreign armies had inflicted on them. Protest, lament, and prophetic words of comfort paved the way for an otherwise unknown figure and his insistence that the survivors begin to rebuild their ruins. As various groups came together to take on modest construction projects, restoring the remains of what their kings had built long ago, they slowly began to realize that they could still be a people in an age of imperial rule. This new community in the South began to think more deeply about their past and the catastrophic rupture that divided them from a more glorious era. They also thought about their relationship to a closely related yet competing community in the North that was reconstituting itself from the former kingdom of Israel. Both sets of questions – 1) what is the continuity between past and present? and 2) what do South and North have in common? – propelled the next stage of the Bible's formation. As scribes collected and combined disparate writings, a wider public slowly embraced them, laying the foundation for the emergence of a "People of the Book."

In Part III, we study scribal efforts to produce a majestic literary monument to Israel's downfall, one beginning with the creation of the world and the liberation of their ancestors from bondage in Egypt. Defeat looms large in this narrative, which introduces a distinction between the nation (or the people) and the state that would become central to modern political thought. We will also see how prophetic messages of doom demolished the foundations of ancient kingdoms and empires, and in so doing, laid the cornerstone for a new covenantal order. Finally, we will consider how by inserting divine laws, scribes transformed what was once a descriptive account of the past into a prescriptive roadmap for the future. The text was henceforth sacred, authoritative scripture since it now contained the deity's verbatim instructions.

Finally, Part IV explores the survival strategies that the last generations of biblical scribes implanted in their corpus. The matters they addressed include new public roles for women, ideals of heroism, relations to outsiders, martyrdom and eternal life, open access, and separation of powers. These scribes created a "Songbook for the Nation" by collecting psalms and laments from both the North and South. They reshaped a body of elite courtly wisdom, making it foundational for the entire nation. They addressed questions of "the one and many" and showed that their people could not flourish without fostering an egalitarian love among couples.

In the end, these final generations of biblical writers made a surprising move: they produced books and texts that encouraged their readers to challenge teachings that their predecessors had developed over centuries. They were convinced that pushback and protest make a system more flexible and resilient. Only when their communities, as a "People of Protest," felt empowered to evaluate and critique their teachings, would they fully appreciate both their merits and their limitations.

At the heart of our story are nameless scribes. They did not live in the same place, or even at the same time. Some were working for kings (both their own and the rulers of neighboring states); others served in the temple or in the imperial administration, writing for their communities in their spare time. The genres they adopted range from historical narrative and law to lyric and lament, from courtly instruction to love poetry. They often differed with each other, even on substantial matters. But what they all had in common was the same set of questions: Who are we? How do we survive in a world ruled by empires, and in which we are the underdogs? Can we still be a people without kings to define our destiny? And what does it even mean to be a people?

In wrestling with such questions, these ancient writers did not tell stories about themselves or even take credit for their work, as the authors of ancient Greece and Rome did. Remaining anonymous, they directed their readers' attention to a wide range of figures in their national history, both real and imagined. It was their stories that they deemed most important.

Nevertheless, we will learn much about the scribes who crafted and curated the collection of writings we know as the Bible. We will explore where their ancestors came from, what they experienced as part of their communities, how they coped with their tragic fate, and what motivated their collaborative efforts. We will also learn how they thought about a wide range of weighty matters, how they both dissented from and dialogued with each other, how they concretely contributed to each other's work, and how their ideas evolved over time.

In keeping with the way these generations of nameless scribes focused on the lives of others, I begin each chapter with biblical personalities (both archetypal and average), whose stories illustrate the respective theme. Each chapter concludes with references to the wonderful scholarship that informed my research – and that I encourage readers to explore for themselves.

FURTHER READING

Anderson, Benedict, *Imagined Communities: Reflections on the Origins and Spread of Nationalism*, Verso, 1991 (1983).

Berti, Monica and Naether, Franziska, "The Digital Rosetta Stone Project," https://rosetta-stone.dh.uni-leipzig.de/rs/team/

Cornell, Collin, "What happened to Kemosh," *Zeitschrift für die alttestamentliche Wissenschaft* 128, 2016, pp. 1–16.

Darmosch, David, *The Buried Book: The Loss and Rediscovery of the Great Epic of Gilgamesh*, Holt, 2007.

Friedman, Richard Elliott, *Who Wrote the Bible*, Simon & Schuster, 1987.

Greenfeld, Liah, *Nationalism: Five Roads to Modernity*, Harvard University Press, 1992.

Kohn, Hans, *The Idea of Nationalism*, Macmillan, 1944.

Kubie, Nora Benjamin, *Road to Nineveh: The Adventures and Excavations of Sir Austen Henry Layard*, Doubleday, 1964.

Kurtz, Paul Michael, *Kaiser, Christ, and Canaan: The Religion of Israel in Protestant Germany, 1871–1918*, Mohr Siebeck, 2018.

Lehman, Reinhard G., *Friedrich Delitzsch und der Babel-Bibel-Streit*, Vandenhoeck and Ruprecht, 1994.

Lepore, Jill, *This America: The Case for the Nation*, Liveright, 2019.

Morgenstern, Mira, *Conceiving a Nation: The Development of Political Discourse in the Hebrew Bible*, Pennsylvania State Press, 2009.

Smith, Anthony, *The Antiquity of Nations*, Polity, 2004.

Smith, George, *Assyrian Discoveries: An Account of Explorations and Discoveries on the Site of Nineveh, during 1873 and 1874*, Scribner, Armstrong & Co., 1875.

Strathern, Paul, *Napoleon in Egypt*, Bantam, 2008.

Taylor, Jonathan, "The Ashurbanipal Library Project," http://oracc.museum.upenn.edu/asbp/

Wellhausen, Julius, *Israelitische und jüdische Geschichte*, De Gruyter, 2004 (1894).

Part I
The Rise and Fall

OUR POINT OF DEPARTURE FOR THIS BOOK is the question why we have a Bible. We will attend to the who, the what, the when, and the where. But our larger concern is why it all began – and why it began in places that were off the beaten path rather than at the centers of ancient civilization. Our answer to that question will involve two primary factors: 1) political *division* and 2) military *defeat*. Without the relationship between a pair of closely related kingdoms, and without their devastating destruction and downfall, we would not have a Bible. In the chapters of Part I that follow, we explore where these two kingdoms emerged, whether they were ever united, what they achieved, and how they perished.

We begin, in Chapter 1, with an introduction to the worlds of ancient West Asia, North Africa, and the strip of land (Canaan) that connected them where the Bible took shape. Chapters 2 and 3 treat Egypt's imperial interests in Canaan, demonstrating how the collapse of impressive civilizations created the conditions for territorial states to take shape there. Chapters 4 and 5 show how an unsung and often vilified dynasty built a powerful kingdom in the region, and how that kingdom (Israel) exerted great influence over a smaller kingdom (Judah) on its southern border. In Chapter 6 we study how the Assyrian Empire conquered the kingdom of Israel, making it possible for Judah to usurp its position and lay claim to its culture. Finally, Chapters 7 and 8 trace the heights that this new kingdom reached before it too faced a catastrophic end at the hand of imperial armies.

1

Abraham and Sarah

From One to the Many

Go from your country,
and from your kindred, and your father's house,
to the land that I will show you.
I will make of you a great nation.
I will bless you and make your name great.
And you will be a blessing.
– Genesis 12:1–3

SO BEGINS THE STORY OF A FAMILY. Destiny calls, even if the destination is unknown. Abraham, the recipient of this promise, is a man in his nineties. He and his wife Sarah are also childless. How then could they be the progenitors of a great nation?

Land, nation, name – these are marks that distinguish mighty monarchs. But Abraham is not being commissioned to reign as a king. His mandate is simply to leave his home, travel to a new country, and become a father there. Such is the prosaic, unheroic fashion in which the biblical story begins.

When Abraham is told to go, he goes, no questions asked. Yet as the account unfolds, this character will prove to be more complex, more conflicted, than the recollection of him as an unflinching "man of faith." Just ten verses later, he appears as a craven narcissist, claiming that Sarah is his sister, not his wife, and allowing the pharaoh to bring her into his household. It will take trials and tribulations before he grasps that the promise depends not just on him but also on Sarah. Her contribution to the project is indispensable.

These details from the book of Genesis expose a vulnerable old man and woman making their way in a precarious world. This is not the stuff that legends are made of. Where are the larger-than-life figures who perform mighty deeds of valor? Such heroic lore is what we would expect for the beginning of a great national saga.

But what a fitting way to begin the *biblical* story. This couple could not have imagined that they would give birth to a child in their old age, and that their descendants, a millennium later, would follow in their footsteps – packing their bags, leaving the prosperity of the East, and making the same long, dusty trek to a stony strip of land, far removed from the centers of civilization.

The voyage of that future generation was different from the one Abraham and Sarah had embarked on. As members of war-torn and exiled communities, they were now returning to a humble habitation in the hill country that had long been their beloved homeland. It was there that their ancestors had built kingdoms that had flourished for centuries, and it was there that they would build a new life after those kingdoms had been destroyed. In the process of restoring their ruins, they would collect broken shards from their past – ancestral lore, royal legends, legal codes, prophecies, poetry, and proverbs – and create what continues to be, now after more than 2,500 years, the most extraordinary and consequential body of literature in human history.

TWO CENTERS OF CIVILIZATION

The story of Abraham and Sarah takes the reader to three intersecting regions that will shape both this family's future and the Bible's formation: 1) West Asia where this aged couple starts out; 2) North Africa where they and their descendants will sojourn in times of famine; and 3) a narrow strip of land connecting them that the Bible calls Canaan.[1] It is this third region where, in the biblical account, Abraham and Sarah establish a family that evolves into the diverse nation whose tumultuous history lies at the heart of our story.

[1] All three areas are known in Arabic as the *Mashriq* ("region of the rising sun") and are often called the "(Ancient) Near East" in English.

Canaan is home to some of the earliest settlements from our species. For example, Jericho, located a few miles to the north of Jerusalem, is one of the world's oldest cities. Some 12,000 years ago, at the beginning of the Holocene period, populations from far and wide migrated to its water source, a spring called Ein es-Sultan. Over the following millennia, the groups that settled there erected the monumental walls that figure prominently in the Bible and in the African American spiritual that the Bible inspired: *Joshua fought the battle of Jericho . . . and the walls came tumbling down.*

While other Canaanite cities emerged early in human history, this region was not home to the most formidable and enduring centers of ancient civilization. This is not where we witness the construction of pyramids and ziggurats, the organization of massive armies, or the invention of sophisticated writing systems. To find these civilizational achievements, we must look elsewhere – to places that boasted more abundant water sources than the modest spring that fed Jericho.

As archeologists in the nineteenth century began to excavate in the Middle East, they discovered the remains of improbably complex and innovative societies, which dated back thousands of years. The grandeur of a mighty civilization came to light in what the Greeks called *Mesopotamia* (literally "the land between rivers"). Some six millennia ago, massive cities rose there between two rivers: the Tigris and Euphrates. This area overlaps with what is today Iraq, Kuwait, and the north-eastern section of Syria.

While Mesopotamia may be home to the oldest West Asian civilizations, competitors would soon emerge in North Africa. Thanks to the Nile's fructifying waters, populations began settling in prehistoric times in what would become known as Egypt, and in the coming millennia, they would achieve incredible architectural feats that still astonish us in the twenty-first century CE.

In times of hardship and famine, the Nile Delta offered sanctuary and sustenance to surrounding populations, and it continued to be a place of refuge over the course of its long history. The Egyptologist Donald Redford notes with respect to the constant incursions of foreign groups:

> Egypt at all periods acted like a magnet on its neighbors. To people like those in [Canaan] whose prime concerns centered on the uncertainty of

> the harvest and the ever-present prospect of starvation, the constancy and super-abundance of Egypt's grain production and the richness of its stock of fish, fowl and wild game could scarcely be resisted. Better to live a well-fed factor in Egypt than die a starving "free man" on the steppes of Asia. Whether emigrating voluntarily, or sold by their village headman, or yet again captured in battle, it is doubtful whether any of the Asiatics [ending up in Egypt] regretted their fate.[2]

The book of Genesis reflects Egypt's historic role. As soon as Abraham and Sarah arrive in Canaan, they face a drought and famine, and to save their lives, they seek refuge in a region with a stable water supply. Mesopotamia, their place of origin, was far away and required a perilous trek. Therefore, they make their way down to Egypt and wait out the famine. (This is also when Abraham attempts to pass off Sarah as his sister.) Genesis concludes with Abraham and Sarah's grandchildren and great-grandchildren facing another famine in Canaan and migrating again to Egypt in search of food. In the book of Exodus, which follows Genesis, they face persecution from a new pharaoh and, after being divinely delivered, return to Canaan.

While Mesopotamia's magnificent cities had to rely on irrigation, Egypt could count on the Nile flooding its banks every year, leaving rich silt on the surrounding plain. The very different rhythms of Egypt's and Mesopotamia's rivers shaped the contrasting political structures and worldviews of the competing civilizations that grew up around them.

But water was not the only reason for the rise of these superpowers; the ability to record and communicate complex information was crucial. Many centuries of experimentation produced two elaborate writing systems: cuneiform in Mesopotamia and hieroglyphics in Egypt. The former is likely older, and thanks to archeological discoveries, we can watch the texts slowly evolve from simple accounting receipts with rudimentary syntax, to elaborate literary productions.

Compared with the many other early innovations, this one was arguably the most important. Writing systems made it easier to manage workforces, command armies, administer economies, petition gods,

[2] Redford, *Egypt, Canaan, and Israel in Ancient Times*, p. 54.

and commemorate rulers. Thanks to their capacity to govern larger populations, the civilizational centers evolved into fearsome empires whose armies campaigned far and wide. Their conquest of two remote kingdoms in the mid-first millennium BCE would, however, pave the way for a new application of writing technologies.

TWO KINGDOMS

The vast Arabian Desert that separates Mesopotamia from Egypt is treacherous to traverse. Therefore, when Mesopotamian traders, emissaries, and armies set out for Egypt, they usually headed northwards to Syria and then descended southward until they reached the Nile Delta. This is the route that Abraham and Sarah take in the biblical story.

The corridor between the Mediterranean coast and the desert was known as Canaan; in modern times, it came to be called Palestine or the Southern Levant. This fertile region functioned as a land-bridge connecting the centers of civilization in Mesopotamia and Egypt (Map 1.1). As a passageway for superpowers, the Southern Levant was also a popular battlefield, and it was there that imperial armies (both ancient and modern) repeatedly came to blows.

At the intersection of the mightiest civilizations, this was a region in which not only many political futures were decided but also the Bible was born. The populations that inhabited the Levant three thousand years ago formed kingdoms that competed with each other for centuries. But as imperial powers consolidated in Mesopotamia, they inevitably set their sights on Egypt. Advancing across the Levantine land-bridge toward this ancient civilization, they destroyed the kingdoms that stood in their way.

The composition of the Bible takes its point of departure from the trauma that imperial armies inflicted on two of these kingdoms. One, called Israel (or the "Northern kingdom"), was a leading power in the region. The other, called Judah (or the "Southern kingdom"), was inferior in size, natural resources, and military strength. It long languished in Israel's shadow, answering to their neighbor's beck and call for much of its history.

The two kingdoms were relatively short-lived, being subjugated by superpowers from Mesopotamia. Israel was conquered first, after existing

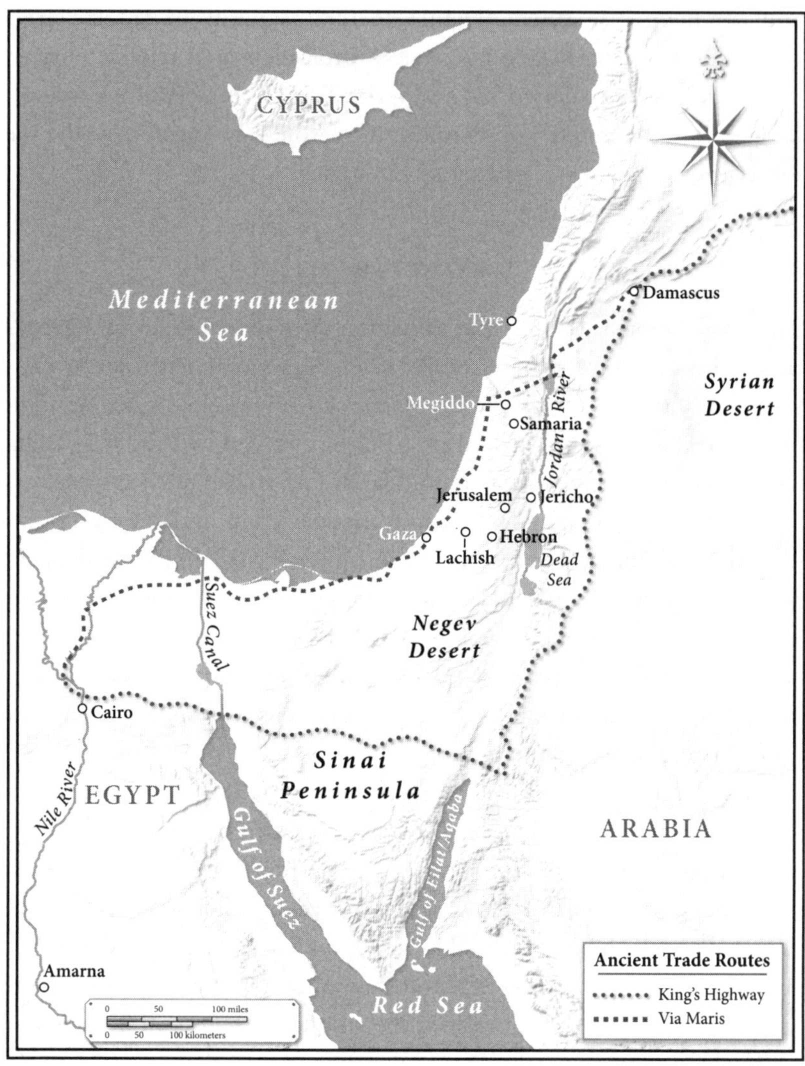

Map 1.1 The Levantine "land-bridge" connecting Mesopotamia to Egypt. Map created by Gerry Krieg (kriegmapping.com).

for just two centuries. Judah managed to escape its neighbor's fate and endured for another 135 years. During those years, it rose to prominence and exerted its influence throughout the region, and as it did, it laid claim to Israel's venerable culture and identity.

If location is everything, Israel and Judah were not predestined for greatness. Although they would later expand, their core territories were just a small part of the Levant. On the periphery of the periphery, they lived in land-locked enclaves, up in the hill country, far removed from the major urban centers in Egypt and Mesopotamia. These two inland kingdoms never managed to build naval fleets, and the main trade routes of the region skirted their borders.[3]

Even if they lay off the beaten path, Israel's and Judah's location on the Levantine land-bridge shaped their destinies. Imperial forces confronted each other on their borders, and when these two kingdoms entered the fray, they did not escape unscathed. Slowly but surely, the superpowers crushed them in military contests and forced them to forfeit their sovereignty.

The scribes who shaped the biblical writings portrayed this imperial subjugation as divine judgment and made it the lens through which they scrutinized their past. As we shall see, the extraordinary attention that these scribes paid to their people's defeat – their willingness to admit and own it, rather than to negate or diminish it – goes a long way toward explaining why we have a Bible today.

THE BIBLICAL NARRATIVE

In the biblical narrative, the family of Abraham and Sarah evolves gradually into a diverse people or nation. After escaping from bondage in Egypt, the nation eventually forms a kingdom, which after just one generation, breaks apart into two rival states, Israel and Judah:

- Abraham and Sarah have a grandson called Jacob, whose name is later changed to Israel.
- Jacob/Israel is the father of twelve sons, and the entire family migrates to Egypt to survive a famine in Canaan.
- In Egypt, the family grows into a large people, with each son becoming a large tribe. Perceiving their prodigious size as a threat, a pharaoh subjects them to bondage and eventually genocide.

[3] One of these routes was the Via Maris ("Way of the Sea"), which ran along the Mediterranean coast where Tel Aviv and Gaza are located today; another was the "King's Highway," which passed along the eastern side of the Jordan River (see Map 1.1).

- After being liberated during the exodus, the tribes of Israel return to their homeland in Canaan.
- There, during the days of David and his son Solomon, they establish a kingdom, which is also called Israel.
- After Solomon's death, that kingdom splits into two: one in the North that retains the name Israel, and the other in the South that is called Judah.
- These kingdoms last for several centuries before being conquered. The Northern kingdom first falls to the Assyrian Empire, and later the Babylonians conquer the Southern kingdom.

This synopsis represents a gross simplification of the complex account that the Bible provides for the origins and demise of the Northern and Southern kingdoms. If the details are fuzzy, do not dismay: the storyline will become clearer as we survey it in the coming chapters of Part I.

As we proceed, it is important that we bear in mind the two, very different, meanings of the name "Israel." One refers to the Northern kingdom, and the other to the nation (the "Israelites") that descended from Abraham and Sarah. This distinction is crucial to understanding the Bible's origins – and to appreciating its vision for a new kind of political community.

The biblical narrative, which begins with the creation of the world in Genesis and ends with the destruction of Jerusalem in the book of Kings, evolved over the ages from smaller, originally independent pieces. Generations of anonymous scribes collected these pieces, embroidered them with new details, and wove them into an elaborate literary tapestry. This work narrates the histories of the two kingdoms, Israel and Judah, portraying their tragic ends. As it does, it blends their separate stories, setting them in relation to an earlier "United Monarchy" from the time of David and Solomon, and beyond that, to a nation that evolved from a single, extended family, beginning with Abraham and Sarah.

As readers, we follow the biblical story from the evolution of a family to the emergence of two kingdoms. But as historians, we begin with these two kingdoms and work backwards, examining how the biblical writers imagined a common past that long antedates these kingdoms. And what we discover is that at the beginning, there was not one family or one nation, as the Bible portrays it, but a wide array of unrelated clans that would later populate these two kingdoms. In their efforts to consolidate the populations of the two defeated states, the biblical writers traced the diverse clans back to common ancestors. Which explains why their work attends so closely to the lives of families and communities, and why it continues to speak to readers today.

Much of what became the biblical narrative originated in the Northern kingdom of Israel. After its downfall, scribes constructed a past of peoplehood that long preceded the palace. These are moving tales of a family becoming a nation, and of liberated slaves making their way as refugees to a new land. Although Northern scribes drafted early versions of these tales, much of their poignancy and power is due to the work of Southern scribes who created a larger "National Narrative" by connecting the competing histories of Israel and Judah. The Bible as we know it is therefore a work from Northern writers that has been filtered through, and decisively shaped by, the experience of Southern writers.

If it had not been for the special relationship between these two defeated kingdoms, there would be no Bible. North and South had long been divided, and the states had repeatedly come to blows in bloody civil wars. What drove the Bible's formation was a vision that the populations of these two vanquished kingdoms could be one people.

E PLURIBUS UNUM

To promote this vision, the book of Genesis holds up Abraham and Sarah as the nation's founders. Similarly, the book of Isaiah points to this couple to illustrate how one could become many: "Look to Abraham your father, and to Sarah who bore you. For he was but one when I called him, yet I blessed him and made him many" (Isaiah 51:2).

E pluribus unum – "From the many, one." Visions of national unity have often inspired works of art and writing projects. What energizes these artistic endeavors (e.g., in Korea, Germany, and the United States) is the will to affirm the existence of one people divided by political borders and factions. The Bible is not only the earliest, and most elaborate, example of these creative endeavors of political imagination, but has also directly inspired many of projects of peoplehood. From Asia and Africa to Europe and America, from colonizing powers to colonized populations, intellectuals and artists have often looked to the biblical model of Israel, imagining themselves as peoples with ancient pasts and hope-filled futures.

While the biblical narrative explains how *the one became many*, as we work our way through this narrative, we face a problem of historical reconstruction: *how the many become one*. What did the host of clans that inhabited North and South have in common? What divided them? And how does the Bible imagine their beginnings?

FURTHER READING

Allen, James P., *Middle Egyptian: An Introduction to the Language and Culture of Hieroglyphs*, Cambridge University Press, 1999.

Blenkinsopp, Joseph, *Abraham: The Story of a Life*, Eerdmans, 2015.

Gates, Charles, *Ancient Cities: The Archaeology of Urban Life in the Ancient Near East and Egypt, Greece and Rome*, Routledge, 2011.

Glassner, Jean-Jacques, *The Invention of Cuneiform: Writing in Sumer* (trans. Zainab Bahrani and Marc Van de Meiroop), Johns Hopkins Press, 2003.

Kratz, Reinhard *Historical and Biblical Israel: The History, Tradition, and Archives of Israel and Judah* (trans. Paul Michael Kurtz), Oxford University Press, 2016.

Rainey, Anson F., *The Sacred Bridge: Carta's Atlas of the Biblical World*, Carta, 2005.

Redford, Donald B., *Egypt, Canaan, and Israel in Ancient Times*, Princeton University Press, 1993.

Schneider, Tammi, *Sarah: Mother of Nations*, Bloomsbury, 2004.

2

Miriam

Empire and Exodus

And Miriam cried to them:
"Sing to Yhwh,
for he has triumphed gloriously.
Horse and rider he has thrown into the sea."
– Exodus 15:21

THE BOOK OF GENESIS ends with the stunning story of Joseph, a son of Jacob whom his brothers sell into Egyptian slavery. In a foreign land, and despite many obstacles, Joseph manages to rise to second-in-command, and when famine strikes Canaan, he makes it possible for his family to find refuge in Egypt.

When the book of Exodus opens, we hear that Joseph's family had not only survived but also thrived there. In fact, they had become such a large population that the new pharaoh perceived their presence as a threat to Egypt's future. The first measure he takes is to afflict the Israelites (or "Hebrews") with arduous labor. When that fails to crush them, he decrees a genocidal program: all their male babies are to be thrown into the Nile.

Unwilling to comply with the law of the land, five women collaborate in acts of insubordinate solidarity, crossing divisions of class and ethnicity.

First, two midwives flout the infanticidal decree, and when they are called to account for their actions, they offer a clever response: "The Hebrew women are not like Egyptians. They're [like] wild animals and give birth before a midwife arrives" (Exodus 1:19).

Simultaneously, one mother hides her male infant in a watertight basket and sets it afloat on the river, while the boy's older sister takes it upon herself to watch over the basket from a safe distance. As the account continues, the pharaoh's daughter goes to bathe with her maidens in the river. Strolling along the bank, she notices the basket, and after her servants fetch it for her, she discovers the baby inside.

At this point in the story, the reader expects the worse. But the child cries, and his tears move the princess to compassion. When she exclaims, "This is one of the Hebrew children!," his sister might have assumed that the princess meant her brother harm. But instead of fleeing, the girl boldly approaches the Egyptian princess with an unsolicited proposal: "Shall I go and hire for you a nurse from the Hebrew women to tend to the child for you?"

Did the princess ever contemplate taking the boy as her own? Or does the Hebrew girl, who shrewdly does not identify herself as the baby's sister, open the eyes of the Egyptian woman to a new possibility? In either case, the girl finds a way to connect to this woman's sense of compassion and turn it into life-sustaining action. As a result, the baby's own mother gets to raise him, and is even paid for it. When the child is old enough, she brings him to the palace, where he joins the family of the ruler who had decreed the extermination of all Hebrew boys.

Later we learn that the girl in this story is Miriam and that her baby brother is Moses, the one who will part the Red Sea and lead Israel to freedom. We often assume that the exodus from Egypt begins when Moses demands from the pharaoh, "Let my people go!" Yet long before this man mustered the courage to speak, a series of women – and one girl in particular – had dared to defy the pharaoh and, in so doing, forged a path to national liberation.[1]

Just as we often fail to remember the pivotal role these five women play in the biblical story of the exodus, so does the biblical memory of this period pass over important historical facts. However, in contrast to our own amnesia, which is the result of centuries of biased or inattentive readings, the biblical authors *consciously* wrote a revisionist account of their people's past. To understand what motivated their revisionism, we need to learn about the dramatic historical events on the eve of Israel's emergence in Canaan.

[1] In Chapter 17, we unpack the significance of Moses' birth-story for the formation of the biblical narrative.

THE EGYPTIAN "PEACE"

Connections between Canaan and Egypt can be traced all the way back to the Stone Age and the Predynastic Period. By the Second and Third dynasties (in the late fourth millennium), at about the same time pyramids began appearing in the Nile Delta, many were already migrating, or being forced to migrate, from the Southern Levant.

To obtain materials and human labor from abroad for their projects at home, Egyptian rulers could engage in trade and gift-exchanges. Or they could carry out military expeditions and take what they needed by force of arms. In resorting to the second method, they demonstrated the undesirable penalties for anyone who might contemplate withholding tribute, gifts, and bodies. Egypt's official iconography and inscriptions emphasize, often to an exaggerated degree, how severe this royal retribution could be. Thus a description of the Canaanite campaign from the Sixth Dynasty (*c.*2340–2180 BCE) reads:

The army returned in peace,
having hacked up the land of them that are across the sand,
having pulverized the land of them that are across the sand,
having razed its fortified towns,
having cut down its fruit trees and vines,
having set all its dwellings on fire,
having slain the enemy troops in the ten-thousands,
the army returned in peace.[2]

Egyptian sources frequently refer to places in Canaan that would become important towns in Israel's history. A fascinating corpus are the Execration Texts from the Twelfth Dynasty (*c.* nineteenth century BCE). As a kind of sympathetic magic, priests wrote the names of Egypt's enemies on clay figurines before pronouncing imprecations on them, breaking and burning them, covering them in urine, and finally burying them. The cursed include centers in Canaan such as Ashkelon and Shechem – two places that will play important roles in both the biblical and the historical lives of Israel and Judah. One of the Execration Texts refers to a "Rushalim," which some scholars identify with

[2] Redford, *Egypt, Canaan, and Israel in Ancient Times*, p. 54.

Jerusalem; others, however, are not convinced by this reading. But what is noteworthy for our story is that the first references to important biblical places are in texts celebrating their doom and destruction.

Eventually, Egypt established an enduring military presence in Canaan, and credit for the feat is due to one of the most sophisticated military strategists of all time, Thutmose III (1479–1425 BCE). Stepson of the famous Hatshepsut (the woman who reigned, and dressed, as a male pharaoh), Thutmose conducted at least seventeen triumphant tours after becoming king. The first one was perhaps his most important as it witnessed a momentous victory at the Battle of Megiddo.[3] Through these feats, Thutmose established Canaan as a province in Egypt's "New Kingdom Empire," whose borders extended to Anatolia (modern-day Türkiye). The contemporary superpowers – Babylon, Assyria, the Hittites, Alashiya on Cyprus – sent diplomatic gifts to Egypt, initiating the *Pax Aegyptiaca* or "Egyptian Peace" (similar to the *Pax Romana*).

From the perspective of Canaan's population, this "peace" meant more pain. Thutmose designated a fixed portion of the harvest to be delivered annually, which ensured an impoverishment of the conquered cities and therewith a weakening of their means of resistance. His demand for human resources depopulated Canaan, especially the hill country. The burden the pharaoh inflicted reminds us of the oppression in the story of Miriam and Moses; the difference is that the ones who suffered were not minorities in Egypt but the denizens of Canaan.

Egypt's domination severely restricted attempts to build native kingdoms in the Southern Levant. Even so, the populations of the central highlands – where the states of Israel and Judah would later emerge – enjoyed a level of autonomy. From Egypt's perspective, hostile hillbillies occupied the region. The pharaohs thought it best to leave this riffraff to its own devices and to interfere only when the local warlords reared their heads too high. More critical to Egypt's imperial strategy were the lowlands and the coast (from Gaza northwards); this corridor was essential to communication and trade with the superpowers abroad.

[3] Megiddo would later belong to the Northern kingdom of Israel. This strategically located site between the coast and the Jezreel Valley persisted through its history (until modern times) as a battleground on which many political fates have been decided. It is also the biblical "Armageddon," a conflation of *Har* ("mountains") and the place name.

Yet, if Egypt allowed turmoil in the highlands to go unheeded, their foes could take advantage of the situation, advance southwards, and eventually end up right at their front door. This scenario had to be avoided at all costs, and hence the palace closely monitored activities in the central hill country.

THE AMARNA LETTERS

A large archive of documents gives us a firsthand glimpse of life on the ground in the Southern Levant a century after Thutmose established Egyptian hegemony there. In 1887 locals were digging among the ruins at a site that we know today as the ancient Egyptian capital of "Amarna." There they discovered a trove of cuneiform tablets and sold them on the antiquities market. When these tablets turned out to be official correspondence with the Egyptian court from the mid-fourteenth century BCE, archeologists eagerly went back to the site and excavated more. Today the dossier includes about 380 separate letters (Figure 2.1).

The most illustrious Amarna Letters originated at the courts of contemporary superpowers, whom the pharaohs addressed as "brothers." Yet most of the missives were sent from small cities in Canaan. The pharaohs had appointed local rulers to serve as town "mayors" and keep an eye on their interests in the region. However, when the court was not looking, these same rulers would refer to themselves as "king" and expected their subjects to address them as such.

Consisting largely of protests and complaints, the Amarna Letters are fun to read. What vexes their senders is the actions of their colleagues, who ruled in neighboring cities yet had ambitions to expand in their own territories. Fearing that they will be forced to forfeit their lands, if not also their lives, these mayors beg the pharaoh to make his annual visitation and send royal archers to establish justice in the land.

The first thing to be noted is that these letters are written not in Hebrew or Egyptian, but in Akkadian, which would persist as the language of diplomacy for many centuries. The scribes who composed the letters were well versed in cuneiform traditions from Mesopotamia, but their formulations often reflect Canaanite idioms and influence. (In many cases, we can ascertain where these scribes were stationed in Canaan by studying the composition of the clay used to make the tablets.)

Figure 2.1 Amarna Letter (EA 288) sent from Jerusalem in the Vorderasiatisches Museum, Berlin. Photo: Einsamer Schütze.

The second, and more significant, point is that these documents mention many *places* of the Bible, such as Shechem, Jerusalem, Hebron, Lachish, Gezer, and Megiddo. Curiously, though, they have nothing to say about the *people* of the Bible – Israel, Judah, or any member of the biblical cast of personalities and clans. Likewise, the archive includes the names of many leading Canaanite rulers and their families, but none of these names appear in the Bible.

Augmenting this disparity is the fact that this dossier dates to a time when major biblical events (e.g., the exodus, conquest, and settlement) were supposed to have taken place. We would expect at least an occasional reference to "Israel," but the mayors in Canaan seem to be unaware of a population bearing this name.

In the past, scholars accounted for the discrepancies between the biblical account and the Amarna Letters by arguing that the Israelites were in Egypt during this period. Their solution represents a facile harmonization of the facts, and most today rightly reject it as a serious option. The Amarna archive confirms what archeologists and historians in the nineteenth century were already starting to realize for other reasons: the biblical account is not a reliable source for Israel's history during these early centuries.

Consider the case of Jerusalem. The Egyptian court had appointed a mayor named Abdi-Ḫeba to govern this town. (His name means "servant of Ḫebat," a goddess widely venerated throughout ancient West Asia, but not mentioned in biblical texts.) Although Abdi-Ḫeba has nothing to do with Israel, Judah, or the Bible, this ruler is the earliest known writer from Jerusalem, and in his six detailed communiqués (composed with the help of his cuneiform scribes), we hear him bemoaning the threats he faced. For example:

> Say to the king, my lord: Message of Abdi-Ḫeba, your servant. I fall at the feet of my lord seven times and seven times...
>
> Consider the lands of Gezer, Ashkelon, and Lachish. They have given my enemies food, oil and any other requirement. So may the king provide for archers and send them against men that commit crimes against the king, my lord. If this year there are archers, then the lands and the mayors will belong to the king, my lord. But if there are no archers, then the king will have neither lands nor mayors.

> Consider Jerusalem! This neither my father nor my mother gave to me. The strong arm of the king gave it to me. . . . Consider, O king, my lord! I am in the right.[4]

Here Abdi-Ḫeba goes to great lengths to reaffirm his allegiance to his Egyptian lord. He avers that Jerusalem belongs to the king, whose "strong arm" (*zu-ru-uḫ*) made it possible for Abdi-Ḫeba to reside there. In separate letter, he pleads for the king not to abandon Jerusalem where he has "placed his name forever."

These documents demonstrate the fundamental problems facing historians of ancient Israel. On the one hand, we find expressions in the Bible similar to those from the Amarna Letters – for example, in relation to Yhwh leading the people of Israel out of Egypt with his "strong arm" and "placing his name (in Jerusalem) forever." The epistles read like prayers to a deity, with the mayors entreating the king to "shine his light" upon them and "save" them from the encroachment of their peers in neighboring towns and districts. In their form and formulation, these letters are strikingly reminiscent of biblical psalms.

On the other hand, the biblical narratives are oblivious to any of the figures or conflicts documented in the Amarna Letters. In fact, they do not even know that Egypt controlled the region at the time. In the biblical memory of this period, Egypt is a place from which Israel escapes, and when the refugees make it to Canaan, they face independent city-states (such as Jericho), which form coalitions without any Egyptian oversight.

From this important archive, we can nevertheless see how Canaanite rulers were eager to break free from imperial control and spread out over wider territories. As long as Egypt was defending its imperial interests in the region, it was able to hold all the chiefdoms from the hill country in check. But when the empire collapsed, new populations would move into the space that Egypt vacated. They include Israel and Judah, as well as neighboring peoples with names such as the Philistines and the Ammonites, Moab and Edom.

[4] Adaptation of Moran, *Amarna Letters*, p. 328.

THE OLDEST REFERENCE TO ISRAEL

In 1896, the celebrated British archaeologist Flinders Petrie made the most sensational discovery of his long and celebrated career. Excavating at Thebes, an ancient Egyptian capital on the Nile's west bank, Petrie's team discovered a temple that the pharaoh Merneptah (1213–1203 BCE) had built. Among the ruins, they found not only this ruler's earliest statue but also an inscribed black granite monument standing over ten feet high (the largest stele found to date; see Figure 2.2).

In a letter to his wife Hilda, a respected Irish Egyptologist, Petrie tells how his colleague came over to read the inscriptions. When he reached the final lines, he stumbled on the name of a population among the peoples whom Merneptah had vanquished. As he slowly pronounced the syllables, Petrie erupted in excitement: "Is-ra-el!" That night at dinner the renowned archeologist declared: "This stele will be better known in the world than anything else I have found."

Petrie's prophecy came true. Headlining newspapers around the world were reports that the earliest reference to Israel had surfaced in the historical records of ancient Egypt. The monument dates to 1207 BCE, not long after the presumed date for the Exodus. It now stands prominently in the Egyptian Museum in Cairo, where one can read its twenty-seventh line in which Merneptah claims that, thanks to his military might, Israel had been completely wiped out:

Canaan is captive with all woe.
Ashkelon is conquered.
Gezer seized.
Yanoam made nonexistent.
Israel is wasted, its seed is no more.

Israel thus takes the stage of world history as a defeated, extinct people. However, reality proved to be the very opposite of Merneptah's claim: far from being rendered extinct, Israel's seed would soon thereafter blossom and flourish, giving its name to a people who not only went on to build a powerful kingdom but also have managed to survive, against all odds, to the present day.

The only thing that was being wiped out at the time was Egypt's empire, and this inscription turned out to be its swan song. Just a decade

Figure 2.2 Merneptah Stele at the Egyptian Museum, Cairo Egypt. Photo: Olaf Tausch.

later, there was little left of an Egyptian presence that Merneptah's predecessors had established in Canaan over the preceding two and half centuries. As Egypt relinquished its claims to the region, local populations formed chiefdoms and kingdoms. These states would jockey for power with each other for the following five centuries, until new empires from the East emerged and reconquered the Levant.

Some scholars date the biblical exodus to the reign of Ramses the Great, Merneptah's father (1279–1213 BCE). Since Merneptah's inscription presents Israel living in Canaan, their migration from Egypt, according to this late dating, would have had to occur shortly before Merneptah's military assault on them. While the Bible has much to say about the former, it is, once again, oddly silent about the latter: Moses and Miriam figure prominently; Merneptah never makes an appearance.

Even if the biblical scribes had known about Merneptah, they probably would not have mentioned him. Their story depicts the nation's liberation from Egypt followed by the conquest of Canaan. The fact that Egypt could continue to harass Israel after it had settled in the Promised Land complicates this neat narrative arc.

Conversely, the Egyptian sources know nothing about Israel's tenure in Egypt or its exodus, even on a small scale. Irritated by this fact, some have attempted to read Merneptah's declaration as a reference to the exodus event, as if Merneptah had claimed to wipe out Israel as a population living in Egypt. Most scholars rightly reject this forced reading.[5]

We cannot be certain that Merneptah actually undertook a campaign in Canaan or encountered Israel firsthand. Yet even if he did, the military tour would have been an exception to Egypt's Levantine policy at this time. Already during Merneptah's reign we witness a weakening of Egypt's grip, marking the beginning of the end of its influence in the region.

Scholars have long mined Merneptah's monument in search of more information relating to Israel's early history and its conflict with Egypt. The results of their efforts have been rather disappointing. Already in 1906 the Egyptologist James Henry Breasted confronted silly suggestions to link the statement in Merneptah's text that Israel's "seed is no more" with the biblical account of the slaying of male children in Egypt (Exodus 1:15–22).

[5] Perhaps a better candidate for the "exodus" is the expulsion of the Asiatic Hyksos three centuries earlier, as Joseph Weinstein and others argue. According to many scholars, the historical kernel of the exodus story may have been the memory of a hero named Moses and a small group that left Egypt to become part of Israel.

More recently, some have suggested that "seed" refers to grain rather than human progeny. Accordingly, the Israelites were engaged primarily in agriculture, and Merneptah focused his aggression on their crops because they did not inhabit cities. The line is, however, a stereotypical expression, and although the name Israel is prefaced with unspoken scribal symbols ("determinatives") that designate Israel as a "foreign people" rather than a "foreign land," we cannot say much about its social constitution. Similarly, while the Merneptah monument refers to both "Canaan" and "Israel," it does not support the Bible's sharp distinction between these two entities. Instead, it simply classifies Canaan as a territory and Israel as a population; to what extent they overlapped is not clear.[6]

The fact that Merneptah's stele mentions Israel suggests that it was a force to be reckoned with. Otherwise, this people's putative annihilation would not have earned them a line on the monument. It's hardly a feat to have wiped out a small band of peasant farmers who did not have the means to engage in combat. Whatever the case may be, Merneptah's monument provides proof positive that a people called Israel existed in the Levant in 1207 BCE, and as we established from the Amarna Archive, they do not seem to have been there – or at least their presence went unnoticed – a century and half earlier.

FROM MERNEPTAH TO MOSES AND MIRIAM

The story of Israel's liberation from Egypt is a part of a larger account that spans five books: Exodus, Leviticus, Numbers, Deuteronomy, and Joshua. It begins with the exodus and culminates with the conquest of Canaan. In Part III, we will learn how this "Exodus-Conquest Account" once competed with the "Family Story" from the book of Genesis. In our Bibles, these two works form a continuous story, with the Family Story segueing to the Exodus-Conquest Account; however, the two works render very different images of the nation's past and likely had separate origins.

[6] The determinative for Israel as a "foreign people" is a throw stick (="foreign"), followed by a sitting man and woman (="people"), over three vertical lines (the plural marker). The determinative for "foreign land" (a throw stick plus three mountains) appears in the inscription before places such as Ashkelon and Gezer.

What is important for our purposes is how scribes created these works by combining earlier traditions. As we shall see, the authors of Family Story took independent figures (such as Isaac and Jacob) and grafted them into a single family-tree. Many of these figures represent independent regions, tribes, and clans. By blending their stories into a larger narrative, scribes affirmed that originally separate and rival groups belonged in the same national fold. Similarly, the Exodus-Conquest Account was formed by linking Moses on the one end to Joshua on the other. It grew to its present proportions as nameless scribes, working over many centuries, amplified it with a host of additional characters.

What drove the formation of the biblical narratives was the will to integrate what was once separate. The synthesis of diverse, originally independent, and often rival traditions is on display throughout the corpus, and it explains why the biblical narratives are less uniform than compositions that have not grown dramatically over time.

Consider again the figure of Miriam. A text from Exodus refers to her as "Miriam, the prophet." After the parting of the Red Sea, she leads the women of Israel in a joyous song and dance: "Sing to Yhwh, for he has triumphed gloriously; horse and rider he has thrown into the sea" (Exodus 15:21). The name of Miriam may have been associated with a particular population, prophetic tradition, or perhaps local cult of some sort. Another text, one that most scholars deem to be old (Exodus 20:1), reports that she died and was buried in Kadesh, an oasis on Israel's border, and it is possible that she was once a venerated figure there.

Later biblical texts conspicuously omit Miriam's prophetic title – perhaps because in that role she challenges her brother's prophetic authority. Thus, the book of Numbers portrays her criticizing Moses for marrying an Ethiopian woman. The deity intervenes, affirming that Moses is his special prophet, and strikes Miriam "white as snow" with leprosy. Moses pleads on her behalf, and she is healed. She is still expelled from the camp, but the people refuse to continue their voyage to the Promised Land until she is readmitted (Numbers 12).

Miriam may have come to represent groups that challenged Mosaic authority and the laws he represents. If so, some would have been tempted to "shut her out of the camp." But instead of omitting her from the nation's story, the biblical authors assigned her an indispensable role. As we saw in the introduction to this chapter, they presented her courageous and clever action at the bank of the Nile as the first step in the nation's liberation from bondage and its voyage to a new land.

The following chapter begins with the figure of Deborah, whose leadership marks the culmination of the deity's direct rule that Miriam celebrated with her song at the Red Sea. Focusing on the conquest and settlement, our survey will once again help us appreciate the biblical account by demonstrating its deep disparities with, and departure from, the archeological record.

FURTHER READING

Cline, Eric and O'Connor, David, *Thutmose III: A New Biography*, University of Michigan Press, 2006.

Cohen, Raymond and Westbrook, Raymond, eds., *Amarna Diplomacy: The Beginnings of International Relations*, Johns Hopkins University Press, 2000.

Drower, Margaret S., *Flinders Petrie: A Life in Archaeology*, University of Wisconsin Press, 1995.

Finkelstein, Israel and Silberman, Neil Asher, *The Bible Unearthed: Archaeology's New Vision of Ancient Israel and the Origin of Its Sacred Texts*, Free Press, 2001.

Goren, Yuval; Finkelstein, Israel; and Na'aman, Nadav, *Inscribed in Clay: Provenance Study of the Amarna Tablets and Other Ancient Near Eastern Texts*, Tel Aviv University, 2004.

Hasel, Michael G., *Domination and Resistance: Egyptian Military Activity in the Southern Levant, 1300–1185 B.C.*, Brill, 1998.

Kamionkowski, Tamar "Will the Real Miriam Please Stand Up?" *TheTorah.com*, 2015, https://www.thetorah.com/article/will-the-real-miriam-please-stand-up

Moore, Megan Bishop and Kelle, Brad E., *Biblical History and Israel's Past*, Eerdmans, 2011.

Moran, William L., *The Amarna Letters*, Johns Hopkins University Press, 1992.

Redford, Donald B., *Egypt, Canaan, and Israel in Ancient Times*, Princeton University Press, 1993.

Tervanotko, Hanna K., *Denying Her Voice: The Figure of Miriam in Ancient Jewish Literature*, Vandenhoeck & Ruprecht, 2016.

Weinstein, Joseph, "We Were Slaves to the Hyksos in Egypt," *TheTorah.com*, 2021, https://thetorah.com/article/we-were-slaves-to-the-hyksos-in-egypt.

3

Deborah

A New Dawn

They ceased living in unwalled towns,
they ceased in Israel,
until I Deborah arose,
until I arose, a mother in Israel.
–Judges 5:7

THESE LINES ARE FROM WHAT MANY CONSIDER to be the Bible's oldest piece of poetry: the Song of Deborah from the book of Judges. In the biblical narrative, the song punctuates an epoch of the nation's past, one that begins with Miriam's song in the book of Exodus.

As we saw in the preceding chapter, the book of Exodus portrays Miriam and the women of Israel celebrating Yhwh's kingship at the Red Sea. His divine reign over the nation continues to the days of Joshua and Deborah, two heroes who act on Yhwh's behalf and lead Israel against Canaan's mighty forces. Yet what follows Deborah is the beginning of a new era. A succession of self-serving men assume power, and as they do, they set their sights on the kingship that until then had been the preserve and prerogative of the nation's deity.

Deborah's paean to divine rule thus plays a pivotal role in the narrative. The poem depicts the kings of Canaan assembling one last time to fight against Israel. Their efforts, however, are in vain. Yhwh soundly defeats them, making his might on the battlefield felt through a diverse host.

Above them all towers Deborah, who refers to herself as a "mother" of the nation. But in contrast to Lady Liberty, this woman does not personify an abstract principle; she is a real-life leader in her people's history.

A prose account of her triumph, which runs parallel to this poem, calls her a prophet, the same title Miriam bears.

As a woman whose husband and children go unmentioned (whether she has either is not said), Deborah governs Israel and commissions an officer to lead the people into battle. In her song, she praises the individual tribes that join the war effort. Those on the periphery are reluctant to contribute, and by chiding them, she affirms that they too are vital members of the nation. In contrast, she curses one group for not sending their mighty warriors, and that group is never mentioned again in the Bible. By commemorating the contribution of a non-Israelite named Jael, she challenges those who would deny Jael's clan (the Kenites) a place in the nation's fold. In these and other ways, her song defines membership in a new political community, one in which the monarchy plays no role whatsoever.

One of the earliest and most influential studies of biblical literature is *The Spirit of Hebrew Poetry: An Instruction for Lovers of the Same and the Oldest History of the Human Spirit.* Published in 1782–1783, this work devotes many pages to Deborah's war memorial. Its author, Johann Gottfried von Herder, is one of the first intellectuals in modernity to think in terms of a national identity. According to Herder, the ancient Song of Deborah demonstrated that a people consisting of diverse "tribes" could be united in spirit even when – and indeed, especially when – it was not united by a ruler and political borders.

Similar to Herder's efforts for German-speaking countries, many political communities across the globe have drawn directly from biblical writings when forming a notion of nationhood that is distinct from, and does not depend on, statehood. Later we will explore how the biblical writers, working after the conquests of their kingdoms, drew this important distinction as they reflected on their pasts and invented a prehistory of peoplehood. To set the stage for that discussion, we need to investigate the expansion of populations in Palestine's central highlands and the eventual emergence of these kingdoms.

COLLAPSE

If we follow the biblical narrative, Deborah would have lived at the end of the Bronze Age, an era known for expansive trade networks, writing systems, bodies of knowledge, military technologies, and cosmopolitan culture that connected communities from the Mediterranean to Mesopotamia, from Egypt to Turkey. The global economy of the Bronze Age was profoundly interdependent, and as such, bears striking similarities to the twenty-first century. Yet this civilization collapsed, and it did so abruptly. What follows is history's first Dark Age.

According to the archeologist Eric Cline, it was the interdependence of Bronze Age communities that assured their demise. They faced a series of connected failures, including invasion, earthquakes, famine, disease, the disruption of international trade routes, local revolts, and internal unrest among the reigning superpowers, such as the Minoans, Hittites, Trojans, Babylonian-Kassites, and Assyrians. Above all, Egypt was beset by low Nile flood levels, food shortages, civil unrest, corruption, increased influence of the priests, and incessant bickering at the court. The crises that characterized this period caused economic hardship and social unrest, which brought the New Kingdom's empire to the brink of ruin.

The onslaught of the so-called Sea Peoples delivered the *coup de grâce* to Egypt's moribund hegemony. Disparaged as migrating marauders, this population comprised at least six different ethnic groups. The turmoil their arrival caused in the Nile Delta is reflected in the frenzied scenes of land and naval battles that we find in temple reliefs.

Egyptian rulers claim to have conquered these intruders from the north and settled them in the Nile Delta. More likely is that they were unable to prevent their migrations and then insisted that it had been all along their idea to have the newcomers reside there. At about this time, Philistines were settling on the Canaanite coast in the region of Gaza. Marking the de facto demise of Egypt's imperial presence in Canaan, this population would later be a major force in the region and one of Israel's and Judah's leading competitors.

The age of Egypt's imperial domination in Canaan did not last much longer. The formidable North African kingdom soon entered a time of decline, division, and political instability. Similar crises plagued competing centers of civilizations. In the wake of the crises, these centers turned their attention inward and operated in much more confined spheres, making space for a new constellation of powers.

POWER VACUUM

By the time the dust of the Iron Age settled (*c.*1100 BCE), several major players of the Bronze Age – the Trojans, Minoans, and Hittites – had vanished forever. The remaining superpowers in Egypt and Mesopotamia were struggling to regain some semblance of the ascendancy that they once took for granted. Their ambitions now faced a dizzying array of smaller players, each eager to make its influence felt in new terrain. Without the channels of trade and exchange that had long linked East and West, the Iron Age was far less cosmopolitan and much more modest in profile.

The collapse of the Bronze Age created a power vacuum in the Southern Levant. Other peoples now had breathing room in which they could stretch out and realize their political potential. During this period, we witness a new phenomenon in Canaan: the evolution of what we call "territorial states" (Map 3.1). Controlling larger regions and often encompassing two or more older "city-states" (such as Jerusalem, Hebron, Lachish, Gezer, Megiddo, or Shechem), these diverse polities include Israel and Judah in the central hill country, Aram-Damascus in the north, and Ammon, Moab, and Edom on the eastern side of the Jordan. City-states persisted, but primarily along the coast, where trade was more feasible: the Phoenicians inhabited the north in the region of modern Lebanon, while the Philistines occupied the south in the coastal plain of Gaza.[1] For several centuries, these players jockeyed with each other for position in the region, and the Bible chronicles many of their coalitions and conflicts, paying special attention to Israel's and Judah's relationship.

Yet eventually superpowers re-emerged in Mesopotamia. As noted in Chapter 1, they all invariably set their sights on Egypt, an ancient civilization with access to rich resources. As they advanced toward Africa, they subjugated all the petty states that had emerged on the Levantine land-bridge. The subjugation of these states re-established the conditions that had once prevailed in the region – a patchwork of vassals and provinces that answered to an imperial power. The only thing that had changed was the location of the imperial center: it was now in Mesopotamia, not Egypt.

[1] The designation for these population groups – "Phoenicians" and "Philistines" – represent attempts by outsiders to classify what were historically diverse populations.

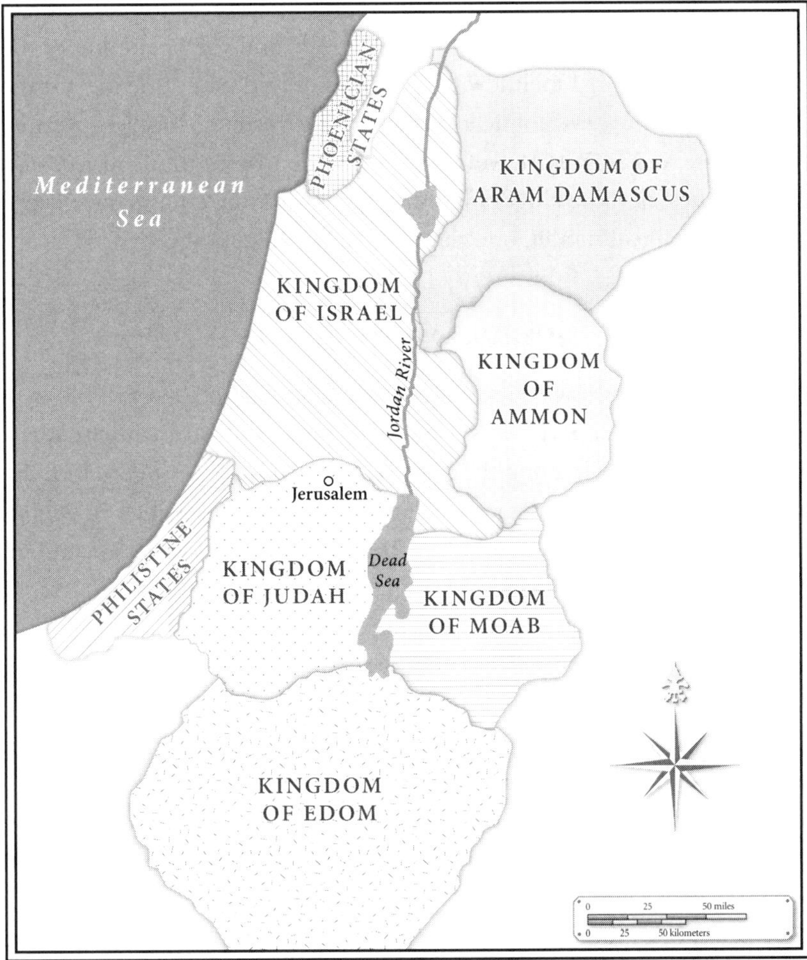

Map 3.1 The territorial states (kingdoms) that emerged in the Southern Levant during the first millennium BCE. Map created by Gerry Krieg (kriegmapping.com).

From the long-term perspective, then, the defeat that decisively shaped the Bible was nothing more than a return to the imperial domination that had been the status quo in the Levant for four millennia. The populations of the Levant of course were not able to view their fates from this historical vantage point, and so they experienced their subjugation and colonization as a cosmic collapse, an abrupt cataclysm, an unprecedented catastrophe. Not surprisingly, most of these Levantine kingdoms and their populations soon vanished from the historical record.

What is important for us at this point in our account are the changes introduced by the collapse of the Bronze Age and the beginning of the Iron Age. The global meltdown during this period paved the way for the emergence of a new political model in the form of locally governed kingdoms. And in Part II, will see how the demise of the Iron Age and the conquest of these kingdoms paved the way for the emergence of yet a different political model, one that we call "peoplehood."

JOSHUA AND THE JUDGES

The Bible has nothing to say about the turmoil from 1200 to 1100 BCE that toppled the superpowers which had long controlled the Southern Levant. Instead of situating the Northern and Southern kingdoms in the new global context that made their breakthrough possible, it depicts newly liberated Israelites invading the land and bringing an end to Canaan's ancient city-states.

The book of Joshua tells how the nation's twelve tribes mount a massive offensive, take the country by storm, and then divide it among their members. Following Joshua, the book of Judges describes the military conflicts that the tribes faced for generations. In this period of turmoil, "judges" (or "saviors") repeatedly rise up to rescue the nation from its foes. These figures represent various regions, tribes, and clans in Israel. Thus, Deborah is from the hill country of Ephraim, while Gideon, who succeeds Deborah, is from the Jezreel Valley north of Ephraim.

Their stories underwent many changes as scribes incorporated them in a national narrative, and the reader can easily see how they were originally independent. Having little to do with Israel as a collective people, the older tales pertain to separate regions and clans, and their ancestral heroes. The biblical authors used them to create an epoch ("the Period of the Judges") that directly precedes the establishment of the monarchy, portrayed in the books of Samuel and Kings.

Why does this biblical narrative not portray the broader picture of the nation's origins? Why do we not learn about the larger geopolitical events, the many population movements, or the major climate changes during these centuries? After all, they are what created the conditions for the rise of the Northern and Southern kingdoms, in tandem with neighboring states.

The answer is simple: even if the biblical authors had some of way of knowing about what happened centuries earlier, an account of those events would have had hardly been relevant to their purposes. They lived during, and especially after, the demise of the territorial states that emerged during the Iron Age, and what they needed was a new way of thinking about themselves. By affirming a direct relationship between a singular deity and the nation's diverse members, and by removing the institution of the monarchy from the nation's formative past, their work provided a blueprint for a new form of peoplehood, one that had the potential to unite rival populations after the downfall of their kingdoms.

Many of the historical factors that shaped Israel's and Judah's formation find no mention in the Bible, while much of what the Bible portrays in considerable detail is far removed from history. Thus, the book of Exodus depicts how the Hebrew slaves became a nation during their liberation, and especially after entering a covenant at Sinai – long before the reign of their kings. That account runs counter to what we know today about the origins of the "Israelites," and many scholars today are convinced that the Bible has little, if any, historical value. Yet rather than summarily dismissing the biblical narrative as a witness to the past, we will be focusing on the divergence of history and story. Only then will we be able to appreciate the creativity, and groundbreaking contributions, of the generations of scribes who shaped the biblical corpus.

THE CONQUEST OF CANAAN

When explaining how the "Israelites" settled in the central hill country, most archeologists today adopt the model of *peaceful infiltration*: the clans that later formed the Northern and Southern kingdoms coalesced from Canaanite groups or migrated from regions east of the Jordan.[2] The process of settlement is thought to have been peaceful at the beginning and to have become more bellicose only after the populations had increased and began to evolve into larger territorial states.

[2] Appealing to a possible etymology of "Hebrew," some philologists suggest that the name originally referred to those who "passed over" this river and settled on its western side.

The Bible, as noted, depicts a unified military campaign during the days of Joshua. However, we lack archeological evidence for hordes of invaders sweeping across Canaan, subjugating its cities, and driving out, or exterminating, the indigenous population. Archeologists have exposed destruction layers at several ancient cities mentioned in the book of Joshua, but most now date these layers to different periods, both long before and long after the time Joshua was supposed to have lived.

Thus, the Bible presents Jericho's massive fortifications tumbling to the ground when the newly liberated nation marches around the city and the priests sounds their trumpets. Kathleen Kenyon (1906–1978) was a British archeologist who pioneered a rigorous methodology for her field, and in her excavations at Jericho during the 1950s, she demonstrated that the city's impressive walls were built centuries before Joshua's time. The biblical tale represents, then, the attempt by later generations to connect the ruins of that great city to pivotal events in their national history.

New research on Israel's origins is much more nuanced than that of earlier generations, and it has developed impressively precise methods for studying the material remains of ancient cultures. But even if many historians now agree that the early Israelites were in a very real sense "Canaanites" (i.e., indigenous to the land of Canaan), they still tend to think in simplistic, binary categories of "Israelite" versus "non-Israelite." Many also assume that the population that formed the Southern kingdom of Judah considered themselves to be Israelites, or at least identified with the population that later inhabited the Northern kingdom of Israel. In doing so, these scholars uncritically adopt the later, national perspective that biblical authors introduced to the materials they inherited.

The starting point in our historical reconstructions should be the inscription of Merneptah from 1207 BCE (introduced in the preceding chapter). We know that at this time a population called Israel was living in Canaan. While we cannot be sure what this population included and what territories they occupied, we can be confident that their members would not have thought of themselves as the later biblical narrative depicts them – namely, as twelve tribes descending from Jacob's twelve sons. Most would have identified solely with their own families, clans, regions, and towns, without ever thinking in terms of a larger political community.

At this early stage, the name Israel appears to have designated a powerful tribe, or even alliance of tribes, that posed a threat to Egyptian armies. Its members may have been semi-nomadic outsiders who lived on the periphery of cities and urban civilizations in Canaan. Thanks to Merneptah's stele, we know that the name long antedates the emergence of the Northern kingdom in the tenth and ninth centuries. We can also be confident that those who bore the name in Merneptah's time possessed some political significance; otherwise, the Egyptian scribes would not have deemed their subjugation worthy of mention. The name lived on and assumed new meanings as groups joined the fold. However, had it not been for kings who, centuries later, used "Israel" to designate the diverse regions and populations that they consolidated and ruled, the name likely would have been long forgotten.

MATERIAL CULTURE OF THE EARLIEST "ISRAELITES"

What, then, can one say about the facts on the ground before the rise of territorial states in the Iron Age?

In the twelfth century BCE, the central hill country suddenly blossomed with roughly 250 new villages, hamlets, farmsteads, and small towns. Beginning likely with less than 10,000 souls, this settlement-wave continued, without interruption, for several centuries and stands in direct continuity with the kingdoms of Israel and Judah that emerged in the same region.[3]

These new highland sites are remarkably uniform. Most could not have sustained more than a hundred inhabitants. They were largely self-sufficient, with all their goods being produced locally. They were also far removed from major trade routes, unfortified, and usually situated on hilltops. Lacking any larger administrative buildings and temples, the sites often had an oval layout: the dwellings surrounded a large courtyard that served as a corral for their flocks. The dwellings themselves were made of uncut fieldstones and often feature columns that could support a second floor (called "Four-Room Houses" or "Pillared Houses") (Figure 3.1). We

[3] This means that the biblical scribes could trace their ancestry partially to this early population.

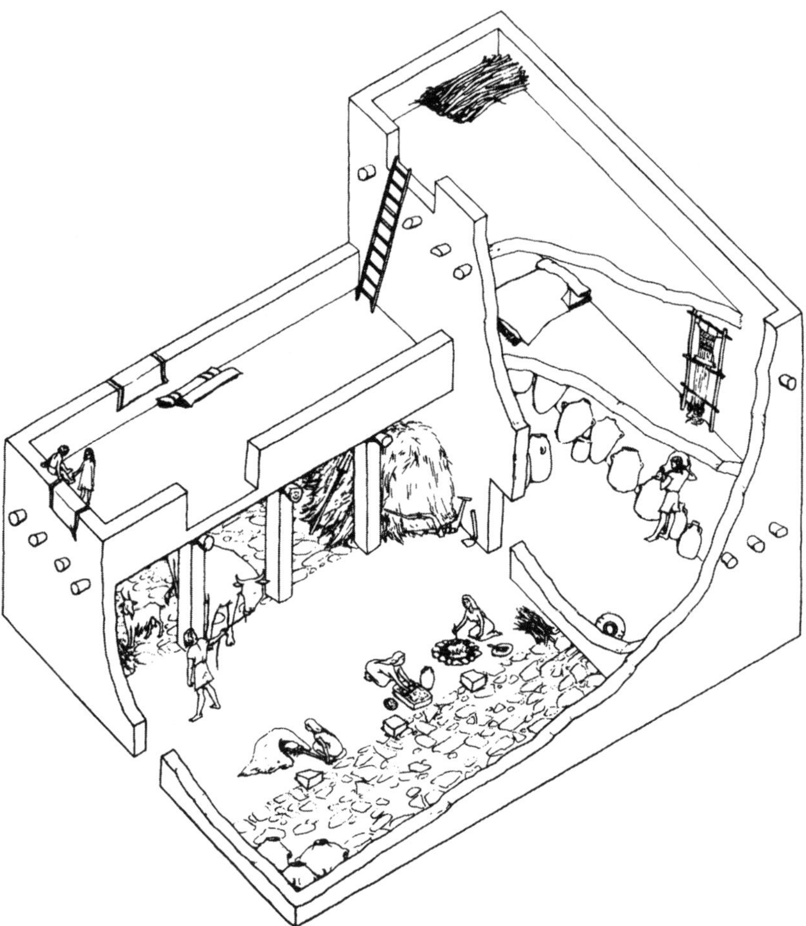

Figure 3.1 Reconstruction of so-called Four-Room House showing daily activities of baking, cooking, grinding grain, and caring for animals, as well as loom and loom weights, storage jars, and use of rooftops. Image from Israel Museum, Jerusalem.

also find many silos for grain storage as well as plastered cisterns for collecting rainwater.

The material culture of these humble highland settlements differs markedly from what we find in the cities on the western coastal plain and in the rich Jezreel Valley. The most abundant archeological evidence is pottery (e.g., fragments of pots, plates, cups, pitchers, storage vessels), and the pottery from the new sites is, in stark contrast to that of the coastal cities, unembellished and much less delicate. Decorations on pottery

Figure 3.2 Examples of simple unadorned pottery, from the Israel Museum, Jerusalem. Photo: Jacob L. Wright.

signal cultural affiliations and mark class divisions. Unadorned pottery, by comparison, is completely utilitarian and functional, and it corresponds to other features of material culture: humble architecture, simple burial customs, crude weapons and technology, dearth of jewelry and "prestige items," and so on. Some scholars claim that this modest culture reflects a distinctive egalitarian ethos, but given the choice, these communities may well have opted for more opulence (Figure 3.2).

To what extent these settlements identified with the name "Israel" or saw themselves as connected is difficult to say. The evidence suggests that they were largely autonomous and did not face military threats that would require them to join forces. The uniformity of the material culture may not reflect a shared identity so much as a shared climate and topography, which demarcates the central hill country from the surrounding regions. It is reasonable to assume that the individual settlements learned technologies and survival skills from their direct neighbors. Marriage pools would have comprised no more than the closest villages. It is not clear whether they came together to celebrate festivals, share harvests, and engage together in ritual activities.

The physical border between North (Israel) and South (Judah) is not pronounced, and so the populations in the hill country would not have been sharply segregated. While we do witness cultural diversity, it corresponds to numerous smaller regions and environmental niches. This does not mean that the populations of North and South thought of themselves as one people. There was in fact little that distinguished them from similar settlement-waves east of the Jordan and in the north. All these peoples spoke basically the same languages and managed well without writing. To the extent that we can speak of a collective identity, one would have expressed it primarily in terms of their village and immediate clan.

It may be tempting to embrace the biblical depiction when we lack data. Yet our reconstructions, chastened by two centuries of scholarship, will have to make do with many gaps in our knowledge and allow the "pottery" – that is, the archeological record and historical sources – to speak with its own voice. While much remains to be explored, we have enough data to offer a compelling and nuanced answer to the question of the Bible's origins and purpose.

FROM POTTERY TO POETRY

We began this chapter with the Song of Deborah, which imagines a battle between Israel and the Canaanites from the pre-state period. The song commemorates various groups that contributed to this national war effort. Strangely, in cataloguing Israel's tribes, it includes only *ten* members; elsewhere the Bible presents Israel consisting of *twelve* tribes. How are we to explain this disparity?

This first thing to note is that the numbers ten and twelve represent the efforts of biblical scribes to imagine a unity from diversity, similar to the way Americans speak about "all fifty states of the Union." The biblical texts that imagine Israel as a people of *twelve* tribes – a natural number corresponding to the months of the year – do so by conceiving of Judah's smaller territory as comprising two tribes. The song may be a response to this larger pan-Israelite identity ("greater Israel"), and if so, it insists that the nation consists of solely ten Northern tribes and does not include Judah!

This observation bears directly on the question of the song's origins. Most agree that it is the work of multiple authors and evolved over time.

Some believe that it dates to the period before the establishment of a centralized state, since it has no place for a native king. But it is more likely that Northern scribes composed the song shortly before or after the downfall of their kingdom in 722 BCE. Without a monarchy to define their collective identity, these circles began thinking of "Israel" in terms of a political community (a "people") in direct relationship with their deity Yhwh, and without a king standing between them.

Just as the "Star-Spangled Banner" commemorates an obscure battle fought in America's history, the Song of Deborah memorializes a military contest with Canaanite kings fought in the twilight of Israel's existence. In doing so it, it conveys a momentous message: if Israel had already coalesced as a nation at an early point, long before the monarchy, it could do so again now after the monarchy had been vanquished.

Northern scribes not only produced this song; they also composed, according to my thesis, the literary cores of the Family Story in Genesis and the Exodus-Conquest Account (introduced in the preceding chapter). Like the song, these writings construct a national identity for Israel by portraying the most formative periods in the nation's past as a time long before the emergence of the monarchy, when Yhwh reigned as king and had non-royal leaders (such as Moses, Miriam, Joshua, and Deborah) as his representatives.

The Song of Deborah, then, does not reflect the structure of Israel's society before the rise of its monarchy. Instead, it was probably composed as a response to the imperial conquests that removed the Northern monarchy from the scene. Yet compared to other biblical texts, the poem is a relatively early composition. For example, it has nothing to say about either the Sinai covenant or the sacrificial cult – subjects that figure prominently in later biblical texts.

In imagining Israel's infancy, this piece of poetry agrees with the pottery on an important point: the ancient communities and clans of the hill country that would later populate the Northern kingdom originally did not have a monarchy that united them. However, in imagining a pre-monarchic people united around Deborah and Yhwh, the song presupposes the monarchy, both its achievements and its demise. The national spirit it breathes was originally awakened by the efforts of Israel's kings to build a centralized state, consolidating the constellation of regions and tribes that this song commemorates.

What's most remarkable about this piece is that its authors *consciously removed the monarchy* from their memory of the nation's early years. Composing an anthem for a vanquished people, they celebrated the nation's deity and "a mother in Israel" – along with a diversity of groups that joined forces under her banner. In the following chapters, we consider the emergence, accomplishments, and eventual demise of the Northern monarchy, all of which shaped the diverse national identity that this anthem elegantly articulates.

FURTHER READING

Ackerman, Susan, *Warrior, Dancer, Seductress, Queen: Women in Judges and Biblical Israel*, Yale University Press, 1998.

Borowski, Oded, *Daily Life in Biblical Times*, SBL Press, 2003.

Cline, Eric H., *1177 BC: The Year Civilization Collapsed*, Princeton University Press, 2014.

Davis, Miriam, *Dame Kathleen Kenyon: Digging Up the Holy Land*, Left Coast Press, 2008.

Dever, William G., *Who Were the Early Israelites and Where Did They Come From?*, Eerdmans, 2003.

Farber, Zev, *Images of Joshua in the Bible and Their Reception*, De Gruyter, 2016.

Faust, Avraham, *Israel's Ethnogenesis: Settlement, Interaction, Expansion and Resistance*, Equinox, 2006.

Finkelstein, Israel, *The Archaeology of the Israelite Settlement*, Israel Exploration Society, 1988.

Kenyon, Kathleen M., *Digging Up Jericho*, Praeger, 1957.

Killebrew, Ann, *Biblical Peoples and Ethnicity: An Archaeological Study of Egyptians, Canaanites, Philistines, and Early Israel 1300–1100 BCE*, Society for Biblical Literature, 2005.

Koch, Ido, *Colonial Encounters in Southwest Canaan during the Late Bronze Age and the Early Iron Age*, Brill, 2021.

Wright, Jacob L., *War, Memory, and National Identity in the Hebrew Bible*, Cambridge University Press, 2020 (open access) – includes several chapters on Deborah and her song.

Yasur-Landau, Assaf; Cline, Eric; and Rowan, Yourke M. (eds.), *The Social Archaeology of the Levant: From Prehistory to the Present*, Cambridge University Press, 2018.

4

King David

Between North and South

David danced before Yhwh with all his might.
– 2 Samuel 6:14

JERUSALEM, *C.*1000 BCE. David, the nation's beloved warrior-poet, is dancing in the streets, reveling in the triumph that he – with Yhwh's help – had secured for his people. The celebration heralds a new dawn. After centuries of wandering, internal chaos, and conflict with neighbors, the nation is now basking in peace and security. This moment simultaneously marks the pinnacle in the bedazzling career of a figure whom the Bible honors as Judah's greatest monarch. His rise to power is a story of the improbable, with a narrative arc corresponding to his people's collective experience.

As the youngest of eight sons, the odds are stacked against this boy from Bethlehem, but the disadvantage makes him only more determined. With one well-aimed shot of the sling, he brings down Goliath, the Philistine giant who had scorned Israel's armies. Thanks to his unwavering faith in his own future, and bolstered by Yhwh's devotion to him, he manages from that point on to surmount every obstacle. On the battlefield and beyond, he displays charismatic charm, unflagging ambition, and an uncanny sense of timing.

In his first act as king, David sets out to take Jerusalem, an ancient Canaanite stronghold situated between the North and the South that had yet to be conquered. The infiltration scheme he devises – sending troops up through the city's water shaft – was a suicide mission, but as always, his instincts do not fail. The fortress is captured and renamed "The City of David." To establish the new capital's prestige, he immediately launches an ambitious building program and erects a palace for himself. When it is finished, he orchestrates a triumphal entry for Yhwh, ensuring Jerusalem's longevity as the deity's eternal residence.

The Bible sets this triumphal moment against the backdrop of an earlier king's tragic demise. His name is Saul, and as a young man standing head and shoulders above his peers, he is initially successful in routing the nation's enemies and consolidating a large kingdom. Yet he's full of self-doubt, and he flouts divine orders. As punishment for his transgressions, Yhwh eventually spurns him and chooses David to reign in his stead.

In contrast to his predecessor, the self-assured David has no trouble crushing all his competitors in the region. Through his many conquests, he builds a mighty kingdom that brings him international renown. But at the end of his impressive reign, he, like his people centuries later, faces catastrophic defeat and manages to return to Jerusalem only after suffering humiliation and exile.

With the lives of David and Saul, the biblical story begins to converge with history. But only on certain points. There is little room for doubt that David built a strong kingdom that endured several hundred years, yet it is unlikely that he ruled over a kingdom that included both the North and the South with Jerusalem at its center. Those who deserve credit for consolidating Israel as a large territorial state are not Saul or David, but rather members of a dynasty that came to power more than a century later. That dynasty is the subject of the following chapter. In the present one, we examine the biblical memory of a "United Monarchy" and compare it to our historical evidence for a plurality of competing polities.

IMAGINING A UNITED MONARCHY

The Bible depicts Saul and David as charismatic leaders who formed large territorial states by appealing to a common "Israelite" national identity. Thus, when the tribal heads of Israel agree to anoint David as king, they declare: "Look, we are bone of your bone and flesh of your flesh!" (2 Samuel 5:1) By adding this line to an older account, editors ascribed the legitimacy of David's kingship to his kinship with the people of Israel.

This is an anachronistic depiction. An Israelite national identity had to be created. That creation was a gradual process, and it owed much to the efforts of non-Davidic monarchs who put the Northern kingdom on the map in the mid-ninth century BCE.

In the book of Samuel, we can reconstruct an older account of David's life. It depicts him consolidating a kingdom in the South out of separate clans, regions, and towns under the banner of "the House of Judah." As a warlord, David secures the throne not by appealing to a national identity (even just a Judean one), but by greasing the palms of rival clans with spoils from his conquests.

In this early account, the place David chooses for Judah's capital is not Jerusalem but Hebron, an ancient city situated directly at the center of the kingdom. David is remembered as the one who captured Jerusalem, which was strategically located on Judah's northern frontier, and the legend of its conquest may reflect his historical achievement. However, this place would not become Judah's capital until (much) later. It is not easy to say when the move from Hebron happened, but it may not have been until the final years of the Northern kingdom, in the late eighth century BCE.

Saul, too, is most probably a historical figure. He likely ruled over a region in Benjamin – a small strip of the hill country running between the North and the South where Jerusalem is located. Over time scribes connected Saul to Jonathan and expanded the traditions into a tale of Israel's first monarch, which tells how Saul brought respite from the nation's enemies but ultimately failed as a ruler and fell tragically in battle.

In a pivotal editorial move, one with profound political implications, scribes combined these separate stories, one about David in Judah and the other about Saul in Israel. In their new unified account, David mounts Saul's throne, and when he does, he brings Judah with him, consolidating thereby the North and the South under one rule. We will have to wait to see who drafted that history, when they did so, and why. Those questions cannot be answered until we learn more about Israel's and Judah's histories.

PLURALITY OF POLITIES

By the end of the early Iron Age (1200–1000 BCE), the archeological record in the central hill country shows signs of significant changes. The population appears to have grown considerably, numbering now *c.*50,000. We can also witness a rise in prosperity driven by more diversified modes of producing olive oil and wine – precious commodities that could be accumulated in large quantities and traded for other goods. This process led to greater social stratification and political centralization. Beginning in the tenth century, and then more rapidly in the ninth century, economic competition and military conflict with neighbors caused groups in the highlands to coalesce into a patchwork of polities, consisting mostly of small kingdoms or "chiefdoms."

The preceding chapter touched on the simple highland pottery found in the remains of early Israelite settlements. Now that pottery starts to appear in the archeological record for cities that had long occupied the lush Jezreel Valley that lies north of the central highlands and that served as the region's breadbasket. This evidence indicates that rulers from the highlands had managed to extend their influence over these important older cities in the lowlands.

Eventually a larger state, with a heterogenous population, would coalesce; we know that state as "the Northern kingdom" or "Israel." In the coming decades, Judah too would begin to emerge as a strong state that controlled a region in the South. However, its territories would be far less diverse than those of its northern neighbor.

All things being equal, we would expect a natural evolution of more than two states in the central hill country, in analogy to many small kingdoms that we encounter in the Amarna archive (see Chapter 2). The recently discovered site of Khirbet Qeiyafa bears witness to an independent (and short-lived) polity just twenty miles from Jerusalem. Some scholars think that it was part of Saul's kingdom; others claim it was part of David's. More likely, the site is evidence for one of many petty states that populated the region up until the ninth century. Although this political plurality is well attested in the archeological record, many historians still have trouble freeing themselves from the past imagined in the biblical narrative.

The Bible may preserve memories for several of these states, but in keeping with its linear narrative, it places them centuries before Saul and David. For example, the book of Judges tells about a figure named Abimelech who established himself as king at Shechem, a city lying at the center of the Northern kingdom. The account depicts him dying a tragic death and failing to establish a dynasty (see Chapter 23). His story is linked in the narrative to Gideon and Jephthah, two figures who may have ruled over small kingdoms in regions that later belonged to Israel.

Recall what we noted about Saul's state: it must have been limited to the small region of Benjamin. Likewise, early biblical texts remember Joshua as a warlord who establishes his rule in the central hill country (see Chapter 17). The biblical account aligns these figures in a succession and assigns to each generation a different leader. Historically, however, many would have ruled at the same time, and some may have lived generations *after* Saul and David.

The inhabitants of these two kingdoms were not united by some primordial identity. There was little that distinguished them ethnically from the populations of neighboring states.[1] In many cases, they could have claimed kinship with groups beyond their political borders just as easily as with their own members. We do, however, observe a lot of regional variation in the realm ruled by these kingdoms. Thus, the peoples that inhabited the deep south (Negev) were culturally different from the region of Jerusalem and had little in common with populations in northern territories (the Samarian hill country, the Jezreel Valley, and the Galilee) and the region east of the Jordan (the Gilead) (Map 4.1).

Rather than strong bonds of culture and kinship, what eventually united the heterogeneous populations of these states was their duty to a *common king*. This first tie that binds was, therefore, not a fellowship of kindred minds. Many of the territories, cities, clans, and communities resented their obligations to the palace, and they would have been eager to break away to pursue an autonomous existence. Taxation, conscription of bodies for building projects and military campaigns, the seizure of

[1] The exception to this rule are the Philistines, who migrated from the Aegean and, originally, had a distinctive culture and diet. Yet in later centuries, even this population was indistinguishable from others in the region.

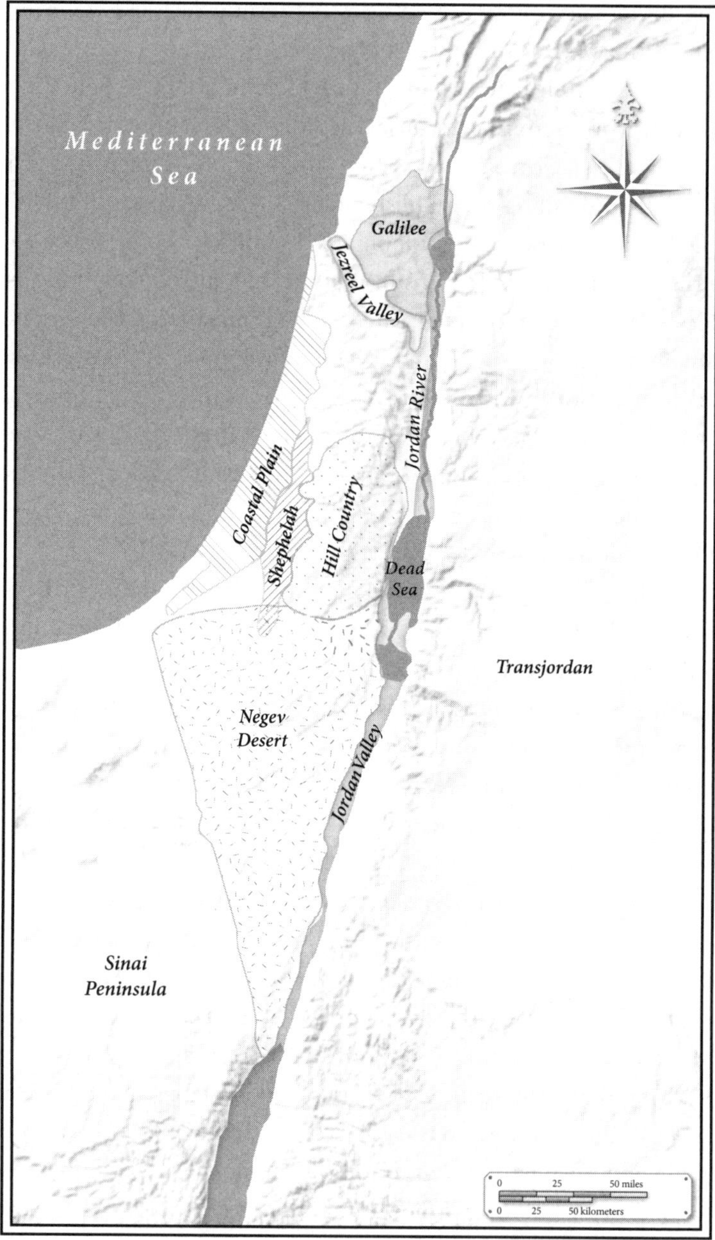

Map 4.1 Geographic regions of Southern Levant. Map created by Gerry Krieg (kriegmapping.com).

ancestral lands, and other essential components of royal government fomented the kind of unrest, dissent, and secession depicted in many biblical texts. The Bible even ascribes the division of the imagined union between the North and the South to precisely this kind of conflict: the Northern tribes cede from the union and "return to their tents" (a symbol of their ancient autonomy) because Rehoboam, David's grandson, demands too much from them.

Historically, it took the Northern kingdom of Israel longer to consolidate, with many power centers competing for hegemony. But as we shall see in the following chapter, it eventually became a mighty state, and it achieved this status while Judah was still struggling to get a foothold.

Founded by David, the kingdom of Judah was older. Whereas repeated putsches plagued the Northern kingdom and produced short-lived dynasties, the Southern kingdom benefited from political continuity. Even if the biblical construction of an unbroken chain of Davidic rulers raises suspicion, the smaller Southern kingdom likely did not face the same struggles among rival regions as the North did. Nevertheless, the Southern kingdom was much less powerful for the first centuries of existence. Its territory was poorer, its towns smaller, and it had just a fraction of the North's population.

A RAID ON JERUSALEM

A military campaign conducted by an Egyptian ruler at this time gives us a glimpse of Judah's inferior position vis-à-vis Israel. It also illustrates how Judean authors put a Jerusalemite spin on the past.

Both the Bible and the Egyptian inscriptions relate that a pharaoh named Shishak (or Shoshenq) campaigned in Canaan in Canaan (c. 925 BCE). Fragments from his victory monument turned up at Megiddo, a major city in what would become the Northern kingdom; Shishak likely placed it there when he passed through. The campaign in Canaan was highly unusually. The Libyan rulers of this time were too occupied with internal issues to think about problems abroad. As we learned in the preceding chapter, Egypt's inability during this period to intervene in Levantine affairs had enabled the emergence of territorial states in this region.

Figure 4.1 The Egyptian ruler Shishak depicted on the Temple of Amun in Karnak (near Luxor). Photo: Olaf Tausch.

The account of Shishak's campaign, which is inscribed on the walls of a temple at Karnak (a city in southern Egypt), catalogues more than 150 towns and peoples that the pharaoh conquered in the Levant, many from the kingdom of Israel (Figure 4.1). Yet none of them refer to Jerusalem or any place in the kingdom of Judah.

The reason the scribes at Karnak omitted these Southern towns is most probably that Judah was not on Egypt's radar by 925 BCE – or at least it had yet to create anything that would divert Shishak's attention from the powerful kingdom of Israel and its neighbors.

The biblical book of Kings, however, knows nothing about Shishak's assault on the Northern kingdom and its neighbors. Instead, it presents him marching up and attacking Judah (see 1 Kings 14:25–27). The book's authors recounted events from their Southern perspective. They were convinced that Jerusalem, thanks to David and his son Solomon, possessed great wealth in the early years of the dynasty. If the capital was much poorer in the following generations, it was because, these Judean scribes cleverly claimed, Shishak had robbed its wealth in the reign of Solomon's son.[2]

Under the assumption that Judah must have been a prominent power at this time, some scholars contend that Shishak's own account consciously omits Judah because it had entered an alliance with Egypt and therefore Shishak circumvented it during his campaign. Others claim that the Karnak inscription, which is damaged in a few places (see Figure 4.1), originally did refer to Jerusalem and towns in Judah. These apologetic efforts present several serious problems and have therefore not convinced most scholars. It seems more reasonable to assume that Shishak, or his armies, never stepped foot in the Southern kingdom.

In the biblical accounts, Shishak's campaign takes place immediately after Solomon's death, when the United Monarchy falls apart. Following his death, the North and the South repeatedly wage war with each other and face incursions from foreign foes. The Southern authors of these accounts imagined David and Solomon as formidable rulers. Why, then, was it so easy for Shishak to have his way with Judah? The fault lies, according to these authors, with Solomon's foolish son, Rehoboam. Through an imperious and foolhardy act, the new king had provoked the Northern tribes to break away from the Davidic dynasty and found a competitor state. That state, the Northern kingdom of Israel, turned out to be stronger than Judah and ended up inflicting suffering on it for two centuries.

[2] The book of Chronicles, which reiterates the account in Kings from the perspective of the temple in post-exilic Jerusalem (see Chapter 12), includes an expanded account of the incident in which Shishak comes with 1,200 chariots and 60,000 horsemen, and innumerable troops of Libyans, Sukkites, and Cushites, and captures all the fortified cities of Judah.

These accounts are part of a larger Southern history that I call the "Palace History." Found in the books of Samuel and Kings, this work does not know of an exodus from Egypt. Instead, it presupposes that the "Israelites" had always lived in their homeland, albeit under foreign domination. The narrative begins with Saul and later David liberating the nation from the Philistines (and Ammonites).

In Part III, we will see that Southern scribes in Judah likely would have been composing this narrative at about the same time that Northern writers were drafting a "People's History," which consists of the Family Story of Genesis and the Exodus-Conquest Account that I introduced in Chapter 2:

- The Palace History imagines a *political* unity centered on the Davidic dynasty and Jerusalem. In contrast, the People's History completely removes the monarchy from Israel's collective identity.
- The Palace History promotes Yhwh's promise of an eternal dynasty to David and his descendants, while the People's History is propelled by Yhwh's promises to the nation's ancestors and a covenant that Yhwh makes with the nation as whole.
- Likewise, the Palace History views the political rupture between the North and the South as the first fall from grace, whereas the People's History, in advanced stages of its composition-history, portrays primordial sins against divine commandments – first in the Garden of Eden and then later, in the wilderness, when the newly constituted nation breaks the covenant by worshipping a golden calf.

Under what historical circumstances were these competing accounts composed? Why would Judean historians have written about Israel's past? And who combined these rival accounts to form a single grand narrative that begins in Genesis and continues to the downfall of the kingdom of Judah? Those are questions that we will be addressing in coming chapters.

LITERATURE AND LITERACY

By this point, readers might be wondering: Why were the earliest biblical texts written so long after the events? Could Moses and Joshua not have penned a few passages in the Pentateuch, and David and Solomon at least some of the psalms and proverbs? And why are our oldest sources for Israel's history Akkadian and Egyptian texts, rather than Hebrew ones? The short answer to all these questions is: Hebrew writing, which presupposes the invention of the alphabet, did not yet exist.

In the preceding chapters, we noted that the earliest writing in human history comes from Mesopotamia and Egypt. These two centers of civilization had innovated rudimentary writing systems, with the temple and palace administrations using them for simple accounting purposes. Over time, the pictographic symbols became more abstract and evolved into "logograms," with hundreds of individual signs representing either complete words or short syllables (e.g., *ma, me, mi, mu, na, ne, ni, nu, pa, pe*) that could be combined to make words.

The non-alphabetic writing system that evolved in Mesopotamia is called "cuneiform" because the writing materials were clay tablets on which scribes, using sharpened styli, impressed tiny "wedges" (*cuneus* in Latin) to render the logograms and compose complex texts. Cuneiform was used widely to conduct foreign correspondence, even in Egypt. (Recall that the Amarna Letters were written in cuneiform Akkadian.) However, Egypt had developed its own non-alphabetic system: hieroglyphs (and its cursive form, hieratic). Instead of being impressed on soft clay tablets, these "sacred engravings" were painted on, or chiseled into, hard surfaces.

Cuneiform and hieroglyphs share many features. For example, both use unspoken symbols or "determinatives" to provide readers with information about the kind of word intended. Thus, as we saw in Chapter 2, when Merneptah declares Israel's extinction in his famous inscription, he deploys the hieroglyphic determinative for "foreign people" rather than for "foreign land."

The earliest Hebrew texts found in archeological excavations use the much simpler writing system that we call the alphabet, which was invented long after the "logo-syllabic" scripts of cuneiform and hieroglyphs. Rather than having to master hundreds of signs and their manifold variations, a scribe writing alphabetic texts needed to learn a minimal number, which consisted mostly of consonants and were much simpler in form.

Despite being less elaborate, alphabetic texts could not reckon with a broader readership – initially, at least. For Mesopotamia and Egypt, experts estimate that literacy was likely less than 1 percent. As for societies that produced alphabetic texts (such as Israel, Judah, and their neighbors in the Southern Levant), most agree that literacy was not much higher, and some claim that it was just as low.

While such was certainly the case in its early phases, by the seventh and sixth centuries BCE, literacy among elites had risen considerably in the Southern Levant. Throughout West Asia at this time, alphabetic Aramaic was also beginning to replace Akkadian as the lingua franca for international diplomacy. With respect to Athens and many of its Aegean neighbors, not everyone could read and write alphabetic Greek, but many (if not most) citizens could. It is hard to imagine this being the case had they been learning cuneiform Akkadian or hieroglyphic Egyptian.

ALPHABETS AND ABECEDARIA

Although frequently trivialized in recent scholarship, the alphabet's significance is considerable not only for the Bible's reception but also for its origins. Even so, its impact was far from immediate and long limited to the periphery.

The earliest evidence for the alphabet was carved into the limestone cliffs of the Wadi el-Hol Valley in Egypt. Pictographic in form and acrophonic in function, the writing dates to the early eighteenth century BCE. From about the same time, we have alphabetic graffiti from an Egyptian mining camp on the Sinai Peninsula (Serabit el-Khadim), where Canaanite prisoners of war worked – and occasionally wrote.

These early inscriptions were written in a Proto-Sinaitic (or Proto-Canaanite) script that spawned multiple iterations of the alphabet. One of the most important ones is from Phoenicia (modern Lebanon), and it was used to write not only Aramaic, Hebrew, and other Levantine languages, but also Greek, Latin, and other European languages. Thus, while Aegean communities achieved extraordinary literacy levels, their Greek alphabet derives from an older one invented on the Canaanite coast.

The earliest Hebrew inscriptions date to the late tenth or early ninth century BCE. An important exemplar is the Gezer Calendar (Figure 4.2),

Figure 4.2 Reproduction of the Gezer Calendar, on display at the Israel Museum, Jerusalem. Photo: Jacob L. Wright.

which lists a sequence of agricultural duties according monthly or bimonthly periods:

Two months: gathering.
Two months: planting.
Two months: late sowing.
One month: cutting flax.
One month: reaping barley.
One month: reaping and measuring grain.
Two months: pruning.
One month: summer fruit.
Abi. . .

The calendar's function is a subject of scholarly speculation, with suggested genres ranging from farmer's almanac to lullaby. The inscription itself was engraved on a limestone plaque and appears to be a scribal exercise. Even though it looks like the work of a novice, epigraphers (experts on ancient writing) assure us that it was performed by a practiced hand.

The Zayit Stone was found in the same region and likely dates to the same time. Measuring some fifteen inches in length, it too is presumably

Figure 4.3 Another abecedarium is the 'Izbet Sartah Ostracon, which is on display at the Israel Museum, Jerusalem. Photo: Jacob L. Wright.

a practice exercise, as it consists of nothing more than the twenty-two letters of the alphabet, in order. We have other Hebrew "abecedaria" from later times, but this is perhaps the earliest one and simultaneously one of our oldest Hebrew inscriptions.

All the early Hebrew inscriptions use a Phoenician script. From the mid-ninth century BCE on, Hebrew writing makes itself increasingly felt in the archeological record, reaching a zenith in the seventh century. During this time, a distinctive script (what epigraphers call "national script") evolved in the Northern kingdom, and surprisingly, its oldest exemplar is the monumental inscription from the neighboring kingdom of Moab that we discuss in the next chapter.

That "paleo-Hebrew" script would endure for centuries. Although it faded from daily use in the post-destruction period, it still appeared on coins and other national symbols from the Greco-Roman period, and it was used to write Yhwh's name (the "tetragrammaton") in the Dead Sea Scrolls. The preservation of the paleo-Hebrew script reflects an attachment to national tradition that is deeply rooted in the Iron Age, and it stands in sharp distinction to the *koine* or "shared" culture of Bronze Age civilizations.

The Bible was born in the Iron Age, and if Hebrew writing was not invented until the late tenth or early ninth century, we can understand why Moses and David were not its earliest authors. In the following chapter, we turn our attention to a little-known dynasty that put Israel on the map and paved the way for the first biblical writings.

FURTHER READING

Edelman, Diana Vikander, *King Saul in the Historiography of Judah*, Sheffield Academic Press, 1991.

Ehrlich, Carl S. and White, Marsha C., *Saul in Story and Tradition*, Mohr Siebeck, 2006.

Garfinkel, Yosef; Ganor, Saar; and Hasel, Michael G., *In the Footsteps of King David: Revelations from an Ancient Biblical City*, Thames & Hudson, 2018.

Krause, Joachim J.; Sergi, Omer; and Weingart, Kristin (eds.), *Saul, Benjamin, and the Emergence of the Monarchy in Israel*, SBL Press, 2020.

Leonard-Fleckman, Mahri, *The House of David: Between Political Formation and Literary Revision*, Fortress, 2016.

Na'aman, Nadav, "Was Khirbet Qeiyafa a Judahite City? The Case against It," *Journal of Hebrew Scriptures* 17, 2017 (open access).

Rollston, Christopher A., *Writing and Literacy in the World of Ancient Israel: Epigraphic Evidence from the Iron Age*, Society of Biblical Literature, 2010.

Sanders, Seth L., *The Invention of Hebrew*, University of Illinois Press, 2011.

Vayntrub, Jacqueline, "'Observe Due Measure': The Gezer Inscription and Dividing a Trip around the Sun," in Jeremy M. Hutton and Aaron D. Rubin (eds.), *Epigraphy, Philology, and the Hebrew Bible*, SBL Publications, 2015 (open access).

Wilson, Kevin A., *The Campaign of Pharaoh Shoshenq I into Palestine*, Mohr Siebeck, 2005.

Wright, Jacob L., *David, King of Israel, and Caleb in Biblical Memory*, Cambridge University Press, 2014.

5

Ahab and Jezebel

Putting Israel on the Map

"Yhwh forbid that I would give up
my ancestral inheritance to you."
– 1 Kings 21:3

THE REIGNING KING OF ISRAEL appears to be a mighty man of valor. But underneath his stately facade, he's a wimp, and a greedy and inept one at that. To his credit, he has an assertive queen at his side, and she knows how to get things done. Her handling of a property sale provides a case in point.

Near the palace there was a vineyard that the king wanted to make into a large herb garden. However, the land did not belong to him. Its owner would not accept a fair offer, as he would be relinquishing rights to his ancestral inheritance. Perturbed by this state of affairs, the king returns home, refuses to eat, lies down on his bed, and turns his face to the wall.

Enter the doughty and indomitable queen. Appalled by her husband's passivity, she takes matters into her hands. First, she cooks up a charge of treason against the vineyard's owner. Then she organizes a trial, bribes witnesses to give false testimony, and in the end, has him stoned. When all is said and done, she goes to her husband, the pouting king, and in her no-nonsense manner, tells him: "Go take possession of that vineyard you wanted. Its owner is dead."

This account is just one of the many unflattering tales that the biblical book of Kings has to tell about Israel's most important monarch. He is Ahab, and the queen is Jezebel. They were members of a dynasty, called the Omrides, that consolidated the Northern kingdom, established its international repute, and promoted a culture in which Yhwh featured prominently. Without these efforts, we would have no Bible today.

The book of Kings, however, lambastes Ahab, Jezebel, and the entire Omride dynasty. When its authors begrudgingly grant Ahab a victory over Israel's enemies, they go on to report that he nonetheless screwed up and failed to finish the job. In their account of his life, they portray the skilled commander as a coward who dies in battle despite his attempt to disguise himself as an average soldier. Likewise, they claim that he and Jezebel ferociously persecuted Elijah and Elisha, two prophets of Yhwh, while spreading the worship of other gods.

What would have prompted this extraordinarily disparaging portrait? To answer that question we first have to examine what the Omrides achieved, and what the biblical authors did to belittle those achievements.

THE CREATION OF A COMPLEX STATE

While the Bible credits David and his son Solomon with the feat of building the first major kingdom consisting of both the North and the South, historically it was Omri who really transformed Israel into a major power in the region. In just four decades, from 884 to 841 BCE, he and his dynastic successors – above all, his son Ahab – carved out a large and complex territorial state. As a testimony to the dynasty's significance, the Assyrians, and perhaps many others, knew the Northern kingdom simply as the "House of Omri" (*Bit-Ḫumri*), and they continued to use this designation long after new dynasties had usurped control of the impressive Levantine state that the Omrides founded.

Omri ended decades of civil wars between rival regions and rulers in the North, built a new capital in Samaria, and established a powerful ruling house that would endure for several generations.[1] He and his descendants expanded Israel's borders from the hill country and the Jezreel Valley further northwards into the Galilee, as well as across the Jordan River to the Gilead in the East.

[1] The name Samaria can refer to both the capital city and its wider region/kingdom.

An inscription from the Assyrian king Shalmaneser III tells about a momentous battle at Qarqar in 853 BCE. (The Bible, notably, does not mention it, as it would have given credence to this dynasty's success.) At that battle, Ahab fought against the Assyrians in an alliance of Levantine kings. He is said to have provided 10,000 foot-soldiers and 2,000 chariots to the coalition – the largest contingent of chariots in the campaign. Egypt appears to have joined the coalition but sent just 1,000 troops and no chariots. Even if the numbers may have been exaggerated, the comparison reveals how mighty Israel had become and how little Egypt was capable of investing in international affairs at this time. In Samaria, archeologists found an alabaster vase with cartouches from the contemporary pharaoh (Osorkon II); it was presumably a gift from Egypt to Ahab. Israel had come a long way since the days of Merneptah.

With its horses and chariots, the military was a major motor of state centralization and societal stratification. Biblical texts frequently feature chariots as a leading emblem of statehood, and their role in Israel's political evolution may be compared to the role of shipbuilding in Athens' rise during the fifth century. Chariots represent the most sophisticated technology of the ancient world. At the nexus of a vast network of knowledge and material goods, they were extremely expensive, and the horses that propelled them required exorbitant amounts of water and food. Evidence of stables and equestrian enterprises at the majestic city of Megiddo and other sites supports the biblical and extra-biblical accounts of Ahab's military might. Indeed, Israel's chariot battalions were so feared that their members were given posts in Assyria's imperial army after the kingdom's downfall.

Closely linked to the introduction of chariots are other important innovations, such as expensive body-armor for the chariot crew and the highly sophisticated composite bow. To fight effectively with these weapons, a standing army was necessary. Therefore, instead of recruiting private armies for ad hoc campaigns, they employed skilled fighters who trained regularly in formation.

The maintenance of a large, professional fighting force established a social hierarchy that relied on taxing the wider population. (The system for levying these duties – above all, grain, wine, and oil – can be studied

Figure 5.1 Assyrian chariots of Shalmaneser II from Balawat Gates. The British Museum, London. Photo: Jacob L. Wright.

in sixty-six receipts from Samaria; see Chapter 6.) Wherever the Omrides went, they undertook impressive building projects, and these efforts would not have been possible without the conscription of large labor forces and a literate bureaucracy.

In putting Israel on the map, the Omrides created a cosmopolitan culture. The kingdom traded their precious crafts and commodities with cities on the Phoenician coast, where, as we saw in the preceding chapter, the alphabetic writing system used for Hebrew was invented. Jezebel, the woman who reigned as Ahab's queen, came from Phoenician city of Tyre. Many cities collected the intricate ivory carvings that artisans produced in Samaria. The Omrides had introduced beautiful volute ("Proto-Aeolic") capitals throughout their kingdom, and the Assyrians adopted the style and spread it throughout their empire. These capitals show up a century later in Judah and in the Transjordan, where rulers either adopted them directly from the Omrides or via the Assyrians.

JUDAH AS ISRAEL'S VASSAL

The Omrides exerted influence over Judah and constantly interfered in its internal politics. In fact, the Southern kingdom that was emerging at this time relied heavily on Omride patronage. It also appears to have been at the beck and call of its Northern neighbor for much of its early history.

As part of its vassal obligations, Judah was expected to participate in Israel's military campaigns. Later, Southern scribes would insist that Judah's kings had agreed freely to join forces with the North. However, even they had to admit that the Omrides had managed to place one of their own on the throne in Jerusalem.

Her name was Athaliah, and she began her career in a political marriage with the Judean king Jehoram (or Joram). After his death, her son became king in Judah, and she exerted considerable influence in her role as queen-mother. When her son was assassinated after one year of his reign, she assumed the throne. In keeping with its anti-Omride polemics, the book of Kings claims that she went to great lengths to eradicate the Davidic dynasty. According to this tendentious account, the daughter of her deceased husband had rescued one of the Davidic descendants, and when the boy was old of enough, a priest in Jerusalem staged a rebellion, placing him on the throne and assassinating Athaliah after she had ruled as Judah's monarch for six years.

Samaria's leverage over Jerusalem goes a long way toward explaining why Judah later inherited Israel's cultural and literary heritage. And as we shall see, this former capital of the Northern kingdom continued to exert influence over Judah after these two states had been conquered and converted into imperial provinces.

While the book of Kings concedes that the reign of the Omrides was a time of power and opulence, it focuses solely on the decadence and the corruption that accompanied the prosperity and has little to say about their accomplishments. It also inveighs against these rulers for forsaking Yhwh, killing his prophets, and introducing the worship of foreign deities. A more scathing censure is difficult to imagine, and what elicited it was, not least, Israel's regional domination, which provoked deep resentment in Judah.

The preceding chapter introduced the Palace History, whose Southern authors brought together the stories of Saul, David, Solomon, and their successors from both the North and the South. Their work claims that it was not the Omride dynasty of Israel but rather the Davidic dynasty of Judah that first built a prestigious international kingdom. And instead of subordinating Judah to Israel, as the Omrides did, the Davidic kings of the Palace History unite them on equal footing.

Some of the legends in the Palace History about Ahab and the Omride dynasty may have been composed by scribes working for subsequent Northern dynasties, but many appear to be the work of Southern scribes writing much later. In their final form, these legends present Ahab, Jezebel, and other Omride rulers as the pinnacle of Northern transgressions. The Palace History does the opposite with King David, portraying him as the paradigm for the monarchy – with both its boons and its banes. David is a courageous fighter and ultimately a successful king; in contrast, Ahab is a coward and failure. As we will see in Part III, the reason for these contrasting attitudes is that the Judean historians who compiled and reworked these accounts needed David to serve as a point of unity in the nation's past – a unity with Jerusalem at its center.

THE MESHA STELE

The Mesha Stele is the most important non-biblical source for the study of ancient Israel and Judah; it also mirrors monarchic ideologies that were shared throughout the Southern Levant. Discovered in Jordan by an Anglican missionary in 1868, the massive stone bears a royal inscription from Mesha, a foundational ruler in the kingdom of Moab who was previously known only from the Bible. The monument, which dates to *c.*840 BCE, commemorates Mesha's military triumphs and ambitious building projects (Figure 5.2). The Moabite king tells how he succeeded in recovering territories that Omri and his son Ahab had occupied east of the Jordan River.

We have yet to discover a lengthy inscription like this from an earlier period, and it is unlikely that we will find one. At this time, the kingdoms of Israel and Judah, and their neighbors, were beginning to assign importance to texts and monumental writing. In the archeological record from the mid-ninth century, we start to see more inscribed artifacts; they range from personal seals to pottery shards (ostraca), which represented a cheap and accessible writing medium. This move toward "textualization" is historically pivotal, as it laid the foundation for the Bible's formation.

We will discuss other aspects of the Mesha Stele in later chapters. For our present concerns, what is most important is how a mid-ninth century ruler from the region used the written word and appealed to a common identity when ruling the heterogenous population of his kingdom. This foreign inscription is even more significant for our story if, as many epigraphers now claim, it is the earliest attestation of the Hebrew script.

Figure 5.2 The Mesha Stele. From the Matson Photograph Collection, Library of Congress.

The Bible shares with Mesha's monument many other commonalities, both conceptual and stylistic. Most likely, rulers in Israel and Judah commissioned inscriptions very similar to Mesha's, and some of these older monarchic sources may form the basis for biblical writings in the Palace History.

The monument foregrounds what may have been a new name for different communities in Mesha's kingdom: Moab. This territorial-ethnic name, which occurs at least six times in Mesha's account, matches the Bible's use of "Israel" to describe a kingdom and its inhabitants. The biblical usage has its origins in Omride rule, when the palace in Samaria adopted the name Israel to designate the expansive state it was creating.

Mesha also appeals to a male deity to unify his subjects. His name is Chemosh, and he exercises divine sovereignty over his land. Mesha had built a temple for him, and this inscription was part of the building project. In his account, Mesha recalls how Chemosh "saved me from all aggressors and made me look upon all mine enemies with contempt." Strikingly similar expressions appear in the book of Psalms and other biblical writings, where they describe Yhwh's salvific interventions. In Mesha's account, the divine deliverance turns out to be a long record of military victories, beginning with the reconquest of land previously forfeited to Omri and the Northern kingdom:

> Omri was the king of Israel, and he oppressed Moab for many days, because Chemosh was angry with his land. Omri's son replaced him. He said, "I will oppress Moab." In my days he said so. But I looked down on him and his house: Israel has been defeated; it has been defeated forever.
>
> Omri had taken possession of the whole land of Madaba, and had lived there in his days and half the days of his son: forty years. Yet Chemosh restored it in my days.

The rest of the inscription continues in this vein, describing how Chemosh restored to Moab territories in the Transjordan that Omri and his son (likely Ahab) had previously conquered.

Mesha was by no means a monotheist. But neither were the kings of Israel. In the same way that Mesha promotes the veneration of Chemosh, the Omride monarchs used Yhwh to consolidate their kingdom.

Circles beyond the palace would have had little if any reason to think in the collective category ("Moab" or "Israel") that the palace promoted. Many groups would have resisted the palace's totalizing claims and have affirmed their older, local identities – or new identities that they fashioned in protest. Clan resistance to centralization efforts is one of the chief concerns for states, both ancient and modern, and it explains why Mesha goes to such great lengths in his inscription to make a case for a collective Moabite identity with Chemosh at its center.

After the downfall of the Northern kingdom, scribes would adopt this monarchic strategy but also take it in a new direction. Whereas those in Mesha's court told the history of Moab from the perspective of a king ("I am Mesha, son of Chemosh-gad, king of Moab, the Dibonite"), scribes from the defeated Northern kingdom would narrate Israel's past from Yhwh's perspective, removing the king from the picture altogether. As the one and only sovereign of the nation, Yhwh makes his will known through prophets and texts, and does not need a human ruler as his representative. The remarkable post-monarchic shift is a subject for future chapters.

Mesha's account thus reveals how Southern Levantine states could 1) construct a collective identity to consolidate their diverse realms and 2) use written narratives to do so. Moreover, his monument joins that of Merneptah and several others in not only providing an ancient nonbiblical attestation of the name "Israel," but also in insisting, counterfactually, that this people had been "defeated forever."

To be sure, the experience of defeat plays a leading role in our story. If Israel had continued to grow and to expand into an imperial power, without long and painful experiences of political subjugation, then its members would never have produced a national literature and lore capable of holding together a people after a crushing defeat. However, the defeat would have been much less crushing had it not been for preceding triumphs that presaged an auspicious future.

SHIFTING IDENTITIES

We have already witnessed how scribes who curated the biblical corpus integrated representative individuals (such as Miriam) into their nation's narrative. The Mesha Stele offers us early external evidence for studying this compositional process.

Mesha begins by identifying himself as "son of Chemosh-Gad." His father's name declares, literally, that the Moabite national deity Chemosh reigns over, and resides in, a territory called Gad. According to his account, the people of Gad had dwelt in a town/region named Ataroth from time immemorial. Later a king of Israel (either Omri or Ahab) came and laid claim to this territory, fortifying its chief city. But with the help of his national deity, Mesha drove Israel out of his territory and re-established its earlier border.

Some of the oldest passages of the Palace History, as well as many prophetic writings, refer to Gad in the same way that Mesha does – as a region across the Jordan that either belonged to Israel or was beyond its borders. But the People's History introduced in the preceding chapter claims something radically different: it presents Gad as the name of one of Jacob's twelve sons. He is the ancestor of a tribe, also called Gad, that was part of the people of Israel during the exodus and that settled in the region east of the Jordan. Gad was a peripheral territory in the Northern kingdom, and the People's History represents this fact by making Gad a child not of Jacob's wives but of these women's handmaids.

As with many other populations, Gad became part of Israel through a complex history of conquest and political negotiations. The courts of Omri and Mesha, and of their successors, fought over the region for many years. The People's History looks back on this protracted conflict and reframes it by describing the genesis of an ancestral figure named Gad, implying that the region of Gad had been part of Israel centuries before the reigns of Mesha and Omri.

Each of the twelve tribes, along with countless other clans, has a different history of how it came to be affiliated with Israel. We can rarely reconstruct that history in any detail. What is most remarkable is how the scribes who produced our texts found a way to construct a collective past that affirms Israel's unity without erasing the diversity of its members.

The Mesha Stele also refers to several places where important events unfold in the Bible. The most prominent is Nebo, from whose heights Moses, at the end of Deuteronomy, views the Promised Land before he dies. Yhwh honors the special relationship with "my servant Moses" by tending to his burial. Since the gravesite is unmarked and hidden, one could use the legend to claim the whole territory for Israel. In most biblical texts, Nebo is understood as belonging to Israel, yet others present it in Moabite hands. Some prophetic texts even pronounce curses on it.

Mesha's victory inscription offers a Moabite perspective on the history of this place. The ruler recalls how he captured Nebo from Israel, slaughtering 7,000 men and offering the women and girls to his god Chemosh. He also tells how he deported Yhwh's sacred objects, which means that Yhwh must have had a sanctuary there.

Mesha's reference to this deity, likely the oldest one in the historical record, provides another clue that the Omrides used Yhwh to consolidate their subjects. Although the Bible denounces Ahab for promoting the veneration of other gods, all our evidence suggests that he did much to establish Yhwh as the central deity of the kingdom. We know that he gave his sons Yahwistic names: Ahaziah ("held by Yhwh") and Jehoram/Joram ("Yhwh is exalted"). And as we have seen, he or his father appear to have built sanctuaries for Yhwh in the territories they occupied east of the Jordan. That they promoted Yhwh as the nation's chief deity does not mean that they excluded other gods. As Mesha did for the land of Moab with the deity Chemosh, the Omrides likely did for the land of Israel with Yhwh, and as in the case of Moab, the worship of other gods would have been tolerated alongside Yhwh.

YHWH AND HIS WIFE

In 1975–1976 archeologists working at an isolated fortress (Kuntillet Ajrud) in the northern Sinai Desert discovered Hebrew writings related to Yhwh (Figure 5.3). The material finds and texts themselves suggest a direct link between this remote place and the Northern kingdom. Scholars debate the date, but most are comfortable with the late ninth or early eighth century – that is, after the Omride effort to promote Yhwh worship.

The inscriptions appear to be scribal exercises, and several lines read, "I have blessed you by the Yhwh of Samaria." The references to the capital of the Northern kingdom leave no doubt that many in Israel

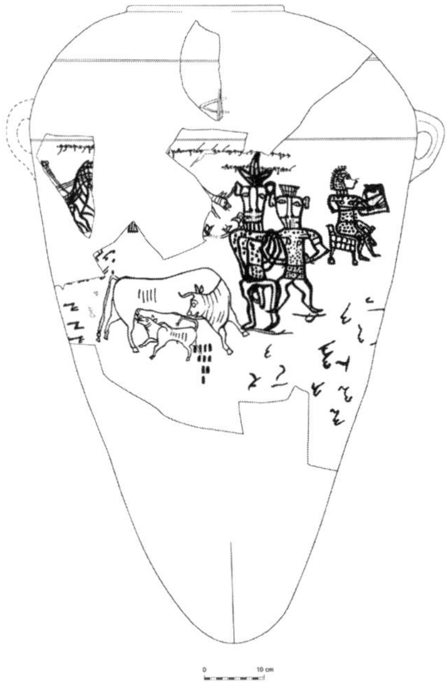

Figure 5.3 Reconstruction of pithos jar from Kuntillet Ajrud with inscriptions pertaining to "Yhwh and his Asherah." Image courtesy of Ze'ev Meshel.

(especially elites) venerated Yhwh. However, this deity is not alone; he's accompanied by "his Asherah."

Asherah is a well-attested West Asian deity. As the consort of the highest god El, who presided over a larger pantheon, she occupied a position of prominence. In the Bible, she is often paired with Baal. Both El and Baal are attested in these inscriptions, with blessings pronounced in their names. However, Asherah is no longer El's or Baal's consort but Yhwh's. The evidence suggests that in being promoted to Israel's national deity, Yhwh had usurped El's (and Baal's) place of honor in the pantheon.

These finds are undeniably shocking and scandalous. The coupling of Yhwh with another deity flies in the face of the Bible's stringent requirements to worship Yhwh alone and its vehement opposition to the veneration of other gods. But then again, such stringency and vehemence would not have been necessary had this veneration not been widespread.

The Bible admits as much, especially with regard to Asherah. According to the Palace History, Ahab had set up her symbol in Samaria and Jehu maintained it even after his political putsch and religious reforms (1 Kings 16:33, 2 Kings 13:6). For the reign of the Judean king Josiah, this history recounts a reform (*c.*620 BCE) in which the king removed Asherah's sacred vessels from the temple and destroyed a sector of the city where a guild of women wove her ritual garments (2 Kings 23:4, 7). Asherah worship was thus firmly entrenched in both Samaria and Jerusalem.

What led to the banishment of this goddess was not some sort of entrenched, macho opposition to a female deity in the societies of ancient Israel and Judah. After all, many macho cultures in antiquity, from Athens to Assyria, had goddesses as their chief deities. Moreover, Asherah had all along been only the consort, with limited power next to Yhwh, and by pairing her with Yhwh (not El), worshippers were affirming Yhwh's preeminence.

The biblical ban on worshipping Asherah along with other male deities was part of an effort to focus on a single transcendent entity that could unite the nation. If Yhwh were allowed to have a consort, then communities would continue thinking in terms of conventional Canaanite cosmologies. The intimate relationship between one people and one deity, which is foundational to the biblical concept of covenant, meant that the longstanding union between Yhwh and Asherah had to be dissolved. As they constructed this new covenantal order, the biblical authors annulled the union and envisioned a new marriage between Yhwh and Israel (see Chapters 20 and 21).

MONOTHEISM?

Biblical religion is, by and large, not monotheistic but "monolatrous," which means that worship focuses on Yhwh but does not deny the *existence* of other gods. Indeed, the existence of these other gods was crucial to the way in which biblical authors developed new political-theologies, as well as to their assertion that Yhwh is superior to his competitors.

In the process of making monolatry, the biblical scribes identified various deities as Yhwh's different titles or manifestations. Notice, for example, how the first lines of Psalm 91 identifies Elyon ("the Most High") and Shaddai ("the Almighty") with Yhwh as "my God":

> You who sit in the shelter of *Elyon*,
> who dwell in the shadow of *Shaddai*,
> will say to *Yhwh*:
> "My refuge and my fortress,
> my God in whom I shall trust."
> – Psalm 91:1–2

Perhaps most telling is the name Israel: while scholars debate its meaning, most agree that the final "-el" refers to the god El. In a wide array of biblical texts, we can witness a development in which El came to mean "God" and be understood as a title for Yhwh. Thus, while the name Israel may have originally meant "El contends," the biblical story of Jacob reinterprets it with the meaning that *Jacob* contends *with the deity* (see Genesis 32:28).

At the beginning, there was more than one Yhwh. Inscriptions from Kuntillet Ajrud and other places refer to "the Yhwh of Samaria" as well as "the Yhwh of Teman (Edom)." We also know of "the Yhwh of Jerusalem" as well as Yhwhs from various other places. Eventually, the authors of Deuteronomy, in an effort to consolidate a nation from competing centers, would declare that all these Yhwhs are one and the same: "Hear O Israel, Yhwh is our God, Yhwh is one" (Deuteronomy 6:4).

One of the most important steps that the biblical scribes took was to portray their people's past as the story of a (rocky) relationship with Yhwh. As we explore that important development in Part III, we must bear in mind that it was the Omrides who laid the foundation for it.

FURTHER READING

Beach, Eleanor Ferris, *The Jezebel Letters: Religion and Politics in Ninth-Century Israel*, Fortress, 2005.

Bean, Adam L. and Rollston, Christopher A., "Ataroth and the Inscribed Altar: Who Won the War between Moab and Israel?" *TheTorah.com*, 2020 (open access).

Dutcher-Walls, Patricia, *Jezebel: Portrait of a Queen*, Liturgical Press, 2004.

Finkelstein, Israel, *The Forgotten Kingdom: The Archaeology and History of Northern Israel*, Society of Biblical Literature, 2013 (open access).

Fleming, Daniel, *Yahweh before Israel: Glimpses of History of a Divine Name*, Cambridge University Press, 2020.

Hadley, Judith M., *The Cult of Asherah in Ancient Israel and Judah: Evidence for a Hebrew Goddess*, Cambridge University Press, 2000.

Lipschits, Oded, "The Origin and Date of the Volute Capitals from the Levant," in Israel Finkelstein and Nadav Na'aman (eds.), *Studies in the Archaeology and History of Israel in the Late Bronze Age, Iron Age, and Persian Period in Honor of David Ussishkin*, Winona Lake, 2011.

Olyan, Saul, *Asherah and the Cult of Yahweh in Israel*, Society of Biblical Literature, 1988.

Parker, Simon B., *Stories in Scripture and Inscriptions*, Oxford University Press, 1997.

Routledge, Bruce, *Moab in the Iron Age: Hegemony, Polity, Archaeology*, University of Pennsylvania Press, 2004.

Römer, Thomas, *The Invention of God*, Harvard University Press, 2015.

Smith, Mark, S., *The Early History of God: Yahweh and the Other Deities in Ancient Israel*, 2nd ed., Eerdmans Publishing, 2002.

Smoak, Jeremy and Schniedewind, William, "Religion at Kuntillet 'Ajrud," *Religions* 10 (2019): 1–18 (open access).

Tobolowsky, Andrew, *The Myth of the Twelve Tribes of Israel: New Identities across Time and Space*, Cambridge University Press, 2022.

6

Jehu and Elisha

Israel's Downfall and Judah's Jubilation

The prophet Elisha called one of the "sons of the prophets," and said unto him: "Gird your loins, take this vial of oil, and go to Ramoth-gilead."

– 2 Kings 9:1

IT IS 841 BCE AND ISRAEL is at war, fighting on the eastern front. Its armies – including those of its Judean vassal – are locked in a showdown with Hazael, the king of the powerful Aramean state that had long managed to keep Israel's northern and eastern territories in its political orbit.

As Israel's commanding officers are meeting to discuss a new strategy, a servant of the prophet Elisha arrives at the military camp. Instead of waiting for the meeting to end, he barges in: "I have a message for you, the commander."

"Which one? We are all commanders."

"For you, *the* commander!" he replies, pointing his finger at an officer named Jehu.

The two withdraw to a nearby residence, and as soon as they are alone, the young man pours oil over Jehu's head and declares: "Hereby I anoint you to be king over Israel, the people of Yhwh." After prophesying that Jehu would destroy Ahab's dynasty, he opens the door and disappears.

When Jehu returns to the council, his fellow commanders ask what had happened. Jehu brushes aside their question: "Nothing. You know how that guy babbles. . ."

"Liar! Come on, out with it!"

When Jehu tells them about the anointing, they take their robes, place it under Jehu's feet, and sound the trumpet, proclaiming, "Jehu is king!"

This account appears in the Palace History (2 Kings 9–10), which portrays Jehu assassinating the reigning Omride king and ordering that his corpse be discarded in the same vineyard that Jezebel had secured for his grandfather Ahab long before.

As we discussed in the preceding chapter, the Palace History goes out of its way to malign the Omrides' memory. For the Southern scribes who drafted this work, the Omrides epitomized all that was wrong with the North. However, these Southern circles owed much to the achievements of this censured dynasty – not least, their promotion of Yhwh worship.

This debt was decisive for the making of the Bible, yet it presupposes the demise of all that powerful Northern kings had managed to create. Their cataclysmic downfall, and the jubilation it elicited in Judah, is the subject of the present chapter.

THE DISCOVERY OF DAVID

Dan is a town on Israel's northern border at the headwaters of the Jordan River near beautiful Mt. Hermon, and an inscribed stele from this place provides critical clues for not only the existence of a historical David but also the relationship between the Southern and the Northern kingdoms. The excavation team recovered several sections of stele; the remaining pieces have yet to be found. Someone in antiquity seems to have shattered the monument and scattered it over the site, presumably when the city was destroyed by the Assyrians in 733/732 BCE.

The person who had originally commissioned the monument was likely Hazael (842–796 BCE), whom the Northern kingdom is fighting in our opening story of Jehu's anointing. A mighty monarch and military leader, Hazael reigned over Aram-Damascus, and the stele commemorates his success in seizing Dan from the Northern kingdom.

Among his great feats, the Aramean ruler claims to have vanquished seventy kings (a conventional number of exaggeration). However, he names just two. Though their names are not fully legible, the first ruled over "Israel," that is, the Northern kingdom. The second belonged to "the House of David." This expression refers to the Southern kingdom

Figure 6.1 The Tel Dan Stele at the Israel Museum, Jerusalem. Photo: Oren Rozen.

(Judah), and it represents our earliest reference to David in the historical record (Figure 6.1):

1. . . .and cut . . .
2. . . . my father went up [against him when h]e fought at . . .
3. and my father lay down, he went to his [ancestors (i.e. became sick and died)]. And the king of I[s-]
4. rael entered previously in my father's land, [and] Hadad made me king,
5. And Hadad went in front of me, [and] I departed from the seven [. . .]
6. s of my kingdom, and I slew [seve]nty kin[gs], who harnessed th [ousands of cha-]
7. riots and thousands of horsemen (or: horses). [I killed Jeho]ram son [of Ahab]
8. king of Israel, and [I] killed [Ahaz]iahu son of [Jehoram, kin-]
9. g of the House of David, and I set [their towns into ruins and turned]
10. their land into [desolation]
11. other [. . . and Jehu ru-]
12. led over Is[rael and I laid]
13. siege upon [ ]

– Translation by Biran and Naveh

Even if the inscription only refers to a member of David's dynasty who lived long after its founder, the appearance of the name "David" in this fragmentary account sparked a media frenzy, making the front page of the New York *Times* in 1993. The find, according to many, confirms not only that David lived, but also that he ruled over the extensive and mighty kingdom portrayed in the Bible. The first conclusion is merited and important, since many "minimalist" historians maintain that David is a mythical figure. But the second – that this find somehow supports the biblical description of David's "United Monarchy" – is unsustainable.

Notice the subordinate place that the House of David occupies in the inscription. By naming this kingdom second, the scribe indicates that the Northern kingdom led the war effort. On this point, the inscription corroborates the biblical portrait of this century before Israel's downfall: as the one who set the terms of the relationship, the Northern kingdom expected Judah to join its coalitions and take part in its campaigns.

The Palace History depicts Judah trying to break free from Israel's domination. A Davidic dynast triumphs over the Edomites, and the success bolsters his confidence. He sends messengers to the king of Israel, inviting him to a face-off on the battlefield. The Northern ruler sends back a cheeky response:

> Once a thistle sent a message to the cedar of Lebanon,
> saying, "Give your daughter to my son as wife!"
> Soon thereafter a large animal passed by
> and unknowingly trampled that thistle underfoot.
>
> You have indeed defeated Edom,
> and now you feel high and mighty.
> Glory in that success.
> But do yourself a favor and stay at home.
> Why should you meddle with trouble so that you fall,
> you and Judah with you?
>
> – 2 Kings 14:9–10

The Judean king refuses to listen, and during the duel, he is trounced. The Northern ruler then marches up to Jerusalem, breaks down its wall, seizes its wealth, and returns to Samaria with the humiliated ruler and other hostages.

While the Southern authors of the Palace History could not deny that Judah was subservient to Israel during these years, they claimed that originally – that is, just a few generations earlier – David and his son Solomon were at the helm. Jerusalem forfeited its ascendancy to Samaria only after a regrettable rupture between the North and the South. For the Palace History, the ideal is a Davidic dynast ruling over, and uniting, the two realms. As so often in biblical narratives, an imagined past becomes the benchmark for the present and future.

The authors of the Palace History were not satisfied with foreign kings conquering the Omrides for strategic reasons; their demise had to be an act of divine judgment. These scribes therefore created an account in which the Omrides fall not only in a contest with foreign armies, but also at the hand of a new dynastic leader (Jehu) whom Yhwh commissions through his righteous prophet Elisha. This account also claims, counter-factually, that Jehu re-established Yhwh worship in the North after it had fallen out of favor during Omride rule.

JEHU AND HIS DYNASTY

Under Jehu and his dynasty (the "Nimshides"), Aramean rulers won the upper hand and began to dismantle what the Omrides had accomplished on the battlefield. Although the Palace History has these foreign kings harassing the Omride kingdom, it may be describing events that actually occurred during the reign of Jehu and his descendants. By projecting them back to the time of the Omrides, the Palace History demonstrates how this dynasty brought suffering on its subjects.

While the Arameans were Israel's chief nemesis for much of the ninth century, the Assyrians, from northern Iraq, gradually assumed this role. A victory monument called the Black Obelisk – which once stood in the Assyrian capital of Nimrud and now can be viewed in the British Museum – portrays either Jehu or his ambassador prostrated and kissing the feet of the mighty Assyrian overlord Shalmaneser III (d. 823 BCE) (Figure 6.2). This is our oldest image of a member of the Northern kingdom, and the accompanying inscription lists the tribute paid to Assyria:

Figure 6.2 Part of Black Obelisk showing Jehu (or his emissary) prostrate before Shalmaneser III, at the British Museum, London. Photo: Jacob L. Wright.

> The tribute of Jehu, son of Omri: I received from him silver, gold, a golden bowl, a golden vase with pointed bottom, golden tumblers, golden buckets, tin, a staff for a king, and spears.

Shalmaneser's court was mistaken about Jehu's genealogy: he was not an Omride, but the one who dethroned the Omrides. Conversely, and more importantly, we hear nothing in the Bible about how Jehu purchased his freedom – and may even have come to power – by bending his neck to Assyria's yoke.

In 803 Assyria under Adad-nirari III besieged Damascus, the Aramean capital. The assault radically weakened Israel's most immediate competitor. As a result, Jehu's descendants (Jehoash and later Jeroboam II) were able to reconquer some of the lost northern and eastern regions and to re-establish the prosperity that the Omrides had enjoyed. In fact, they managed to bring the kingdom to an unprecedented level of luxury. The affluence of the age was due not only to military achievements but also to the increased production of olive oil and wine. A wide range of stamps, seals, and other objects (often engraved with names and dates) attest to this economic surge. The Samaria Ostraca, for example, are receipts for the delivery of wine and oil that have been painted or scratched on potsherds. Historians continue to mine this large corpus for data about the administration and economy of the Northern kingdom. The personal names on them reveal also that Yhwh enjoyed pride of place among the elite members of this society. They also illustrate how figures in biblical narratives frequently represent larger clans and regions.

For five decades, Israel complied with Assyria's demands, and the imperial records attest to the tribute Jehu's successors paid as vassals to this foreign power. Assyria was by this time far greater than any state in the Southern Levant. Samaria, the capital of Israel, was about fifty times smaller than the Assyrian capital in Nimrud, whose city walls were five miles long. As for Egypt, it was politically in disarray. The influential North African kingdom did, however, keep a close eye on the political tumult in the region. Eventually, it would take part in the conflict that was moving ever closer to its borders.

The long period of Northern prosperity came to an end with the rise of the expansionistic ruler Tiglath-pileser III (745–727). He is the de facto founder of the Neo-Assyrian Empire, and his sweeping military and political reforms revived Assyrian hegemony. In a hitherto unmatched show of arms and with unflinching terror, he swept over much of the Southern Levant. This was the beginning of the end. Soon enough this emerging empire would begin to annex Israel's territories, and within less than century, it would conquer its capital, laying waste to the entire kingdom and deporting its inhabitants.

The Palace History claims that King Menahem (d. 737 BCE) paid an enormous sum of silver when Tiglath-pileser (called "Pul") advanced on the Northern kingdom. Originating in Tirzah, a powerful city in the Jezreel Valley, Menahem had usurped the throne, and by paying Assyria the generous amount, he secured imperial sponsorship for his rule. Moreover, we are told that to raise the funds for this payment he had to impose heavy duties on Israel's propertied classes:

> Menahem exacted the money from Israel, from every Man of Valor/Might, to pay the king of Assyria. Each head paid fifty shekels of silver. The king of Assyria then turned back and did not stay in the land.
>
> – 2 Kings 15:20

In the biblical narrative, this is the first encounter between Assyria and the Northern kingdom. Yet as we noted earlier, payment of gifts and tribute had begun already during Jehu's reign – another fact that did not fit the Palace History's favorable portrait of the one who deposed the despised Omrides.

THE FINAL YEARS

In *c.*740 BCE, a captain in Israel's army named Pekah staged a putsch from the Transjordan and seized the throne. In the fifth year of his reign, he entered into an alliance with Aram-Damascus. The strategic goal was to thwart Assyria's advance into the Southern Levant. Judah, however, was an obstacle. Its king was Ahaz, father of the famous Hezekiah (the subject of the next chapter). Because he refused to join the Israel–Aramean alliance, the allied armies laid siege to Jerusalem, with the objective of deposing Ahaz and replacing him with a ruler who would do their bidding.

This incident is known as the Syro-Ephraimite War, and the prophetic book of Isaiah treats the clash at length in it oldest portion (the "Isaiah Memoir" of chapters 7–9). The account begins with the prophet addressing Judah's deep fear of Israel's aggression:

> The heart [of Ahaz] and the heart of his people shook as the trees of the forest shake in the wind. Then Yhwh said to Isaiah: Go out to meet Ahaz ... at the end of the conduit of the upper pool on the highway to the Fuller's Field, and say to him:
>
> Take heed, be quiet, do not fear, and do not let your heart be faint because of these two smoldering stumps of firebrands [the king of Israel and the king of Aram-Damascus] ... because they have plotted evil against you, saying, "Let us go up against Judah and cut off Jerusalem and conquer it for ourselves and make the son of Tabeel king in it." Therefore, thus says my lord Yhwh: "It shall not stand, and it shall not come to pass ... Within sixty-five years Ephraim [Israel] will be shattered as a people. If you do not believe, you will not remain."
>
> – Isaiah 7:2–8

Isaiah promises Ahaz that the enemy's plan would come to naught, and that Israel eventually would be destroyed. The king, however, does not believe the prophet. Taking matters into his own hands, he allies himself with Assyria, paying Tiglath-pileser to intervene militarily against Israel and the Arameans.

The book of Isaiah is deeply concerned with the relationship between Judah and Israel, which explains why the incident lies at the heart of this mammoth prophetic work. Likewise, the conflict represents one of the lowest points in the Palace History. It corresponds to a clash depicted immediately after the division of the United Monarchy, with the Judean king paying the Arameans to assault Israel after Israel had begun to build up a military presence on Judah's border (1 Kings 15). Whether this earlier event ever occurred is difficult to say, but it was important for the authors of the Palace History to show how the chain of events leading to Israel's downfall is a direct result of conflicts with Judah: in response to Northern aggression, Judah made alliances with foreign powers, which proceeded, slowly but surely, to dismantle their competitor. The Palace History also demonstrates how these same foreign powers that Judah invited to the region would eventually set their sights on Jerusalem and in the process destroy much of the Southern kingdom.

Contrary to the biblical depiction, Assyria's advance against Israel had little if anything to do with Judah's invitation. The empire had already begun – a decade earlier – to establish its hegemony in the region. As the Assyrian kings seized Israel's northern and eastern territories, they deported many of their inhabitants. In 732 BCE, the Syro-Ephraimite conflict concluded with Assyria attacking Damascus, annexing all of Aram, executing its king, and deporting much of its population. Likewise, they reduced the Northern kingdom ("Ephraim") to Samaria and its direct environs. On the throne they placed a new ruler named Hoshea and exacted from him heavy tribute. Recovered records from the Assyrian palace show that the kingdom of Judah was a dutifully paying imposts to the empire at this time.

In 727 Hoshea stopped sending tribute and sought to form an alliance against Assyria with Egypt's help. These audacious moves proved catastrophic. Under Shalmaneser IV and Sargon, the empire waged war on the Northern kingdom (likely with Judean auxiliaries serving in their ranks). After being beleaguered for several years, Samaria capitulated sometime around 722.

A once mighty kingdom had fallen. In the two centuries of existence, it had exerted considerable influence throughout the Southern Levant. In the reign of Ahab, it had even challenged Assyria's advance as the leading member of a powerful coalition. But those days were long gone. Samaria was now an imperial province, with foreign governors presiding in the place of native kings.

Some five hundred years later, a native monarchy would be re-established in the region, as members of the Maccabean family carved out a kingdom that included territories from both the North and the South. Yet in contrast to what the Omrides and Nimshides had achieved, the kingdom would be ruled from Jerusalem, not Samaria, and it would have a pronounced Judean profile.

Even though the biblical corpus is ultimately a work of Judean scribes, it has hardly anything to say about the Maccabean state. As we will see in Chapter 25, the circles of sages responsible for shaping the contours of this corpus excluded the books of the Maccabees, with their ideologies of statist power and political martyrdom. The writings that these circles included in their collection focus instead on the first kingdoms of Israel and Judah, the imperial provinces that replaced them, and above all, the families and clans that lived long before them. At the center of the Bible's political landscape is a new kind of community, one capable of surviving the downfalls of kingdoms – whether it be the one that the Maccabees re-established or the ones David and Omri created long before.

THE FATE OF THE DEFEATED

What happened to the local populations after Assyria conquered the Northern kingdom? How many were deported to Mesopotamia? Did the exiles assimilate into their new environments and vanish for good? What kinds of new communities formed in the wake of destruction? And how did they think about their past? These are the questions that we will be examining in coming chapters. For the present, it suffices to note a few details.

Our first and most important sources of information are the official Assyrian records. They are poorly preserved and not always consistent, but from them we can glean valuable details about the fate of Samaria and its inhabitants. Thus, a royal "prism-inscription" discovered at the Assyrian palace in Nimrud, Sargon describes how he conquered Samaria for his god and exiled 27,290 of its inhabitants. Among this population, he equipped soldiers to man two hundred chariots for his royal corps. He resettled the rest in Assyria, placing one of his officers as governor over them and "counted them among the citizens of Assyria" (which means that he imposed upon them heavy taxes).

Regarding Samaria itself, Sargon claims to have rebuilt it "better than it was before and settled therein people from countries which I had conquered." Whereas the later Babylonian deportations kept the Judeans together, the Assyrians severed the ethnic cohesion of the populations they conquered. Beginning with Tiglath-pileser III, the empire practiced a policy of "two-way deportations," resettling the inhabitants of subjugated kingdoms in sparsely populated regions far from their homelands while bringing in new groups to colonize the conquered territories. Reflecting this program of forced migrations, the biblical book of Kings reports that Assyria transferred peoples from "Babylon, Cuthah, Avva, Hamath, and Sepharvaim, and settled them in the towns of Samaria in place of the Israelites; they took possession of Samaria and dwelt in its towns" (2 Kings 17:24; see discussion in the next chapter).

For the region of Samaria, archeologists estimate that the Assyrians deported little more than 10–20% of the population. This means that many would have been around to carry on Israel's traditions – something to bear in mind as we think about the formation of the Bible in the coming chapters. Recent archeological finds also shed light on the settlement of Mesopotamian populations in the former Northern kingdom. Ido Koch has helpfully surveyed these finds, which include not only cuneiform tablets and seals but also Mesopotamian-style vessels and Assyrian architecture.[1]

The empire's chief concern were the corridors and trade routes that ran through Gaza on the coast as well as Megiddo, which had been an important city in the Northern kingdom. Scholars are divided on the

[1] Koch, "Assyrian Deportation and Resettlement."

issue of Assyria's economic interest in the Southern Levant. Some insist that the empire was eager to exploit the resources of the region and even encouraged its economic development. Others argue that it was interested in little else than collecting tribute from its client states, and that it left most lands (especially those that did not serve a strategic purpose) to languish under the imperial "yoke" it imposed on them.

Sargon's assignment of Israel's soldiers to Assyria's royal chariot divisions is especially significant. We noted in the preceding chapter that Israel was famous for its chariots and horses, and when Assyria conquered Samaria, and in a body of texts from Nimrud called the "Horse Lists," we find many references to high-ranking Samarian officers in equestrian divisions. According to Stephanie Dalley, an expert on the Horse Lists, the Samarian battalion is "the only known unit from outside Assyria proper that is known as a national unit under its own city name."[2] The Samarian battalion consists of thirteen equestrian officers with the title "commander of teams." It was larger than all the others and therefore "a very significant part of the Assyrian army." Foreign officers deported from other countries joined the imperial army, yet according to Dalley, none of them maintained their "national" affiliation as those from Samaria did.

These texts related to the Assyrian army thus provide us with important data. They indicate that Samaria's downfall did not mean the extinction of the collective identity that the Omride kings had created two centuries earlier to unite their diverse kingdom. Many of the vanquished still took pride in their origins, in coming chapters, we will explore how that Israel-focused identity made itself felt in literature.

A NEW DAY FOR JUDAH

Israel's disintegration elicited jubilation in Judah. The *schadenfreude* is palpable not only in the Palace History, which details at length all that Israel had done to deserve its fate, but also in the prophetic writings: some of the earliest portions of this corpus, as we saw for Isaiah, promise

[2] Dalley, "Foreign Chariotry and Cavalry," p. 32.

salvation to the Southern kingdom in the form of its Northern competitor's destruction (see further discussion in Chapter 21).

The decision of the Judean king Ahaz to invite Assyria to intervene in Levantine affairs turned out to be a costly mistake. The empire may have wiped out Judah's longstanding rival, but it was a difficult master to serve. In just two decades, during the reign of his son Hezekiah, Assyria's armies would overrun the Southern kingdom.

Judah, however, would manage to escape that encounter intact and go on to become a major power in the region, taking the prominent position that Israel had long held. The sensational rise of the Southern kingdom, which is the subject of the next chapter, made its fall all the more dramatic. It occurred in the span of 135 years, what historians call "the long seventh century."

That politically volatile period witnessed the growth of many of the most important biblical writings, which consisted of two very different types: those drafted by members of the defeated Northern kingdom and those written in the employ of the Judean court. Both sets of texts addressed central questions of what it means to be a people and what role the state has to play in a people's life. Their very different perspectives impart a complexity and diversity to the biblical corpus that go a long way toward explaining its longevity and influence.

FURTHER READING

Athas, George, *The Tel Dan Inscription: A Reappraisal and a New Introduction*, Sheffield Academic Press, 2003.

Biran, Avraham and Naveh, Joseph, "The Tel Dan Inscription: A New Fragment," *Israel Exploration Journal* 45 (1995): 1–18.

Dalley, Stephanie, "Foreign Chariotry and Cavalry in the Armies of Tiglath-Pileser III and Sargon II," *Iraq* 47 (1985): 31–48.

Elayi, Josette, *Tiglath-Pileser III, Founder of the Assyrian Empire*, SBL Press, 2022.

Ghantous, Hadi, *The Elisha-Hazael Paradigm and the Kingdom of Israel: The Politics of God in Ancient Syria-Palestine*, Routledge, 2014.

Hagelia, Hallvard, *The Dan Debate: The Tel Dan Inscription in Recent Research*, Sheffield Phoenix, 2009.

Hasagawa, Shuichi; Levin, Christoph; and Radner, Karen (eds.), *The Last Days of the Kingdom of Israel*, De Gruyter, 2019.

Kleiman, Assaf, "King Hazael of Aram-Damascus Subjugates Israel, 9th Century B.C.E," *TheTorah.com* (2022), https://thetorah.com/article/king-hazael-of-aram-damascus-subjugates-israel-9th-century-bce.

Koch, Ido, "Assyrian Deportation and Resettlement: The Story of Samaria," *TheTorah.com*, 2019, www.thetorah.com/article/assyrian-deportation-and-resettlement-the-story-of-samaria.

Leonard-Fleckman, Mahri, *The House of David: Between Political Formation and Literary Revision*, Fortress, 2016.

Mandell, Alice and Smoak, Jeremy D., "Reading Beyond Literacy, Writing Beyond Epigraphy: Multimodality and the Monumental Inscriptions at Ekron and Dan, *MAARAV* 22 (2018): 79–112.

Nam, Roger, *Portrayals of Economic Exchange in the Book of Kings*, Brill, 2012.

Oded, Bustenay, *Mass Deportations and Deportees in the Neo-Assyrian Empire*, Reichert, 1979.

Robker, Jonathan Miles, *The Jehu Revolution: A Royal Tradition of the Northern Kingdom and Its Ramifications*, De Gruyter, 2012.

7

Hezekiah and Isaiah

Putting Judah on the Map

The Assyrian came down like the wolf on the fold,
And his cohorts were gleaming in purple and gold;
And the sheen of their spears was like stars on the sea,
When the blue wave rolls nightly on deep Galilee.
– Lord Byron, "The Destruction of Sennacherib"

THESE LINES ARE FROM THE POEM that the English poet and peer Lord Byron published in his *Hebrew Melodies* from 1815. What inspired this unusual treatment of an Assyrian monarch was Byron's interest in the Middle East (he died helping Greece in its war with the Ottoman Empire), his interest in Jewish emancipation, and the biblical account of Assyria's assault on ancient Judah.

In the biblical account, the Assyrians had just conquered the Northern kingdom and deported its population. Now they are back with a vengeance, devastating most of Judah's territory. Jerusalem is still standing, but Assyria's armies have it surrounded, and their general is offering terms of surrender. The Davidic dynast whom they are up against is Hezekiah, a political opportunist with unrelenting ambition. From atop the Broad Wall that he had built to protect his capital, the people of Judah listen to the foreign general taunt him. The Assyrian challenges Hezekiah's masculinity and scorns him for counting on the help of Egypt – "a broken reed of a staff that pierces the hand of anyone who leans on it."

When the Judean officials urge the general to speak Aramaic (instead of "Judean") so that the people on the wall could not understand their negotiations, the general insists that he was sent to speak not only to the king but also "to this people sitting on the wall, who, like you, are doomed to eat their own dung and drink their own urine." In effort to incite an uprising, he warns the beleaguered inhabitants of the city:

> Do not let Hezekiah deceive you, for he will not be able to deliver you out of my hand . . . Do not listen to Hezekiah, for thus says the king of Assyria: "Make your peace with me and come out to me. Then every one of you will eat from your own vine and your own fig tree, and drink water from your own cistern."
>
> – 2 Kings 18:31

The situation was at its bleakest. That night, however, something strange happened. The biblical account describes an angel of death going through the Assyrian camp and striking down 185,000 troops: "In the morning, they were all dead bodies." The account contains two other, and perhaps older, explanations for Jerusalem's salvation: the Assyrians heard a rumor of the Egyptians coming to rescue Hezekiah, or, alternatively, Hezekiah paid Assyria an exorbitant amount of tribute. To complicate matters, a legend reported by the Greek historian Herodotus tells about mice who overran the Assyrian camp in Egypt, while the Jewish historian Josephus ascribed the outcome to a "pestilential distemper that God visited upon the army."

Whatever happened, Jerusalem escaped unmolested. The encounter, however, left the kingdom's resources severely depleted, with major cities razed to the ground and vital territories forfeited. If Hezekiah hoped to regain international influence, he needed to ally himself with a major player. He appears to have reached out not only to Egypt but also to Assyria's emerging competitor, Babylon.

Later generations knew of Hezekiah's flirtations with Babylon – the same power that, a century later, would besiege Jerusalem twice as it dismantled the Southern kingdom. The suffering that Babylon's armies inflicted on Judah impelled the authors of the Palace History to expand the account of Hezekiah's reign. They drafted an episode in which the ruler, after his bout with Assyria, seeks to impress the Babylonian king by hosting his ambassadors and showing them the wealth and weaponry he had amassed. When the prophet Isaiah hears of the diplomatic visit, he marches before the throne and prophesies Judah's future demise. Days were coming when all that was in his house would be carried off to Babylon: "Nothing will remain, says Yhwh. And some of your own descendants, your own flesh and blood, shall be taken away and serve as eunuchs in the palace of the king of Babylon" (2 Kings 20:19).

Undaunted by oracles of his own family's doom and suffering, Hezekiah responds in a manner that reveals his self-serving shortsightedness. His response is one of the most cynical and disturbing in the entire Bible: "Then Hezekiah said to Isaiah, 'The word of Yhwh that you've spoken is acceptable.' For he thought, 'At least there will be peace and security in my days!'" (2 Kings 20:19).

The long reign of Hezekiah (728–687 BCE) marks the point when Judah became a truly independent and powerful kingdom in its own right. If Ahab and the Omrides put the Northern kingdom on the map, Hezekiah did the same with the Southern kingdom. This was an age of state centralization and growing Judean pride, developments that were crucial to the emergence of the earliest biblical writings. The present chapter examines the major changes that Judah underwent after the conquest of the Northern kingdom, an important find related to the increasing importance of writing in Judah, and the tensions between the North and the South reflected in the two very different histories at the heart of the biblical narrative.

AN INVASION

Largely the achievement of the Omride dynasty, the Northern kingdom endured for two centuries before its conquest by the Assyrians in *c.*722 BCE. While the Southern kingdom may have been modest by comparison, it lasted more than century longer, and as David's creation, it could claim to be more than a century older. The antiquity, continuity, and longevity of the Davidic dynasty must be kept in mind as we seek to understand why Hezekiah's reign figures so prominently, and favorably, in biblical memory. As we will see, these years were an important turning point for the Southern kingdom.

In 2015, Eilat Mazar – an archeologist who excavated for years in Jerusalem before her untimely death in 2021 – announced that her team had found a stamp impressed with Hezekiah's personal name and signet; it features the Egyptian ankh symbol of eternal life, reflecting perhaps his alliances with the pharaohs (Figure 7.1).

Beginning in Hezekiah's reign, Judah bloomed with signs of more widespread literacy among its elites. From an administrative center at

Figure 7.1 An impression (bulla) of King Hezekiah's seal. Photo: Ouria Tadmor, courtesy the Madain Project.

Ramat Rachel to the capital of Jerusalem and scores of sites throughout the region, excavations turned up hundreds of jar handles impressed with personal names and official stamps reading "For the King." They attest to a highly developed administrative infrastructure that controlled the supply and transport of olive oil, wine, and other precious commodities.

Jerusalem grew into a thriving metropolis, increasing almost ten times in size. The fortifications of the city – its walls and the gates – were now quite impressive, and measures were undertaken to protect the city's water supply, which was the first thing that a besieging army would target.

In many ways, Judah's growth and prosperity was a direct consequence of Assyria's expansion. For centuries Israel had overshadowed its neighbor to the south. Now that the Assyrian Empire had wiped Israel off the map, many inhabitants of the former Northern kingdom may have made their way to Judah's borders. While scholars debate the extent of these migrations, all agree that the Southern kingdom at this time seized the opportunity to become one of the leading military and political players in the region.

The palace began by pursuing peace with Assyria. In the preceding chapter, we saw how Hezekiah's father Ahaz had dutifully paid tribute to the empire. In the first decades of his reign, Hezekiah pursued his father's policy and proved to be a faithful tributary. But then he revolted, and he likely did so with the expectation of Egypt's assistance.

The insurrection grew after Sargon's reign suddenly ended in 705 BCE. As one of Assyria's greatest kings, his astonishing death on the battlefield – his corpse was never recovered – sent shockwaves throughout the empire, giving rise to numerous rebellions. By 703 BCE, his son Sennacherib had consolidated his power and gone on the warpath to punish transgressors. In Judah, his armies laid waste to its richest region – the Shephelah (see Map 4.1 on page 62). Located between the coastal plain and the mountains, these soft-sloping, rolling hills were home to Judah's lucrative olive oil industry. Because of Hezekiah's rebellion, Judah forfeited much of this industry to the Philistines (their competitors on the coastal plane).

While the Palace History features a lengthy account of the showdown between Hezekiah and the Assyrians at Jerusalem, it conspicuously avoids any mention of the more important battle fought at Lachish, a Judean city that protected the Shephelah. Imperial troops invested the impressively fortified place and brought it to its knees. Graphic scenes of siege and destruction were later carved into the palace walls at Nineveh and now can be viewed in the British Museum. They show in stunning detail the efforts of Sennacherib's soldiers to infiltrate the city by breaching its fortifications. They also portray Assyrian troops deporting the population, with women and children riding in carts, and men walking beside them (Figure 7.2). Dating to the early seventh century BCE, they are our earliest depictions of Judeans.

Excavations at the site uncovered not only countless Assyrian arrowheads but also a mass grave containing about 1,500 corpses, with their heads inhumed separately.[1]

[1] Three of the skulls show signs of surgical perforation – a procedure known as "trepanation" – that had been successfully performed years earlier.

Figure 7.2 Part of the Nineveh reliefs at the British Museum showing Assyria's conquest of Lachish in Judah, with the population being deported. Photo: Jacob L.Wright.

In his annals, Sennacherib boasts of having trapped Hezekiah, "who did not submit to my yoke," behind the walls of Jerusalem "like a bird in a cage." The lengthy account, which is quoted in abbreviated form here, recounts how the Assyrian king had his way with Judah:

> 200,150 people, great and small, male and female, horses, mules, asses, camels, cattle and sheep without number, I brought away from them and counted as spoil.
>
> . . .
>
> [Hezekiah's] cities, which I had despoiled, I cut off from his land, and to the king of Ashdod, the king of Ekron, and the king of Gaza, I gave (them). . . .
>
> In addition to the thirty talents of gold and eight hundred talents of silver, gems, antimony, jewels, large carnelians, ivory-inlaid couches, ivory-inlaid chairs, elephant hides, elephant tusks, ebony, boxwood, all kinds of

Figure 7.3 Ivory plaque decorated with a lotus flower, discovered in Jerusalem. Photo: Eliyahu Yanai, courtesy of the City of David.

> valuable treasures, as well as his daughters, his harem, his male and female musicians, which he had brought after me to Nineveh, my royal city.[2]

Notably, evidence for the ivory-inlaid furniture – the most coveted prestige objects of the time – was discovered in Jerusalem in the summer of 2022. Some of the pieces that are currently being published witness to an astounding level of geometric precision, as one can see in Figure 7.3.

While Sennacherib's account provides a reliable inventory of what he deported, the figures are exaggerated for the exiles: at its demographic peak, the entire population of Judah likely never exceeded 125,000 souls. Yet we can glean from the Assyrian account several important facts: 1) by this time Judah boasted considerable resources, with its affluence bringing international influence; 2) the empire deported and resettled many Judeans abroad as they had done with inhabitants of the Northern kingdom; and 3) Judah's rich western territories were transferred to Philistine control. Although Jerusalem was spared the fate of its

[2] Translation by Luckenbill, *The Annals of Sennacherib.*

Northern neighbor, the Assyrians reduced the kingdom of Judah to a rump state in the hill country, just as they had done with Samaria in the decades before its conquest.

THE WATERS OF SILOAM AND NORTHERN SCRIBES

In the aftermath of Assyria's wars in the Southern Levant, the environs of Jerusalem and the southern territories of Judah became densely populated. During the extraordinarily long reign of Hezekiah's eldest son, Manasseh (697–643 BCE), Judah demonstrated unwavering loyalty to the Assyrian Empire, and this demographic development resulted in unprecedented levels of prosperity and growth.

When the Northern kingdom fell, many of its artisans, skilled laborers, soldiers, and scribes, who had made Israel famous for its vibrant culture, left their homeland (either voluntarily or by force) and resettled in places where they could practice their craft and trades. Many would have served the Assyrians, either in Mesopotamia or back in the province of Samaria. Others, however, would have found employment at the Davidic court in Jerusalem. Some scholars think that Northern scribes may even have had a hand in the drafting of a remarkable inscription that a sixteen-year-old student discovered in 1880, when Jerusalem was under Ottoman rule.

Jacob Eliahu, a gifted pupil at the London Society for Promoting Christianity Amongst the Jews, had been exploring the Siloam tunnel, a human-made, subterranean canal stretching some 580 yards below East Jerusalem that brings water from the Gihon Spring to the Pool of Siloam. In a dark, narrow corridor, he stumbled one day over rocks and fell into the water. When he rose up, he spotted what appeared to be an ancient text engraved on the wall. As his important discovery became known, a resident of Jerusalem attempted to sever the inscription from the wall but ended up breaking it into six pieces. When the fragments were finally recovered, the Ottoman government organized a well-attended public exhibition in Jerusalem before shipping the inscription off to Istanbul.

The Siloam Inscription, as it is known today, is an invaluable find for the history of writing in ancient Judah. The fragmentary account is formulated in the third person (he, she, they), rather than the conventional first-person form of monarchic inscriptions ("I am Mesha, king of Moab"). Moreover, it relates not to a triumph on the battlefield but to a much more quotidian, yet nevertheless symbolic, feat: workers quarried stone in two narrow tunnels deep under the surface, and coming from opposite directions, they managed to meet in the middle.

> [...] the tunnel ... And this is the story of the tunnel:
>
> While ...the axes were against each other and while three cubits were left to cut ... Then the voice of a man ... called to his counterpart, (for) there was crack in the rock, on the right ... And on the day of the tunnel (being finished), the stonecutters struck each man towards his counterpart, ax against ax, and water flowed from the source to the pool for 1,200 cubits. And 100 cubits was the height over the head of the stonecutters.[3]

As we shall see in Part II, public building projects played a pivotal role in the history of Judah after the kingdom's downfall. Whereas before these construction programs had been conducted at the behest of the crown, members of the Judean province during the Persian period took the initiative themselves to rebuild their ruins, without a native king to take credit for their work.

The work on the Siloam tunnel in the time of Hezekiah was part of a larger effort to fortify Jerusalem and its water sources, and that effort would most likely have been initiated, and funded, by the crown rather than a collective body of citizens (as in post-exilic Judah). The account in the Palace History admits as much. Even if it refers to a different project from the one commemorated in the Siloam Inscription, it leaves no doubt that work on the capital's water supply was a royal initiative:

> And the rest of the events of Hezekiah and all his mighty deeds, and how he made the conduit and the pool, and brought the water into the city, they are written in the chronicles of the kings of Judah.
>
> – 2 Kings 20:20

What is remarkable about the Siloam Inscription is that it seems to have omitted any reference to Hezekiah or the palace. The first lines are unfortunately missing, and we cannot be sure what they contained.

[3] See translation and discussion in Schniedewind, *How the Bible Became a Book*, pp. 64–90.

They may have mentioned the king, but they may very well have omitted him, and if so, this would represent a highly unusual case for ancient West Asia: a monumental inscription that does not acknowledge, let alone extol, the achievements of a ruler.

Here then a prosaic, third person, account of communal collaboration has usurped the place in formal inscriptions that usually reported a ruler's words. In this respect, our "story of the tunnel" stands in direct continuity with building accounts from Judah during the Persian period that we study in Part II. In all these cases, including the monument of the Moabite king Mesha, we witness a close connection between physical construction and literary production – a point to bear in mind when we turn to the pivotal writings that emerged from Judah's post-defeat building activities.

With the move of Samarian scribes to Jerusalem, we have finally hit on the social location of the first generations of the biblical writers. Many of the earliest biblical writings are the work of Judean scribes who wrote on the behalf of Davidic kings in Jerusalem. But in addition to these Southern circles working for the crown, an important body of biblical writings were composed by scribes from the North – not only by those who served the Assyrian bureaucracy in the province of Samaria, but also by those who would have worked in Jerusalem.

The Judean scribes were working as spin-doctors for Davidic dynasts. They were not only on the payroll of the palace, but the writings they produced, such as the Palace History, were also monarchic and statist in their perspective. In contrast, Northern scribes who were serving in both Samaria and Judah produced for themselves a corpus of texts that emphasize the role of the people and its direct relationship to Yhwh. These writings include the Family Story in Genesis and the Exodus-Conquest Account, which the preceding chapters introduced.

When did the Northern scribes find the time for these extracurricular literary endeavors? The same question must be posed for some of the most important intellectual works in human history. We know of many writers throughout history who have completed groundbreaking works by carving out time from their daily duties. They include Classical writers such as Callimachus, Cicero, and Pliny; the rabbis who composed the Mishna and Talmud; philosophers from the Middle Ages, such as

Maimonides and Abravanel, who served at royal courts; poets from the nineteenth century, such as Goethe, Herder, and Schiller who worked at the court in Jena; and a host of authors from more recent times. In the case of German philosophers and poets from the nineteenth century, the writing projects they pursued for their own interests often produced their most influential publications, and many of these publications were at odds with their patrons' politics.

AN INVITATION TO THE NORTH

Thus, while Judah was radically reduced in size, the population density around Jerusalem increased significantly, and this process of urbanization created the conditions for a more robust exchange of ideas that crystalized in the biblical writings. To map the differences between Northern and Southern literary activities, we need to resume our discussion of the competing histories that form the larger biblical narrative.

We begin here with the most Judean of them all: the Palace History. This work would eventually grow to significant proportions, comprising much of the books of Samuel and Kings. But at its core is the synthesized story of Saul and David in which David mounts the throne of Israel that Saul had first occupied. The history has a clear political message. It argues that David and his line are the rightful rulers of all Israel, and that the nation's deity approved of David's decision to make Jerusalem the place where he was to be worshipped. Following Yhwh's instructions, the same prophet who had previously anointed Saul now anoints David, and later Yhwh promises to never take his love from his descendants, as he did from Saul.

Closely related to the declarations of the deity's devotion are the episodes in which David outdoes his predecessor, both in his martial feats and in his moral conduct. David spares Saul's life, shows him honor, is close to his son Jonathan and his daughter Michal, mourns his death, and performs acts of benefaction for his household.

These tales represent some of the finest storytelling in the entire Bible, and they continue to attract many readers and retellings. The intended audience would have discerned parables of Israel's and Judah's history. Being the youngest of eight sons from the small town of Bethlehem, David (like Judah) is an underdog. Nevertheless, Yhwh chooses him to replace Saul. The Bethlemite eventually creates the kingdom of Judah in the South. However, the population of the North (Israel) that had been loyal to Saul embrace him as their king only after a foreign foe (the Philistines) subjugates Saul and the armies of Israel.

In all these episodes (as well as the accounts of David's dealings with two other Northern figures, Absalom and Sheba ben Bichri), we can hear representatives of David's royal line summoning communities from the defeated Northern kingdom and asserting their authority over "all Israel." Thus, when the tribal chiefs of the North go down to Hebron to make David their king, they make a statement that spoke directly to their descendants living after 722 BCE:

> We are of your own flesh and bone. For some time, while Saul was king over us, it was you who led out Israel to battle and also brought it home again. Moreover, Yhwh has said to you: "It is you who shall be shepherd of my people Israel, you who shall be ruler over Israel."
>
> – 2 Samuel 5:1–2

Yhwh had all along designated the Davidic dynasty to rule the nation, and by abandoning Jerusalem, the Northern kingdom had turned their backs on their own God. Now that Assyria had deported these secessionist kings, those who remained in the North could finally return and submit themselves to the authority of the divinely chosen, royal line ruling in the South.

It is possible that this literary activity pre-dates Israel's downfall in 722 BCE, yet it is not likely. Up to that point, Judah's kings were much weaker than those in Israel, and they were not in the position to expect communities in the North to recognize themselves as their legitimate rulers. Not until Hezekiah's reign were the conditions propitious for Judean scribes to compose these elaborate appeals to a kingless Northern community.

ANTI-NORTHERN POLEMICS

In time, the Palace History was expanded with accounts of David's successors (his son Solomon and grandson Rehoboam) and the two separate lines of rulers after the division of the United Monarchy. When appending these accounts, scribes modified the work's orientation and message. Whereas the first iterations of the Palace History had appealed to communities from the North and affirmed that the Davidic dynasts were the rightful kings of Israel, the new expanded editions pillory the North with scathing polemics.

We have already seen how Southern historians vilified the Omrides, the dynasty that put the Northern kingdom on the map and made Samaria its capital. The account of that kingdom's downfall (2 Kings 17) claims that the Assyrians undertook a major repopulation program after conquering Samaria. They deported *all* the defeated population and settled them throughout Mesopotamia. In return, they brought in populations from far beyond Israel's borders and settled them in the region of Samaria. This account denies that any of the former inhabitants of the kingdom – in other words, "true Israelites" – continued to live in the region after the Assyrians colonized it with foreigners.

The polemical intent is obvious. The authors were writing from a Judean perspective, and their antipathy for the North was severe. Yet in claiming that the populations living now in Samaria lack any genealogical ties to the people of Israel, the Palace History creates a problem: if the new colony consists entirely of non-natives, why do its members worship Yhwh and claim to be members of Israel?

To solve this contradiction, the Judean circles who produced the Palace History fabricated a bizarre legend: Yhwh had been angry that the newcomers did not worship him, and as punishment, unleashed lions against them. Soon enough, the imperial court in Assyria was informed that "the god of the land has sent lions against this population because they do not know the law of the god of the land." What to do? Eventually the emperor came up with a plan: a native Northern priest should be sent back to this conquered territory with instructions to "teach the population the law of the god of the land." The royal orders were carried out, and a priest took up residence in Bethel, an important cultic site on the border to Judah. There he taught the foreign population how to worship Yhwh. The account goes on to describe this population's "syncretistic" practices. They begin to worship Yhwh, but they also continue to serve their own gods and behave in keeping with their foreign customs. "To this day their children and their children's children continue to do as their ancestors did," revering Yhwh while also engaging in idol worship (2 Kings 17:32–41).

Bits of truth lie buried in this account, but they are veiled in polemical falsehoods. First, we know that the Assyrian kings sent officials to instruct subjugated populations, but the purpose was to teach them to fear *the Assyrian kings and the Assyrian gods*, not the gods of the lands to which they had been deported. Second, we saw in the preceding chapter that the Assyrians engaged in "two-way deportations" in the places they conquered; however, they did not displace all of Samaria's inhabitants and replace them with non-natives. Finally, Samaria's religious practices were in some ways different from those in Jerusalem, but those differences have little, if anything, to do with Mesopotamian colonists and their foreign influence on an older, "orthodox" form of Yhwh worship.

These kinds of assaults on Samaria's history would continue for centuries to come, and they appear in a variety of biblical texts. Many in Judah (including some of the scribes who shaped the biblical corpus) opposed cooperation with Samaria, especially as Samaria had long been, and continued to be, economically and militarily superior to Judah. But taken as a whole, the biblical writings are not anti-Northern; to the contrary, they champion a vision of unity between North and South.

In sum, there was no "parting of the ways" between true and false worshippers after the Northern kingdom's downfall, as the Palace History asserts. Its authors, writing from Jerusalem, went to great lengths to cast aspersions on both Samaria and the important cultic site of Bethel directly on Judah's border. Their malice toward these places reflects the threat they posed for Jerusalem, as the Davidic dynast was laying claim to Israel's preeminent position in the Southern Levant. That threat only intensified after Judah's downfall in 586 BCE, when the powerful province of Samaria overshadowed its southern neighbor.

NORTHERN RESPONSES

We could look at further examples of Judean writings from this period, such as prophetic texts that inveigh against the sins of the Northern kingdom. But what we have discussed in this chapter and the preceding ones suffices to demonstrate that Southern writings, which lambasted communities from the North and asserted a statist ideology centered on the Davidic kings and Jerusalem, would have incensed Northern scribes, adding insult to injury for those living after the painful destruction of their society.

While we cannot say much about the friction on the ground, we do know how Northern scribes responded to the insults hurled at their communities in Southern writings: they drafted poetry and narratives – such as the Song of Deborah, the Family Story in Genesis, and the Exodus-Conquest Narrative – that remove the king from Israel's national identity. We have already touched on these texts in preceding chapters, but we are now in better position to appreciate their distinctive messages.

The Song of Deborah provided Israel with a national anthem that celebrates a diverse host of groups coming together around Yhwh and "a mother in Israel." Yet as we saw in Chapter 3, it conspicuously omits any reference to Judah or Southern communities.

The Family Story in Genesis contains an older core that focuses on the life of the patriarch Jacob/Israel. Some of the Jacob traditions must have emerged before Samaria's downfall in 722 BCE, and the court in Samaria may even have put them to use as a unifying myth of origins for the Northern kingdom's diverse populations. The stories affirm that all members of the kingdom belong to the family of Jacob, live in places where he roamed, was blessed by Israel's God, and as such, are natural members of one nation that the kings of the North managed to consolidate. After 722 BCE, the simple act of collecting and preserving these traditions – and, later, amplifying them with new material – made a groundbreaking political statement that would become central in later biblical writings: *Our king is gone, but Israel is still alive. We were a people before we had a king, and we can continue to be a people now that our kingdom has been conquered.*

Traditions of migrations from Egypt and of heroes like Joshua who had long ago liberated their clans from enemy oppression in Canaan may have once circulated among communities in the Northern kingdom. Northern scribes drew on these traditions as they drafted the narrative of the exodus and conquest that is transmitted – in a highly emellished form! – in the books of Exodus, Numbers, Deuteronomy, and Joshua. This "Exodus-Conquest Account" presents Yhwh directly intervening to rescue Israel from its enemies, and his only representatives are non-monarchic leaders (Moses, Miriam, and Joshua). The removal of a royal figure from this story of national liberation stands in stark contrast to the Palace History, which depicts two royal figures (Saul and David) delivering Israel from its enemies and establishing in the process a centralized state.

Over time, Northern scribes would continue to add new representative figures to the narrative, and they would extend it by attaching many of the accounts in Judges of non-monarchic figures who Yhwh raises up to deliver the nation (Deborah as well as Ehud, Barak, Gideon, and Jephthah). But the most impactful move, as we shall see in Part III, was the introduction of divinely revealed law (the Covenant Code in Exodus 20–23). Containing now the very words that Yhwh spoke in his inaugural instructions to the nation, these writers transformed a historical narrative into sacred scripture, with rules and a roadmap for rival communities that had lost their bearings through conquest and colonization.

THE CONVERGENCE OF TEXTS AND TRADITIONS

With their very different perspectives, these early generations of scribes from the North and the South got the ball rolling. All that the Bible would become over the following centuries evolved on the bedrock they laid. The tension in the biblical writings between "all Israel," on the one hand, and the Davidic king and the Jerusalemite temple, on the other, owes itself to these two competing circles of writers.

Our story will eventually take a twist: after the Southern kingdom suffered the same fate as the North, Judean scribes would begin to embrace the ideas of their Northern congeners and transmit their writings. Not only that, but these Southern scribes would also make them their own by inserting their own figures into the narrative: Abraham and Sarah, Moses' brother Aaron (the ancestor of priests who served in Jerusalem), Caleb (a non-royal figure that became an alternative to David as Judah's greatest hero), and a host of others. They would also expand these narratives with new corpora of laws, such as the Deuteronomic Code, the Holiness Code, and the Priestly Source. In contrast to Northern writings, much of this later material asserts the centrality of Jerusalem's temple. However, its authors also embraced the originally Northern conception of a direct covenant between Yhwh and the nation, as well as the kinship and solidarity that this covenant fosters among all members of the nation.

Later we will study the steps by which these writings came together to form a grand "National Narrative," which imagines a shared past for the North and South. But to understand why all these competing works would ever converge in the first place, we first must consider the final dramatic chapter in the history of the Southern kingdom.

FURTHER READING

Elayi, Josette, *Sennacherib, King of Assyria*, SBL Press, 2018.

Farber, Zev I. and Wright, Jacob L. (eds.), *Archaeology and History of Eighth-Century Judah*, SBL Press, 2018.

Fleming, Daniel E., *The Legacy of Israel in Judah's Bible: History, Politics, and the Reinscribing of Tradition*, Cambridge University Press, 2012.

Grabbe, Lester L. (ed.), *Like a Bird in a Cage: The Invasion of Sennacherib in 701 bce*, Bloomsbury, 2003.

Kahn, Dan'el, *Sennacherib's Campaign against Judah: A Source Analysis of Isaiah 36–37*, Cambridge University Press, 2020.

Lipschits, Oded, *Age of Empires: The History and Administration of Judah in the 8th–2nd Centuries BCE in Light of the Storage-Jar Stamp Impressions*, Penn State University Press, 2021.

Luckenbill, Daniel David, *The Annals of Sennacherib*, Oriental Institute Publications, 1924.

Matty, Nazek Khalid, *Sennacherib's Campaign against Judah and Jerusalem in 701 B.C.: A Historical Reconstruction*, De Gruyter, 2016.

Park, Song-Mi Suzie, *Hezekiah and the Dialogue of Memory*, Fortress Press, 2015.

Russell, Stephen C., *The King and the Land: A Geography of Royal Power in the Biblical World*, Oxford University Press, 2017.

Schniedewind, William, *How the Bible Became a Book: The Textualization of Ancient Israel*, Cambridge University Press, 2005.

Ussishkin, David, *Biblical Lachish: A Tale of Construction, Destruction, Excavation and Restoration*, Israel Exploration Society, 2014.

Young, Robert Andrew, *Hezekiah in History and Tradition*, Brill, 2012.

8

Josiah and Huldah

Judah's Downfall and Deportation

Then they brought her response to the king.
– 2 Kings 22:20

JOSIAH ASSUMED THE THRONE OF JUDAH at the age of eight. One can readily imagine the court intrigues around the child-king, with different factions and institutions jockeying for influence. The Palace History, however, glosses over that period and focuses instead on the reforms he introduced in the eighteenth year of his reign (*c.*623 BCE).

At the center of the account is the "discovery" of a Torah scroll in the temple. When Josiah hears its contents, he rends his robes and issues an order:

> Go, inquire of Yhwh for me, for the people, and for all Judah, concerning the words of this scroll that has been found. For great is Yhwh's wrath that is kindled against us, because our ancestors did not obey the words of this scroll, to do according to all that is written concerning us.
> – 2 Kings 22:13

Instructed to "inquire of Yhwh" (an expression for seeking a divine oracle; see Chapters 13 and 26), the chief-scribe Shaphan and a delegation from the palace and temple promptly head to Huldah. This woman was a prophet who lived in Jerusalem's New Quarter, and the delegation apparently recognized her as a leading authority.

In a lengthy oracle, Huldah foretells two things: 1) "Yhwh, the God of Israel" would soon bring disaster on "this place and this people" in keeping with the warnings issued in the scroll and 2) Josiah himself would die in peace because he had humbled himself before Yhwh.

When the delegation brings back Huldah's response, Josiah promptly assembles the kingdom. After reading the scroll publicly, he makes a pact with the people and reaffirms the terms of an earlier covenant inscribed in the discovered document. Thereafter, he launches a campaign to centralize the worship of Yhwh. As the culmination to these reforms, he orchestrates a national festival.

Although scholars rightly do not take this account at face value, we have good reasons to identify the "discovered" scroll with the laws of in what is now the fifth book of the Bible (Deuteronomy). Using a common book-finding scheme, the authors made a claim for the antiquity of a text that, historically, may have begun to coalesce during Josiah's reign.

Within this emerging text-based culture, the role that the prophet Huldah plays is noteworthy. With unmatched authority, her words suffice to authenticate the document, and Josiah launches major reforms in direct response to her seal of approval.

Strangely, however, the second part of Huldah's prophecy did not come to pass: Josiah met an early and tragic death when he attempted, like Hezekiah, to expand his sphere of influence. The consequences were disastrous. The following years were filled with chaos, placing Judah at the vortex of a conflict between Babylon and Egypt. Within three decades, the Babylonian Empire would raze Jerusalem to the ground, inflicting on Judah the monumental defeat without which the Bible would not have been written.

This final chapter of Part I surveys the events leading up to Josiah's reign and the catastrophes that followed it. The Bible contains many (prophetic) texts from this period, and as we shall see, they testify vividly to this tumultuous time.

AN ECONOMIC BOOM

With a reign lasting fifty-five years, the longest in Judah's history, Manasseh mounted the throne in 687 BCE after the death of his father Hezekiah. At the beginning of his reign, Sennacherib still ruled the Assyrian Empire, and the records of his successors (Esarhaddon and Ashurbanipal) reveal that the Judean monarch remained a loyal vassal, contributing both to Assyria's building projects and its conquest of Egypt in 673–663 BCE.

Manasseh's loyalty and cooperation redounded to Judah's benefit, with the kingdom experiencing an economic boom. At this time, the hill country around Jerusalem and the arid regions of the south, which previously had been only sparsely settled, experienced a tenfold population growth.

The demographic shift occurred in direct response to Sennacherib's ferocious demolition of the towns that oversaw the rich farmlands of the Shephelah. This region of Judah had long been a major center of olive oil production, and after Sennacherib ravaged it, he established a new center at the Philistine city of Ekron (see his inscription quoted in Chapter 7), which quickly became the leading oil producer in the world. Even if it was not part of Judah, the thriving industry on its border boosted its economy.

By this time, another Philistine city, Gaza, had become a major entrepôt for the caravan routes conveying incense and precious items from Arabia and Africa. The routes ran along the Mediterranean coast and cut through Judah's southern frontier, and during the seventh century, we witness the establishment of forts and settlements in the Negev and the Beersheba Valley.

Manasseh's primary wife is the first of five queen-mothers for whom the Palace History provides both the father's name and his place of origin, and this location in Jotbah/Jotbathah may reflect Judah's maneuverings in relation to the Arabian incense. It is also possible that the famous story of an unnamed queen bringing Solomon incense and spices from the South Arabian kingdom of Sheba (1 Kings 10, discussed in Chapter 19) reflects the time of Manasseh's reign.

The restructuring of the Southern kingdom did not happen on its own; rather, it was a result of centralized planning by the palace in Jerusalem. Testimony to such state-building initiatives by the Davidic court is provided by the thousands of "Judean Pillar Figurines" that turn up at almost every site in Judah from the seventh century (Figure 8.1). (They completely cease from the archeological record after the end of the Southern kingdom in 586 BCE.) With respect to their function, they may have been related to fertility rituals or even a state-sponsored

Figure 8.1 Judean Pillar Figurines, on display at the Israel Museum, Jerusalem. Photo: Chamberi.

"natalism." The leading expert on the figurines, Erin Darby, rightly cautions against attributing a single meaning and purpose to them. Even if we do not know how ancient communities viewed these objects, they are so clearly Judean that archeologists have used them to identify the borders of the Southern kingdom during the seventh century.

Manasseh is thus an important piece in our puzzle, and his reign represents, next to that of the Omrides and Hezekiah, a pivotal period in the making of the Bible. While his pro-Assyrian politics brought – and bought – peace and prosperity, they came at a high price. Cooperation with the empire enmeshed the kingdom in messy international affairs, and from the perspective of later generations, Judah would have done well to keep to itself as much as possible.

ASSYRIA'S FALL AND BABYLON'S RISE

The Palace History excoriates Manasseh, comparing him to Ahab, accusing him of child-sacrifice, and even blaming him for the kingdom's downfall (although it happened decades after his death). When his son Amon is assassinated by his servants after two years of his reign, the landed nobility (*am ha-aretz*, literally "people of the land") manage to place the young Josiah on the throne. While the Palace History has high praise for Josiah's reforms, it depicts his tragic demise when he enters the fray of international politics during the final years of the Assyrian Empire.

Following Ashurbanipal's death in 631 BCE, wars of succession had severely weakened the Assyrian Empire, and in 626, Chaldean tribes crowned Nabopolassar king of Babylon. The events surrounding the coronation encouraged cities throughout southern Mesopotamia to shrug off Assyria's imperial yoke. With this major menace on its doorstep, Assyria's final king, Ashur-uballit II, was forced to retrench and leave Levantine affairs to Egypt. Over the course of the next fifteen years, Babylon would continue to harass Assyria and in 612, a combined force of Chaldeans, Medes, Persians, Scythians, and Cimmerians sacked the capital of Nineveh. In the process, they also torched its magnificent libraries, whose discovery in modern times was treated in this book's Introduction.

Nineveh was at the time the largest city in the world, and its cataclysmic fall reverberated far and wide. The city symbolized a mighty empire and rulers who had ruthlessly imposed their will on the world. During their annual campaigns, Assyria's armies had brought suffering to populations far and wide, and many of these peoples took pleasure in the pain that their oppressors now felt:

> There is no assuaging your hurt; your wound is mortal.
> All who hear the news about you clap their hands over you.
> For who has ever escaped your endless cruelty?
> – Nahum 3:19

These lines conclude the biblical book of Nahum, a prophetic work whose three chapters celebrate Nineveh's humiliation with a poetic force matching the intensity of Judah's elation:

> Look! On the mountains the feet of one
> who brings good tidings,
> who proclaims peace!
> Celebrate your festivals, O Judah, and fulfill your vows.
> For never again shall the wicked one invade you;
> he is utterly cut off.
> – Nahum 1:15/2:1

Despite Nahum's promise, a "wicked one" did invade the country. In 609, while the Babylonian Empire was dominating in the east, a pharaoh named Necho came up from Egypt to assist Assyria in the west. As his armies advanced northwards, with his ships flanking the coast, they pivoted inland at the strategic site of Megiddo. For two centuries, this city had belonged to the Northern kingdom, and it was here that Josiah of Judah came out to meet Necho. His intentions were either to affirm his loyalty or to stop his advance. Given that Megiddo was the scene of so many important battles (see Chapter 2), the latter seems more likely. Whatever his intentions may have been, it did not go well: Necho suspected him of a treasonous affair with Babylon and had him summarily executed. The untimely death of this ambitious Davidic dynast crushed the messianic hopes that accompanied his reign, and according to the book of Chronicles, the nation mourned his passing:

> All Judah and Jerusalem grieved for Josiah. Jeremiah [the prophet] uttered a lament for him, and all the male and female singers speak of him in their laments to this day. They became a custom in Israel and are recorded in the Laments.
>
> – 2 Chronicles 35:24–25

Joining forces with the Assyrians, Necho proceeded to cross the Euphrates – the first Egyptian ruler to do so since Thutmose III invaded the Mitanni kingdom in 1446 BCE. The combined force made what was by then a second attempt to defend the new Assyrian capital of Harran, but it failed. And that failure marks the historical end of the once great Assyrian Empire, which had gone from the pinnacle of its power to complete and utter ruination in less than three decades.

The turbulence and confusion that characterize the Southern kingdom's final decades mirror the geopolitical chaos of the time. Caught in a political maelstrom, the next mistake Judah made was to misjudge Necho's ambition and determination. According to the Palace History, the landed nobility that had placed Josiah on the throne did the same for his son Jehoahaz – apparently because they opposed compliance with Egypt. That reign lasted less than a year: as Necho was returning home from Harran, he had Jehoahaz deported in chains to Egypt and replaced him with a new monarch named Jehoiakim who held onto the throne for eleven years. Necho also imposed a massive tribute on Judah, which Jehoiakim purportedly paid by taxing the landed nobility (see 2 Kings 23:33–35).

With Assyria eliminated, the stage was set for a showdown between Egypt and Babylon, and the site of that contest was the Syrian city of

Carchemish – the place where Thutmose had crossed the Euphrates eight centuries earlier. Under Egypt's control, and despite receiving support from former Assyrian forces, the fortress fell in *c.*605 BCE to Nebuchadnezzar II, son of the Nabopolassar and commander of Babylon's armies. On his way to the throne, Nebuchadnezzar proceeded to drive Necho out of the Levant, thereby dashing Egypt's dream of restoring the empire that Thutmose had established long before.

The humiliation that Babylon inflicted on Egypt's armies in the following years figures prominently in biblical literature. Thus, the books of Jeremiah and Ezekiel contain lengthy and spirited poems celebrating the fall of a pharaoh who had, from their perspective, murdered Josiah and manhandled Judah:

> Go up to Gilead, and take balm,
> O virgin daughter Egypt
> In vain you have used many medicines;
> there is no healing for you.
> The nations have heard of your shame,
> and the earth is full of your cry,
> for warrior has stumbled against warrior;
> both have fallen together.
> – Jeremiah 46:11–12

After inheriting Assyria's imperial holdings, the Babylonians set their sights on annexing Egypt, the perennial holy grail for Mesopotamian powers (see Chapter 1). Assyria had managed to hold sway over Egypt for less than a decade, and Babylon never succeeded in conquering the renowned North African kingdom. That feat would remain for the Persians, who brought the Babylonian Empire to its knees just fifty years later.

BABYLON'S CONQUEST OF JUDAH

Babylon's frustrated attempts to annex Egypt frame the final two decades of Judah's existence as an independent kingdom. Indeed, had Babylon not pursued that strategic goal, Jerusalem would not have suffered the defeat that produced, and dramatically shaped, the biblical corpus.

While Jehoiakim owed his throne to Necho, he dutifully transferred his allegiance to Nebuchadnezzar and served as a loyal vassal for several years. In 601 Babylon sustained heavy losses during a failed campaign to conquer Egypt. The fiasco inspired Jehoiakim's insubordination, and soon thereafter Judah had to face Babylon's fury. During those turbulent years, Jehoiakim died or was deported, leaving the throne to his son Jehoiachin. In 597, Nebuchadnezzar laid siege to Jerusalem and according to the official Babylonian annals, the city fell three months later, on March 16:

> The seventh year: In the month Kislimu, the king of Akkad [Babylon] mustered his army and marched to Hattu [Syria]. He encamped against the city of Judah [Jerusalem], and on the second day of the month Addaru, he captured the city and seized its king. A king of his own choice he appointed in the city, and taking the vast tribute, he brought it into Babylon.

The biblical Palace History provides more details about Babylon's first siege of Jerusalem:

> King Nebuchadnezzar of Babylon came to the city while his servants were beleaguering it. King Jehoiachin of Judah gave himself up to the king of Babylon, along with his mother, his servants, his officers, and his palace officials. The king of Babylon took him prisoner in the eighth year of his reign. He carried off all the treasures of Yhwh's house as well as the king's house; he cut in pieces all the vessels of gold in Yhwh's sanctuary that King Solomon of Israel had made, as Yhwh had foretold. He carried away all Jerusalem, all the officials, all the warriors, ten thousand captives, all the artisans and the smiths; no one remained except the poorest people of the land. He carried away Jehoiachin to Babylon; the king's mother, the king's wives, his officials, and the elite of the land, he took into captivity from Jerusalem to Babylon. The king of Babylon brought captive to Babylon all the men of valor, seven thousand, the artisans and the smiths, one thousand, all of them strong and fit for war. The king of Babylon made Mattaniah, Jehoiachin's uncle, king in his place and changed his name to Zedekiah.
>
> – 2 Kings 24:11–17

The Babylonian annals agree with the biblical Palace History on three issues: Nebuchadnezzar did not destroy the city; he placed a new king on the throne; and he carried off a massive amount of tribute. The main point of difference relates to the deported population: while the Babylonian annals have nothing to say about a forced migration, the biblical account claims that "no one remained except the poorest people of the land," with all the warriors, skilled laborers, palace officials, and royal family taken captive to Babylon. While we must reckon with extensive deportations already in 597 BCE, the Palace History clearly exaggerated the figures. And what motivated the exaggeration was an ideological battle with a second group of exiles – those captured ten years later during the final conquest of the Southern kingdom.[1]

During this first bout with Babylon, Jerusalem was not destroyed since Jehoiachin, along with "his mother, attendants, nobles, and officials," were quick to surrender. (The appearance of "his mother" in this list is in keeping with the influential role that the queen-mother played in the palace.) We would expect Zedekiah, the Davidic dynast whom Babylon appointed as its puppet, to have been even more eager to pursue peace with the empire. While such seems to have been the case at the beginning of his reign, things changed after Necho's death in 595.

With Babylon's failed invasion of Egypt in recent memory, Necho's successors – Psamtik II and Apries (Hophra) – felt emboldened to challenge the empire's hegemony in the region. In 590, Psamtik conducted a royal procession in the Levant. This was brazen provocation, yet Nebuchadnezzar let it go unpunished. A year later, Zedekiah allied himself with the pharaoh and withheld tribute, inspiring the Phoenician kingdom of Tyre to do the same. The insubordination of these Levantine states demanded a response, and the empire delivered a resolute and powerful one. While Tyre managed to escape destruction, Judah did not. When Babylon descended on Jerusalem, Egypt's pharaoh Apries dispatched an army to assist. His help was short-lived, and over the course of a grueling eighteen-month siege, which ended in the summer of 586, Babylon brought the Judean capital to its knees.

Unfortunately, we have not found Babylonian records relating to these events, yet we have uncovered graphic primary sources from

[1] In line with this ideological battle, the Palace History concludes with a notice that Jehoiachin, who represents the first group of exiles, was released from prison and awarded a prominent position in the imperial palace; see discussion in Chapter 19.

Judah. Thus, in a letter likely dating to 586 BCE, an army officer writes from an unknown location to his commander in Lachish, and he concludes his report with a haunting statement about smoke signals:

> May Yhwh cause my lord to hear, this very day, tidings of good.
>
> And now, according to everything which my lord has sent, this has your servant done. I wrote on the sheet according to everything which you sent to me...
>
> ...
>
> My lord should know that we are observing the smoke signals from Lachish according to the codes that my lord has provided. But Azekah we do not see.[2]

The cessation of Azekah's signals likely means that this Judean fortress had fallen. In the following days, the smoke signal from Lachish would be snuffed out as it too fell to Nebuchadnezzar. A prophecy from the book of Jeremiah is dated to the time "when the army of the Babylonian king was fighting against Jerusalem and against the cities of Judah that remained, Lachish and Azekah, for these were the only fortified cities of Judah that were left" (Jeremiah 34:7).

The Palace History recounts how the Babylonians built siege engines to beleaguer the city. After three years, the famine had become severe, and Zedekiah faced a mutiny. When members of the landed nobility no longer had anything to eat, the king decided to abscond. A breach was made in the wall, and he waited until nightfall to head out:

> All the soldiers fled by night by the way of the gate between the two walls, by the Royal Garden, though the Chaldeans [i.e., Babylonians] were all around the city. Zedekiah went in the direction of the Arabah, and the Chaldean army pursued and overtook him in the plains of Jericho; his entire army was scattered, deserting him.
>
> After capturing the Judean king, they brought him up to the king of Babylon at Riblah where they passed sentence on him. They slaughtered

[2] For more on this letter, see the first pages of Chapter 14.

Figure 8.2 Archeologists from Tel Aviv University excavating Jerusalem's destruction layers in the "Givati Parking Lot" (2020). Photo: Shai Halevi.

> Zedekiah's sons before his eyes, and then they gouged out his eyes. Thereafter they took him to Babylon bound in bronze fetters.
>
> – 2 Kings 25:4–7

The account goes on to describe how the Babylonian army returned to Jerusalem to torch the temple, palace, and prominent homes, and tear down the city wall (Figure 8.2). With respect to the city's inhabitants, we are told that all were exiled, both those who resisted and those who previously had defected. The only ones who remained were the poor, whom the conquerors left behind to labor in the vineyards and fields. What follows the account are two lists that seem to have been added at a later point. The first registers the precious vessels that the army plundered from the temple and hauled off with the exiles to Babylon. Of more historical significance, the second names the individuals who, instead of being exiled, were executed by Nebuchadnezzar in Syria:

> The Captain of the Guard took the Chief Priest Seraiah, the Second Priest Zephaniah, and three "Keepers of the Door." From the city he took one eunuch in command of the soldiers; five men of the king's council who were found in the city; a scribe-commander who enlisted the landed nobility; and sixty members of the landed nobility who were found in

> the city. Nebuzaradan, the Captain of the Guard, took them and brought them to the king of Babylon at Riblah. The king of Babylon assaulted and executed them at Riblah in the land of Hamath.
>
> – 2 Kings 25:18–21

If this list provides reliable information, Babylon deemed the highest-ranking priests and the landed nobility among those most culpable in the insurrection that led to Judah's downfall.

POLITICAL DYNAMICS OF JUDAH'S FINAL DECADES

The Palace History reports an incident in the immediate aftermath to Judah's destruction. Nebuchadnezzar had appointed a governor named Gedaliah to oversee the population that remained behind in Judah. The seat of his government was in the town of Mizpah, not far from Jerusalem in the region of Benjamin. Gedaliah's father (Ahikam) and grandfather (Shaphan) play a central role in the account of Josiah's scroll and reforms, and in the book of Jeremiah, his father is a close ally of Jeremiah. The name Gedaliah also appears in stamped storage jars from this time and region; whether this is the same Gedaliah is difficult to say given that his tenure was brief.

The biblical account tells how this figure had made an oath with a retinue of Judean army officers and their men, adjuring them to cooperate with Babylon: "Dwell in the land, serve the king of Babylon, and it will go well with you" (2 Kings 25:24). The account is puzzling: How could Judah have had army officers and soldiers still living in the land after the conquest? The Palace History leaves the impression that all were either executed or deported.

What makes this account even more baffling is that the most prominent of these army officers, Ishmael, is a member of Davidic dynasty. In keeping with the royal house's longstanding policy of resisting Babylonian rule, this prince leads a group of ten men to Mizpah and assassinates Gedaliah, along with Judeans and Babylonians who were with him there. Implying that the land was now truly empty, the account concludes: "At this time, all the people, from the least to the greatest, together with the army officers, went to Egypt for fear of the Babylonians" (2 Kings 25:26).

The book of Jeremiah (chaps. 40–42) contains an older and much longer version of this dramatic episode, including details that undermine the Palace History's impression of post-destruction Judah as a howling wasteland. For example, it reports that instead of being deported to Babylon, many Judeans had taken up residence in countries that surrounded Judah. When they hear how "the king of Babylon had left a remnant in Judah and had appointed [Gedaliah] over them," they return to the land of Judah and harvest "grapes and summer fruits in great abundance."

The version in Jeremiah also provides a wider perspective on the assassinations, linking Ishmael to the Transjordanian politics of the Ammonites and its king Baalis. It describes Ishmael murdering a group of eighty male mourners who come from the former Northern kingdom bearing oblations for Yhwh's house. (The enigmatic account raises important questions about the relations between the North and the South during these years.) In the end, those who had been loyal to Gedaliah – including many Judean princess, eunuchs, and palace officials – approach Jeremiah and petition him to deliver Yhwh's directions. However, the oracle he receives after ten days is not what their leaders wanted to hear: instead of seeking asylum in Egypt, all were to remain in their Judean homeland. The account concludes with a figure named Johanan, along with army commanders, forcing a large company of Judean survivors, including Jeremiah, to migrate to Egypt.

The book of Jeremiah paints an intimate portrait of Judean politics directly before and after the destruction. Its perspectives evolved over several generations and are clearly partisan, but when appreciated as such, they are invaluable for our interest in the post-destruction scribes who produced many biblical writings. In both its prose and poetic parts, the book consistently takes a confrontational stance. The prophet's opponents include not only the palace, but also priests and other prophets. At the center of the book are several chapters in which he contends with prominent prophets, both from Jerusalem and Babylon, who were encouraging Zedekiah to revolt. He also writes a letter to the first group of exiles, urging them to not listen to those who were promising an imminent return to the homeland. These deported communities were to build homes, plant gardens, raise families, and "seek the peace of the city to which I have carried you into exile. Pray to Yhwh for it, because in its prosperity, you too will prosper" (Jeremiah 29:7).

FROM TERRITORIAL STATE TO IMPERIAL PROVINCE

The Israeli archaeologist Avraham Faust describes Judah after the Babylonian conquest as a "Post-Collapse Society," and the material record clearly demonstrates that Jerusalem and its environs suffered extensive destruction and devastation. Only seven out of fifty excavated sites show continuity between the seventh and fifth centuries. The population declined drastically from its peak in the seventh century BCE. Oded Lipschits, a leading expert on the period, estimates that Judah declined from about 110,000 to about 40,000. Others contend that the population in the post-destruction period was even more meager.

As for the region of Benjamin, to the north of Jerusalem, archeologists generally agree that much of the rural sector suffered decline, while the urban centers remained intact and even served as a new administrative center for the local government, as we saw in our discussion of Gedaliah. The Rephaim Valley, to the southwest of Jerusalem, had become a vital agricultural area (perhaps as a royal estate) after Judah became an Assyrian vassal, and the discovery of winepresses, storage caves, and plastered cisterns from the post-destruction period demonstrate that it continued to produce wine and oil.

Our excavations have also unearthed many stamped jar handles (along with bullae), which provide important data on both the economy and the administration. Lipschits and his colleagues have indexed and catalogued the finds, revealing how a system that had served the Southern kingdom during the seventh and sixth centuries was wiped out in 586 BCE. The imperial administration that replaced it likely had its headquarters at Ramat Rahel, which lies on a hill just to the south of Jerusalem and where occupying forces could keep a close eye on activities in the capital. At this site we have discovered over three hundred stamped jar handles, and its occupation layers suggest that it served as a collection point for oil and wine already for the Assyrians, becoming a major imperial post in the Babylonian and Persian periods.

Other than a few lines of continuity, Judah's archeological record testifies to a major rupture after 586. No longer do we witness the characteristic features of the society that emerged over the preceding centuries: the four-room house, burial caves, pillar figurines, (Greek) imported pottery, and so on. The new farmsteads that emerge at this time are humble habitations. Many would have been living as squatters among the ruins of their erstwhile kingdom, a phenomenon that Eli Itkin, a student at Tel Aviv University, has recently demonstrated for the years following Assyria's onslaught.

With Judah's subjugation, the Levant was once again what it had long been and would continue to be: a land-bridge controlled by imperial powers from Egypt and Mesopotamia. The age of territorial states – which gave rise to the kingdoms of Israel, Judah, and their neighbors – had now come to an end.

The Babylonian Empire itself would endure for just another half century, making way for a succession of new imperial powers: the Persians, the Hellenistic kings who succeeded Alexander the Great, the Romans, the Christian Byzantines, the Muslim caliphates, the Ottomans, and finally the British. In the twentieth century, territorial states would re-emerge in the form of Jordan, Israel, Lebanon, and Syria, but the fate of those states now hangs in the balance with several players reviving their ancient imperial ambitions.

A territorial state formed itself already in antiquity: in the second century BCE, the Maccabees liberated Judah from the rule of the Hellenistic kings and established an independent kingdom, as noted in Chapter 6. The Maccabees, however, would not have been able to build this kingdom had it not been for the pivotal developments after 586 BCE that we will now learn about in Part II.

FURTHER READING

Albertz, Rainer, *Israel in Exile: The History and Literature of the Sixth Century B.C.E.*, Society of Biblical Literature, 2003.

Barstad, Hans M., *The Myth of the Empty Land: A Study in the History and Archaeology of Judah during the "Exilic" Period*, Scandinavian University Press, 1996.

Birdsong, Shelley L., *The Last King(s) of Judah, Mohr Siebeck*, 2017.

Crouch, C. L., *Israel and Judah Redefined: Migration, Trauma, and Empire in the Sixth Century* BCE, Cambridge University Press, 2021.

Faust, Avraham, *Judah in the Neo-Babylonian Period: The Archaeology of Desolation*, Society of Biblical Literature, 2012.

Frame, Grant, *Babylonia 689–627 B.C.: A Political History*, Nederlands Historisch-Archaeologisch Instituut te İstanbul, 1992.

Grayson, A. K., *Assyrian and Babylonian Chronicles*, Eisenbrauns, 2000.

Itkin, Eli, "Post-Destruction Squatter Phases in the Iron Age IIB–C Southern Levant," *BASOR* 388 (2022): 51–72.

Lipschits, Oded, *The Fall and Rise of Jerusalem: Judah Under Babylonian Rule*, Eisenbrauns, 2005.

Monroe, Lauren A. S., *Josiah's Reform and the Dynamics of Defilement: Israelite Rites of Violence and the Making of a Biblical Text*, Oxford University Press, 2011.

Na'aman, Nadav, *Ancient Israel and Its Neighbors: Interaction and Counteraction*, Eisenbrauns, 2005.

Schipper, Bernd U., *A Concise History of Ancient Israel: From the Beginnings through the Hellenistic Era*, Eisenbrauns, 2019.

Schoors, Antoon, *The Kingdoms of Israel and Judah in the Eighth and Seventh Centuries B.C.E.,* Society of Biblical Literature, 2013.

Part II
Admitting Defeat

Having traced the rise and fall of two related kingdoms, we are now in a better position to address more directly the why and wherefore of the Bible's beginnings. Part I began to demonstrate that the primary factors behind the Bible's formation are political *division* and military *defeat*. As we explore these factors more directly in Part II, we will learn how they are closely related to the Bible's distinctive *didactic* qualities.

In its constitution and function, the kingdoms of Israel and Judah resembled their rivals throughout the region. State and society worked together in relative harmony, and their purpose was to preserve a political order with the palace at its center. What held together competing communities was their shared duty to the throne, not covenantal commitments or a collective consciousness. Identity was demarcated in terms of physical borders with forts and garrisons. A Judean was thus one who lived in Judah. The Jew had yet to be invented.

When these kingdoms fell, there was little left – in either institutions or ideology – that could reconstitute its clans and communities. As the mother of invention, necessity forced survivors to turn their attention elsewhere as they struggled to build a new existence. In both the diaspora and their homeland, they now lived in the "shadows of the empire."

Owing allegiance to foreign kings and without a Davidic dynasty to define their destinies, Judah's clans and communities initially went their separate ways. The story of their recovery from the Babylonian devastation is not one of a phoenix rising from the ashes, liberating itself from foreign bondage, and restoring what had been demolished. Instead, we witness a gradual exodus from an old order and the discovery of something new.

Part II explores how the Southern community of Judah dealt with the trauma that foreign armies – and according to some texts, their own God – had inflicted on them. In Chapters 9 and 10, we begin to see how defeat is a pervading presence in the biblical corpus, and how its presence is closely connected to the new role that scribes assigned to language and texts in the post-destruction period. Chapters 11 and 12 treat the words that a prophet and later a lay leader spoke that inspired their communities in the South to rebuild their ruins, and how these building projects fed tensions with competing communities in the North. Thereafter, in Chapters 13 and 14, we turn to the central theses of our study, namely that 1) the Bible is to be appreciated as a "project of peoplehood," and 2) this project is fundamentally a *pedagogical* one.

As Judeans rebuilt the ruins of their destroyed capital and reflected upon the demise of an earlier, more glorious age, scribes in their midst pieced together the fragments of their past. The way they came to think about that past, and the narrative they created to express their vision for the future, is the story we will explore later in Part III. Those literary labors, however, presuppose both communal lament and physical labors – the subjects with which we now begin in the following chapters.

9

Daughter Zion

Finding One's Voice

How the Lord has covered Daughter Zion
with the cloud of his anger.
He has hurled down the splendor of Israel
from heaven to earth;
he has not remembered his footstool
in the day of his anger.
– Lamentations 2:1

HOW? HOW COULD WE SUFFER THIS WRETCHED FATE? How could our hallowed city be reduced to rubble, and its streets, once teeming with life, be empty?

These questions lie at the heart of a little biblical book that many know as Lamentations. In Hebrew, it is called by its incipit: *eichah,* literally "how." Translators do injustice to the word by rendering it with the stoic "alas." *Eichah* is desperation, interrogation, exasperation, shock in the face of unfathomable brutality, a frantic search for a way out, a plea to be seen and heard:

How – lonely sits the city!
Once full of people,
how is she now become a widow!
She who was great among the nations,
a princess among the provinces,
how is she now a vassal!
–Lamentations 1:1–5

The piercing *cri de coeur* reverberates through the book, introducing three of its five poems. The problem of "how" also unifies this work. It refers to a past of violence, a present of psychic torment, and a future of uncertain answers.

In this portrait of a people's pain, Daughter Zion sits bereft, with no one to comfort her. The enemy laid his hand upon her treasures and violated her sanctuary. Her highways mourn because no one comes to her festivals. Her gates are desolate, her ramparts grieve, and she is bitter.

Although these laments may have been composed long after the depicted events, they capture the upheaval and agony of Judah's downfall in their most immediate and intense forms. Their enduring impact is due in large part to the disturbing bluntness with which they express pain. Its poetry repeatedly reaches a fever pitch as various voices call the deity to account for failing to show pity. In chanting its scripts, readers relive the experience of Judah's destruction and devastation.

This attention to defeat is by no means limited to Lamentations. Loss is the lens through which biblical scribes contemplate the past. As we will see, this is a highly peculiar feature of the corpus they created: the stories commonly told by political communities culminate in triumph, not defeat.

The "how" of Lamentations thus bring us back to our "why" – why is defeat so central to biblical memory? In this chapter, we begin exploring that question, which bears directly on our larger problem of explaining why the Bible began.

ABECEDARIA AND ACROSTICS

With its poetry recreating chaos and confusion, Lamentations describes Judah's disintegration more vividly than any other biblical book. At the same time, this book is more orderly and tidier than others, consisting of five highly structured poems. By giving some semblance of structure to their sorrow, these poems pay tribute to the power of the (spoken and written) word in the process of recovery.

The book's authors worked through their national trauma by literally working through the alphabet (*aleph-bet* in Hebrew). Four of the five poems are ordered acrostically: the first letter of each strophe corresponds to the alphabet, with the strophes proceeding from A to Z (or from *aleph* to *tav*). This poetic structure, lost in translation, shows how the authors turned to the basic building blocks of language. After all had been swept away, one had to rebuild the foundations. And for the scribes who were using texts to fashion a new community, there was nothing more foundational than the alphabet. It may be rudimentary, but it possesses potentiality. By piecing together its phonetic components, the bereaved bring light to darkness and vitality to an empty void.

Lamentations' rehearsal of the alphabet at the nadir of loss and defeat takes us back to the dawn of Israel's and Judah's history. In Chapter 4 we saw that the earliest Hebrew writings were abecedaria. These inscriptions, consisting solely of the alphabet, date to the period directly before the emergence of the Northern and the Southern kingdoms. Now after the rise and fall of these two kingdoms, the alphabet makes its presence felt again, albeit in fuller form.

Much had happened over the six centuries since the appearance of those first abecedaria. Hebrew had evolved into a literary language as scribes, from both the North and the South, used it in many different forms. These developments were foundational for the many biblical writings that emerged in the post-destruction period.

In Lamentations, the alphabet functions as a prism, reflecting and refracting the many dimensions of defeat. The ancient abecedaria had been etched in stone and painted on potsherds to showcase scribal skills. Not surprisingly, their fate was very different from the new, amplified incarnations of the alphabet in Lamentations: instead of being eventually forgotten and abandoned, they were passed down from generation to generation, prompting their readers to reflect on Judah's downfall and to make the experience of defeat foundational to their collective self-understanding.

In using an alphabet to comfort their people, the authors of Lamentations were contributing to what is, without exaggeration, a revolution in the history of writing. In the fourteenth century CE, the "Three Crowns" of Italian literature (Dante, Petrarch, and Boccaccio) innovated a new use of texts as they composed literature in vernacular Latin that was enjoyed, circulated, and edited among notaries working in the towns of northern Italy. Similarly, Northern scribes, after the conquest of their kingdom in 722 BCE, discovered for themselves a new use of texts. Rather than focusing on the needs of the state and its administration, they drafted an account of a people being liberated and migrating to their homeland without a king of their own other than Yhwh.

Northern scribes composed this story (and others) to be shared, primarily, among themselves. But over time, and especially after the defeat of the Southern kingdom in 586 BCE, scribes who were once employed by the palace in Jerusalem started to expand these works and composed new ones. The corpus that coalesced from their collaborative efforts would eventually have a wider social impact, as it became central to an emerging "People of the Book" – a subject that we study later in Part II. As a late addition to this corpus, Lamentations challenges the deity, and as such, it joins several other books that are formative for the "People of Protest" that we explore more fully in Part IV.

SUFFERING, SPEAKING, AND SURVIVING

Order dissipates in the fifth and final lament. A guiding acrostic is gone, but we still have twenty-two verses, the number of letters in the Hebrew alphabet. It is as though language itself, after striving to re-establish some semblance of order, finally gives up.

As the acrostic falls apart, another element of poetry gathers strength: the community finds its voice. What began as the lonely Daughter Zion struggling to speak now erupts in a collective uproar. When the community cries out, the order is no longer coherent or tidy. Yet even if everyone is not speaking in unison, they all participate in the pain:

Remember, O Yhwh, what has befallen us;
look, and see our disgrace!
Our inheritance has been turned over to strangers,
our homes to aliens.
We have become orphans, fatherless;
our mothers are like widows.
We must pay for the water we drink;
the wood we get must be bought.

With a yoke on our necks we are hard driven;
we are weary, we are given no rest.
–Lamentations 5:1–5

Rage unites. Joining forces, the diversity of voices in Lamentations share their anguish and make a corporate plea for redress and restoration. Despite the distance of time and place, the specificity in these laments make them universally familiar and painfully applicable. They furnish a scattered and divided people – separated not only by space but also by time and social differences – with a common script. By using the rhythm of a funeral dirge (three stresses followed by two, known as *qinah*), this poetry creates a community not only of mourners but also of protestors, who come together in their collective outrage.

Lamentations is both survivors' literature and survival literature – that is, it is not only produced in the wake of disaster but also for life thereafter.[1] That life is imagined as a shared one, and thus instead of the solitary work of an individual, the process of recovery requires the participation of the entire community, with the present generation joining their ancestors as co-witnesses to catastrophe.

Trauma makes one mute and numb, and recovery is not feasible without the victim finding his/her/their voice and naming his/her/their suffering. Kathleen M. O'Connor, an expert on Lamentations, parses out the importance of voice in the process of recovery:

> To gain a voice means to come to the truths of one's history corporately and individually, to recover one's life, to acquire moral agency by naming one's world. The voice brings from the deaths of silence the creative power, energy, and the wholeness of a person or a people in the midst of its world.[2]

Lamentations allows the deity to speak only once, and then merely in passing (3:57). By omitting the divine voice, it creates space for the community to express its collective anger. Even so, victims need to know that they are being heard, and in keeping with this insight, the authors

[1] On the prophets as survival literature, see Chapter 20.

[2] O'Connor, *Lamentations and the Tears of the World*, p. 83.

addressed their laments to the one they considered to be the paramount audience: their God.

This threnody is no requiem for a forsaken city, like Hecuba's lament after the fall of Troy. By inveighing against the decree of history, and fulminating against the deity, Daughter Zion reveals her will and strength to live another day. She may have no one to comfort her, but when she raises her voice in protest and anger, we know that she is not destined to perish.

Thanks to archaeological discoveries, we have many laments from the ancient Near East. The most famous exemplar mourns the destruction of Ur, composed after the fall to the Elamites in 2004 BCE. In comparison with their biblical counterparts, the Mesopotamian laments have little to do with a vanquished people. They focus instead on temples and their deities, and they were performed as liturgies when a sanctuary was being renovated, which, as we shall see in Chapter 11, was a precarious activity. Moreover, whereas the Mesopotamia laments ventriloquize various deities, the biblical laments give their voice entirely to the community. They do not wait for Yhwh to speak; rather, they expect him to listen.

ASSIGNING BLAME

Lamentations refers frequently to the perpetrators of violence yet never identifies them by name. Focusing on the experience of conquest, not the identity of the conquerors, its authors were convinced that their deity was ultimately responsible for Judah's fate:

How [*eicha*] the Lord [*adonai*] in his wrath
Has shamed Fair Zion…
The Lord has laid waste without pity
All the habitations of Jacob;
He has razed in his anger
Fair Judah's strongholds.
He has brought low in dishonor
The kingdom and its leaders.
– Lamentations 2:1–2

Setting aside political disputes that might imperil repair and reconciliation, this work asserts that everything happened in accordance with Yhwh's will. Since he is ultimately responsible, the defeated should call him to account, and do so in a manner that will move him to remorse and mercy:

> He has made my teeth grind on gravel,
> And made me cower in ashes;
> My soul is bereft of peace;
> I have forgotten what happiness is;
> So I say, "Gone is my glory,
> And all that I had hoped for from Yhwh.
> – Lamentations 3:16–18

To induce a change in the deity, the laments enroll not only emotion and heart-rending pleas but also direct challenges to the justness of divine justice:

> Our ancestors sinned and are no more,
> and we bear their punishment.
> – Lamentations 5:7

In directing anger at the nation's deity, the objective was not to spiritualize or depoliticize it. To the contrary, the authors were working to consolidate their communities first by provoking a collective outcry and second by formulating the outcry in a covenantal framework: Babylon, the actual destroyer of Jerusalem, may take pride in its might, but it is a mere instrument of Yhwh's punishment. This poetry strips the enemies of power, transforming the experience of trauma into material evidence for a direct and ongoing relationship between a people and their God. Judah succumbed to its fate not simply because its enemies are superior; this was an ordeal that Yhwh himself was forcing them to endure.

Amidst outpourings of anger at the deity's refusal to take pity, voices of optimism make itself heard. If all had come to pass because Yhwh had willed it, then there's reason for hope, for this deity is a merciful one:

> But this I call to mind,
> And therefore I have hope:

> The steadfast love of Yhwh never ceases,
> His mercies never come to an end.
> They are new every morning.
> Great is your faithfulness!
> – Lamentations 3:21–23

To generations living long after the destruction, when things had taken a turn for the better, the laments reminded them that Yhwh had indeed responded to their ancestors' incensed outcry. The performance of the laments affirmed the reality of the relationship and the power of protest to bring about change:

> Why do you always forget us?
> Why do you forsake us so long?
> Restore us to yourself, O Yhwh,
> And we will return.
> Renew our days as of old.
> You cannot have utterly rejected us,
> And be angry with us beyond measure!
> – Lamentations 5:20–22

This effort of prompting the community to cry out collectively, and call the deity to account, is an essential component of the biblical project.

A PENTATEUCH OF SUFFERING

Consisting of five individual units, the structure of Lamentations corresponds to the Five Books of Moses (the Pentateuch), which claim to bear the divine revelation received at the culmination of the nation's liberation. The five poems of Lamentations offer a new revelation – a revelation not delivered by one from on high at a moment of triumph, but fathomed by many in the depths of defeat.

This little book does not permit its audience to avert their eyes from the suffering or to silence it with easy solutions. No voice from the whirlwind responds to the searing challenges, as in the book of Job (see Chapter 27). It will be for others to offer answers, to pick up the hints about the power of language and community, and to create for the survivors a body of literature as a foundation for their new nation.

Indeed, as we will see, the Hebrew Bible contains a range of responses to the questions posed by this little book.

Scholars generally agree that the five laments could not have originated in the direct wake of 586 BCE and that they were not written at the same time. According to a compelling proposal, the five laments evolved in the following order: 2 > 1 > 4 > 5 > 3. The criterium used to establish this relative chronology is the way one lament presupposes another (or alludes to other biblical texts). Some of laments may date to the fourth century or later, which means that they were still being composed more than two hundred years (!) after Judah's defeat.

That the book evolved over centuries means its authors continued long after 586 BCE to dwell on the Babylonian conquest. Their preoccupation with defeat – their will to commemorate it and to make it the cynosure of their collective consciousness – goes a long way toward explaining why we have a Bible.

THE PERVASIVE PRESENCE OF DEFEAT

The vantage point of the vanquished indeed shapes the entire corpus of biblical writings. As introduced in Part I, the National Narrative, which begins in Genesis and ends in Kings, does not have a happy ending. Its conclusion describes Judah's downfall and exile, and it has nothing to say about the period of reconstruction that followed. The narrative begins with auspicious promises and great triumphs: the creation of the world, the birth of a family, liberation from bondage, the formation of a nation, the rapid conquest of Canaan, the hope-filled establishment of a mighty United Monarchy under David, and the completion of a glorious temple under Solomon. Yet things go awry thereafter. The United Monarchy cleaves into two competing states, which wage war with each other for generations. Eventually the Assyrian and Babylonian armies conquer these two states and deport their inhabitants. In the end, nothing remains.

Such is the biblical version of Israel's and Judah's history, and this National Narrative comprises the first half of the Hebrew Bible, encompassing the Torah and the Former Prophets (Joshua, Judges, Samuel, and Kings). As we will see in Part III, the account of a people's past is distinctive in the ancient world, not only in its length and subject matter, but also in its basic structure. The pattern of most monarchic inscriptions begins with defeat and ends in triumph. The biblical narrative presents the opposite, with the liberation and success at the beginning, and destruction and downfall at the end.

The Latter Prophets (Isaiah, Jeremiah, Ezekiel, and the Twelve "Minor" Prophets) not only make defeat the focus of their penetrating discourses, but also place responsibility for it squarely on the nation. By identifying the sins of the past, they lay out survival strategies for the future. As such, they can be read as the deity's responses to Lamentation's accusations.

Defeat, life in exile, and national restoration are also formative themes for much of the "Writings," the third and final section of the Hebrew canon (to which Lamentations belongs). The works in this section depict the consequences of defeat and the means of surviving in a new age of foreign rule. Daniel and Esther relate to life in exile. The book of Chronicles retells the story of the nation's rise and fall, albeit from a very different perspective. Ezra-Nehemiah depicts exiles returning to Judah and rebuilding the ruins of Jerusalem; this restoration proceeds, however, in the shadow of foreign hegemony. The order of the Psalms follows the nation's history, with the final ones offering thanksgiving for return and restoration. The book of Job describes trauma inflicted on an individual in a manner that mirrors the nation's collective experience.

The only three books that do not relate explicitly to defeat are Proverbs, Ecclesiastes, and the Song of Solomon, but as we shall see in Part IV, these works are important parts of the pedagogical project that the biblical scribes initiated in response to the conquest of their kingdoms.

OBLIVION

With its unusual attention to loss, biblical literature lends itself as an exceptionally rich resource for studying what the cultural historian Wolfgang Schivelbusch calls "an empathetic philosophy of defeat [that] seeks to identify and appreciate the significance of defeat itself."[3]

In antiquity, we rarely, if ever, hear about the experience of defeat from the survivors. Most kingdoms consigned their downfall to oblivion;

[3] Schivelbusch, *The Culture of Defeat*, p. 2.

it was something that they wished to forget. With few exceptions, the vanquished vanished from the historical record. The only reason we know about them today is because 1) other societies preserved information about them (above all, in the Bible), or 2) we discovered remains from them in recent years.

Thus, the Achaemenid Empire made Persia a world power, with well-known kings like Cyrus and Darius. But when it fell, even the communities that continued to live in the erstwhile empire's heartland forgot everything about it, and did so in a very short time. The Parthian and Sassanian Empires that succeeded the Achaemenids knew little if anything about Cyrus and Darius, and if the name of the latter appears in later Persian epic traditions, it was because of the influence of Greek traditions about Alexander the Great.

In official sources from the Assyrian Empire, we hear of a king of Elam (from the region of Iran) who sat in a "place of lament" after the Assyrians destroyed his capital and country. Similarly, we are told that people of Urartu (biblical Ararat in the region of Armenia), after they too were defeated by the Assyrians, engaged in self-effacing mourning rites. In both cases, and in countless others, we know about the hardships faced by the defeated only because their conquerors recorded it. And the only reason we have records from their conquerors (the Assyrians) is because many in recent times have labored tirelessly to unearth their archives and decipher the cryptic cuneiform languages they used to memorialize their achievements.

While the Assyrian monarchs lauded their military feats that drove enemy rulers and their subjects into a state of confusion and desperation, the victims themselves remained silent, fading away into the shadows of history. The imperial records take pride in telling, for example, how the king of Urartu committed suicide in the aftermath of Assyria's assault. Moreover, when the defeated did speak, they commonly downplayed the extent of the loss. Thus, we know that Sennacherib destroyed Babylon and treated it in an unusually harsh manner. However, the scribes of the Babylonian Chronicle recorded only that the city was captured; the devastation and the deportation of the Marduk statue is passed over in complete silence. (On the Marduk Prophecy, see Chapter 26.)

It is possible that these conquered communities reflected on their fate in some literary form. Yet it is equally likely that they were eventually discouraged from speaking about the catastrophe, let alone fully admitting and commemorating it. Some societies punished those who summoned memories of defeat. Take the case of Phrynichus, often considered the founder of tragedy. He wrote *The Capture of Miletus* to call to mind the devastation of this beloved colony of Athens in 499 BCE. According to Herodotus, the Athenians imposed a heavy fine on the playwright for composing a work that "reminded them of familiar misfortunes," and forbade any future treatment of the subject.

One cannot help but wonder: if neighboring peoples had not only admitted defeat but also made it central to a new collective identity, as the biblical scribes did, would they too have produced corpora of literature that continued to be transmitted for generations?

A NEW CONSCIOUSNESS OF DEFEAT

Like beauty, victory is in the eye of the beholder, and the definition of defeat depends on one's perspective. After 586 BCE, most of Judah's inhabitants would not have acknowledged that a new era in their history had begun. As we saw in the final chapter of Part I, the Judeans staged a rebellion against the Bablyonians and assassinated the governor. Many would have expected the kingdom's rapid recovery.

The same probably could be said for the situation after 722 BCE, when the Northern kingdom fell to the Assyrians. In that case, though, we have evidence for Northern scribes who reimagined Israel as a nation that established itself long before the monarchy, and who composed key components of the Family Story in Genesis and the Exodus-Conquest Account. Some of these scribes likely came from Samaria and found employment in the service of the Davidic palace in Jerusalem. They were certainly working after 722 BCE, but how long after is not clear.

The ideas of these Northern writers did not immediately take hold among circles in Judah. The destruction of the temple and cultic sites would have been a huge blow initially, but it is difficult to determine how long the force of that blow was felt among non-priests, even for those who had been exiled or who had migrated elsewhere. Most would have been busy rebuilding their lives, tending to the affairs of their families and communities, and adapting to new social conditions.

Those connected to the palace and the Davidic family would have been the last ones to proclaim that a new post-monarchic era had dawned. For many of the scribes who served in the administration and bureaucracy of the kingdom, defeat in 586 BCE meant de facto unemployment, and perhaps it is among this group that a consciousness of defeat began to gain traction as they turned to new kinds of scribal activity. However, some of these same Southern scribes seriously undermined the implications of defeat. Thus, the Palace History concludes with an addended notice reporting that a Davidic dynast was still living in Babylonia, where he was enjoying a privileged place in the foreign palace (2 Kings 25). The authors of this early addition were convinced that if Judah was to reconstitute itself, the monarchy should play a central role.

Northern scribes set the biblical project in motion by constructing a *prehistory of peoplehood*, one in which Israel had flourished as a nation or people long before establishing a kingdom (a subject treated more fully in Part III). Yet we owe the Bible's preoccupation with defeat primarily to circles in the South that operated outside the palace.

The book of Jeremiah presents the prophet, on the eve of Judah's downfall, petitioning women to teach each other dirges:

Thus says Yhwh of Armies:
Consider, and call for the Women Lamenters,
Send for the Wise Women so that they come.
Let them quickly raise a dirge over us,
So that our eyes may run down with tears,
And our eyelids flow with water.
For a sound of wailing is heard from Zion:
"How we are ruined!
We are utterly shamed,
Because we have left the land,
Because they have cast down our dwellings."
Hear, O women, the word of Yhwh,
And let your ears receive the word of his mouth.
Teach to your daughters a dirge,

And each to her neighbor a lament.
"Death has come up into our windows,
It has entered our palaces,
To cut off the children from the streets
And the young men from the squares."
–Jeremiah 9:17–21

"The Wise Women" (*haHachamot*) appear to have constituted a class of venerated communal consultants, and several passages in the Palace History highlight their crucial interventions (see Chapter 23). The reference to "Women Lamenters" (*Mekon'not*) is even more significant if, as now many agree, laments belong to the earliest iterations of the book of Jeremiah and many other prophetic writings. In some cases, and similar to what we see in this passage from Jeremiah, scribes transmitted older laments that communities performed after defeat (or during unrelated catastrophes), and they reformulated them as oracles of oncoming destruction that prophets delivered prior to the event (see Chapter 20).

NOT THE FINAL WORD

An early and foundational building block in the biblical project is the focus on the nation's collective defeat, and that focus may have its origins in traditions of professional lamenters. At some point in the post-exilic period, and perhaps thanks to these women's efforts, groups in Judah slowly began to admit defeat. While many in the province were intent on rebuilding a kingdom, with a Davidic dynast on the throne, others began to think outside the box and to ask what it means to be a people. The work of Northern scribes writing after their own defeat had taught them that what is essential was not territorial sovereignty but a new kind of political community.

With limited sources, it is impossible to know what things were like on the ground and to gauge the impact of women's laments among the various sectors of Judean society. What we do have though is a body of texts in which defeat makes its presence felt throughout. Although Northern scribes laid the groundwork, Southern scribes richly embellished it. And as they worked, they reflected deeply on the lessons of lament.

The pervasive presence of defeat is an important clue to the enigma of the Bible's existence. It suggests that the most formative time for biblical literature was the period following the destruction of the kingdom of Israel in 722 BCE, the decades leading up to the destruction of the kingdom of Judah in 586 BCE, and especially the centuries thereafter, during which new communities re-emerged in both the North and the South.

The flourishing of two kingdoms was, to be sure, a necessary precondition for the development of biblical literature. By consolidating disparate groups with unified calendars, festivals, music, law, cult, and language, the palace created new occasions for writing. But if the kingdoms of Israel and Judah had continued to grow and expand, and their members had not suffered long and painful experiences of political weakness and subjugation, scribes would have never produced a body of writings capable of creating and sustaining a new nation.

By reminding their audience of the destruction and suffering that their ancestors witnessed – especially after things had started to take a turn for the better – Lamentations and other biblical writings issue a warning: place your hope not in ephemeral kingdoms but in something more enduring. That something is not heaven or a new earth but belonging to a people whose members are committed to each other and to the deity who dwells in their midst. In the coming chapters, we examine how this project of peoplehood took shape in the centuries after Judah's defeat.

Lamentations may decry depredation and devastation, but the composition and transmission of its five laments bespeak a community with a lot of life left. Its members had survived, even if they now included many mourners and protestors; moreover, there were still poets to record their voices. In the aftermath of defeat, the act of putting pen to paper – or stylus to papyrus – required courage. Indeed, without the courage to look defeat in the face, to lament, to protest, and to write, all would have been lost.

While defeat is perhaps the most important factor in the making of the Bible, a close second is the complex and often tense relationship between the North and the South. Part I traced the contours of this relationship during the history of the two kingdoms. Now in Part II, we will see how a vision of a larger national unity emerged in the post-exilic period. Along the way, we will add to these two factors others that, while rarely receiving attention, played an immensely important role in the Bible's formation.

The Bible's project of peoplehood grew out of the will to admit defeat, yet also the refusal to allow it to be the final word. In Lamentations and the important works that preceded it, we witness how generations of anonymous scribes denied that military might was all-determinative in world affairs, and how their denial laid the foundation for a new kind of political community.

FURTHER READING

Dué, Casey, *The Captive Woman's Lament in Greek Tragedy*, University of Texas Press, 2006.

Goiten, S. D., "Women as Creators of Biblical Genres," *Prooftexts* 8 (1988): 1–33.

Hens-Piazza, Gina, *Lamentations*, Liturgical Press, 2017.

Linafelt, Todd, *Surviving Lamentations: Catastrophe, Lament, and Protest in the Afterlife of a Biblical Book*, University of Chicago Press, 2000.

Mandolfo, Carleen R., *Daughter Zion Talks Back to the Prophets*, SBL Press, 2007.

Meyers, Carol (ed.), *Women in Scripture*, Houghton Mifflin Harcourt, 2000.

Nguyen, Kim Lan, *Chorus in the Dark: The Voices of the Book of Lamentations*, Sheffield Phoenix, 2013.

O'Connor, Kathleen M., *Lamentations and the Tears of the World*, Orbis, 2002.

Samet, Nili, *The Lamentation over the Destruction of Ur*, Eisenbrauns, 2014.

Schivelbusch, Wolfgang, *The Culture of Defeat: On National Trauma, Mourning, and Recovery*, Picador, 2004.

Wright, Jacob L., "The Commemoration of Defeat and the Formation of a Nation in the Hebrew Bible," *Prooftexts* 29 (2009): 433–473 (open access).

10

The Creator

Comforting the Afflicted

Comfort ye, comfort ye my people, saith your God.
Speak ye comfortably to Jerusalem,
and cry unto her,
that her warfare is accomplished,
that her iniquity is pardoned.
– Georg Frideric Handel,
Messiah (HWV 56)

THESE FIRST LINES OF HANDEL'S *Messiah* are drawn from poetry that an anonymous group of Judean scribes known collectively as Second Isaiah composed to comfort their people in the wake of Babylon's devastation of Judah. The first half of Isaiah (chapters 1–39) concludes with a foretelling of Judah's suffering and downfall. Without pausing to describe the fulfillment of that disturbing forecast, the book begins anew with Second Isaiah's stirring poems and prophecies.

The preceding chapter considered the book of Lamentations. In the Jewish calendar, communities chant that book during a fast (called Tisha be'Av) that commemorates the defeat of 586 BCE and subsequent catastrophes in Jewish history. On the following Sabbath, the synagogal readings include the first passages of Second Isaiah, which begin with "Comfort ye, comfort ye my people" (Isaiah 40:1). These words of consolation and reassurance provide an emotional antidote and ritual response to Lamentations and the memories of defeat and destruction worked through in the days prior.

What could one say to a bereaved and ravaged nation? Repeatedly in Lamentations we hear that there's no one to offer consolation. The deity's deafening silence now erupts in a chorus of voices charged with compassion and solace. They call Jerusalem to know that soon she will be filled to the brim with inhabitants, that her shame will be forgotten, and that the God who once assailed her has been moved to pity and sorrow.

In Lamentations, the image of the widow bereft of both partner and children dominates several of the poems. In Second Isaiah, the widow finds reassurance in declarations that her spouse, none other than the nation's deity, is now right beside her.

In Lamentations, the bitter agony of defeat was envisaged as a woman forced to witness the starvation of her own children. In Second Isaiah, the barren mother is told she will have many children who will come from afar to soothe her in her period of mourning:

> The children born in the time of your bereavement will yet say in your hearing:
> "The place is too crowded for me.
> make room for me to settle."
> Then you will say in your heart,
> "Who has borne me these [children]?
> I was bereaved and barren,
> exiled and put away –
> So who reared these?
> I was left all alone –
> where then have these come from?"
> Thus says Yhwh, God:
> I will soon lift up my hand to the nations,
> and raise my signal to the peoples;
> They shall bring your sons in their bosom,
> and your daughters shall be carried on their shoulders.
>
> – Isaiah 49:20–22

To those accustomed to biblical prophets spelling out the nation's transgressions, the message of Second Isaiah must come as a surprise. There are no accusations, no demands. The only expectation is that one does not relinquish hope.

Speaking to a community convinced that their God had abandoned them, Second Isaiah calls attention to Yhwh's activities long before the emergence of nations:

Have you not known?
Have you not heard?
Has it not been told to you from the beginning?
Have you not understood from the foundations of the earth?
It is he who sits above the circle of the earth,
And its inhabitants are like grasshoppers.
It is he who stretches out the heavens like a curtain,
And spreads them like a tent to live in.
It is he who brings princes to naught,
And makes the rulers of the earth as nothing.
Have you not known?
Have you not heard?
Yhwh is the everlasting God,
The Creator of the ends of the earth.
– Isaiah 40:10–23, 28

Once again, the contrast to Lamentations is stark. In that work, words decry suffering; in Second Isaiah, words declare consolation. Lamentations blares a bitter cacophony, to which Second Isaiah responds with a sweeping symphony. Its celebration of creation counters the former's preoccupation with destruction.

In a lyrical outpouring of comfort, the prophet points his war-torn, exiled people to the abiding word of their God:

A voice says, "Cry out!"
And I said, "What shall I cry?"
All flesh is grass.
And its love/loyalty [*chesed*] is like the flower of the field.
The grass withers,
And the flower fades,
When the wind/spirit of Yhwh blows upon it.
Surely this people are grass.
The grass withers,
The flower fades,
But the word of our God will stand forever.
– Isaiah 40:6–8

The breathtaking poetry of Second Isaiah features the major themes of the biblical narrative: creation, the patriarchs and matriarchs, the exodus, and so on. Many of the poems date to the time of the Persian Empire, which conquered Babylon in 539 BCE, reversed many of its imperial policies, and cleared the way for Judah's new beginning.

The present chapter treats another monumental tribute to the creative word, one composed by priests in the post-destruction period. This text may be one of the best known in the Bible, but the manner in which it responds to the trauma of defeat needs to explored. In doing just that, we will engage the work of a scribal school that left a deep imprint on the biblical corpus.

GENESIS 1

One would be hard pressed to find a more resplendent homage to language than the first chapter of the Bible. In it, we watch words create worlds.

Enemy armies had brought an end to a way of life that had endured for generations. Cosmos turned to chaos as they dismantled the institutions that had long defined space and time. The destruction of the palace erased the land's political borders, and without a temple and altar, communities could no longer celebrate the annual festivals that structure time.

The authors of Genesis 1 responded to the disorder and desolation, the confusion and chaos, that imperial armies inflicted on Judah by going back to the very beginning of time, when a voice pierced the primordial darkness with the most magnificent words ever spoken: "Let there be light!"

The remarkably ordered and structured account of creation introduces the National Narrative, which concludes in the book of Kings with Jerusalem's catastrophic destruction. This poetic prologue to that narrative portrays the deity, here as the one and only God of all ("Elohim" in Hebrew), looming over a dark chaos and bringing into existence a vast cosmos. The Creator achieves this titanic feat through a modest medium: the spoken word.

Elohim said: Let there be light!
And there was light.
Elohim saw that the light was good.
Elohim separated the light from the darkness.
Elohim called the light "Day."
The darkness he called "Night."
There was evening,
There was morning:
Day one.
– Genesis 1:3–5

From this first light we proceed through an entire week, with each day corresponding to a realm of the cosmos. In its simple elegance, this account of creation calls a defeated and dispersed people to reflect on the essentials: the seasons and cycles of time, the goodness of the natural order, and, similar to Second Isaiah, the power of the divine word.

The authors of this text knew that with their words they too wielded generative power. Imperial armies may have been able to deal death to their kingdom, but a majestic myth that speaks profound truths could bring life to a nation.

CREATION THROUGH COMBAT AND COPULATION

In their account of creation, the authors of Genesis 1 repudiated a conventional cosmology and its glorification of conquest. Thanks to our archeological discoveries, we know how the Babylonians, who conquered Judah, conceived of the world's beginnings. We also know that deported Judean elites were likely familiar with the general contours of these cosmologies.

Enuma Elish, one of the most influential Babylonian epics, portrays a battle among the gods, a "theomachy." But it is also a cosmology, describing the world as a product of combat and copulation. As in Genesis 1, *Enuma Elish* depicts the origins of the heavens and earth, of the heavenly hosts, and of humans. (The title is drawn from the opening words,

"When on high [*enuma elish*] heaven was not yet named, and below the earth did not yet bear a name.") But it is also an explanation for Marduk's rise to the supreme place in the Babylonian pantheon – and by extension, a call for Babylon to assert its control over the rest of the world.

In this myth, the goddess Tiamat, who represents chaotic oceanic waters and simultaneously the empire's enemies, becomes too powerful and upsets the divine order. Marduk agrees to combat her if all the gods agree to make him their champion and chief. With the terms accepted, Marduk challenges Tiamat to a duel.

Sure enough, Marduk triumphs over the goddess, and the battle is gory. In the aftermath, he rips apart her corpse, dividing it into the heavens and earth. Thereafter he institutes divisions of time, seasons, and the cultic calendar, regulated by the planets, stars, sun, and moon. All the gods who had allied themselves with Tiamat are forced to toil for others. Later Marduk slays Tiamat's husband and from his blood creates humans; their sole duty is to relieve the gods of their labors. In keeping with a common ancient Near Eastern sentiment, work is a drudgery that the gods are eager to impose on inferiors.

The myth instructs its Babylonian audience that underlying the surface of reality is the corpse of a goddess that Babylon's male hero-god had slain when she became too powerful. Marduk had long ago created the natural order in the same way that Mesopotamian rulers now carve out the borders of the political world: through force of arms. The myths and rituals, in fact, link Marduk's instruments of violence to the symbolic weapons Babylon's kings are handed as they embark on their campaigns of conquest.

This paean to Babylonian power provoked the authors of Genesis 1 to pen a counter vision. In it, there is no combat and no triumph; there is just one Creator who, instead of contending with competitors, crafts a cosmos according to a grand architectural vision. First there is light, and then land and the heavens, and finally planets and creatures to fill and govern these new habitats.

The creation is performed at ease. Instead of weapons being wielded, only words are spoken. The poem's proclamation asserts more than the supremacy of Israel's deity; its authors made language itself a force superior to Babylon's arms.

Enuma Elish conveys the mythic pattern for warrior-kings and imperial rule. Genesis 1 offers an alternative: labor and creativity. Elohim designs the cosmos, brings it into existence over the course of time, has pleasure in artistic exertion, and then rests to enjoy the fruits of six days of labor. The repose is the reward for a week of work, not a victory on the battlefield.

After each act of innovation, the deity steps back, considers the progress, and recognizes it to be "good." At the very end of his labors, "Elohim saw all that Elohim had made, and behold, it was very good!" This evaluation includes humans, who are formed not as an afterthought, to alleviate the gods of their travails, but as the crowning achievement: "Elohim created the human in his image, and in the image of Elohim, he created him. As both male and female he created them" (Genesis 1:27).

That Elohim created humans in his image was a radical claim. Traditionally, only the king is made in the divine image; here it is all humans. This assertion, which extends royal honor to humanity as a whole, has important implications not only for the ineradicable self-worth of all persons but also for the way that the readers of this account are to view the other peoples who inhabit the earth. Moreover, Elohim creates humans simultaneously as male and female, and the latter are not derivative or inferior. Together, they are to fill the earth and govern the animals:

Elohim blessed them.
Elohim said to them:
"Be fertile and increase.
Fill the earth and master it.
Rule the fish of the sea,
the birds of the sky,
and all the living things that creep on earth."
– Genesis 1:28

That humans are to have dominion over the animals does not mean that they have free rein. To the contrary, Elohim lays out a strictly vegan diet: only things that grow from the ground and from trees may be eaten.

If what predestines literature to a long afterlife is its ability to tell a thrilling story, then we would expect *Enuma Elish*, not Genesis 1, to be the creation account to be read, without interruption, to the present day. Beyond Genesis, the Bible alludes to other cosmologies in which Yhwh slays a male dragon (such as Leviathan or Rahab) that represents not only natural forces of chaos (such as drought and pestilence) but also enemies that threatened the kingdom's borders. Genesis 1 may be less exciting than these competing cosmologies, but it offered a powerful framework for thinking about the world and one's place in it. A cosmos created through language and labor, and declared to be good, offered more hope to a conquered people than a cosmos created through combat.

CREATIO EX PROFUNDIS

The authors of Genesis 1 articulated a new way of looking at life. While it may seem that existence is all about physical might and (violently) imposing one's will on others, their cosmology declares that peace, not war, is the natural order of things. As a model to be emulated, Elohim works not as a warrior but as an artist and architect.

Genesis 1 introduces the Priestly Source – an alternative account of Israel's origins that defines the final shape and contents of Pentateuch. This work constructs a precise chronology of the nation's history, going all the way back to the first week in history, and when drafting it, its authors drew directly upon, and modified, earlier materials.

The older materials included a creation account. Found now in Genesis 2, that account is less cosmic in proportions. It addresses the needs of agrarian communities from the Southern Levant and says nothing about the creation of light, its separation from darkness and chaos, the formation of the planets, and the beginning of time.

The earlier creation account begins, as does Genesis 1, with the earth already in existence. However, "Yhwh-Elohim had not sent rain upon the earth, and there was not yet a human to work the ground." The deity begins by creating a human and then planting a garden in Eden that the human is instructed to plant and till. When creating the human, Yhwh-Elohim does not use words as in Genesis 1 but rather the dust of the ground and his own divine breath. He physically forms the human as a potter works with clay. (In this respect, he resembles the Egyptian god Khnum, who, as "the Divine Potter," creates human fetuses from clay and implants them in the womb.)

Just as the older account presents all humans with the breath of Yhwh-Elohim, the new Priestly version in Genesis 1 depicts Elohim creating all humans in the divine image. Both accounts assign humans an indispensable role in the creative process and ascribe dignity to labor. Furthermore, both portray the deity as an artist who works with pre-existing material.

In the older account, this material is a barren land, while in the Priestly version, this material has agency and a name: Tehom. The word is most often translated as "the deep," but many traditional and modern scholars have understood it to be a proper name. One reason is that the Hebrew formulation lacks the definite article "the." Another reason is that Tehom bears a striking resemblance to Tiamat, even if the etymological relationship remains a matter of scholarly debate.

Tehom's personality, and her potential to not only destabilize creation but also contribute to it, is explored in Catherine Keller's brilliant work of theological imagination, *Face of the Deep: A Theology of Becoming.* In the place of the traditional doctrine of *creatio ex nihilo* ("creation from nothing"), Keller proposes a *creatio ex profundis,* a creation out of the deep.

At the beginning, the earth is an unformed chaos (*tohu va-vohu*) with "darkness covering Tehom." This primordial age endured for an indefinite period with the spirit (or wind) of Elohim "sweeping over the surface of the water." The unusual word for "sweeping" would be better translated as "brooding or hovering," the activity of a mother bird over her young. (The same word is used to describe Yhwh hovering like an eagle over his nation of nestlings at the time of the exodus; see Deuteronomy 32:11.) The verb is a participle, expressing enduring action. We are not told how long Elohim had been engaged in this mystical cohabitation with Tehom, but her presence is crucial to creation in the Priestly imagination.

Tehom underlies the cosmic order, and she can reappear in the form of a flood that inundates the earth and consumes it with her raging waters. This is precisely what happens six chapters later in the lifetime of Noah, when a deluge annihilates all living things: "The fountains of 'great Tehom' burst forth, and the windows of heaven were opened" (Genesis 7:11). The created order is undone when Tehom is set free. But as Keller shows, Tehom's enduring presence holds recreative potential, and Elohim draws on this potential rather than mastering and dominating it (as in traditional paternal theologies of what Keller calls "Creator-creation dominology").[1]

Elohim creates not only by speaking but also by separating (*havdil*), by pushing back the darkness and blocking the waters. The divine activity of partitioning makes room for light and life. It is also central to the thought of the Priestly Source, with its dual principle of *imago Dei* and *imitatio Dei* – that is, just as all humans are created in "the image of God," they are expected to "imitate God" in their conduct. All are to engage in the sacred, creational activity of *havdil* as they navigate their way in the world. One of the primary purposes of the Priestly Source is to provide the people of Israel with guidelines for this activity, and in doing so, it addresses all realms of human life: from conventional cultic matters of holiness and purity to matters of public health (e.g., the treatment of contagious diseases through quarantine).

Many of the Priestly applications of *havdil* anticipate fundamental features of Cartesian thought and Enlightenment principles of "scientific analysis." But *havdil* also has an esoteric quality, especially when it is applied to the political realm: the nation has been separated from others in the world and entrusted with special, secret knowledge. When it follows instructions revealed to its leaders (Moses and Aaron) – for example, when it builds a sanctuary for the deity in the wilderness according to the deity's own blueprint – it engages in the sacred activity of labor, mimicking Elohim's creative labor in Genesis 1 (a point that the authors underscore with their distinctive terminology).

This Priestly theology o*f imitatio Dei* gave a vanquished nation a new purpose and direction. It tasked its members with making space for the sacred and bringing light to the darkness, momentous acts of creation that they could perform even as – or perhaps *especially* as – a conquered

[1] Keller, *The Face of the Deep*, p. xvii.

nation. (In the following chapters of Part II we will see how competing communities discovered what it means to be a people through collaborative building efforts.) A society may have been destroyed and its members exiled from their homeland, but the cosmos had not disintegrated fully into chaos: the sun still governed the day, just as the moon and stars still ruled the night. And in the world that Elohim created and declared to be good, there was much work to be done.

TIME VERSUS SPACE

One of the most unusual features of Genesis 1 is that Elohim creates the cycles of nature (days, months, seasons, and years) in the framework of an *unnatural* cycle. The latter is the same cycle that Yhwh, during the revelation at Sinai, makes known to Israel: the covenantal order of the week, culminating in the Sabbath.

Elsewhere, the Priestly Source identifies the Sabbath as the sign and symbol of the eternal covenant between the nation and Yhwh (see Exodus 31:16–17). By introducing it at the very beginning of the National Narrative, the Bible's first chapter provides the lens through which the hundreds of chapters that follow are to be interpreted. Babylon's subjugation of Judah, recounted in the final chapter of the National Narrative, is not the result of Marduk's triumph. It was brought about rather by the nation's actions. Its members had failed to abide by the terms of the covenant – the one written, ratified, and transmitted in the narrative that begins with the Sabbath.

During the centuries before Judah's defeat, the Sabbath appears to have been a monthly festival celebrating the Full Moon, parallel to the New Moon. Similar to other festivals in monarchic times, it was intimately linked to the land, its seasons, harvests, agrarian communities, altars, and sanctuaries. The destruction of the temple meant therefore the disruption of the festival calendar, with its monthly Sabbath. This point is made when the community mourns in Lamentations 2:6, "Yhwh has abolished in Zion festival and Sabbath, and in his fierce indignation has spurned king and priest."

For the Sabbath to survive conquest, it had to be reinvented. As I show elsewhere, this full-moon Sabbath was combined with a seven-day cycle of labor. Prescribed in the older "Covenant Code" (see Exodus 23:12), the requirement to rest after six days of labor, which extends to not only servants but also (work) animals, represents one of the earliest, and most ambitious, labor laws in human history, and it was not until recent times that a weekly rest day established itself as the norm.[2] Whereas the seven-day rest cycle was originally not linked to a national calendar, in the post-exilic period, it was standardized across communities and combined with the old monthly Sabbath. And as such, it became a central feature of Judah's collective identity. The authors of the Priestly creation account trace this new weekly Sabbath back to the beginning of time:

> Elohim ceased on the seventh day from all *the work that Elohim had done.*
> Elohim blessed the seventh day and declared it holy,
> because on it Elohim ceased from all *the work of creation that Elohim had done.*
> – Genesis 2:2

The repeated reference to Yhwh's *work* in this passage is striking. Elohim labors, finishes, and then rests. By blessing the day of rest and declaring it sacred, the Creator does not undermine the value of the preceding six days of labor, but rather celebrates them. Through this new Sabbath-structure, work replaced war as the most noble activity, one performed by the deity at the beginning of time and one in which even the defeated could take pride.

Time transcends space. Among the reasons why the weekly cycle of labor and Sabbath-rest became so important was that exiled, dispersed communities could observe it wherever they were. As the saying goes, "I'm never free, but I *make time.*" For a people without land, the temporal order took on a new importance. By making time with a shared calendar, communities separated by great distances could be united in both spirit and action. According to the biblical narrative, the nation began to keep the Sabbath in the wilderness, when they did not yet possess a territory of their own. Similar to dietary restrictions, ethical behaviors, and a host of other divine mandates, the Sabbath did not require being in the sacred land that the nation's deity inhabited. Whether at home or abroad, one

[2] See Wright, "Shabbat of the Full Moon," and "How and When the Seventh Day became Shabbat."

could participate in the divine activity of labor and rest. And because this Sabbath-structure was already fixed at the creation of the world, and later secretly revealed to the nation at the time of its liberation, it could withstand repeated efforts of native kings and foreign empires to reorder time and restructure the calendar according to their ephemeral rule.

WHEN GOD SPOKE HEBREW

Genesis 1 affirms the power of words and the primacy of time over space, but it also promotes a particular language – the one of the biblical corpus.

Yeh-hee or – "Let there be light!" The biblical writers recognized the potential of language to unite communities and form a people. The story of the Tower of Babel, a few chapters later, describes how at the beginning of history "everyone on earth had the same tongue and the same words." Yhwh does not desire a world whose inhabitants all dwell together in one city speaking the same language, and he therefore scatters them throughout the earth.

When Yhwh enters into a covenant with one of these peoples, he writes with his fingers on tablets, using the language of the biblical scribes. Conventionally, deities reveal knowledge that humans record, but here Yhwh engages in the actual writing. That he has pleasure in reading Hebrew is affirmed in the jewel-encrusted breastplate that the high priest dons when entering the Holy of Holies. The rows of precious stones represent the nation's twelve tribes, and the priest bears their names on his heart ("a memorial before Yhwh continually") when he approaches the deity.

When Jerusalem was besieged in the time of Hezekiah (701 BCE; see Chapter 7), the Assyrian commanders announced the terms of surrender to the people standing atop the city wall. When the Assyrians speak in "Judean" (a dialect of Hebrew), Hezekiah's officials implore them to switch to Aramaic, the lingua franca of diplomats; otherwise, the citizens of the city, who did not speak Aramaic, could understand their negotiations (and the way the Assyrians were trash-talking Hezekiah).

Over the course of the following century, average Judeans learned Aramaic and began using it in their everyday exchanges. By the time of

Babylonian and Persian rule, most spoke Aramaic and many had ceased using "Judean" altogether. If the language survived in that age of globalization, it was because some made efforts to revive it and the culture that went with it.

One of the figures who sought to resuscitate and reform Judean culture was Nehemiah. In his memoir, the focus of Chapter 12, he reports that many children in Judah no longer knew how to speak "Judean." For him, language was the key to culture, and without speaking "Judean," one was at a disadvantage when participating in Judah's new public life. His reforms to remedy the problem are depicted as the culmination of his many initiatives to foster a sense of kinship and solidarity among Judah's inhabitants.

We might be tempted to view these preservation efforts as conservative, growing out of an anxiety toward the future and outsiders. But actually these were highly innovative measures. Language did not play the same socially formative role in monarchic times, but after the kingdom's downfall, it would gradually become a key strategy with which communities resisted imperial domination.

There is no universal language, there are only languages, and in periods of social rupture and displacement, they easily die out. This "linguicide" usually goes hand in hand with the culture in which it was once spoken. In recent years, UNESCO has invested substantial resources to rescue imperiled languages. Languages contain within themselves not only rich cultural histories but also important insights on life, and thus their preservation is no less important than the protection of endangered wildlife.

The biblical scribes championed a similar language program by portraying Yhwh speaking, writing, and reading in Hebrew. These writers argued again according to the principle of *imitatio Dei*: if our God knows the language of the biblical scribes, then we should too. And it is in this language that they tell their people's story.

A BIBLICAL VERNACULAR

In *Imagined Communities*, Benedict Anderson observes how vernacular tongues (e.g., Italian, French, German) replaced Latin among the pan-

European elite, and thereby facilitated the emergence of national communities. An example is Martin Luther's translation of the Protestant Bible, which in the following centuries provided a common language and means of expression for disparate communities (including Roman Catholics) as they came together to form a "German" nation.

The Hebrew used in biblical texts has a similar story. It represents a distinctive scribal construction, and it should not be confused with the way most inhabitants of the Northern and Southern kingdoms spoke and wrote. Hebrew narrative style presupposes developments from the official chancelleries in the kingdoms of Israel and Judah, and its peculiar syntax, as we will see in Part III, made it easy for future generations to expand the texts they inherited.

When collecting, editing, and expanding older writings and creating new ones, many scribes would no longer have been using Hebrew in their daily routines. It is really remarkable, then, that in their literary efforts, they sought to create continuity with the language of the oldest biblical writings. Perhaps one of the reasons they did so is because they were convinced that these writings bear the sacred words of the nation's deity.

In the remaining chapters of Part II, we survey the historical and literary landscape of Judean life after the Babylonian conquest of 586 BCE. Our aim is to understand how the biblical writings came to be central in Judean society. The two texts we have discussed in the present chapter, Second Isaiah and Genesis 1, were originally circulated in very small circles. Genesis 1 belongs to an esoteric account that was originally restricted to priests at the temple in Jerusalem. Second Isaiah was heavily amplified by later generations, and its oldest parts may have been shared exclusively among scribes, presumably in Babylon.

The early post-destruction period was, as we shall see, far from biblically literate, and it would take centuries for Judah's population to evolve into a "People of the Book." The first steps they took involved a lot more doing than thinking, more rebuilding than reading. The construction projects they undertook were modest, but they laid the foundation for their collective future. In the following chapter, we begin our exploration with the little-known figure of Haggai, whose words inspired a people to come together and erect a dwelling for their deity.

FURTHER READING

Anderson, Benedict, *Imagined Communities: Reflections on the Origin and Spread of Nationalism*, Verso, 1983.

Blenkinsopp, Joseph, *Isaiah 40–55: A New Translation with Introduction and Commentary*, Doubleday, 2002.

Burrows, Donald, *Handel: Messiah*, Cambridge University Press, 1991.

Cuéllar, Gregory Lee, *Voices of Marginality: Exile and Return in Second Isaiah 40–55 and the Mexican Immigrant Experience*, Peter Lang, 2008.

Fried, David, "Man is not God: The Limits of Imitatio Dei," *Lehrhaus*, 2021 https://thelehrhaus.com/jewish-thought-history/man-is-not-god-the-limits-of-imitatio-dei/.

Keller, Catherine, *The Face of the Deep: A Theology of Becoming*, Routledge, 2003.

Lambert, Wilfred G., *Babylonian Creation Myths*, Eisenbrauns, 2013.

Landy, Francis, "Death and Exile in the Book of Isaiah," lecture at University of Victoria 2018, https://soundcloud.com/universityofvictoria/death-and-exile-in-the-book-of-isaiah-francis-landy

Landy, Francis, "The Prologue to Deutero-Isaiah," *TheTorah.com*, 2020, https://thetorah.com/article/the-prologue-to-deutero-isaiah

Schniedewind, William M., *A Social History of Hebrew: Its Origins through the Rabbinic Period*, Yale University Press, 2013.

Smith, Mark S., *The Priestly Vision of Genesis 1*, Fortress, 2009.

Thiong'o, Ngugi wa, *Something Torn and New: An African Renaissance*, Basic Books, 2009 (a rich study of "linguicide" in Africa's colonialist history).

Tiemeyer, Lena-Sofia, *For the Comfort of Zion: The Geographical and Theological Location of Isaiah 40–55*, Brill, 2010.

Wright, Jacob L. "Shabbat of the Full Moon," *TheTorah.com*, 2015, https://thetorah.com/article/shabbat-of-the-full-moon

Wright, Jacob L., "How and When the Seventh Day Became Shabbat," *TheTorah.com*, 2015, https://thetorah.com/article/how-and-when-the-seventh-day-became-shabbat

11

Haggai the Prophet

Laying the Foundation

Is it a time for you to live in your paneled homes,
while this house lies in ruins?
– Haggai 1:4

HE LIVED IN THE LATE SIXTH century BCE, he was a prophet, and his name was Haggai. That is all we know about a figure who played one of the most pivotal roles in Judah's history. As we will see, it was his exhortations, not an edict of the empire, that laid the foundation of the temple and paved the way for the dramatic developments of the post-destruction period.

"This people say the time has not yet come to rebuild [Yhwh's] house." The communal apathy angers the deity: "Is it the time for you to live in your paneled homes, while this house lies in ruins?" The population in Judah was consumed with quotidian affairs. Life was a struggle in the province, and the economic conditions were dismal. One labored all day long yet had nothing to show for it:

You sowed much — and harvested little.
You eat — but never have enough.
You drink — but never have your fill.
You clothe yourselves — but no one is warm.
And you that earn wages — earn wages to put them in pockets with holes.
– Haggai 1:5–6

Speaking for Yhwh, Haggai presents an explanation for their economic struggles:

"You have been expecting much,
And getting little.
When you brought it home,
I would blow it away.
Because of what?" says Yhwh of Armies.
"Because my house lies in ruins,
While you all hurry off to your own houses."

The solution is to build:

"Go up to the hills,
Collect timber,
And rebuild the house.
Then I will look on it with favor,
And I will be glorified," says Yhwh.
– Haggai 1:7–8

In the preceding chapter, we studied the work of scribes who were writing primarily for their own circles. As we saw, those erudite texts ascribe great power to language and the (divine) word. In the present chapter, we consider the work of someone who spoke and likely never wrote anything. Yet as we will see, the words he delivered in the deity's name prompted his community to take their first step together as a people.

A COMMUNAL ENDEAVOR

One might be tempted to interpret Haggai's prophecies as a predecessor to televangelist sermons that promise prosperity to those who financially support "the work of God." Although Haggai may have been connected to the temple (his name means "my festivals," perhaps indicative of priestly birth), such a reading fails to grant him a fair hearing. His words have been transmitted because they have a deeper rationale and significance.

Inasmuch as the natural order was closely linked to the land's temples and sacred places, the construction and reconstruction of divine dwellings was fraught with danger. One wrong move could anger the deity, and wrathful gods wreak havoc on human society. Many texts from Mesopotamia (especially the Babylonian lament traditions) reflect anxieties about rebuilding temples or making changes to existing ones. An unwarranted disturbance to these revered residences was bound to have negative repercussions.

Should we not wait for an auspicious sign? Is this a good time to be building temples? Do we not want to save our precious resources, instead of spending them during this economic recession? To these concerns, the prophet responds: divine goodwill is not the precondition for our building activities; it is the result.

Haggai's prophecies are not about poor people giving their resources to priests in the hopes of receiving a divine blessing. They are also not about waiting for a ruler to make the first move. The construction of temples was conventionally a royal duty. The great kings who had once reigned over Judah – Solomon, Hezekiah, and Josiah – are known for their work on the temple that once stood in Jerusalem. In Haggai, however, we see the community coming together and building on their own. To be sure, the people had always done the work, but now they take the credit for it.

"If you build it, he will come." In the film *Field of Dreams*, these words prompt Ray to undertake a quixotic venture: the building of a baseball diamond in the middle of an Iowa cornfield, with nothing else for miles around. The message – which evolves over the course of the film into "if you build it, they will come" – is counterintuitive. Should not at least a small crowd precede a grand construction effort?

The most significant part of Haggai's words is seemingly trivial: the use of the plural forms of address (something lost in translation). He refers, and then directly speaks to, "this people" (*ha'am hazeh*) as a whole, not solely their leaders. He urges all the members of his destitute community to go up into the hills, fell timber, and start building. When their leaders respond, they do so as their representatives, not their rulers.

Some scholars claim that Haggai knew of a decree from Darius and was addressing primarily the governor (Zerubavel) and high priest (Jeshua). According to this interpretation, the royal decree prompted Haggai's prophecy, but he presented as if it were solely from Yhwh. However, recent research has demonstrated that we must distinguish older prophecies from the book's later editorial framework (1:1, 12–14 and 2:1–2, 10, 20–21a). If Haggai had known about a decree from Darius, he could have found a way to present Yhwh inspiring the decree, as the authors of Ezra-Nehemiah did with the Cyrus Edict. As we will see, the Cyrus Edict likely represents a creation of the biblical authors. While Darius' decree may be more historical, it would have been issued sometime after Haggai's prophecies.

Had it not been for the modest triumph that Judah witnessed in raising up a small temple, and later in rebuilding Jerusalem's ramparts (the subject of the following chapter), it is unlikely that the community would have ever gone on to commit themselves to more thoroughgoing social reforms and embrace new ways of thinking about themselves.

This is not the only example of a people rebuilding a temple on their own. During this same period, the population in the province of Samaria was building a sanctuary (which was also for Yhwh). Likewise, we know of a Jewish community Egypt from the same period that had built a Yhwh temple. (The local population destroyed it, and when the community began to rebuild, their representatives sought support from leaders at both Jerusalem and Samaria.) As we will see in the coming chapters, these two comparative cases have much to teach us about the unique state of affairs in Judah, where most of the biblical corpus took shape.

THE VOLUNTARY NATION

In the days of Haggai, scribes were just beginning to flesh out the book of Exodus with passages that promote ideals of volunteerism. The passages, which appear in the Priestly Source, imagine an ideal past when the Israelites come together to construct a dwelling, or "tabernacle," for Yhwh, who had just delivered them from an Egyptian despot. As a communal undertaking, the building project marks their first achievement as a nation after their liberation from bondage.

In this imagined past, the people are eager to contribute to the effort. Moses does not need to apply pressure or make threats; he simply summons the nation's members to donate precious metals and materials: "Everyone who is of a willing heart shall bring them . . . Let all among you who are wise come and make all that Yhwh has commanded." The call is heeded widely: "And they came, both men and women, as many as were of willing heart; and all brought noserings and earrings and signet rings, all of solid gold" (Exodus 35:21–22). The response is so enthusiastic that Moses must order the people to stop.

The repeated references to women in these texts are striking. After the downfall of the Judean kingdom in 586 BCE, building activities replaced war efforts as the primary theater of communal action. These peacetime enterprises offered more opportunities to participate in public life, and not surprisingly, the texts from Exodus repeatedly draw attention to the crucial part played by the nation's women:

> And all the women who were wise-hearted did spin with their hands, and brought what they had spun – blue, purple or scarlet yarn or fine linen. And all the women whose hearts had moved them to use their skill spun the goats' hair.
>
> – Exodus 35:25–26

In Part IV we will see that women figure prominently in biblical texts that emerged after Judah's defeat, and the reason was a pragmatic concern. Enemy armies had decimated the populations of the former Northern and Southern kingdoms, and even as they began to recover, they could not compete with imperial powers. To survive, the entire nation had to be mobilized for its future. As a sparsely populated ship set sail on stormy seas, all hands were needed on deck. Not only were their contributions needed in new ways, but also they had much to teach men about collaborating and surviving in a world in which the cards were stacked against them.

In the liturgy of later Jewish synagogues, the story of the tabernacle came to be read alongside the story of how King Solomon, centuries later, built the temple. The combination of these epochal episodes should cause one to compare and contrast: on the one side, the people as a whole building the tabernacle in the wilderness; on the other side, a monarch who builds the temple at the pinnacle of political power. The first is achieved through voluntary action, the second through conscription and violent coercion. Now, after being conquered by imperial armies, and without a native king to set the agenda, the community in Judah could "return" to the ideals of their imagined past and become the people envisioned in their wilderness charter.

We have arrived here at another crucial factor in the Bible's origins. Sociologists often make a basic distinction between *conscription* and *volunteerism*: kings and states conscript bodies and resources; communities and nations volunteer their time and donate their resources. A nation exists only to the extent that groups are willing to come together for collective action. Such is what the Breton philosopher and historian Ernest Renan concluded in his lecture, from 1882, "What is a Nation?":

> A nation is a soul, a spiritual principle. Two things, which in truth are but one, constitute this soul or spiritual principle. One lies in the past, one in the present. One is the possession in common of a rich legacy of memories; the other is present-day consent, the desire to live together, the will to perpetuate the value of the heritage that one has received.[1]

Notice how Renan underscores both the sacrifices of the past and the voluntary actions of the present. He also links this volunteerism to the role of defeat in the making of a nation: "Where national memories are concerned, griefs are of more value than triumphs, for they impose duties, and require a common effort."[2]

We saw how memories of "grief" loom large in biblical writings (Chapter 9). The scribes who shaped these writings wanted their readers to reflect on their national trauma more than their triumphs. They needed everyone to take an active part in the work at hand, and with this goal in mind, they created a past that long precedes the palace. Their elaborate narrative of the nation's beginnings in the wilderness portrays the nation coming together to build a dwelling for the deity who had just saved them from their suffering in Egypt.

Thanks to this imagined prehistory, the poverty-stricken community in the province of Judah should know that their building project has an ancient precedent. What they were doing now is what their ancestors had done long ago at Mount Sinai, at the moment it all began. In their literary labors, the biblical authors refashioned and reframed their community's physical labors – and the monotony of this post-monarchic age – as a new, and auspicious, chapter in the nation's ongoing story.

[1] Bhabha, *Nation and Narration*, pp. 18–19. [2] Ibid.

REVISIONIST HISTORY IN EZRA-NEHEMIAH

The rebuilding of the temple was a turning point in Judah's history. After the Babylonian exile, this institution became a central hub of Judean life, taking the place once occupied by the palace. Priests and the scribes who served at the temple had a direct hand in shaping the Bible's emphases and final contours. They also penned the most prominent history of the post-exilic period: Ezra-Nehemiah.

Though citing many sources and purporting to render a factual account of the period, Ezra-Nehemiah proves upon closer inspection to be a revisionist und unreliable history. Its authors sought to correct the witness of Haggai's oracles and Nehemiah's memoir (the subject of the next chapter). This new account of the restoration presents the community in Judah as the descendants of the Babylonian exiles, who are eager to return to their homeland and to rebuild the temple in Jerusalem. For it authors, Yhwh has only one legitimate temple, and it is in Jerusalem; all others are illicit. These writers wanted their readers to believe that the deity looked with contempt on other temples built to worship him, especially on the one at Mount Gerizim in the province of Samaria.

This revisionist history ascribes the impetus to none other than to Cyrus, the king who conquers Babylon and establishes a new world empire in its place. The first chapter of the book, which is cited in the final chapter of Chronicles, presents the Persian ruler issuing this decree already in the first year of his reign:

> Thus says King Cyrus of Persia: Yhwh, the God of heaven, has given me all the kingdoms of the earth, and he has charged me to build him a house at Jerusalem in Judah. Any of those among you who are of his people, may their God be with them. They should go up to Jerusalem in Judah and rebuild the house of Yhwh, the God of Israel (he is the God who is in Jerusalem).
>
> – Ezra 1:2–4

Yhwh's house should be built in Jerusalem, nowhere else. Those who belong to Yhwh's people must contribute to that building project. That the decree is the work of a Judean scribe rather than the Persian court would explain why it dovetails so neatly with the wider narrative of Ezra-

Nehemiah. The book describes how a throng of exiles, in response to the king's instructions, enthusiastically migrates to Jerusalem and makes generous contributions to the construction project. This community of returnees also longs to celebrate the mandated festivals, restore the city's breached ramparts, and commit themselves anew to Yhwh's teachings.

Such is Ezra-Nehemiah's portrait of the restoration. In the coming chapters, we will see how its themes and emphases are central components of the survival strategies that developed in the wake of Judah's defeat. However, we will also see how a range of sources allow us to be quite confident that: 1) the people of Judah were not united; 2) they were apathetic about the temple; and 3) they did not consult the Torah and ancient textual traditions as they rebuilt their society. From archives found in both Babylon and Egypt, we know now that many had built a stable existence in the diaspora, and they were not inclined to return to a distant and destitute homeland.

THE CYRUS DECREE AND TENSIONS WITH THE NORTH

In Ezra-Nehemiah, the community eagerly begins building after Cyrus gives the word. However, after they lay the foundation, the work comes to a halt. The reason for the unexpected pause is that the project provokes envy among "the adversaries of Judah," whom the book links in various ways to the population of Samaria in the North (Map 11.1).

As we saw in Chapter 7, the book of Kings polemicizes against the Samarian province by declaring its inhabitants to be ethnic groups from Mesopotamia that the kings of Assyria settled in the land after deporting the inhabitants of the Northern kingdom. While we know that the Assyrian kings actually did engage in large-scale resettlement of subjugated territories, by no means did they deport the entire population of Samaria. In fact, Northern scribes did much to pave the way for the biblical project, a point that Part I introduced and Part III will unpack.

The authors of Ezra-Nehemiah, however, embraced the polemics against Samaria that they found in the book of Kings. In their account of the restoration, these groups identify themselves as non-natives who long ago had begun to sacrifice to Yhwh and now want to participate in the building of the temple at Jerusalem:

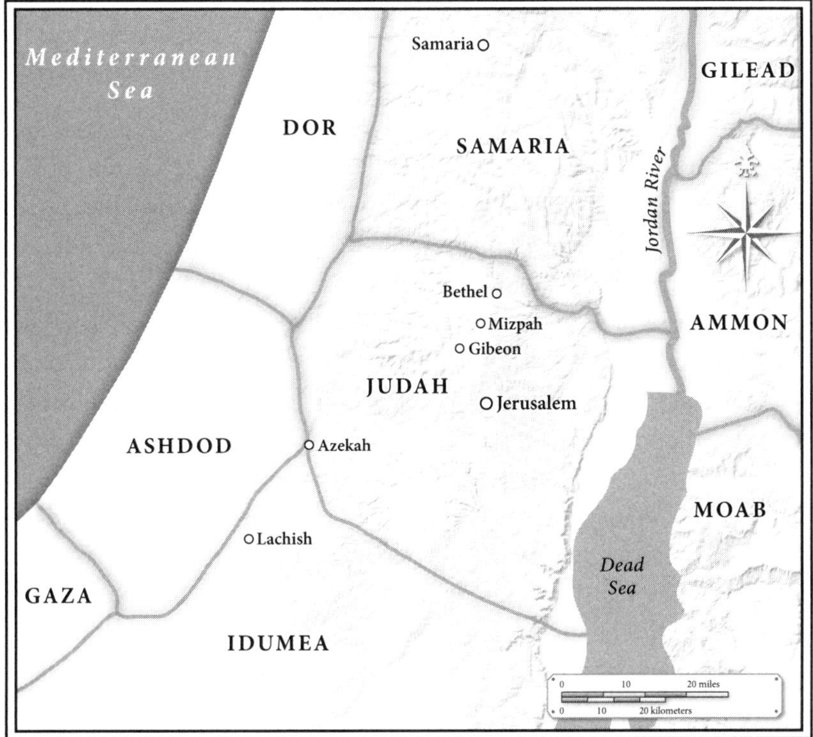

Map 11.1 Imperial provinces in the Southern Levant. Map created by Gerry Krieg (kriegmapping.com).

> When the adversaries of Judah and Benjamin heard that the returned exiles were building a temple to Yhwh, God of Israel, they approached Zerubbabel and the chiefs of the clans and said to them, "Let us build with you, since we too worship your God, having offered sacrifices to him since the time of King Esarhaddon of Assyria, who brought us here."
>
> – Ezra 4:1–2

The leaders of Judah resolutely reject the offer from these "adversaries." Claiming to represent the ancestral houses of all Israel, they insist that both Yhwh and Cyrus had commissioned them to build the one and only authorized temple:

> But Zerubavel, Jeshua, and the rest of the heads of the ancestral houses of Israel said to them: "It is not for you and us to build a house to our God,

> but we alone will build it to Yhwh, God of Israel, in accord with the charge that the king, King Cyrus of Persia, laid upon us."
>
> – Ezra 4:3

This Judean narrative reflects a deepening rift between Jerusalem and Samaria in the post-exilic period. Its authors traced the "parting of the ways" between their communities to both the Cyrus Edict and the resentment that Judah's leaders incited when they appealed to the Edict in their response.

On the basis of terminology, we can confidently identify the Cyrus Edict as a fabrication from the authors of Ezra-Nehemiah. The Edict should not be confused with the Cyrus Cylinder, an important ancient artifact on display at the British Museum (Figure 11.1). The Cylinder, although often thought to refer to the Judeans, is concerned solely with the temple of Marduk (the deity who slays Tiamat in the Babylonian creation epic discussed in preceding chapter). Without a doubt, the Persians reversed the policies of their Babylonian predecessors and generally pursued a policy of tolerance with their subjects. As Judah became more important in their imperial politics, later kings, beginning with Darius, may have made special arrangements with the province, just as they did with many of their subjects. But the community Haggai addressed knew nothing about an imperial decree from the reign of Cyrus.

The Cyrus Edict grew out of an anxiety about Jerusalem's place in relation to its Northern neighbor. Judah had long been inferior, and occasionally even a vassal, to the kingdom of Israel, and its secondary status persisted into the Persian period. At this time, the province of Samaria was much more affluent and influential, and when they built a temple to Yhwh, they likely did not pay much heed to Judean sentiment.

Writing on the behalf of the temple in Jerusalem, the authors of Ezra-Nehemiah responded in a dramatic way, claiming that already Persia's first king, Cyrus, made it an administrative priority in the first year of his reign to recognize Jerusalem as the rightful location for Yhwh's house to be built, and that Cyrus' successors went all out in donating their wealth to support ongoing work on the temple. Historically, many (even in Judah) would not have embraced the temple's ambitious claims about Jerusalem being the sole place where Yhwh's altar should be. Even so,

Figure 11.1 The Cyrus Cylinder bearing a cuneiform inscription that is often mistakenly thought to pronounce freedom for the Judean exiles. The British Museum, London. Photo: Mike Peel.

these claims had already started to gain purchase in wider circles and become central to the biblical project. Thus, in the next chapter, we will see how the authors of Chronicles promoted Jerusalem's temple. However, for them, this place was to be a point of unity for the entire nation (including the population in the North), not a cause of division, as the authors of Ezra-Nehemiah conceived it.

BY THE RIVERS OF BABYLON

Both Haggai and Ezra-Nehemiah portray communities of builders forming around construction programs, but what can we say about the identity and origins of these builders? The answer that the Hebrew narrative of Ezra-Nehemiah offers is straightforward, and it contradicts the depiction in Haggai: the builders were not those who *remained* in the land, but those who *returned* from exile in Babylon.

While the Hebrew narrative of Ezra-Nehemiah goes to great lengths to emphasize this identity, the older Aramaic sources that are embedded in this narrative tell a different story. They have nothing to say about returning exiles. Only the leader, a man named Sheshbazzar, comes to Judah, and he does so because King Darius commissions him to rebuild the temple. The older Aramaic sources agree with what we witnessed in Haggai: his prophecies never even mention a return from exile; they address a population that had long resided in Judah.

The number of the exiles who returned to the province in the two centuries after the Babylonian conquest would have been small. A handful of prominent repatriates from Mesopotamian communities took leading roles in the affairs of Judah. We know of Sheshbazzar, Zerubavel, Jeshua, Ezra, and Nehemiah, and there were likely quite a few others who go unmentioned in our sources. However, the archeological record shows no signs of significant demographic growth until much later. On top of this evidence, we know of many Judean exiles who planted deep roots in Babylon. In doing so, they followed the counsel that the prophet Jeremiah purportedly provided in a letter to the exiles:

> Build houses and settle down. Plant gardens and eat what they produce. Marry and have sons and daughters. Find wives for your sons and give your daughters in marriage, so that they too may have sons and daughters.

> Increase in number there; do not decrease. Seek the peace and prosperity of the city to which I have carried you into exile. Pray to Yhwh for it. Because if it prospers, you too will prosper.
>
> –Jeremiah 29:5–7

Babylonia was home to a flurry of literary activity whose creations are important parts of the biblical canon. In addition to the prophecies of Second Isaiah and Ezekiel, the Palace History was read and reworked there, as we saw in our discussion of Jehoiachin (Chapter 8). Moreover, the first chapter of the Bible engages directly with Babylonian mythology that the exiled Judeans encountered after 586 BCE, as we saw in the preceding chapter. Unfortunately, we know little to nothing about the identity of these authors. We cannot be sure exactly where they lived, who supported them, or how their writings made it from Mesopotamia to Judah. As so often in our story, these are mysteries that we may never solve. But the evidence of a cultural exchange between the homeland and the diaspora tells us something important: the biblical writings were starting to be shared more widely in the early Persian period, even if this circulation was still confined primarily to scribes.

What was life like for the exiles in Mesopotamia? Unfortunately, we lack a corresponding body of evidence for life in Babylonia like that for a Jewish colony in Egypt (see Chapter 13). Yet the Babylonian communities are not completely lost to history: a few historical, non-biblical sources shed light on their lives.

Most of the material comes from assorted contracts and banking records that include Judean names. Thus the Weidner Ration Lists mention Jehoiachin, the Judean king exiled to Babylon according to the book of Kings. These texts, found in Babylon and dating to 592 BCE, refer to food rations given to exiled elites and craftsmen living in Babylon. Among the list of captives receiving rations is "Ya'u-kīnu, king of the land of Yahudu." Apparently Jehoiachin and his five sons (also listed) survived for some time in Babylon and were treated respectfully. The fact that the ration tablets refer to him as king most likely indicates that he was viewed as royalty, and perhaps as the legitimate heir to the Davidic throne.

The Murashu Texts from the Babylonian city of Nippur in the fifth century provide evidence of a sizable Judean community. In these tablets, which are records of financial transactions spanning generations, we find the names of approximately a hundred Judeans among other ethnic minorities. The texts are helpful for two reasons. First, despite the fact the community had lived in Mesopotamia for generations, their names contain references to Judah and the deity Yhwh, which means that they still retained some aspects of their Judean identity. Second, it is clear that Judeans worked in various business ventures, and some seem to have prospered.

The newest body of evidence consists of about two hundred tablets that appeared on the antiquities market rather than being discovered in archaeological excavations. While we cannot be sure where they were originally found, they refer to several places in the region of Nippur, with the most prominent being Al-Yahudu ("Judahville"). Dating from 572 to 477 BCE, these texts feature hundreds of Judean names. Many appear to have been relocated from Judah to lands near the Tigris River owned by the crown. In particular, they, like other populations from the Southern Levant, were settled in regions where they could develop palace land, establish infrastructure, and increase royal revenue through taxes.

Past research on all these texts has focused on name-giving patterns, looking particularly at how Judeans named their children with either their own native, or new Babylonian, elements. This study of the available data is helpful, but new methods give us a fuller picture of life among the exiles. For example, Caroline Waerzeggers has reconstructed social networks in the available texts, discerning degrees of separation. For instance, she demonstrates how we can connect a Judean in a remote place by three degrees of separation to a high-ranking official at the center of the empire. Moreover, she explores what these connections might have meant for cultural connections among Judeans in a rural context.[3]

[3] Waerzeggers, "Social Network Analysis of Cuneiform Archives: A New Approach." See also Alstola, *Judeans in Babylonia*.

Religious life continued for these communities, and scholars agree that they would have had temples of some sort in their villages, as there was at the Judean colony in Egypt from this time (see Chapter 13). A few of the exiles were quite successful in their business ventures. Most, however, worked on estates that they did not own.

Even when this population had lived there for generations, their names frequently include references to Yhwh, which means that many were still perpetuating their ancestral identity. However, some of these same families could name their children with references to other deities. We lack any evidence that biblical traditions were known to them, let alone central to their collective life. Likewise, the members of these communities do not seem to have been in a hurry to return to Judah. They had built a new existence in Babylonia along with new institutions, distinctive identities, and survival strategies, and they were prepared to stay there for generations to come.

There can be no doubt that many exiles made their way back to Judah; however, most of this returning population did not originate in Babylonia. They migrated instead from lands that bordered Judah, where they had sought asylum during the long period of armed conflict and economic calamity, directly before 586 BCE and the century that followed Judah's collapse (see Jeremiah 40:11–12 and discussion in Chapter 8). This means that we should not imagine "the return to Zion" with mass migrations from Mesopotamia as portrayed in many biblical texts.

A HUMBLE BEGINNING

Our survey in this chapter has made it clear that the one who deserves credit for motivating the rebuilding of the temple was not Cyrus or the revered rulers of the Persian Empire, but an unsung hero named Haggai. He had the courage to speak at a time when no one cared. And when he spoke, he addressed the people as whole.

The temple erected in these first years was modest in size. It was not the grand complex that Judah's kings had built. Haggai's words admit as much: "Who is left among you that saw this house in its former glory? How does it look to you now? Is it nothing in your sight?" The lackluster edifice disheartened the community. Speaking to their despondency, Haggai prophesied that one day that structure would be resplendent:

> In a little while, I will shake the heavens and the earth,
> the sea and the dry land.
> I will shake all the nations,
> so that their treasure shall come here,
> and I will fill this house with splendor," says Yhwh of Armies.
> "The latter splendor of this house
> shall be greater than the former," says Yhwh of Armies.
> "And in this place I will grant prosperity."
> – Haggai 2:6–7

To watch the wealth of nations pass into the coffers of the Persian kings would have been demoralizing. Providing hope for his impoverished people, Haggai foretells a time when that wealth would flow to Jerusalem – not to the palaces of their kings but to the dwelling of their deity. He assured them, "It may not look like much now, but if you [plural!] build it, they will come."

Those who collected Haggai's prophecies and formed them into a book wanted to show their readers how a community banded together around a common building venture. As the temple grew in size and influence, and as the book of Haggai evolved, the authors of Ezra-Nehemiah penned a rejoinder to ensure that this prophetic writing did not have the final word about the temple's origins. Ezra-Nehemiah's new narrative, drafted by priestly circles, portrays this institution in much grander proportions and as the object of generous support, from both the community and the Persian court.

To be sure, facts on the ground were often demoralizing. The new house for their God was but a humble replica of its former glory, and the economy did not take a sudden turn for the better. But we should not lose sight of what both works highlight: the new temple is the achievement of the people, not the king. Repeating the feat of their liberated ancestors who had long ago built a tabernacle in the wilderness, a war-torn, struggling population had taken its first step as a reborn nation, without a native king guiding the way.

The moderate success gave this fledgling community a much-needed boost of confidence. Eventually they took on new building projects, and as they participated in them, they began to think – and write – about their past, about their place in the world, and about what it means to be a people. At the time Haggai was exhorting the community to build, the biblical writings discussed in the preceding two chapters were beginning to take shape: Lamentations, Second Isaiah, and the Priestly Source that begins in Genesis 1. These writings join older works that we have touched on in Part I and will treat in greater depth in Part III. All these texts were not widely circulated in Judean society during these years, but they were gradually becoming known beyond the confines of scribal circles.

The building of the temple in Jerusalem was a major achievement, but not an unparalleled one. We observed that the community in Samaria built a temple on their own, and in the following chapter, we consider a similar building project for a related community in Egypt.

What was determinative for Judah, which had long seen itself as an underdog in the region, was that it went "from strength to strength." Long after Haggai addressed "this people," they would continue to work on the temple, eventually taking great pride in it and making it a central institution of their society. Most importantly, they would find ways of connecting it to the story of their ancestors.

FURTHER READING

Albertz, Rainer; Nogalski, James D.; and Wöhrle, Jakob (eds.), *Perspectives on the Formation of the Book of the Twelve: Methodological Foundations, Redactional Processes, Historical Insights*, De Gruyter, 2012.

Alstola, Tero, *Judeans in Babylonia: A Study of Deportees in Sixth and Fifth Centuries BCE*, Brill, 2020.

Bhabha, Homi K., *Nation and Narration*, Routledge, 1990 (includes translation of Renan's lecture).

Davis, Stacy and Dempsey, Carol J. (eds.), *Haggai and Malachi*, Liturgical Press, 2015.

Gilhooley, Andrew M., *The Edict of Cyrus and Notions of Restoration in Ezra–Nehemiah and Chronicles*, Sheffield Phoenix, 2020.

Hilprecht, H. V. and Clay, A. T., *Business Documents of Murashu Sons of Nippur Dated in the Reign of Artaxerxes I (464–424 B.C.)*, Penn Press, 2017 (1898).

Jacobs, Mignon R., *The Books of Haggai and Malachi*, Eerdmans, 2017.

Kessler, John, *The Book of Haggai: Prophecy and Society in Early Persian Yehud*, Brill, 2014.

Knoppers, Gary N., *Jews and Samaritans: The Origins and the History of Their Early Relations*, Oxford University Press, 2013.

Meyers, Carol, *Exodus*, Cambridge University Press, 2005.

Pearce, Laurie E. and Wunsch, Cornelia, *Documents of Judean Exiles and West Semites in Babylonia in the Collection of David Sofer*, Eisenbrauns, 2014.

Waerzeggers, Caroline, "Social Network Analysis of Cuneiform Archives: A New Approach," pp. 207–233 in *Social Network Analysis of Cuneiform Archives, Oxbow*, 2014.

Wright, Jacob L., "Ezra," in *NIB One-Volume Commentary*, Abingdon, 2010.

Wright, Jacob L., "The Cyrus Cylinder and a Dream for the Middle East," Huffington Post, 2012.

12

Nehemiah the Builder

Restoring Judean Pride

If it please the king,
and if your servant has found favor in his sight,
let him send me to the city in Judah
where my ancestors are buried,
so that I can rebuild it.
– Nehemiah 2:5

IT WAS THE MIDDLE OF NIGHT, and the city was fast asleep. No one knew what Nehemiah was planning to do under the veil of darkness. Just several days before, he and his entourage had crossed the borders into the province of Judah. News of his arrival had created a stir. Not often did the small, struggling community in Jerusalem welcome such a high-ranking dignitary from Iran's snowcapped mountains.

In his colorful first-person account, the core of which dates to the late fifth century BCE, Nehemiah describes a night excursion he undertook soon after arriving in the province.

I got up at night, I and a few people with me,
and telling no one what my God had put in my heart to do for Jerusalem,
and taking no other beast than the one on which I was riding,
I set out through the Valley Gate.
– Nehemiah 2:12–13

A royal cupbearer who had served all his life in the Persian palace, Nehemiah had lived far removed from this important city of his homeland. As he informed Artaxerxes when asking for a leave of absence, his ancestors lay buried in this place. It was here that the Davidic dynasty established a capital from which they had governed the kingdom of Judah for centuries. Yet now only vestiges of that former glory remained.

The most imposing feature of an ancient city was its walls. They made the first impression on visitors, and their strength was a source of pride for the local inhabitants. Jerusalem's fortifications once towered proudly, glistening in the sun, her unique palette of pale limestone giving her the appearance of gold. Yet during his night ride, all Nehemiah could make out were silhouettes of ramparts razed to the ground. Gaping breaches separated the sections that were still standing, with heaps of finely hewn ashlar now providing refuge to jackals and foxes. The terrain was so impassable that he had to dismount and walk much of the way.

It was among these ruins that Jerusalem's few inhabitants resided. The preceding generation had managed to build a temple in the sacred precinct, but the city was still hardly populated: they numbered in the hundreds, not thousands.

Some might have been doing well for themselves. Members of Judah's nobility and priesthood lived in fine homes overlooking estates on the hills surrounding the city. Others worked in the administration of the Judean province. Yet most were impoverished, residing in makeshift dwellings, and barely earning enough to eat as they served the priests and provincial administration.

Once the sun had risen over the city, Nehemiah addressed this diverse population in a public assembly, revealing his ambitious plans:

> You see the trouble we are in,
> how Jerusalem lies in ruins
> with its gates burned.
> Come, let us rebuild the wall of Jerusalem,
> so that we may no longer suffer disgrace.
> – Nehemiah 2:17

After he informed them that the Persian court had granted him permission to repair the city's ramparts, they embraced his plan: "They said, 'Let us rise up and build!' So they prepared their hands for the good work."

At least such is how Nehemiah recalls these events. His memoir asserts that a modest building project, which dates to *c.*440 BCE, prompted a series of major reforms, restored Judah's self-confidence, and marks its de facto resurrection as a people. This rebirth was, however, an exclusively Judean one, focused on Jerusalem as the capital of the province. And the one who initiated it was at loggerheads with the leaders of Samaria, the imperial province that had replaced the Northern kingdom of Israel.

What regenerated a Judean collective consciousness was robust competition with neighboring provinces – in territories from the North, South, and Transjordan where the kingdoms of Israel and Judah had staked claims in centuries past. Yet this communal competition is only half the story: the biblical corpus represents, in large part, a concerted effort to rise above these rivalries.

Focusing on this unusual firsthand account by one of the few known biblical authors, the present chapter examines how Nehemiah worked to reconsolidate Judah and restore Judean pride, and how others built on that foundation and expanded the national fold to include communities beyond Judah.

THE FIRST KNOWN BIBLICAL WRITER

Nehemiah's Memoir stands apart from other biblical texts in an important aspect: this is the only case in which we know something about the author. Even if he had a scribe doing the actual writing on his behalf (although this may not have been the case), and even if later scribes added new material to his account (as I have demonstrated elsewhere[1]), he directly oversaw much of the composition.

We know precious little about the lives of those who composed the People's History and the Palace History, and those who later synthesized them to form the National Narrative – momentous literary achievements that we will study in Part III. Likewise, we would not have the words of Haggai and other prophets if anonymous scribes had not preserved them on papyrus and parchment.

Not so with Nehemiah. He identifies himself by name, speaks in the first person, and does so in the most direct, idiosyncratic manner. Not

[1] See Wright, *Rebuilding Identity*.

only are his diction and his approach unconventional, but he also rails against the family of the high priest and members of the aristocracy.

Because his memoir ruffled so many feathers, a revision of Ezra-Nehemiah undertaken in the Hellenistic period (called "First Esdras") erased his memory from the history of Judah's restoration. Much later, the rabbinic sages would find him to be egoistical. Yet the enduring significance of his contribution is evident not only from the opposition it provoked, but also from the fact that later generations preserved his work and expanded it with new material.

At the heart of his memoir is an account of the construction campaign he initiated and directed. In Part I, we witnessed the close connection between building and writing. Thus, in the Mesha Stele, a Moabite king from the ninth century commemorates a series of military triumphs that he celebrates with the construction of cities and temples – a conventional sequence in the royal ideologies of ancient West Asia. The seventh-century Siloam Inscription, in contrast, describes how two excavation crews, working in tandem, managed to meet in the middle when digging a water shaft in Jerusalem. The project, as noted in Chapter 7, may have been part of Judah's preparations for a showdown with the Assyrian Empire during the days of King Hezekiah. Remarkably, the authors of the account, writing in the third person, had nothing to say about the king or palace, and that omission represents a major milestone in the evolution of commemorative inscriptions.

While Nehemiah formulates his memoir in the first person, he too describes a community coming together around a building project. As in the Siloam Inscription, the workers meet at the halfway point. Yet in the memoir, the communal dimensions are on display more dramatically than ever before. The heightened drama serves, as we shall see, paradigmatic and pedagogical purposes.

According to his romanticized, and heavily embellished, account of the events, it all started with a conversation in the imperial capital of Susa. His brother Hanani, along with a few others, had returned from a voyage to Judah, and he describes what they had witnessed: "The survivors there in the province who escaped captivity live in great distress and shame. And the wall of Jerusalem is broken down, with its gates destroyed by fire" (Nehemiah 1:3).

The report took Nehemiah by surprise. He had assumed that everything was going well in his native country. After all, it had been about a century and half since Nebuchadnezzar and his Babylonian armies conquered their kingdom and laid waste to Jerusalem. Persian rule had brought peace and prosperity to the world, and the empire's bounty was on display everywhere in the Persian capital.

Nehemiah had spent all his life at the imperial court. He likely belonged to a group of Judean lads whom the Persian court seized from their parents at a young age (similar to the later Devshirme system, in which Ottoman rulers recruited boys from their Balkan Christian subjects to serve at the palace and in the army). To prepare him for palace service, they would have made him a eunuch. One of the purposes of castration was to sever a boy's ties to his biological family and tether him to the throne. Eunuchs were often highly competitive, and the names they made for themselves in their careers were supposed to serve as a substitute for their inability to sire a genealogical namesake.

Nehemiah was certainly ambitious, having climbed to the preeminent position of "Cupbearer to the King." Devoted to the Artaxerxes' welfare and enjoying his favor, Nehemiah remained oblivious to issues facing his ancestral community. Life was good for him at the center of the world, and no old sweet song kept Jerusalem on his mind. But in the days following his fateful conversation with Hanani, he realized that there was something that his years as a palace eunuch had not erased: he was still a son of the South.

WHY A WALL?

The project Nehemiah initiated consisted mostly of cosmetic repairs to Jerusalem walls, and it was finished, according to his account, after just fifty-two days. A more substantial construction effort was not needed: Judah was now a province in a world empire; it was no longer an independent kingdom with garrisons guarding its borders and a fortified capital towering over the countryside.

A thousand years earlier, most cities in the Southern Levant were unwalled. They did not require fortifications because Egypt governed the region. When problems arose, the "mayors" of the towns wrote to the

Egyptian court, as we learned in our discussion of the Amarna Letters (see Chapter 2). Now that Persia had conquered the world, establishing a *Pax Persica* ("Persian Peace") that antedates the *Pax Romana* by almost five centuries, capital cities could once again afford to be unfortified.

Much had transpired since the Amarna Age. The millennium had witnessed the emergence of a new political constellation: a patchwork of independent territorial states in the form of kingdoms. Judah was one such state, and in Part I we retraced its rise and fall in relation to the similar fate of its Northern competitor. Thanks to the *Pax Persica,* which replaced these kingdoms with imperial provinces, the populations of the Southern Levant could handle their local disputes as they did in the Amarna Age – by writing letters to a foreign power and petitioning them to intervene. Such official correspondence between local administrators and imperial authorities is on display in the Aramaic documents archived both in Ezra-Nehemiah and in the Jewish colony at Elephantine (discussed in the following chapter).

What began to define Judean identity in this age of imperial rule was not a physical border but a common consciousness. In the remainder of Part II, we consider how the biblical authors fostered this consciousness by adopting a new approach to education, before exploring how they created memories of a common past in Part III and a new national culture in Part IV.

Now if the population in Judah did not need a securely fortified capital, why would they have consented to Nehemiah's project? Remember that they were not eager to build the temple, and Haggai had to chasten them with divine oracles before they commenced the work. Nehemiah admits later that not everyone was enthusiastic about the work. But why does the community appear to have been much more motivated to come together and invest their time and resources to rebuild something that served little, if any, pragmatic purpose?

What impelled them, according to the memoir, was their desire to "no longer suffer disgrace" (Nehemiah 2:17). This was a social world shaped by the quest for honor more than wealth, and that feared humiliation more than much else. Thus, as the Judeans build, neighbors ridicule their efforts to remove the reproach that the destroyed ramparts of their capital city represented: "What are these feeble Judeans doing? ... Will they revive the burned stones out of the heaps of rubbish?" Another said, "Even what they're building – a fox could break a wall of their stones!" (Nehemiah 3:34–35/4:2–3).

For Nehemiah – and perhaps many others in Judah – Jerusalem's wall was more central to their collective dignity and corporate identity than even the temple. Indeed, he hardly even mentions the sanctuary, describing Jerusalem as a wasteland and writing as if earlier generations had done nothing to make Yhwh's dwelling the center of Judean society.

Of course, these aspersions perturbed the priests of Jerusalem, and they made every effort to set the record straight. They wrote the larger narrative of Ezra-Nehemiah to show their readers that long before Nehemiah (and Haggai), hordes of exiles had flocked to the city with the sole purpose of rebuilding the temple. What unified Judah, according to their narrative, was not the work on the wall but devotion to the temple. As noted earlier, the priestly authors of First Esdras completely removed Nehemiah and his wall from their account of the restoration. For the authors of Ezra-Nehemiah, however, this erasure of Nehemiah's memory went too far. His account of Judah's rebirth was not to be forgotten, even if it was not the final word.

The genius of Nehemiah's political approach was also a prominent feature of his own identity: pride. His memoir repeatedly calls the deity to remember "all that I have done for this people," and such self-adulation has long irritated his readers. However, he succeeded in galvanizing a community of builders, and he did so by appealing to the sense of collective shame they and their ancestors had endured after the conquest of their kingdom. Whatever personal vanity may have motivated him, his larger objective was to restore collective Judean pride, and that objective likely would not have been achievable without him first convincing a defeated and humiliated population to rise up and rebuild their ruins.

FROM BATTLES TO BUILDING

In the preceding chapter, we noted that after an imperial province replaced the kingdom of Judah, building activities assumed the formative role once played by battles and war efforts. This choice of a new theater for public life – building sites instead of battlefields – was not a natural one: it owed much to the initiatives of communal leaders like Haggai and Nehemiah, but even more to the nameless scribes who shaped the biblical corpus.

At the heart of Nehemiah's memoir is a long list of names, which pays tribute to individuals, districts, clans, priestly groups, and professional guilds in the province of Judah. The names are linked to portions of the wall whose repairs they sponsored, and this structure is highly symbolic. By charting the course of the wall, it portrays the political community as a joined circle encompassing Jerusalem, with each group working hand-in-hand along the wall's circumference and two sides meeting in the middle.

We may compare this impressive literary monument to ancient pillars, columns, and steles that Aegean city-states commissioned to commemorate their war efforts. A good example is the Serpent Column. Standing today in Constantinople, it was originally erected in Delphi after the victory over the Persians in the Battle of Plataea (479 BCE). The monument (or more precisely "trophy") has a long and fascinating literary history, negotiating status and belonging by honoring those who participated in the war effort. One community was added later, while five others are conspicuously absent – likely for political reasons.

With its selective constellation of names, the list in Nehemiah's memoir negotiates membership in a similar way to the Serpent Column and other war memorials. Yet it differs from them in that the communities it commemorates contributed to a building project rather than a war effort. Moreover, its authors inscribed the contributors' names on a portable memoir, not a fixed monument. As such, it was easier to reproduce, circulate, and amplify than a memorial carved in stone and planted in the ground. These are, indeed, features of the larger biblical corpus, which I describe in a recent book as a "movable monument" and – following the nineteenth-century German poet Heinrich Heine – a "portable homeland."[2]

The work on the wall was not completely voluntary. Nehemiah became governor at Judah at some point, and he expected everyone to

[2] See Wright, *War, Memory, and National Identity.*

share the burden. Those who shirked their duties were subjected to public opprobrium. His memoir not only pays tribute, but also casts aspersions. For example, it calls out the nobles of Tekoa (a district on the province's southern border), claiming that they "refused to shoulder their share of their lord's labor." In this way, the memoir records for posterity that the aristocratic members of a prominent community failed to participate at a time when everyone else was coming together for collective action.

As we will see in Chapter 24, the biblical authors created many memories of war and military conflict as they negotiated belonging and status among a wide range of communities. The Bible's most majestic war monument is a poem, the Song of Deborah, and as we saw in Chapter 3, it celebrates a great victory over the Canaanites in Israel's early history. Just as the register in Nehemiah's memoir censures the Tekoans, Deborah's song curses one community (Meroz) for failing "to come to the aid of Yhwh, to the aid of Yhwh among the warriors" (Judges 5:23). Furthermore, both the song and the memoir honor those who "volunteered themselves" and fulfilled their duties – one to a war effort and the other to a construction project. Through both activities, battle and building, one accumulated public honors and political capital. Conversely, those who dodged their duties could forfeit their social status – if not also their membership.

Although building accounts make for less thrilling reading, the authors of Ezra-Nehemiah imbue the work on Jerusalem's temple and wall with a martial quality. The people battle through building.

In the first section of the book, the earliest generations of builders quickly erect the altar because they live in "terror from the peoples of the land." After they lay the temple's foundations, their adversaries make every effort obstruct their work – first by maligning them in letters to the imperial court, and then, after receiving authorization to stop the construction, with military force.

In the second section, a priest and scribe named Ezra (the subject of the following chapter) organizes a caravan to bring Judeans and donations to Jerusalem. Before departing, he proclaims a fast, "because I was ashamed to ask the king for soldiers and horsemen to protect us against enemies on the road."

The book's third and final section consists mostly of Nehemiah's memoir, which punctuates each stage in the construction of Jerusalem's wall with notices of the enemy's reaction. First they resort to insults and trash-talk, as we saw earlier. Later the Judeans have to arm themselves against physical assaults, building with one hand while bearing a weapon in the other. When addressing them as their captain, Nehemiah incorporates standard themes of battle speeches: "Have no fear of them. Remember the Lord, the great and awesome one, and fight for your kin, your sons, your daughters, your wives, and your homes." The completion of the wall is viewed as a great triumph over Judah's foes: "All our enemies heard about it, and all the nations around us were afraid and lost their morale." The city's settlement is likewise depicted as a form of voluntary military service: not only do they cast lots (a typical method of selecting soldiers for a dangerous assignment), but also the new residents are designated "valiant warriors."

All this is more than mere saber-rattling for rhetorical effect. By incorporating martial features into these portraits of post-exilic life, the memoir and other texts in Ezra-Nehemiah ascribe to construction projects the same gravity and significance that major war efforts had had in the nation's past.

Nehemiah, and those who wrote in his wake, transformed the tedium of building activities with the grandeur and drama of battle. In doing so, they contributed to a new culture that, after Judah's defeat, began to supplant a deeply entrenched warrior-ethos – a subject we explore at greater length in Part IV.

FROM BUILDING TO REFORM

Internal rivalries debilitated Judean society at this time. In addition to rival clans, regions, and guilds, a deep chasm separated the wealthy from the poor. Nehemiah saw his building program as way to heal these rifts. A wall that imperial armies had rent asunder could be pieced back together as competing factions came together to restore their capital: "The entire wall quickly came together to half its height, for the people had a mind to work." Yet right at this halfway point, part of the population raises a complaint:

> There was a great outcry of the men and their wives against Judean kin/brothers. ... They were saying: "We are having to borrow money on our fields and vineyards to pay the king's tax. Our flesh is the same as that of our kin/brothers, and our children are the same as their children. Yet we are forcing our sons and daughters to be slaves, and some of our daughters have been ravished. We are powerless, and our fields and vineyards now belong to others."
>
> – Nehemiah 5:1–5

Nehemiah describes his reaction after learning of the economic injustice that threatened to undo Judah's newfound solidarity:

> I was furious when I heard their outcry and these complaints. Once I got hold of myself, I brought legal charges against the nobles and the officials: "You are all taking interest from your own kin/brothers." I then summoned a massive jury against them and continued: "We, according to our ability, have redeemed our Jewish kin/brothers who had sold themselves to the nations, and now you are selling them back...?"
>
> – Nehemiah 5:6–8

If Judah was to experience a full restoration, it had to take aggressive financial measures against the spiritual decay that plagued the community. Throughout this account, Nehemiah not only reminds the Judeans that they are "brothers" but also spells out the economic implications of their kinship. Later we hear about other radical reforms he introduced to repair a wide range of communal injustices. In each case, he takes formal legal action, suing the (aristocratic) offenders and forcing their hand with contractually binding commitments.

Similar to what we observed for Haggai and the building of the temple, Nehemiah's wall is an example of a grassroots movement organizing for collective action. At this time, Judeans had little to be proud of. The wall may not have been as formidable as the one King Hezekiah fortified in the eighth century. (One can still see in Jerusalem portions of this "Broad Wall" that are twenty-feet thick.) But the success of coming together to repair the city's ramparts had laid a concrete foundation for more ambitious social, economic, and religious reforms.

There are many examples of communal building projects catalyzing social change and economic recovery. Two prominent cases in Israel's and Judah's histories are the massive architectural feats that the ninth-century Omride kings achieved throughout the borders of their diverse kingdom and Hezekiah's construction efforts in Jerusalem in the late eighth century. In both instances, a financial boom is closely tied to building initiatives.

In American history, the best-known case of construction activities sparking growth is President Franklin Roosevelt's "New Deal" during the Great Depression of the 1930s. These domestic programs focused on the "3 Rs" – not only on *Relief* and *Recovery* in terms of many different construction projects, but also on *Reform* of financial abuses. When Roosevelt introduced the initiatives, he declared: "This is more than a political program. It's a call to arms."

Roosevelt's words recall the way Nehemiah's memoir connects battles and building. The latter makes a case for the role of a provincial governor, one that not only initiates construction projects but also introduces wide-ranging reforms and ensures that the community abides by its resolutions. With the authority to compel compliance, this political role distinguishes Nehemiah the governor from Haggai the prophet.

Nehemiah represents this new form of government just as David embodied the monarchic state from an earlier era. What distinguishes Nehemiah is that he acts under the jurisdiction of the Persian king and thus must convince, rather than conscript, others for collective action. A new era had begun, and a new deal was needed. It was the time for Nehemiahs, not Davids – for governors and provinces, not kings and kingdoms.

ARISTOCRACY AND INTERMARRIAGE

Nehemiah's building project may have reconsolidated Judah, but it also appears to have aroused jealousy from abroad. His memoir, often in secondary passages, claims that several groups sought to obstruct the project, and the main culprit is a figure named Sanballat.

Extra-biblical sources confirm what we can glean from Nehemiah's memoir: Sanballat and his sons were governors of the powerful province of Samaria in the North. In the final passage of the memoir, Nehemiah tells how he "chased away" a son of the High Priest in Jerusalem who had married Sanballat's daughter. The immense influence that this family and Samaria exerted in the region explains the fevered pitch of Nehemiah's polemics.

The memoir links Sanballat to a leader from the Transjordan named Tobiah. His name means "My fortune is Yah [or Yhwh]" and the community he governed had strong ethnic and religious ties to Judah. Notable figures from the upper classes in Judah had formed marriage alliances with Tobiah. As part of his campaign to create a "Judah for Judeans," Nehemiah claims that the first thing he did after arriving in Jerusalem was to drive Tobiah from his pied-à-terre in the temple precincts.

His memoir even goes so far as to claim that Sanballat and Tobiah organized a regional confederation and resorted to violence in a collective effort to halt the construction of the wall. According to later supplements, both Sanballat and Tobiah were deeply distraught that "someone [i.e., Nehemiah] had come to seek the welfare of the children of Israel." The indictment implies that these two figures, and the communities they represent, are Israel's enemies. A more scathing denouncement is difficult to imagine.

Taken as a whole, the memoir promotes an exclusivist, in contrast to an assimilationist, identity – for both the province of Judah and the people of Israel. For Nehemiah, and for those who transmitted and amplified his work, what impeded the restoration were efforts among the wealthy to advance their own interests by entering into political marriages with foreign elites.

Throughout history, the betrothal of one's progeny with prominent families abroad has been one of the primary means by which nobility and elites demarcate themselves from others in their countries. In modernity, nationally minded intellectuals and activists, in their efforts to consolidate autonomous political communities, have often resented and called out precisely this practice.

If the Judean province was to consolidate and assert itself in the region, it had to address the political alliances that the aristocracy had forged by marrying nobility in neighboring lands. Thus, the critique of intermarriage in Ezra-Nehemiah consistently focuses on the culpability of the upper classes (including priests) that arranged these unions. If these texts do not denigrate the foreign wives as culturally inferior, it is because these men were marrying "out" in order to marry "up."

THE NATIONAL CONSCIOUSNESS OF CHRONICLES

In the preceding chapter, we saw how the book of Ezra-Nehemiah, which was likely composed after 400 BCE, depicts Samarians thwarting the work on the temple. The way they describe themselves as immigrants echoes the account of their origins in the book of Kings, which tells how the Assyrians settled foreigners in the province of Samaria after conquering the Northern kingdom. Committed to the revitalization of Judah, the authors of these texts saw Samaria as a potential threat to their project of unifying their community, and when they vilify Samaria, they deny that its inhabitants belonged to the people of Israel. As ones who worshipped Yhwh and identified themselves as members of the nation, the Samarians would have taken umbrage at such imputations.

The Southern, or "Judah-centric," perspective that shapes Ezra-Nehemiah occasioned counter visions that were more latitudinarian or "pan-Israelite" in purview. The book of Chronicles is the most elaborate one. This work recapitulates the biblical narrative from Adam to Cyrus' decree to rebuild the temple in Jerusalem. Although it was drafted in the South, and not long after Ezra-Nehemiah, its authors embraced communities in Samaria, throughout the North, and across the Jordan as part of their people.

What motivated Chronicles' more open posture toward non-Judeans was, surprisingly, the temple in Jerusalem. Like Ezra-Nehemiah, this book asserts that this temple is the only legitimate one. Yet in contrast to Ezra-Nehemiah, it also presents this temple as a point of unity for "all Israel." The greatest moments in the nation's past, according to their account, was when Northern tribes, especially those farthest removed from Judah, united around major Judean kings (such as David, Solomon, Hezekiah, and Josiah) to lend support to this institution.

In making their "assimilationist" case, the authors of Chronicles composed remarkable new tales portraying rival communities overcoming their antipathies and affirming their kinship and solidarity. One of these stories depicts Samaria winning a war against Judah and then capturing 200,000 Judeans, including men, women, boys, and girls. A prophet of Yhwh appears and censures their callous behavior: "Do you seriously intend to subjugate the men and women of Judah and Jerusalem, and make them your slaves?" Not wishing to offend Yhwh, the Northerners submit dutifully to the prophet's warning and release "their kin" to return home. But before they let the Southerners go, these "Good Samarians" clothe them, put sandals on their feet, provision them with food and drink, anoint them with oil, set the feeble ones on donkeys, and escort them all the way to the border town of Jericho (2 Chronicles 28).

Tales such as these counter an anti-Samarian sentiment that was deeply rooted in many Judean circles. Their authors were convinced that the Northern communities belong to Israel. If they are different from Judah, it is because they abandoned worship of Yhwh at his sole authorized altar and temple in Jerusalem. By shifting the point of contention from national belonging to unorthodox worship, Southern scribes could make a case for the inclusion of Northern communities in a larger political community.

Numerous biblical texts express the expectation that Northern communities would eventually return to the orthodox fold. In them, many from Samaria make pilgrimages to Jerusalem for national festivals. Some even emigrate there, convinced that Yhwh was on Judah's side, and these texts may reflect actual ongoing movements of Northerners to and from Judah. But we must remember that, historically, Judah was inferior to Samaria, both as a kingdom in the Iron Age and later as a province in the Persian Empire.

"YOU SHALL LOVE YOUR NEIGHBOR AS YOURSELF"

The Bible is ultimately a Judean product. Its authors drew upon and learned from the works of Northern writers, but they revised and expanded them from a Southern, and especially Jerusalemite, perspective.

In Ezra-Nehemiah and Chronicles, we see how circles in Judah were struggling to come to terms with others who worshipped Yhwh and identified as the people of Israel. These books do not advance completely opposite programs. Indeed, the first one, advanced in Ezra-Nehemiah, makes the second one, in Chronicles, possible. Before groups could form larger corporate or national identities, they had to come together in their own communities. Accordingly, the authors of Ezra-

Nehemiah pushed for Judah's consolidation, despite the centrifugal forces that pulled it in all directions. If Judah had not first united as a provincial community, it would not have been able to join others to form a larger people.

This tension between individual communities and the collective nation lends the Bible much of its intellectual force and enduring political relevance. The scribes who shaped this corpus sought ways to rise above deep distrust and division in order to form a more perfect union.

The North and South never managed to overcome their rivalry. For centuries, they continued to compete with each other, often stridently. While both sides could perhaps agree on Yhwh being the nation's transcendent object of affection and locus of unity, the Southern side, which had the final say in this corpus, insisted that Jerusalem should be the nation's capital. In the second century, Hasmonean kings conquered Samaria and incorporated it into their Judean kingdom. As we observed in Chapter 6, this was a radical reversal in the long history of the North's domination.

Mutual hostility was harbored for centuries thereafter. When asked about the greatest commandment, a first-century Jewish teacher named Jesus told a parable in which a Samaritan cared for an assaulted man on the roadside who was on his way to the border town of Jericho (compare 2 Chronicles 28, which we just discussed). Speaking to a Judean audience, this teacher from Nazareth showed that a member of the Northern population behaved in keeping with the ethos of national kinship affirmed in the Torah:

> You shall not take vengeance or bear a grudge
> against the members of your own people.
> You shall love your neighbor as yourself.
> For I am Yhwh.
> – Leviticus 19:18

FURTHER READING

Burt, Sean, *The Courtier and the Governor: Transformations of Genre in the Nehemiah Memoir*, Vandenhoeck & Ruprecht, 2014.

Fried, Lisbeth S., *Nehemiah: A Commentary*, Sheffield Phoenix Press, 2021.

Fritz, Volkmar, *The City in Ancient Israel*, Bloomsbury, 1995.

Guy, Jordan, *United in Exile, Reunited in Restoration: The Chronicler's Agenda*, Sheffield Phoenix, 2019.

Japhet, Sara, *From the Rivers of Babylon to the Highlands of Judah: Collected Studies on the Restoration Period, Eisenbrauns*, 2006.

Japhet, Sara, *The Ideology of the Book of Chronicles and Its Place in Biblical Thought*, Eisenbrauns, 2009.

Levin, Yigal, *The Chronicles of the Kings of Judah*, Bloomsbury, 2017.

Lynch, Matthew *Monotheism and Institutions in the Book of Chronicles: Temple, Priesthood, and Kingship in Post-exilic Perspective*, Mohr Siebeck, 2014.

Tiemeyer, Lena-Sofia, *Ezra-Nehemiah: Israel's Quest for Identity*, T&T Clark, 2017.

Wright, Jacob L., "Nehemiah," in *NIB One-Volume Commentary*, Abingdon, 2010.

Wright, Jacob L., *Rebuilding Identity: The Nehemiah Memoir and Its Earliest Readers*, De Gruyter, 2004.

Wright, Jacob L., *War, Memory, and National Identity in the Hebrew Bible*, Cambridge University Press, 2020 (open access).

13

Ezra the Educator

Forming a People of the Book

All the people gathered as one at the square before the Water Gate, and they told Ezra the scribe to bring the Scroll of Moses's Teaching that Yhwh had enjoined upon Israel.

– Nehemiah 8:1

THE YEAR IS 444 BCE. Athens is now busy establishing an empire, and its leader Pericles has sponsored a building plan to refortify its main ports and the Long Walls that provided the city with a secure access to the sea. Meanwhile in Jerusalem, the inhabitants of Judah have just finished rebuilding the municipal fortifications of Jerusalem. Both its walls and temple had long languished in the rubble to which Babylonian armies had consigned them, but now they are standing again.

Today is the first day of the sacred seventh month, and on this occasion, the laws of Moses call for a fanfare of trumpets and ceremonious sacrifices at the central sanctuary. Strangely, however, the crowds converging on Jerusalem have little regard for the temple and annual rituals performed there. After assembling at the plaza in front of the Water Gate, they petition a priest and scribe named Ezra to make an appearance, and what they want him to do is not perform a cultic rite at the altar, but to read from the text he brought from Babylon. It is "the Scroll of Moses's Teaching/Torah that Yhwh had enjoined upon Israel." At the community's behest, Ezra ascends a high platform and reads aloud to all those who had gathered there – "men, women, and all who could understand."

The scribes responsible for capturing – or more accurately, creating – this scene keep the attention focused on the text Ezra bears: the people's longing to hear it read; those who help Ezra read it; and the people's response to the reading. When Ezra opens the Scroll, all the people rise, and after a blessing is pronounced, they lift their hands and respond "Amen, Amen!" Then they all bow and prostrate themselves "before Yhwh." After the Torah is read and explicated, the leaders exhort the people not to mourn, "for this day is holy to Yhwh, your god!" All are to go their ways and celebrate by "eating the fat, drinking the sweet, and sending portions to those without."

Many may find it difficult to appreciate the drama and emotion of this account. Ritual reading of a sacred text is not unusual for many of us. Jews, Christians, and Muslims have worshipped this way for millennia. But the reason why texts are central to their religious traditions is what happened 2,500 years ago.

Even if more imagined than real, this moment represents a tectonic shift: a scribe, scroll, and the activity of reading usurp the place long occupied by high priest, altar, and the performance of sacrifices. The people are no longer mere spectators, looking on while priests carry out rites and rituals; they now actively participate in the proceedings. And their participation includes communal prayer (in the place of priestly sacrifice) as well as cognition and comprehension: when they celebrate at the end of the day, it is "because they understood the words that [Ezra and others] had imparted to them."

However, this moment is about more than religious history. What we witness here is nothing less than the birth of "the People of the Book" (perhaps more properly, "the People of the Scroll"), along with a new approach to education that informs this text-based identity. The present chapter and the following one conclude Part III by exploring this pedagogical program. The ways in which biblical scribes democratized textual study was a foundational move for the biblical project, and we will situate it in the context of ancient scribal training.

THE TEACHER AS A NEW ARCHETYPE

With Jerusalem's ramparts now repaired, the narrative of Ezra-Nehemiah shifts its focus to the reading and study of the Torah. In the account I just rehearsed, the Judeans lay claim to their ancestral traditions and make them the cornerstone of their collective life. Nehemiah, the builder and governor, must therefore take backstage to a different kind of communal leader: the teacher.

In the person of Ezra, the luminary at the center of our story, we come closest to the profile of those who crafted the biblical corpus. This figure is first and foremost a priest with an illustrious heritage. But more important than this inherited status are the skills he acquired as a scribe and teacher. After tracing his genealogical line back to Aaron (the legendary brother of Moses and the nation's first priest), the authors introduce him with a statement about his preparation for that historic moment in Jerusalem: "he was a scribe who devoted himself to study the Torah of Yhwh, and to observe it, and to teach laws and justice to Israel."

Ezra was not a typical member of his profession. Instead of training other scribes, he formed a larger community of learners. The account of him reading the Torah in Jerusalem repeatedly underscores broad participation. Twice in the opening verses, we are told that "both men and women, and all who could understand," had assembled on this momentous occasion. The expression, "all the people," occurs no less than seven times; indeed, they are the primary protagonists. Torah study is the prerogative of the entire community; all, not just a select few, should be involved. And indeed what's portrayed in this scene is actual learning, not just a ceremonious reading: the Levites who join Ezra on the podium translate (presumably into Aramaic) and explicate the meaning of what is read to the people (literally, "help the people to understand").

As this highly symbolic account continues, the community learns to read on their own. First, the leaders gather around Ezra and read the text he brought from Babylon. At that time they discover and reclaim a long-neglected festival, and as they observe it, Ezra continues with public readings. At the end of the month, the community assembles again, yet now they are reading and studying without his help. The text is firmly in their hands, and together they have embraced a groundbreaking paradigm for their future as a people.

These scenes are truly remarkable. Across the Bible's rich narrative tapestry, with its tales of lives both great and small, one activity is conspicuously absent: learning from books or teaching others about the past. For the eight or more centuries connecting the age of Moses and Joshua to that of Ezra and Nehemiah, the people had never petitioned a scribe to read the Torah to them; indeed, they hardly seem aware of its existence.

To appreciate the heightened emotion in the account of Ezra's reading, we have to step back and consider what the event would have meant to the scribes who imagined it.

The scribal profession was one among many, and its practitioners would never have expected their trade skills and technologies to be embraced so widely and passionately. From our vantage point, we might think of the development as predestined from the beginning, but scribes had been making texts for millennia before this moment in Jerusalem. Against any simple teleology, with humans inevitably evolving into literate societies bearing bodies of writings in their bosoms, we have to acknowledge that a broader consumption of texts – or a "reading public" – has continued to wax and wane throughout history.

The scribes who produced the biblical corpus, with its innovative didactic dimensions, had long envisioned that the texts they held so dearly, and that they had long shared among themselves, would one day migrate from the shadows of their writing chambers to the spotlight of their communities. Our account expresses this vision in spectacular proportions, with the Torah mounting the podium in Ezra's hands and towering above a huge crowd. The reverence, the choreographed performance, the cries of jubilation, the tears, and the feasting that follows – these behaviors are reminiscent of a modern music concert. If authors of this account went all out in their portrait of Ezra as a scribal rockstar, it is because this was the moment for which they had long waited.

In this scene, the Torah scroll and rituals of reading bear a striking resemblance to the processions of gods at festivals. The authors wanted their readers to regard the scroll as a new kind of icon. The difference from conventional icons is that this one was reproducible and not confined to a singular sacred space. The scroll served merely as the medium and repository for a written text whose words should ideally be inscribed on the heart. The fabrication of temple icons (such as representations of deities) required secret knowledge that was guarded by a priestly caste. In this new textual garb, what was esoteric is now exoteric: circles with a wide range of affiliations and perspectives produced these scrolls, and they bequeathed them to the wider community.

ARCHIVES FROM A COLONY IN EGYPT

Most political communities have had to deal with defeat, yet few have responded by reorienting their collective identities around bodies of texts, and none have done so on the scale that we witness in ancient Judah. Even so, the emergence of a community of learners in this province was by no means immediate.

Important witnesses reveal that it took time for its inhabitants to make the Torah central to their collective life and to evolve into the text-focused community portrayed in Ezra-Nehemiah. For example, the book of Haggai features both a prophet who speaks in the deity's name (what we might call "charismatic authority") and priests making pronouncements based on their own professional expertise, which is the original form of *torah* or "teaching." Yet there is nothing in this book about heeding the authority of a text.

The same can be said for a number of other biblical texts that date to this period (such as the earliest editions of Nehemiah's Memoir), but also for the trove of texts from an ancient Judean community that archeologists discovered in Egypt. These texts reveal a very different state of affairs from the society imagined in Ezra-Nehemiah.

When the classical archeologist Otto Rubensohn in the early 1900s unearthed an archive of papyri documents on one of the rocky islands of the Nile's First Cataract, little could he or anyone else anticipate how dramatically these documents would alter our understanding of the Bible's formation. The place where Rubensohn made this groundbreaking discovery, known today as Elephantine, is located not far from the Aswan Dam (Figure 13.1). There, on the southern frontier of the Persian Empire, about a thousand miles from Jerusalem, Judean soldiers and their families took up residence in c.540 BCE. Their mission was to patrol the transport of imperial goods on the Nile. Over the following century and a half, they created a tight-knit community, in close proximity to other imperial soldiers as well as to the native Egyptian population.

Figure 13.1 The island of Elephantine, located on the Nile in the Aswan region, where rich remains of a Judean community in the Persian period have been found. Photo: Marc Ryckaert.

For no other group from Judah or Israel prior to Greco-Roman times do we have such an abundance of documents. In addition to these papyri, other texts appeared on the antiquities market, and later excavations have discovered inscribed potsherds ("ostraca"). The texts consist of mostly ad hoc writings, including business memoranda, marriage contracts, correspondence with authorities abroad, and family letters. Many of the latter are both poignant and tender: "Why did you not write when I was sick?" writes a brother to his sister. "Thank you for the coat that you sent," writes a son to his mother.

Written in Aramaic, these documents date to 495–399 BCE, the century in which Ezra and Nehemiah were active in Jerusalem. Yet unlike our biblical writings, the Elephantine papyri and ostraca are what historians call "primary sources," discovered in situ, rather than being transmitted, and edited, by generations of readers.

The community in Elephantine was called the "Jewish Garrison." Its members were loyal to the Persian kings who sent them to Egypt, where they faced attacks from the native population. Their correspondence divulges how these Egyptians had already razed the Judeans' temple to the ground even while the Persians were in control

Figure 13.2 Part of the letter, written on papyrus, requesting help from Jerusalem after the destruction of the Judeans' temple at Elephantine. From *Abhandlungen der Königlich Preussischen Akademie der Wissenschaften,* 1901.

(Figure 13.2). When the Persian Empire fell, the community did not fare well. The life built there over the centuries was wiped out, and nothing was known about their experiences until their papyri were discovered 2,500 years later.

The habits, laws, and religious behaviors of the Elephantine community differ starkly from biblical teachings. In fact, some of their most common practices are precisely those that many biblical books proscribe most fervently: they work on the Sabbath; the priests are engaged in intermarriage with outsiders; there is a temple to Yhwh (or "Yahu"); the community makes regular contributions to this deity in addition to a number of other deities (Anat-Bethel and Ashim-Bethel); and Yhwh/Yahu appears to have a wife (her name is Anat-Yahu).

What makes these facts even more shocking is that the Jews of Elephantine maintained close relations with the homeland. When their leaders had questions about cultic practice, or when they needed support for their communal affairs, they wrote to the priestly and lay authorities in both Jerusalem and Samaria. From what we can piece together, the responses from these authorities surprisingly never condemned the community's worship of Anat-Yahu or their labors on the Sabbath. This is therefore not a case of a diasporic community backsliding from "orthodoxy" and embracing a syncretistic form of "paganism," as some scholars claim.

Literacy is also not the issue. Many at Elephantine could read and write, reflecting a wider trend throughout the Persian Empire. The cosmopolitan literature they read included the widely transmitted Proverbs of Ahiqar and the famous Behistun Inscription of King Darius. However, all their texts are in Aramaic, not Hebrew. And closely connected to this fact is a more obvious, yet all the more astounding, one: the biblical writings were not available on this island in the Nile. In fact, no one there seems even to know of their existence, nor do the leaders in Jerusalem ever refer to them!

The community at Elephantine clearly ascribed much honor to Jerusalem and Samaria, and they viewed the population of their homeland as "brothers/kin." They were also eager to act in accordance with ancestral traditions. Reverence for tradition and solidarity among members of the nation were driving forces behind the Bible's formation, but when the communal leaders at Elephantine wanted to know something, instead of consulting sacred scriptures, they asked a living authority. Thus a leader named Hananiah (presumably from Jerusalem) answered questions from the Judean community in Egypt about how to observe the laws of Matzoth, a fall festival linked to Passover:

> [To] my [brethren Yedo]niah and his colleagues the [J]ewish gar[rison], your brother Hanan[iah]. The welfare of my brothers may God [seek at all times]. Now, this year, the fifth year of King Darius, word was sent from the king to Arsa[mes...]
>
> Now, you thus count four[teen days in Nisan and on the 14th at twilight ob]serve [the Passover] and from the 15th day until the 21st day of [Nisan observe the Festival of Unleavened Bread. Seven days eat unleavened bread. Now,] be pure and take heed. [Do] n[ot do] work [on the 15th day and on the 21st day of Nisan.] Do not drink [any fermented drink. And do] not [eat] anything of leaven [nor let it be seen in your houses

> from the 14th day of Nisan at] sunset until the 21st day of Nisa[n at sunset. And b]ring into your chambers [any leaven which you have in your houses] and seal (them) up during [these] days. . . .
>
> [To] my brothers, Yedaniah and his colleagues the Jewish garrison, your brother Hananiah s[on of ??].

In this letter, which was found on a piece of papyrus with writing on both sides, Hananiah informs the leaders in Elephantine about various rules, some of which coincide with biblical laws. But he skips over important parts and does not seem to know these laws in their written form. His source may have been verbal communications or perhaps priestly manuals that were being reworked and incorporated into the Pentateuch at this time.

Another text, written on a pottery shard, refers to Passover, yet it too does not seem to know this festival in its biblical form. This is doubly surprising since Passover is so closely connected to the exodus from Egypt where this community lived. Why then do we not hear about the larger story and the laws linked to that story?

At this time (*c.*400), the worship of Yhwh in Jerusalem most likely did not include his wife, yet for all we know, the authorities in Jerusalem never thought to castigate the community in Elephantine for not worshipping in the ways prescribed by biblical texts. They merely offered guidance on cultic matters related to the temple. And they never appealed to the Torah's authority. Instead of citing biblical texts, these letters refer to the authority of the imperial command. Even more surprising, the Jerusalem community acknowledged temples to Yhwh outside of Jerusalem. In fact, they encourage the Elephantine Jews to rebuild their temple "on the place where it once stood." In assuming this supportive position, they stand in direct contradiction to the book of Ezra-Nehemiah and the laws of Moses, which stipulate that there be only one temple to Yhwh.

The Elephantine documents reflect a concern that all be done in keeping with the command of the Persian king. The same can be said for Ezra-Nehemiah, but this biblical book reflects a second concern: that all be done "as it is written (in the Torah of Moses)." That formula is conspicuously absent in the correspondence from Elephantine.

To summarize our findings, the Judeans at Elephantine were educated and literate, yet what is conspicuously absent in the many texts we discovered from their community are biblical writings. They were not cognizant of a body of authoritative "scripture" that they could consult for direction in social and religious matters. Nor did the authorities in Judah and Samaria to whom they wrote ever suggest that they acquire copies of these writings and make them the centerpiece of their collective life.

As such, this archive stands in stark contrast to another important archive that we found: the Dead Sea Scrolls. These texts, which date to the turn of the Common Era, are products of a community at Qumran that spent their days studying and copying most of the writings that would become part of the biblical canon (in addition to a host of others). Elephantine and Qumran are the most important finds of ancient Judean texts, and together they provide concrete evidence for the dramatic cultural and political impact of what began as an exercise of scribal imagination.

SEEKING AND FINDING IN WRITINGS

Even though we cannot take Ezra-Nehemiah at face value, the book reflects a pioneering vision among a group of ancient scribes, namely to make their beloved body of writings an object of affection for a new nation. What propelled Judah's restoration, according to the narrative, were texts, and those who interpreted them, and in depicting how texts played this formative role, its authors made a compelling, and creative, case for their culture of writing and reading.

The book begins with Cyrus decreeing that all Yhwh's people should rise up and rebuild the temple in Jerusalem, and the narrator makes a point of reporting that the decree "was also in writing." After hearing of the building project, Judah's "adversaries" approach them with the petition to participate in the project. The leaders in Jerusalem reject their offer by appealing to Cyrus' mandate. In their anger, the rebuffed petitioners attempt to thwart the progress. During the reign of Artaxerxes, provincial administrators write to the king, advising him to search in the royal annals and find Jerusalem's rebellious record. The king follows their advice, commands a search to be made, and sure enough finds what he was looking for. He then orders the construction of the city to cease.

Later, in the reign of Darius, the work on the temple resumes thanks to the prophecies of Haggai and Zechariah. But then the provincial administrators approach the builders and inquire whether the construction project had been authorized. In response, the Judean elders claim that Cyrus had authorized the project. To verify this claim, the local officials write again to the imperial court, petitioning Darius to search the archives in Babylon for a record of the decree, and as before, the crown complies with these directions and orders that a search be conducted.

After looking in Babylon and not finding it, the long-lost Cyrus Edict finally turns up in an archive of another city (Ecbatana). Darius then responds by issuing a new decree that quotes the first one and supplements it with generous benefaction on the behalf of Jerusalem. Without further delay, the temple is then brought to completion.

This story of "seeking and finding" should not be confused with history. As we saw in the preceding chapter, Cyrus likely never announced the temple-building mandate, and the Judeans initiated and completed their project without much, if any, imperial benefaction or interference. What is most improbable about the narrative is its portrayal of powerful rulers, who govern a world empire, conducting searches in their state archives before determining their policies toward a tiny and insignificant province. If the Persian kings had wanted to stop or support construction activities in Jerusalem, they did not need to study records of the city's past, or conduct an extensive search for an earlier decree, as local officials direct them to do.

While it may not be historically reliable, the account of these archival searches would have made the quoted documents seem authentic to its ancient readers. Yet the account also has a larger pedagogical purpose, modeling a modus operandi for Judah's leadership. The lesson is clear: if rulers of a world empire showed deference for their written traditions, and never made a decision or decree without consulting their archives, how much more so should the Judean community, now without a king of their own, study their own texts as they plod forward under the aegis of these foreign rulers?

The texts in which the community of Ezra-Nehemiah "seek and find" range from registers and records to the narratives of their nation's past and the text par excellence – the Torah. Thus, in the first section, the community conducts research in their genealogical records when determining membership, and as they re-establish both cult and community, they do so "as it is written in the Torah of Moses." Throughout the remaining narrative, the protagonists repeatedly refer to events recorded in the National Narrative, which begins with the creation of the world and ends with Jerusalem's destruction.

The heart of the book focuses on Ezra, the paradigmatic figure with expertise in both "studying" (literally "seeking/inquiring") the Torah and "teaching" it to others. The king grants him permission to go up to Jerusalem with anyone who wishes to accompany him, to "seek/inquire" in Judah according to "the law of your god that is in your hand." When he gets there, he and the leadership in Jerusalem "seek/inquire" in communal records to expose the marriage alliances that some leading priests had made with Judah's competitors in the region. His account culminates in the scene of him studying the Torah with the community and "finding/discovering" what had been forgotten.

In late supplements to his account, Nehemiah demonstrates a command of Israel's written traditions and can even cite biblical texts verbatim. Likewise, when populating Jerusalem after the completion of the wall, he consults Judah's written records that he happens to "find/discover" and that he reproduces at length. And in the book's final chapter, when the community "seeks/inquires" in the Torah, they "find/discover" laws demanding them to separate themselves from surrounding peoples. The authors prefaced this passage to an older account of Nehemiah's reforms, and by doing so, they reinterpreted these reforms as a reinforcement of prior communal resolutions, in keeping with written precedents (both the Torah and their own corporate pact).

For a community negotiating its survival in a world empire, such concern with identity and tradition is to be expected. In the absence of clearly demarcated, political borders, and a native Judean army to defend those borders, its members notably turn to their *written* traditions. By means of ancestral texts, and sophisticated methods of interpretation, they demarcate their identity and determine how they should proceed into an unprecedented future.

What is remarkable about Ezra-Nehemiah's depiction of the imperial court and the Judean community consulting written records is that the terminology for "seeking/inquiring," both in this work and in many other post-exilic writings, is the same terminology used to describe divination practices in pre-exilic writings. Thus, when King David decides whether to launch military campaigns, he first "seeks/inquires of Yhwh." The method of oracular inquiry usually goes unsaid, but at certain points we hear of the Ephod, the Urim and Thumim, and *teraphot* – ancient divination paraphernalia that remain shrouded in mystery. Now when members of the Judean province desire to know the divine will, rather than engaging in divination, they seek/inquire in written texts.

This is a major development with wide-ranging implications, both for an emerging text-based religion and for the wider culture. Michael Fishbane calls it "a new stage of legal rationality, when a text becomes an *oraculum* for rational-exegetical inquiry."[1] What made the development possible was the occupation of David's throne by foreign kings, which in post-exiling writings goes hand in hand with the transformation of David's divination practices to the communal study of (sacred) texts.

In Chapter 26 we explore this transformation in relation to prophecy and the Bible's principle of "open access." But for our present purposes, it is important to bear in mind how the archeological evidence from Elephantine, as well as biblical texts like Haggai, relativizes Ezra-Nehemiah's account to a vision scribes had for their communities in which texts played a pivotal role. That vision was not fully realized at this time. A scriptural consciousness and culture had yet to take root. Even so, the seeds were being planted.

MAKING A PACT

As noted, all the Elephantine documents are written in Aramaic; none are in Hebrew. The book of Ezra-Nehemiah, however, consists of

[1] Fishbane, *Biblical Interpretation in Ancient Israel*, p. 244.

Aramaic sources surrounded by a Hebrew narrative, and this composite form communicates an important point: the Judeans were now to be bilingual, in the fullest sense of the term. Their new home was within a global empire. Without their own kings to protect and guide them, their welfare depended upon good relations with the powers that be.

The community of Ezra-Nehemiah conducts its correspondence with the empire in the language of the empire, but when they tell their own story, they write in their native tongue. The inclusion of the older Aramaic materials demonstrates that many Judean activities required imperial authorization, while the Hebrew narrative in which these Aramaic materials are embedded illustrates how the community must establish new institutions and ways of doing things.

Thus, in both the form and language of Ezra-Nehemiah, we witness how Judean scribes began to recognize the opportunities their fate afforded them. The downfall of their kingdom and the favor of foreign kings created conditions for a new form community with biblical writings at their center.

The space and autonomy that foreign rulers granted this community was to be used to foster study of ancestral traditions – the very ones that the biblical authors were collecting, revising, and expanding at this time. (Not only the Persians but also their Hellenistic successors – at least until the second century – permitted their subjects to live under their "ancestral laws.")

The account of Ezra reading the Torah in Jerusalem includes a public prayer – the longest in the Bible – that reviews the nation's tumultuous past. Part praise, part protest, it culminates in a plea that their God would not take lightly the suffering that Judah has endured "from the time of the Assyrian kings to this day." The community is said to be slaves in their own land. Their fields yield abundant crops to foreign kings whom the deity had set over this people as punishment for their sins: "They rule over our bodies and our beasts as they please, and we are in great distress."

This is a rare criticism of the Persian kings. The next step the community takes is to draw up a written pact. This document is not the founding document for a liberation movement or a charter to stake out a claim in a new country. They long to be free, but in meantime they come together to corporately commit themselves to the Torah and to support their own institutions (above all, their temple).

Representing broad support, the pact begins by listing the signatures of Judah's many leaders, and then goes on to include every group in the community: "their wives, their sons, their daughters, and all who have knowledge and understanding." The pact speaks with the voice of the "we" as it lays out specific duties:

> – We lay on ourselves the obligation to charge ourselves yearly one-third of a shekel for the service of the House of our God . . .
>
> – We have also cast lots for the wood offering, to bring it into the House of our God, by ancestral houses, at appointed times, year by year, to burn on the altar of Yhwh our God, as it is written in the law.
>
> – We obligate ourselves to bring the first fruits of our soil and the first fruits of all fruit of every tree, year by year, to the House of Yhwh.
>
> – Nehemiah 10:32–35

Here, as so often elsewhere in the book, the point pertains less to the *what* than the *how*, as members of the province negotiate new ways of caring for their institutions and corporate life.

In contrast to the earth-shattering covenant ratified on Mount Sinai, this pact is made solely among the people themselves. Yet even if they do not hear the voice of Yhwh thundering from a cloud above, the ideals inscribed in the Torah were now being realized. Judah had witnessed devastation, the loss of native sovereignty, and now a humble new beginning under foreign rule. Although its inhabitants had seen a new dawn, their future was far from certain. They recognized in their plight as a vanquished nation the moral imperative to commit themselves to their collective welfare and ensure that all do their part to shoulder the load.

AN AGE OF PROSE

These episodes represent the culmination not only of the events portrayed in Ezra-Nehemiah but of the National Narrative, which begins in Genesis and continues to Judah's defeat in the book of Kings. The inclusion of the lengthy prayer, which selectively rehearses the National Narrative, reveals how the authors want us to understand their account: as the sequel to that Narrative, yet one that does not diminish its emphasis on defeat.

The signing of the pact is followed in the book by the festive dedication of the wall, marking the completion of many years of building activities in Jerusalem. However, the story does not conclude on that celebratory note. Instead, the final chapter describes several religious and social reforms that Nehemiah undertakes because the community failed to abide by the terms of their pact.

This anticlimactic conclusion is in keeping with the general tenor of Ezra-Nehemiah. This book portrays no glorious triumphs, no retrieval of lost glories. It does not recount the restoration in mythic proportions, with Judah rising from its ruins and returning to its former glory. The tale of Judah's comeback is not spectacular, and in telling it, the authors went to great lengths to ensure that their readers resisted the temptation to mythologize the events. They depicted a much more modest restoration, a life lived in the shadow of foreign rule, without heroes like David to save the day. Defeat is an abiding presence, and reconstruction takes place "In an Age of Prose" (the title of an important book on Ezra-Nehemiah, by Tamara Cohn Eskenazi[2]). In keeping with the consciousness of defeat they sought to cultivate, the scribes who shaped the biblical corpus identify this age as not only a formative era but also an abiding one.

FURTHER READING

Becking, Bob, *Identity in Persian Egypt: The Fate of the Yehudite Community of Elephantine*, Penn State University Press, 2020.

Eskenazi, Tamara Cohn, *In an Age of Prose: A Literary Approach to Ezra-Nehemiah*, SBL Press, 1988.

Fishbane, Michael, *Biblical Interpretation in Ancient Israel*, Clarendon, 1985.

Folmer, Margaretha (ed.), *Elephantine Revisited: New Insights into the Judean Community and Its Neighbors*, Eisenbrauns, 2022.

[2] Eskenazi, *In an Age of Prose: A Literary Approach to Ezra-Nehemiah.*

Fried, Lisbeth S., *Ezra and the Law in History and Tradition*, University of South Carolina Press, 2014.

Hasler, Laura Carlson, *Archival Historiography in Jewish Antiquity*, Oxford University Press, 2019.

Himmelfarb, Martha, *A Kingdom of Priests: Ancestry and Merit in Ancient Judaism*, University of Pennsylvania Press, 2006.

Jones, Christopher M., "Embedded Written Documents as Colonial Mimicry in Ezra-Nehemiah," *Biblical Interpretation* 25 (2018): 158–181.

Kratz, Reinhard G. and Schipper, Bernd U. (eds.), *Elephantine in Context: Studies on the History, Religion and Literature of the Judeans in Persian Period Egypt*, Mohr Siebeck, 2022.

Laird, Donna, *Negotiating Power in Ezra-Nehemiah*, SBL Press, 2016.

Polaski, Donald C., "'What Mean These Stones?': Inscriptions, Textuality and Authority in Persia and Yehud," in Jon L. Berquist (ed.) *Approaching Yehud: New Approaches to the Study of the Persian Period*, SBL Press, 2007.

Porten, Bezalel, *The Elephantine Papyri in English*, Brill, 1996.

van der Toorn, Karel, *Becoming Diaspora Jews: Behind the Story of Elephantine*, Yale University Press, 2019.

Wright, Jacob L., "Seeking, Finding, and Writing in Ezra-Nehemiah," in Mark J. Boda and Paul L. Reddit (eds.), *Unity and Disunity in Ezra-Nehemiah*, Continuum, 2007.

14

Hoshayahu the Soldier

Peoplehood as a Pedagogical Project

As Yhwh lives,
no one has ever had to read a letter to me!
– Lachish Letter 3

IN 1938, JUST WEEKS BEFORE BEING MURDERED, the British archeologist James Leslie Starkey discovered a stockpile of ancient texts. He had been excavating at Lachish, which was a once powerful city in the Southern kingdom, second only to Jerusalem. As Starkey was digging in the guardroom of the gate complex, he happened upon a cache of inscribed pottery shards (ostraca) from Judah's final days, when Nebuchadnezzar was preparing his siege of the capital. One of these texts is a letter that an officer in Judah's army named Hoshayahu sent to his commander (Figure 14.1):

> Your servant, Hoshayahu, sends to inform my lord, Yaush: May Yhwh cause my lord to hear a report of peace and of good tidings!
>
> And now, please explain to your servant the meaning of the letter you sent to your servant yesterday evening, because your servant's heart has been sick since you sent it to your servant. My lord said, "You do not know how to read a letter." As Yhwh lives, never has anyone ever had to read a letter to me! Also every letter that comes to me, surely I am the one who reads it. Moreover, I can repeat it completely . . .
>
> To your servant it has been reported saying: The commander of the army has gone down to go to Egypt, and he sent a letter to . . . And as for the letter of Tobiyahu, the servant of the king, [which quotes] the prophet saying, "Beware!" – your servant is sending it now to my lord.[1]

[1] See Schniedewind, "Sociolinguistic Reflections."

Figure 14.1 Lachish letter III. Image from the Matson Photograph Collection at the Library of Congress.

Many of the officers in Judah's army must have been illiterate, and Hoshayahu is unsettled to learn that Yaush, his commander, assumes he is one of them. His response sets the record straight: not only does he not need to rely on someone else to read the official memos he receives, but he even commits their contents to memory. Because he could read and remember things so well, there was no opportunity for a third party to modify the messages he was receiving.

We could not wish for a more telling testimony to the way education functioned in the monarchic society that imperial armies obliterated just a few months later. At the center of the *ancien régime* was a well-oiled war machine. The military spent its days studying strategy and practicing tactical maneuvers with their chariots, compound bows, and siege machines. Prophets, priests, scribes, and everyone else were expected to do their part to ensure the state's security and triumph. Literacy was not only critical to the many functions of this society, but also the trademark – and trade secret – of the ruling class.

The only text David handles in the biblical memories of the monarchic age are dispatches from the front lines, similar to the officer's letter from Lachish. Yet when all that David built had been destroyed, and when it was no longer possible to re-establish a native monarchy and military force, a new kind of text takes center stage, and with it, a new kind of readership.[2]

In the preceding chapters of Part II, we examined the pervasive presence of defeat in the Bible, from Lamentation's People of Protest to Ezra-Nehemiah's People of the Book. The present chapter lays the foundation for Part III by considering the larger implications of the Bible's vision for an educated nation. We begin with a survey of scribal training before turning to the new model of education introduced in biblical writings, which we will situate in a larger historical context and compare with educational reforms from later times.

SCRIBES AND SCHOOL LIFE

An oft-repeated Babylonian account tells how a schoolboy struggled to do his best and yet repeatedly failed. Everyday he was caned for submitting sloppy work, speaking without permission, appearing in slovenly attire, and loitering in the streets. His wealthy father eventually invited

[2] In keeping with this shift, the final editions of Psalms differ dramatically from the older book of Samuel by presenting David as one who studies and meditates day and night on the Torah.

the schoolmaster to their home where he anointed him with a fine fragrance, clothed him in new raiment, put a ring on his finger and money in his pocket. Pleased with the demonstration of generosity, the schoolmaster blessed the man's son and proclaimed: "You have carried out well the school's activity. You have become a man of learning. Nisaba, the queen-goddess of learning, you have exalted." Before leaving, he assured the student that he had a bright future.

Called "tablet-houses" in Mesopotamia and "houses of life" in Egypt, ancient schools were not hospitable places of learning. Instructors were not immune to venality, lessons were monotonous, and pupils faced corporal punishment for the slightest misdemeanors. Teachers were likened to creator deities who physically formed and inscribed their students as if they were clay tablets. Although students often came from the most propertied families, they were expected to do their utmost to secure the title of scribe, which might be compared to a modern university degree.

Training began at an early age. Most were boys, but exceptions were made occasionally for girls. The students spent their days learning how to prepare materials used for writing, memorizing texts, and practicing hundreds of cuneiform and hieroglyphic signs that formed the basis of non-alphabetic writing systems. In Mesopotamia, the tutor would impress signs on the frontside of a clay tablet, and the student would attempt an exact replication on the backside. From such practice exercises, we can witness firsthand how pupils struggled to keep up and often distracted themselves with doodling.

After mastering long lists of technical vocabulary, advanced students moved on to literary texts, wisdom sayings, model letters, legal documents, trial proceedings, and display inscriptions. They also learned mathematics, astronomy, incantations, myths, and music. Yet here too the emphasis was on duplication, memorization, and preservation, not creativity. Whereas Apple's motto was once to "think different," Babylonian and Egyptian students were expected to "think ancient." Like Roman students who learned Greek, scribes in Babylonia were expected to have a command of Sumerian, a language that was no longer spoken. A popular proverb asked: "A scribe who does not know Sumerian, what kind of scribe is he?"

Education in ancient West Asian and North African societies was primarily about training a select group of scribal elites for administrative positions in the temple and palace. Not all scribes served in these two leading state institutions; many spent their days as "street scribes" producing business documents, drafting marriage contracts, or writing letters for private clients (as one can still witness today in the Jerusalem's Old City and in marketplaces throughout the Middle East). The scribal craft emerged, and to a certain extent evolved, independently of the infrastructure provided by state administrations; in this regard, it was not any different from many other professional trades, such as pottery and metalworking. But once kings began to consolidate their dominions, their military and political feats accelerated the growth of complex societies, which in turn increased the demand for literate professionals. Indeed, scribal expertise was instrumental to the growth of mighty kingdoms and empires, and the assignments scribes most coveted were those in the palace, temple, and army.

In the "Parody of the Professions" (Papyrus Lansing), a widely transmitted Egyptian school-text from the eighteenth century BCE, the teacher pits the soldier's life against the scribal profession. When the soldier is called up for a campaign in Canaan, his officer promises him a good name as an incentive: "Quick, forward, valiant soldier! Win for yourself a good name!" In the end, however, the commander's promise is empty: "The soldier dies on the edge of the desert, and there is none to perpetuate his name." The scribal profession, in contrast, promises a mansion, fine clothes, slaves, a beautiful boat, and, most importantly, a grave in the Egyptian homeland. The teacher urges his student: "Look, I make you into a staff of life! Put the writings in your heart, and you will be protected from all kinds of toil."

Scribes not only played essential administrative roles; they also transmitted among themselves literary and legal texts that they copied and expanded. We can be confident that those serving in official capacities of the kingdoms of Israel and Judah also produced such texts.

A range of evidence suggests that Northern scribes, after the downfall of their kingdom in 722 BCE, found employment at the Davidic court in Jerusalem, and that they reacted to its propaganda by composing core components of the National Narrative. Their work, as we noted in Part I, imagined Israel becoming a people and establishing itself in the Promised Land *without* the institution of the monarchy.

As we prepare to probe that work in Part III, we need to consider here how the biblical authors collectivized the competitive advantage of text-based learning.

EDUCATION AND NATION

Noblesse oblige – with privilege comes duty. In antiquity, the upper echelons distinguished themselves from the masses by what they deemed to be their special obligation of safeguarding a cultural legacy. The monarchic societies of Israel and Judah were not fundamentally different from their neighbors when it came to education, yet the scribes who produced the biblical corpus saw a different potential in their training. Instead of promoting education as a way of demarcating themselves from others in their society, they adapted and applied it to their project of creating a people. Education is still about the competitive advantage it promises, but the contest is no longer primarily between individuals and groups within their society. The goal is rather that everyone learns and internalizes the nation's history, laws, songs, and wisdom, so that *together* they will be able to make a name for themselves on a global stage.

Throughout history the "upwardly mobile" have discovered education on their quest for public honor and societal privilege. Thus the society of Classical Athens was characterized by an agonistic struggle for recognition, and in their competition with each other, citizens embraced ideals of education (*paideia*) and excellence (*arete*) from the upper echelon.

What we witness in biblical literature, however, is very different from the parvenu's pursuit of honors in high society. This is not about a general democratization of aristocratic virtue. Nor is it about elites immersing themselves in a foreign cultural tradition – such as Akkadian scribes memorizing Sumerian texts, Romans appropriating Greek *paideia*, or privileged students in modern preparatory schools learning Greek and Latin.

Rather, the scribes who curated the biblical corpus consciously took what priests and palace members had long guarded as their special heritage and made it available, and indeed mandatory, for the education and edification of the entire nation. Their aim was to transform a legacy and cultural canon to promote wider participation in public life. As part of this process, the ancestors of the few became the ancestors of all; proverbs and wisdom teachings were reworked for the instruction of the wider community; and the secret rules that governed the performance of priests were now accessible in a public document (subjects we explore in Parts III and IV). In addition to new content, the authors shaped this corpus with a standardized language (or "vernacular"), a simplified prose style for narrative, and media of publication that made it easier to reproduce writings and disseminate ideas.

This novel, national orientation of education is, as we saw, embodied in the person of Ezra. It is also explicitly delineated in Deuteronomy as Moses delivers laws and lectures to the people as they prepare to cross the Jordan. In what many scholars agree is a late addition to the book, Moses identifies himself as the nation's teacher. He knows that he must die without entering the Promised Land, yet he assures his audience that one day Israel would be known far and wide as a "great nation." Their claim to fame, however, will not be architectural feats or military might, but the wisdom embodied in the teaching they received from him:

> See, just as Yhwh my God has charged me, I now teach you statutes and ordinances for you to observe in the land that you are about to enter and occupy. You must observe them diligently, for this will show your wisdom and discernment to the peoples. When they hear all these statutes, they will say, "Surely this great nation is a wise and intelligent people!" For what other great nation has a god so near to it as Yhwh our God is whenever we call to him? And what other great nation has statutes and ordinances as just as this entire Teaching/Torah that I am setting before you today?
>
> – Deuteronomy 4:5–8

This remarkable text collectivizes, or nationalizes, the competitive edge that education promises. The wisdom, discernment, and intelligence traditionally restricted to the nobility, ruling classes, and scribal elite, are here defining features by which the people of Israel demarcate themselves corporately from other peoples. The nation may not be able to compete on the battlefield, yet it will hold its own if it displays the awe-inspiring wisdom revealed in the Torah's statutes and ordinances.

Developing these new media of communication, Deuteronomy prescribes that communal leaders regularly read the Torah to all the people, including "men, women, and children, as well as the non-natives residing in your towns" (31:10–13). Parents are to teach it to their children and grandchildren, and its words are to be worn on the body in the place of amulets and inscribed in the most conspicuous places of egress. In Moses' final days, Yhwh instructs this leader to write down and teach the Israelites a song – "and have them sing it so that it may be a witness between me and them" (31:19). Similarly, Moses instructs the nation, after it crosses the Jordan, to write "all the words of the Torah" on large stones coated with plaster (27:1–8). Later, when Israel enters the land, we are told that they took twelve stones from the Jordan and piled them up as a memorial at Gilgal:

> When your children ask in time to come, "What do those stones mean to you?," then you shall tell them that the waters of the Jordan were cut off in front of the ark of Yhwh's covenant. … So these stones shall be to the Israelites a memorial forever.
>
> – Joshua 4:6–7

The monument's purpose was to provoke "teaching moments." The account may refer to an actual memorial at Gilgal, which would have had nothing to do with the Exodus, yet the authors of Deuteronomy and Joshua have pressed it into the service of their pedagogical project – as a prompt for parents to tell their inquisitive children about their people's past.

THE ORIGINS OF THE BIBLE'S PEDAGOGICAL PROGRAM

The authors of Ezra-Nehemiah recognized the radical innovations related to textual study when they depicted the inhabitants of the imperial province yearning to learn. In their narrative, all members of the community, both men and women, immerse themselves in written traditions. And as they do, they bloom into the People of the Book that, according to the authors of Deuteronomy, Moses had envisaged long before.

In the preceding chapter, we noted that the account of Ezra reading the Torah cannot be taken at face value. Yet even if it is more aspirational than factual, the depiction of a people committed to textual study makes us wonder about the absence of comparable scenes in the National Narrative. How are we to explain this epochal transformation from a society occupied with everything under the sun except education, to one that is passionate about learning and that plants a text at the center of their collective lives?

When accounting for the Bible's distinctive pedagogical principles, along with the demotic dimensions of biblical peoplehood, many appeal to primordial qualities – like monotheism and an egalitarian ethos – that supposedly characterized Israel's collective consciousness from the beginning. However, as we saw in Part I, the archeological evidence reveals that the societies of the Northern and Southern kingdoms were hardly different from their neighbors.

If we cannot appeal to some primordial principle that shaped Israel's identity from the beginning, then perhaps the Bible's educational ideals go back to an initiative during the period of statehood. Would not the kings of Israel and Judah have sought to bring together rival populations in their realms by promoting a shared body of texts? We know that the "tyrants" who seized control of many Mediterranean city-states (at about the same time as the kingdoms of Israel and Judah existed) consolidated their rule by weakening the aristocracy's control, codifying laws, enlarging the state cults, promoting the arts, and, not least, canonizing Homeric writings. Therefore, it is possible that powerful Judean monarchs did the same in their own realms. In our survey of King Josiah's reign (Chapter 8), we saw how the biblical authors depicted the priests of Jerusalem finding a Torah scroll in the final years of the kingdom of Judah.

To be sure, various developments from the monarchic societies of Israel and Judah laid the groundwork for the Bible's distinctive educational ideals. But even the biblical account of Josiah's reign (2 Kings 22–23) does not depict the people yearning to learn or taking concrete measures to educate themselves, such as we see in the book of Ezra-

Nehemiah. During the monarchic period, what defined Judah's identity were the borders of the kingdom, taxes paid to the palace, service in the king's armies, contributions to royal construction projects, celebration of national festivals, and so on. Some texts, though not the Torah as we know it, circulated during this period, but these did not function as a broad identity marker, and access to them was limited to a few circles.

Instead of Israel's and Judah's kings, then perhaps it was the foreign empires that, after conquering Israel and Judah, promoted these new educational ideals. This scenario is again improbable. What we know of imperial education programs is very different from the biblical approach. Thus, after conquering Egypt in 525 BCE, the Persian king Cambyses sought the help of his Egyptian physician Udjahorresne in an effort to win the allegiance of the local population. One of the strategies he adopted was an educational reform for scribes. Describing how he fulfilled Cambyses' orders, Udjahorresne reports in an autobiographical inscription that he filled schools with only "sons of fine people and no sons of common men." This restriction of education to the nobility contrasts sharply with the biblical vision of the people as a whole internalizing the nation's traditions of law, and history, and wisdom. Udjahorresne and Ezra represent, as such, very different pedagogical models.

The Assyrian king Sargon describes in a monumental inscription how, after conquering Samaria, he sent officials from the court to teach the subjugated population "proper behavior." The same goes for the masses of deportees throughout his empire: he commissioned officials to "teach correct behavior along with the fear of god and the king." This Assyrian program involves collective civic education, not dissimilar to what we find in the Bible. Yet the objective of Sargon's educational initiative was to fashion submissive subjects for the state. In stark contrast, the Bible's pedagogical program mobilizes a people after the *demise* of the state – in response to the very same imperial encroachment on Israel's and Judah's sovereignty that Sargon himself so dramatically achieved.

Recently, some scholars have attempted to explain the Bible's origins in terms of an educational curriculum for Judah's upper echelon in the Hellenistic-Roman period. Without a doubt, elites would have been eager both to distinguish themselves in their own societies and to demonstrate to peers in neighboring societies the antiquity and prestige of their own culture. Yet such would have been the case already in the kingdoms of Israel and Judah; it was not new to the Hellenistic-Roman period. Most importantly, the Hellenistic-Roman educations ideals were not national, as they are in the Bible.

Much more determinative for the biblical model was the move of Judean scribes in the post-destruction period to make education the means by which their defeated communities corporately compete on the international stage and demarcate themselves from surrounding peoples. Having forfeited territorial sovereignty, communities in both the North and South needed to create for themselves a space in a foreign empire. The space they carved out is not so much territorial and political as it is social, one demarcated by practice and behavior. And because this project was by and large the work of scribes, the tools they used for demarcating it were written traditions.

EDUCATIONAL REFORM IN RESPONSE TO DEFEAT

Military defeat has often elicited educational reform. The most instructive case is from modern Germany. In 1807 Napoleon's imperial armies had conquered Prussia's forces at Jena and were occupying Berlin, the capital. In response to the humiliating subjugation, the philosopher Johann Gottlieb Fichte stood up and delivered his "Addresses to the German Nation." In his lectures, Fichte identified literature, law, language, and tradition as the cornerstones for a collective political identity. Educational reforms were needed if the populations of all the politically divided principalities were to begin thinking of themselves as Germans. Three years later, when Wilhelm von Humboldt introduced educational reforms and founded a new university in Berlin, he made Fichte its first rector in recognition of the influence he exerted on his holistic approach to education (the so-called Humboldtian Ideal).

Fichte's orations giving birth to a nation reminds us of Moses addressing Israel at the beginning of its history or Ezra forming a new community of learners among the defeated in Jerusalem. Yet while both the form and the content of Fichte's lectures bear affinities to the biblical writings, there are important differences: Fichte's aim was (military) mobilization and liberation. He proclaimed Germany's superiority. Only the German *Volk* ("people") have what it takes to do profound and rigorous thinking; they must prepare to unshackle themselves from the French occupation and become the rightful heirs of the Holy Roman Empire.

In stark contrast, both Moses and Ezra emphasize Israel's weakness and inferiority. In Deuteronomy 4, as we just saw, Moses reminds Israel that they are the most unimportant of all peoples and that Yhwh did not set his affection on them because of any special quality of excellence. Similarly, Ezra describes the community as a small remnant of slaves who had been spared from calamity. Instead of seeking liberation, they must be careful not to jeopardize the favor their God had extended them with the Persian kings.

What the Prussian state needed were disciplined and duteous subjects, and as an intellectual forefather of fascism, Fichte called for a "national education" that would destroy the freedom of the will. His ideas have much in common with the corporal punishment that molded youths like clay tablets into skilled scribes in Babylonia and formed young men into educated citizens in Greece. In contrast to this top-down, statist approach that forms obedient and willing subjects, the biblical model of peoplehood relies on individual actors collaborating for the good of the community. Consistent with this model of education, the Bible extols characters who, instead of being passive and pliant, courageously stand up to human and divine authority.

Some European thinkers set forth educational views more in harmony with the biblical model. Perhaps the best example is Jean-Jacques Rousseau. In 1770 the Genevan philosopher began drafting his final major political work, an essay entitled "Considerations on the Government of Poland and on Its Proposed Reformation." As he completed it, Russia, Austria, and Prussia had invaded Poland, occupying and partitioning its territories. With an eye to these events, the Genevan philosopher conceived a constitutional blueprint for the Polish-Lithuanian Commonwealth. Asserting the necessity of creating a national identity in the aftermath of defeat, he declared:

> The virtue of its citizens, their patriotic zeal, the particular way in which national institutions may be able to form their souls - this is the only rampart which will always stand ready to defend her [Poland], and which no army will ever be able to breach. If you see to it that no Pole can ever become a Russian, I guarantee you that Russia will not subjugate Poland.[3]

Rousseau's strategy for ensuring "that a Pole can never become a Russian" meant that individuals had a voice in the political process and a share in future prosperity. For this to happen, Poles had to become self-conscious citizens, and the means for achieving this transformation in consciousness was education. The collective could responsibly determine its fate only if its members were properly instructed in the nation's history and laws. Rousseau had long ascribed an indispensable role to education, and he articulated his influential pedagogical philosophy in *Émile, Or Treatise on Education* (1762), the book he considered to be "the best and most important of all my works."

Compare now Rousseau to Fichte. The Prussian philosopher wanted the German people to rise up and assert themselves, both culturally and militarily. In contrast, Rousseau wanted the Polish people to inculcate virtue, zeal, and solidarity so that they could survive conquest at the hands of military superpowers like Prussia. Viewed in this light, Rousseau's thought comes remarkably close to that of the anonymous biblical scribes who collectivized the competitive edge that education offers and were convinced that their communities, like the Polish people, needed not only to know their nation's history and laws but also nurture new virtue and vision.

DEFEAT AND LITERACY

In Ezra-Nehemiah, as well as Exodus and Deuteronomy, the ones who attend public readings at national assemblies are, as we noted, not ony men and women but also "all who could understand." Conventionally, it was only men of fighting age and bearing arms who attended public assemblies. By highlighting the presence and participation of a much

[3] Rousseau, "Considerations," p. 5.

broader cross-section of the community, the biblical writings promote a momentous shift in ethos: a People of the Book supplants a People in Arms, and the ability to understand replaces the capacity to bear weapons as the criterion for participation.

What prompted this dramatic development was not a philosophical insight pertaining to equal rights, but a pragmatic strategy of survival. A thriving kingdom perhaps could afford to exclude many within their society, but a vanquished and exiled people struggling to hold its own against kingdoms and empires needed to include as many as possible in public life. All had to feel a part of this new nation and be given an opportunity to contribute – not only to building projects but also to public life more generally.

This is where education comes into play. Emerging hand in hand with a narrative capable of uniting rival communities and encouraging its members to imagine themselves as one people (the task of storytelling), it is the means to promote collective participation (the task of education). The members of the new society were to spend time learning their people's history, studying its law, internalizing its wisdom traditions, and mastering its poetry and songs.

Education, more than anything else, has the capacity to equip citizens to engage in communal life, offering "the keys to the kingdom." Whereas imperial powers use arms and creeds to carve out their kingdoms, the biblical authors created a community with texts and the vibrant, persisting conversations that these texts prompted. A similar point about literacy and belonging was made by the journalist Abigail Pogrebin in a talk she gave at the 2014 Open Hillel Conference:

> When you're literate, you're in the game. And when you're in the game, you can add your two cents. And when you can add your two cents, you're in the conversation. Suddenly you realize the conversation has been going on for generations, and you're moved. And when you're moved, you keep coming back.

I began this book by dispelling the common assumption that the Bible is a collection of religious writings and that all religions need scriptures. The chapters of Part II have shown that the raison d'être of the Bible lies in the realm of education. As a pedagogical project, the biblical authors consolidated a people in the aftermath of defeat by reshaping earlier writings into a national curriculum. This suggestion can best explain the diversity of writings contained in the biblical canon: its historical narratives, laws, songs, poetry, and wisdom collections. In Part III, we turn our attention to how a group of writers in this newly constituted community of Judah pieced together literary traditions to create a grand narrative for the nation, consisting of both North and South.

FURTHER READING

Allon, Niv and Navratilova, Hana, *Ancient Egyptian Scribes: A Cultural Exploration*, Bloomsbury, 2017.

Blackman, Aylward M. and Eric Peet, T., "Papyrus Lansing: A Translation with Notes," *The Journal of Egyptian Archaeology* 11 (1925): 284–298.

Boyd, William, *The Educational Theory of Jean Jacques Rousseau*, Russell & Russell, 1963.

Carr, David M., *Writing on the Tablets of the Heart: Origins of Scripture and Literature*, Oxford University Press, 2008.

Charpin, Dominque, *Reading and Writing in Babylon*, Harvard University Press, 2011.

Crenshaw, James L., *Education in Ancient Israel: Across the Deadening Silence*, Doubleday, 1998.

Garfinkel, Yosef, "The Murder of James Leslie Starkey near Lachish," *Palestine Exploration Quarterly* 148 (2016): 84–109.

Kleinerman, Alexandra, *Education in Early 2nd Millennium BC Babylonia: The Sumerian Epistolary Miscellany*, Brill, 2011.

Kraus, Nicholas L., *Scribal Education in the Sardonic Period*, Brill, 2020.

Moore, Gregory (ed.), *Fichte: Addresses to the German Nation*, Cambridge University Press, 2008.

Robson, Eleanor, "The Tablet House: A Scribal School in Old Babylonian Nippur," *Revue d'assyriologie et d'archéologie orientale* 95 (2001): 39–66.

Rousseau, Jean-Jacques, *Considerations on the Government of Poland*, 1772, translation from International Relations and Security Network, Zurich, www.files.ethz.ch/isn/125482/5016_Rousseau_Considerations_on_the_Government_of_Poland.pdf.

Schniedewind, William M., "Sociolinguistic Reflections on the Letter of a 'Literate' Soldier (Lachish 3)," *Zeitschrift für Althebraistik* 13 (2000): 157–167.

van der Toorn, Karel, *Scribal Culture and the Making of the Hebrew Bible*, Harvard University Press, 2007.

Williams, Ronald J., "Scribal Training in Ancient Egypt", *Journal of the American Oriental Society* 92 (1972): 214–221.

Zhakevich, Philip, *Scribal Tools in Ancient Israel*, Penn State University Press, 2020.

Part III
A New Narrative

WHEN EZRA APPEARED ON THE PODIUM before the assembly in Jerusalem, it was, according to the biblical narrative, almost a thousand years after Moses had ascended Mount Sinai to receive the Torah. The nation first had to take possession of the Promised Land, and then lose it, and finally return to it and attempt to build a new society under very different circumstances, before the words of that Torah could come to life. Without loss, there is little learning.

The communities that inhabited Judah after its conquest could have easily forgotten the past and started all over again. Yet instead of recreating themselves *ex nihilo,* they understood their work as rebuilding the ruins – similar to the *creatio ex profundis* in Genesis 1 that we examined in Part II. The blocks of stone with which they worked were once part of walls and a temple that the kings of Judah had built. Now they lay strewn about as memorials to the might of imperial armies that marched through the region. These communities were living among the ruins of a bygone age, and they knew that if they were ever to regain the former glory, it would not be anytime soon.

What unifies our history? What thread connects the dismal present to our illustrious past? Without our fearless kings, formidable cities, high-tech chariots, valorous warriors, and all the glory and grandeur they brought to us, who are we? The National Narrative, which stretches from the creation of the world in Genesis to the destruction of Jerusalem in the book of Kings, reflects how generations of scribes, from both North and South, asked and answered these foundational questions. The creative manner in which they did so is what we will explore in the following chapters of Part III.

We begin in Chapter 15 by examining not only who wrote the Bible but how this question bears directly on the shape and character of the larger corpus. Chapters 16–19 compare competing accounts of the past and how scribes combined these accounts to create the larger National Narrative. Chapter 20 explores how this work would not have been possible without the prophetic writings and the radically new relationship to the deity they introduced. Finally, in Chapter 21, we study this relationship and how its conception of covenant left a deep imprint on not only codes of ethics but also the understanding of the people's past.

Together the chapters of Part II reveal how the Bible represents an interweaving of two master narratives. There is the familiar monarchic story, familiar because of its ubiquity in human civilization. It lingers on the exploits of the great men (and occasionally, great women) who have defined history – their architectural achievements, their military triumphs, and the powerful states they created. The second, however, is something altogether new and unique: the people's story. With it, the biblical authors undercut the monarchic story and made their most enduring contribution. While acknowledging the benefits of statehood, they relegated it to a supporting role, and in the process, made a groundbreaking political discovery.

15

Jeremiah and Baruch

A Monument to Defeat

> Then Jeremiah called Baruch ben Neriah, and Baruch wrote on a scroll at Jeremiah's dictation all Yhwh's words that he had spoken to him. . . . And many similar words were added to them.
>
> –Jeremiah 36:4, 32

WHO WROTE THE BIBLE? That is the question taken on in the best-selling book bearing this title. Its author, Richard Elliott Friedman, argues that the most extensive source in the biblical narrative was written either by the prophet Jeremiah or his scribal secretary, Baruch ben Neriah, or both working in tandem (see introduction to Chapter 25).

In 1975, a clay "bulla" that bears the imprint of Baruch's personal seal ("Belonging to Berachyahu ben Neriyahu, the Scribe") appeared on the antiquities market. No one knew where it was found, and some argued that it must have originated near the "Burnt House" in Jerusalem where similar bullae and seals had been found. In 1996, a second clay bulla came to light that had been impressed by the same seal. This one also had a fingerprint, and several scholars speculated that it was from none other than Baruch himself. It now turns out that both of these artifacts are most likely fakes, counterfeited by someone eager to create buzz and make a buck.

In contrast to these bullae, biblical narratives may bear Baruch's imprint. But as we have seen and will continue to see, the Bible betrays very different views of the nation's history, and many writers had a hand in the composition of this work. Some of the scribes may be mentioned among the host of names found in the book of Jeremiah. We also saw how two figures, Ezra and Nehemiah, provide us with profiles of those who belonged to the circles of biblical writers. But for all practical intents and purposes, the biblical authors are anonymous. Even in the case of Baruch, we cannot say much about his life, social location, or political agenda (and the bullae would have added little to his biography had they been authentic).

The anonymity of the biblical writings stands in stark contrast to the single-authored works of Greece, such as the histories of Herodotus and Thucydides. The authors of the National Narrative intentionally concealed their identity in an effort to focus their audience's attention on the representative figures they portrayed in their account – figures such as Abraham and Sarah, Joshua and Rahab, Josiah and Huldah.

Our aim in Part III is to understand how this account, corresponding to the Pentateuch and Former Prophets, evolved from older precursors that originally competed with each other. Picking up threads introduced in Parts I and II, we identify in what follows some of the most salient features of the National Narrative. In comparing it to monarchic monuments, we will see how this literary memorial stands apart not only in being portable but also in commemorating defeat. We will also witness how its architects uncovered a categorical distinction that would prove crucial to later political and theological thought.

POLITICAL AGENDAS

The Bible is nothing if not a revisionary work. It grew as multiple textual memories were compiled. Later it was redacted from new perspectives, and thereafter the process continued in the form of commentary and retellings.[1]

For the documents that modern archeologists unearth in excavations, the identity of their authors is not always clear. Hence philologists must work hard to reconstruct the exact historical circumstances and circles in which a given text emerged. Yet they can often be much more confident than biblical scholars about the groups and historical circumstances that produced the texts they study – ranging from letters, laws, and lists, to myths, oracles, and treaties.

[1] A stunning homage to this process is James Goodman's *But Where Is the Lamb?*

The Lament of Inanna illustrates the point. In this text, the Mesopotamian goddess recalls how enemy forces penetrated the innermost area of her temple, purloining her cultic objects and using them for profane purposes. In its attention to matters of purity, the Lament leaves little room for doubt that representatives of the widespread Inanna cult (possibly temple singers) were responsible for its composition and transmission.

With respect to the biblical book of Lamentations, we saw in Part II that scholars cannot say much at all about the circles that composed its poetry over the centuries. Although the work has much in common with Mesopotamian lament traditions (in both form and content), it differs from them by being only minimally concerned with the temple cult and priests. The destruction of the temple, along with the interruption of the cultic calendar, is mentioned just once in its five laments, and then only in passing. The priests, along with the king and prophets, are even made partly responsible for the divine ire.

The memories of defeat in the biblical book focus on the plight of a people. Although we cannot be sure exactly when the Lament of Inanna was composed, we can nevertheless reliably assign it to a specific societal group and institution. Conversely, we can date the biblical book of Lamentations to a time after the destruction of the Southern kingdom, yet we are nevertheless at a loss to explain *who* composed this work, which condemns the same institutions and classes that were traditionally responsible for literary production.

The same goes for much of the biblical corpus. Scholars use general designations – such as Yahwist, Elohist, Deuteronomist, Priestly, Exilic, and Nomist – to describe the complex authorship of biblical texts. Some biblical texts (or portions of these texts) are easier to assign to Northern versus Southern scribes, and to various priestly, prophetic, or palace circles. Yet these texts are rarely transmitted alone; they are usually part of a larger work with often opposing perspectives. There have always been some who are sanguine about the possibility of identifying the authors of biblical writings (e.g., Moses, Solomon, Ezra, Baruch), but by and large, the field of biblical scholarship is skeptical about these claims.

We can therefore recognize from the outset that 1) our texts have been heavily expanded and reworked in the early history of their transmission, and 2) these texts address concerns of an imagined political community and its diverse constituents, rather than primarily promoting the interests of the palace and priests. The biblical writings are just as political as those discovered in archeological excavations, but their purposes and agendas are very different.

A camp of scholars within biblical studies called "Minimalists" deny any continuity between the post-exilic community in Judah and the inhabitants of the former kingdom. They claim that most of the returnees were outside groups who sought to divest the local population of their land, and the biblical narrative is, accordingly, is a fanciful fiction through which new arrivals in the Persian province of Judah fabricated a connection to Israel's past. Working within a (post-)Christian tradition, these scholars are well aware of how outside groups throughout history have gone to great lengths to identify themselves as the "new" or "true" Israel, and this history of Christian supersessionism directly informs the ways in which they interpret biblical texts to undermine the legitimacy of the modern state of Israel.

What we have already seen seriously undermines the Minimalists' claims. As we turn now to the formation of the National Narrative, we will witness how its authors worked by connecting and expanding older writings that they inherited from earlier generations, many of them going back to monarchic times. The way they shaped this literary legacy, in their efforts to come to terms with defeat, was radically new. But to focus on the new while completely diminishing the old is intellectually irresponsible. Both tradition and innovation – what the scribes preserved and what they created – must be held in balance as we reconstruct the evolution of the National Narrative.

WRITING HISTORY

The National Narrative has passed through multiple hands, from different times and places, and this composition-history has imbued it with a quality similar to political writings from modernity. National memories are – or at least pretend to be – pluralistic, latitudinarian, and demotic. Though they do not necessarily silence the voice of the palace or religious authorities, they amplify it with other voices and subsume it to the broader perspective of the people.

The ancient inscriptions and images from West Asia and North Africa tend to focus on the feats of rulers. Thus Darius the Great, a usurper who reformed the Persian Empire, tells of his feat in not only conquering Egypt but also cutting a canal (the direct predecessor to the modern Suez Canal) to facilitate shipping between this conquered territory and his Persian homeland:

> King Darius says: I am a Persian; setting out from Persia, I conquered Egypt. I ordered to dig this canal from the river that is called Nile and flows in Egypt, to the sea that begins in Persia. When this canal had been dug as I had ordered, ships went from Egypt through this canal to Persia, as I had intended.[2]

The biblical scholar John Van Seters helpfully distinguishes between the historiography of monarchic inscriptions (such as this one from Darius) and what he calls "history proper." In the former, the concerns for personal identity and self-justification "involve the person of the king – his right to rule or his giving of an account of political actions before gods and men." To be sure, this kind of history writing is very different from works in which a people or nation renders account to itself:

> It may even be argued that history writing arises at a point when the actions of kings are viewed in the larger context of the people as a whole, so that it is the national history that judges the king and not the king who makes his own account of history.[3]

The National Narrative provides an excellent example of this genre. It is indeed the earliest and most breathtaking attempt to write history from the perspective of a people, with its authors relativizing the role of monarchy.

Despite making important contributions to our understanding of ancient history writing, Van Seters unfortunately falls prey to an established pattern in academic biblical studies of making the biblical narrative the achievement of isolated individuals, celebrated as masterminds and geniuses. One was the "Yahwist," who drafted the narrative from

[2] Kuhrt, *Persian Empire*, pp. 485–486. [3] Van Seters, *In Search of History*, p. 2.

Genesis to Numbers, and the second was the "Deuteronomist," who is responsible for the remaining narrative in Deuteronomy to Kings.

In the first half of the twentieth century, two German scholars, Gerhard von Rad and Martin Noth, published influential works that minimized the contributions of later scribes (Noth referred to them as "gravel"). Their interest was to restore the works of the Yahwist and Deuteronomist to their original contours and brilliance. The Yahwist was thought to have worked in the court of Solomon, and his account represents the acme of ancient Israel's cultural achievements, while the Deuteronomist was writing in the direct wake of Judah's defeat (like Noth himself, who wrote the most important work on the subject while serving as a German soldier on the eastern front during the Second World War). Van Seters argues that both the Yahwist and the Deuteronomist were writing in the post-exilic period, and he goes much further than his predecessors in diminishing the presence of earlier sources as well as later additions. One of his most recent books denies any significance to later editing.[4]

This approach to biblical authorship is problematic. By reducing a complex narrative to the achievement of a singular genius (my student Ian MacGillivray calls this the "von Rad-icalization of biblical authorship"), it fails to appreciate how these scribes not only collaborated across space and time, but also did so anonymously. In contrast to Greek historiography, they did not write in the first person and introduce themselves at the beginning of their accounts, which would be expected if these accounts were in fact the achievement of one or two individuals. These writers also worked in community – sharing materials, connecting them to form larger narratives, and embellishing them in a typically modest yet thoughtful manner.

Rather than referring to their own lives, these nameless scribes invested their creative energies in a cast of characters that represents the heterogeneity of their people and with which everyone could identify. The closest they came to describing themselves was, as we have seen, in their portrait of Ezra, the scribe who devoted his career to teaching the nation. While Nehemiah's memoir is one of the few cases in which

[4] Van Seters, *The Edited Bible.*

the author identifies himself and writes in the first person, his work was not transmitted alone. The authors of Ezra-Nehemiah integrated it and other materials into a larger account of the post-exilic period, which, like the National Narrative, they narrated in the third person.

Moreover, it is the thoroughly edited character of the biblical narrative that, perhaps more than anything else, qualifies it as "history" according to Van Seters' own useful definition. Indeed, if we should define a nation primarily in terms of broader participation, as well as competition between hegemonic memories and counter-memories, then we may compare the augmented, anonymous quality of the National Narrative to monuments, war memorials, and other public spaces in which members of modern political communities engage each other as they construct their national identities (see Chapter 24).

A MONUMENT TO DEFEAT

The inherent resistance of the National Narrative to clear authorial identification is its hallmark, and it speaks volumes to its agenda of representing the nation as a whole (and thereby also forming an "Israelite" audience for itself), rather than defending a particular institution or social class. This work reflects a shared wisdom negotiated in an intergenerational community of scribes, instead of the insights of a genius compelled by a new form of faith (following von Rad and Noth) or the ideology of an elitist who fabricated collective memories to manipulate the masses (following Van Seters).

The National Narrative's distinctiveness is most evident when we place it side by side with monarchic narratives from the time of the Northern and Southern kingdoms. An instructive example is the ninth-century Mesha Stele from the neighboring kingdom of Moab, which we discussed in Chapter 5. It begins by introducing its author: "I am Mesha." This king goes on to recount the many victories he achieved for Moab after the Omride rulers of Israel had managed to occupy its territories.

The theological explanation Mesha offers for Moab's prior defeat is essentially the same as what we find in the Bible: the enemy triumphs because the deity is *angry* with his land/people. The National Narrative makes this point central to its account. At each step of the way, it is the people's transgressions vis-à-vis Yhwh that are the ultimate cause for their military losses and the eventual downfall of their kingdoms.

Additional similarities may be observed in the way Mesha fights in accordance with a divine oracle: "And Chemosh said to me: 'Go, take Nebo from Israel.' And I went." This line reminds us of the oracles that David and other kings in the Bible receive before they launch a military campaign. Mesha also slaughters an entire population as a sacrifice to his national deity; likewise, biblical texts describe the ritual dedication of conquered peoples, along with their livestock and valuables, to Yhwh, using the same Semitic term (*herem*).

All these features are so common to biblical accounts that we must reckon with the probability that kings of Israel and Judah composed very similar inscriptions. However, the National Narrative differs from monarchic inscriptions on three important points.

First, portions of this Narrative may have been originally inscribed on stone, tablets, pottery shards, and steles. Yet its lengthy and composite character – which already says much about its purpose – required a lighter medium. Produced and reproduced in parchment or papyrus, this work was not only much more portable but also easier to edit, expand, and duplicate. In contrast to this "movable monument," Mesha inscribed his account on a massive stone (measuring almost a meter in height) implanted in the ground to which he laid claim as king. As such, his memorial constitutes a conventional expression of monarchic rule and emblem of statecraft, and it stood alongside temples and palaces that he, like other ancient rulers, erected when performing kingship.

Second, the National Narrative is not narrated in the first person, and the one doing the narration is not a king. Instead, it portrays a people's past in the third person, and from the perspective of an anonymous narrator – the *vox populi*. This "voice of the nation" is, in some ways, also the *vox dei* – the voice of Yhwh reminding his people of their story. It is also polyphonic inasmuch as it has been heavily edited and expanded to incorporate contrasting, and often conflicting, perspectives.

Without downplaying this diversity, traditional Jewish interpreters over the ages have identified the biblical authors with a faithful prophet from each generation (e.g., Lamentations is said to have been composed by Jeremiah, "the weeping prophet"). Few scholars today would embrace these attributions, and rightly so. But since the Bible imagines the ideal prophet as independent of any institutional affiliation, representing its transcendent source of truth, these traditional claims capture the distinctive character of the narrative's voice and vantage point.

Third, and most remarkably, the National Narrative does not stop where Mesha concludes. Rather than culminating in a great victory, it proceeds to recount the nation's political decline and ultimate demise. While Mesha begins with a past period of defeat followed by his own triumphs, the biblical account begins with great victories and concludes with defeat. The book of Kings uses scenes of the royal table to portray the demise of native sovereignty: it begins with Solomon hosting the illustrious Queen of Sheba at his table in Jerusalem and ends with his descendant being hosted in Babylon by those who conquered Jerusalem (see Chapter 19). Likewise, the wider National Narrative begins with the people's liberation from Egypt and miraculous conquest of the Promised Land; these inaugural triumphs render the culminating exile from the land all the more tragic.

The sequence of defeat followed by triumph in Mesha's narrative prevails in all the monuments we know from ancient West Asia. By reversing that sequence, and concluding with present defeat rather than past conquest, the biblical authors were not aiming merely to incite anger and antipathy for their enemies. Rather, they wanted their readers to reflect on their collective identity, their past mistakes, and their shared future. This pedagogical purpose explains why the final conquest of the two kingdoms is recounted in such succinct terms compared with the lengthy account of the nation's origins that precedes it.

As we noted in Chapter 5, Mesha's monument may provide the earliest attestation of the Hebrew script, and Israel's and Judah's courts probably produced state inscriptions like the one Mesha commissioned. Some of these state-sponsored texts may, in fact, form substrata in the National Narrative; if so, scribes have thoroughly reworked them with the state's defeat in view. Thanks to the new layers of meaning they superimposed on older materials, this grand saga functioned as a kind of "survival guide" for communities struggling to make it in a brave new world. To sustain themselves, these communities had to reconsider their long-held values, reimagine their identity, and come together as one people.

THE PRIMACY OF PEOPLEHOOD

Drafted in anticipation of and in response to defeat, the National Narrative holds alive the memory of a more glorious age during which their ancestors flourished in their homeland. It tells the story of a people, its deity, its territories, and the various institutions and social groups that constituted its existence as a nation. But its greatest accomplishment moves beyond such nostalgia to a "prospective memory" that responds to downfall and destruction by simultaneously demonstrating the culpability of the whole nation and laying out a roadmap for a viable future.

When all that one had once taken for granted was gone, communities were forced to answer the question: who are we? The architects who designed the biblical monument to defeat responded to this question by constructing an extensive account of their people's diverse origins and the events leading up to two major catastrophes: the conquest of the Northern kingdom in 722 BCE and of the Southern kingdom in 586 BCE. Most of the National Narrative treats the period before the rise of the monarchy, and it portrays Israel existing as a political community long before it established a centralized state.

The first impulse for collecting and transmitting texts would have been simply to preserve the memories of ancestral communities. Some of these memories would have been erased and many others created as new generations came to terms with their trauma and mobilized their members.

The National Narrative places those institutions that cannot withstand the threat of imperial subjugation, such as the monarchy or the military, in relation to a prehistory in which those institutions did not yet exist. In this way, these institutions are shown to be historically important yet not essential to the nation's existence. The Pentateuch, Joshua, and Judges never refer to an Israelite standing army and have very little to say about an Israelite monarchy. While the books of Samuel and Kings do not erase the important role played by monarchy and the professional army, the reader has to heed the historical sequence: both the monarchy and the standing army represent *secondary* developments.

Likewise, the Pentateuch does not portray the conquest of the Promised Land, leaving it to be reported in the Former Prophets that follow it. The narrative sequence and literary division affirm a larger point: Israel constitutes a people not limited to its historical territory and longstanding monarchies, and it can survive without its temple and armies. A simple equation between people or nation, on the one hand, and the state and land, on the other, is therewith radically severed.

The expansive literary tapestry unfurled in this effort of scribal collaboration articulates and painstakingly illustrates, for the first time in history, a cardinal categorical distinction that we take for granted today: the nation and the state are two separate entities, with the nation being greater than the state that governs it. The state has a responsibility to serve and protect the people; it is not an end to itself and hence must not be hallowed.

The biblical authors thus strictly severed peoplehood, on the one hand, from statehood, on the other. By affirming the priority and primacy of the nation, they removed any doubt that Israel (including both North and South) could still be Israel even when it was conquered and dispersed abroad. By virtue of a covenant with their God, Israel had become a people long before it established a kingdom, a nation long before a state.

Although this narrative runs counter to what we know today about Israel's and Judah's political evolution, the biblical authors wanted their readers to understand that, with the help of their narrative and the divine laws embedded in it, a vanquished and exiled population can unite and flourish as a nation even when imperial domination prohibited the reestablishment of the sovereign state and political independence that their narrative ascribes to the reigns of David and Solomon. The survival and bolstering of a national identity after defeat is, according to their penetrating political analysis, the presupposition for a return to the land and the reestablishment of territorial sovereignty, even if that sovereignty may assume a different form from the independent kingdoms that their communities inhabited in the past.

PLAN B

The kingdoms of Israel and Judah brought secure borders, weakened local allegiances, standardized language and writings systems, integrated competing laws, sponsored national festivals, promoted collective rituals and religious practices, and regularly conscripted diverse groups for royal building projects and military campaigns. All these factors were necessary conditions, yet they were not sufficient ones. They would hardly have sufficed to produce the Bible and inspire the new forms of collective life that its authors imagined. The most important factor was a very different one: collapse, rupture, and the loss of much that the states of Israel and Judah had achieved over the centuries.

The Bible does not cast aspersions on statehood per se. On the contrary, the critiques of the scribes who produced this corpus reflect their solicitude for a state that is properly governed. The legal material in the Pentateuch (Deuteronomy, in particular) sets forth a vision for such a polity. Similarly, the prophets affirm the importance a life-sustaining and well-defended land in which the nation and its members can "dwell in safety, each under his own vine and under his own fig tree," as in the days of Solomon (see Micah 4:4 and 1 Kings 4:25/5:5).

As scribes were piecing together the National Narrative, the communities of Judah and Samaria were busy rebuilding their ruins and re-establishing their collective lives. Their achievements prompted some to expect a return to former glory, with their kings ruling over the (re-) united people of Israel. The National Narrative responds to these expectations. It demonstrates that statehood serves a supporting role. When the state loses sight of subservient function, it swallows up the nation so that nothing remains when it is conquered. And a basic truth documented both in this history and in the equally complex works of prophecy is that all kingdoms end up either being conquered or collapsing under their own weight.

An independent state may be the ideal. But in a world dominated by superpowers, native sovereignty is not a given. It must always be negotiated, and often it is not even on the table as on option. In the coming chapters we will see how the Judean authors of National Narrative drew directly on earlier work from Northern scribes. What unites these writers, as well as biblical corpus as a whole, is their quest for an alternative to statehood – a Plan B. What they deemed to be most urgent, and what occupied their attention, is the constitution for a new form of political community that could persist through the repeated rise and fall of kingdoms.

Even though there is no Hollywood happy ending to the National Narrative, there is still hope. By admitting defeat and devoting so much attention to its causes and the process of decline, they called exiled and dispersed communities back to their homeland where they could finally reinvent themselves as the new nation imagined in the Pentateuch.

In the coming chapters, we study the formation of the National Narrative. In the coming chapters, we study the formation of the National Narrative. We begin with a case study that some readers will want to skip (Chapter 16), as it provides an immersive course in the analysis of biblical texts.

FURTHER READING

Baden, Joel, *The Composition of the Pentateuch: Renewing the Documentary Hypothesis*, Yale University Press, 2012.

Banks, Diane Nunn, *Writing the History of Israel*, Bloomsbury, 2006.

Barton, John, *A History of the Bible: The Story of the World's Most Influential Book*, Viking, 2019.

Brettler, Marc Zvi, *The Creation of History in Ancient Israel*, Taylor & Francis, 2002.

Friedman, Richard Elliott, *Who Wrote the Bible*, Summit, 1987.

Goodman, James, *But Where Is the Lamb? Imagining the Story of Abraham and Isaac*, Knopf Doubleday, 2013.

Kugel, James L., *How to Read the Bible: A Guide to Scripture, Then and Now*, Free Press, 2007.

Kuhrt, Amélie, *The Persian Empire: A Corpus of Sources from the Achaemenid Period*, Routledge, 2010.

Van Seters, John, *In Search of History: Historiography in the Ancient World and the Origins of Biblical History*, Eisenbrauns, 1997.

Van Seters, John, *The Edited Bible: The Curious History of the Editor in Biblical Criticism*, Eisenbrauns, 2006.

Wright, J. Edward, *Baruch Ben Neriah: From Biblical Scribe to Apocalyptic Seer*, University of South Carolina Press, 2003.

16

Isaac and Rebekah

The Family Story

So she is your wife!
Why then did you say, "She is my sister"?
– Genesis 26:9

THE PRESENT CHAPTER IS AN OUTLIER. It treats a single story from the book of Genesis, using it as a case study for the composition-history of the National Narrative. With our focus on the texture of the text, we will witness how scribes, working across both generational and geographical gulfs, synthesized and supplemented originally unrelated materials to create a sweeping saga of one family. The editorial techniques on display in this account have shaped the entire biblical corpus, and thus one can apply what is learned here to the interpretation of other biblical writings. (Some readers may wish to skip this chapter, as it dives deep into the details of textual analysis.)

A STORY FROM GENESIS

Our story relates to the patriarch Isaac, and it explains for his descendants how he, starting with very little, became not only wealthy but also the head of a clan, with a longstanding claim to the border town of Beersheva and its precious water source.

The tale begins with Isaac dwelling in Gerar, a town to the west of what was to become the kingdom of Judah. Isaac resides here as an outsider, and one day the locals approach him and ask about Rebekah. Instead of telling them the truth, he claims she is his sister. Why? Because he thinks she is so attractive that the locals might kill him to get her. It is all about saving his own skin; Rebekah's fate is not an issue for him. Strangely, however, after he announces that Rebekah is not married, no one seems keen to court her.

A long time passes, and still no one has shown any interest. Then one day the king, named Abimelech, happens to be gazing out his window and spots Isaac "playing" with Rebekah. In using this verb, the narrator plays on Isaac's name (*Yitzhak* – "he will laugh/play"). Isaac, however, is engaged in erotic play with Rebekah, not word games, and when the king realizes that Isaac had lied about their relationship, he demands an explanation: "So she is your wife? Why then did you say, 'She is my sister'?" Isaac's explanation – that he feared for his life – provokes the king's consternation: "What is this you have done to us? One of the people might easily have slept with her, and you would have brought guilt upon us!" Straightaway he issues a decree: "Whoever touches this man or his wife shall surely be put to death."

With royal protection, "this man" prospers. When the Philistines grow envious of Isaac's flocks, herds, and huge household, Abimelech tells him "you have become too powerful for us" and asks him to move elsewhere.

Everywhere the patriarch wanders in the parched environs, he has to dig wells. Yet when he strikes water, the herders of Gerar become jealous and contentious. Instead of mobilizing his servants to fight and defend his right to the land, Isaac peaceably moves on.

After excavating wells in two different places, he finally ends up in the most arid region of the South. There, in a place that was barely habitable, he digs another well, but this third time, he does not strike water.

In the final episode, the king pays Isaac a visit with one of his advisers and his military commander. Although Isaac expects hostility, Abimelech announces his desire to make a treaty. The patriarch had become a rich and powerful player in the region, and fearing that one day Isaac might seek vengeance, the king wants him to promise that he would never do his people harm. After eating and drinking all night, they exchange oaths of friendship at daybreak, and Isaac sends Abimelech on his way in peace.

That same day, Isaac's servants bring him the good news: the well they had been digging had now started to produce water! The story concludes on this happy note, attributing the name of this important place, Beer-sheva, to the two events: "well of water" (*be'er*) combined with the "oath" (*sheva*) between Isaac and Abimelech.

THE EVOLUTION OF GENESIS 26

In retelling the tale, I omitted details that were likely added at a later point, and in what follows, I demonstrate why they seem to be secondary. One might ask: why not just leave the story as it is, instead of attempting to reconstruct its evolution? Should we not just assume that it has evolved over time, while also being skeptical about the possibility of ever getting at its original formulation?

I share this skepticism. But my objective is not to isolate *the* earliest version. Indeed, there is more than one way to imagine its origins, and scholars may never reach a consensus on this matter. What is more important, and also more feasible, is to identify parts that clearly have been added, even if, in the end, the original formulation remains an open question.

In fact, the postulation of "the original formulation" of a biblical account is methodologically problematic given the way ancient texts evolved: two or more scribes could simultaneously work on the same text, and they would have expanded it in different ways, producing competing versions.[1] What complicates the matter even more is that early readers (i.e., other scribes) often attempted to harmonize these competing versions.

Given the entangled histories of transmission in an age before copyrights and printing presses, we must proceed cautiously and begin with the parts that are easiest to identify as supplements. The reward for our labor is considerable: many of the parts that seem to be secondary provide invaluable clues for our attempt to understand the composition-history of the National Narrative.

The reconstruction presented in the following represents my best attempt to account for all the problems in our text. In the end, the

[1] These competing versions, which we must postulate, constitute a precursor to the phenomenon of what scholars call "Rewritten Bible," represented in non-canonical works such as Jubilees.

puzzle is not solved if pieces remain on the table. It usually takes experts years to come up with compelling solutions to the many issues posed by complex texts like Genesis 26. Anyone can pick and choose lines to postulate a putative older version. What separates play from serious analysis is that the latter begins and ends with *the entire array of problems* the text presents. Explaining one problem is easy if we do not have to worry about the others. But the objective is to develop a hypothesis for how all the interconnected interpretive issues emerged and then to test the hypothesis from different perspectives.

What I consider to be an early iteration of the story is printed in the next section in bold font and begins in the farthest left margin. Lines that I identify as later additions are indented, and possible supplements to those lines are indented further to the right or printed in italics.

GENESIS 26

1 Now there was a famine in the land,
besides the former famine that had occurred in the days of Abraham.
So Isaac went to King Abimelech of the Philistines in Gerar.
2 Yhwh appeared to Isaac and said, "*Do not go down to Egypt; settle in the*
land that I shall show you. 3 Reside in this land as an alien, and I will be
with you, and will bless you; for to you and to your descendants I will
give all these lands, and I will fulfill the oath that I swore to your father
Abraham. 4 I will make your offspring as numerous as the stars of
heaven, and will give to your offspring all these lands; and all the
nations of the earth shall gain blessing for themselves through your
offspring, *5 because Abraham obeyed my voice and kept my charge, my*
commandments, my statutes, and my laws."
6 Isaac had settled in Gerar. 7 When the men of the place asked him about his
wife, he said, "She is my sister." For he was afraid to say, "My wife," thinking,
"the men of the place might kill me [for Rebekah] **because she is attractive in**
appearance." 8 When Isaac had been there a long time, King Abimelech of the
Philistines looked out of a window and saw him fondling his wife [Rebekah].
9 So Abimelech called for Isaac, and said, "So she is your wife! Why then did
you say, 'She is my sister'?" Isaac said to him, "Because I thought I might die

because of her." 10 Abimelech said, "What is this you have done to us? One of the people might easily have lain with your wife, and you would have brought guilt upon us." 11 So Abimelech warned all the people, saying, "Whoever touches this man or his wife shall be put to death."

> 12 Isaac sowed seed in that land, and in the same year reaped a hundredfold. Yhwh blessed him…

13 And the man became rich. He prospered more and more until he became very wealthy. 14 He had possessions of flocks and herds, and a great household, so that the Philistines envied him.

> 15 (Now the Philistines had stopped up and filled with earth all the wells that his father's servants had dug in the days of his father Abraham.)

16 And Abimelech said to Isaac, "Go away from us; you have become too powerful for us." 17 So Isaac departed from there and camped in the valley of Gerar, and he settled there.

> 18 Isaac dug again the wells of water that had been dug in the days of his father Abraham; for the Philistines had stopped them up after the death of Abraham. And he gave them the names that his father had given them.

19 Isaac's servants dug in the valley, and there they found a well of spring water. 20 The herders of Gerar quarreled with Isaac's herders, saying, "The water is ours." So he called the well "Esek," because they contended with him. 21 Then they dug another well, and they quarreled over that one also, so he called it "Sitnah."

> 22 He moved from there and dug another well, and they did not quarrel over it. So he called it "Rehoboth," saying, "Now Yhwh has made room for us, and we shall be fruitful in the land."

23 From there he went up to Beer-sheva.

> > 24 That very night Yhwh appeared to him and said, "I am the God of your father Abraham. Do not be afraid, for I am with you and will bless you and make your offspring numerous for my servant Abraham's sake." 25 So he built an altar there, called on the name of Yhwh.

And he pitched his tent there.

As Isaac's servants were opening a well there, 26 Abimelech went to him from Gerar, with Ahuzzath his adviser and Phicol the commander of his army. 27 Isaac said to them, "Why have you come to me, seeing that you

hate me and have sent me away from you?" 28 They said, "We see plainly that Yhwh has been with you; so we say: **Let there be an oath between you and us, and let us make a covenant with you 29 so that you will do us no harm, just as we have not touched you. We have done to you nothing but good and have sent you away in peace.** You are now the blessed of Yhwh." **30 So he made them a feast, and they ate and drank. 31 In the morning they rose early and exchanged oaths. Isaac set them on their way, and they departed from him in peace. 32 That same day Isaac's servants came and told him about the well that they had dug, and said to him, "We have found water!" 33 He called it "Shibah" – therefore the name of the city is Beer-sheva to this day.**

> 34 When Esau was forty years old, he married Judith daughter of Beeri the Hittite, and Basemath daughter of Elon the Hittite. 35 They made life bitter for Isaac and Rebekah.

ABRAHAM'S PRESENCE

When studying the growth of a biblical text, the first step is to begin with what is most obvious. Which lines, if any, stick out and interrupt the flow of the narrative? In our story, there are number of them, and they provide an easy point for departure for analyzing the remaining portions.

The second step is to start with full clauses, which are formed with a conjunction, rather than with smaller phrases or isolated lexemes.[2] This prevents us from assigning parts that pose historical problems to a putative glossator. For example, a critic could claim that a given account originally related to an entirely different figure and simply swap out the names. Such hypotheses are speculative, difficult to demonstrate, and best left as our last resort.

[2] What made biblical texts easy to expand was the simple yet innovative system of joining independent clauses using the Hebrew letter *vav*. When this letter is followed by an imperfect verb, it usually is to be translated as "and." When it is followed by a noun, it is usually to be translated as "but." Our translations introduce complexity that is largely absent from these texts, which consist of a series of loosely linked clauses.

The third step is to ask what may have prompted the postulated supplement. For this chapter from Genesis, it is relatively easy to discern, in most cases, what motivated the addition of secondary material. When we study the text in class, students have little trouble in both isolating what many experts agree are additions and offering compelling reasons why scribes would have made these additions.

The most obvious cases of supplementation in Genesis 26 relate to Abraham. Thus, v. 15 is so intrusive that most translations place it in parentheses; the line may have originated as a marginal gloss before someone moved it to its present location. Both it and v. 18, which seems to have been secondarily prefaced to vv. 19–21, anticipate an incongruity that would have disturbed the attentive reader of the wider narrative: if Isaac's father had roamed this same region with his large flocks and herds, would he not have already dug wells that Isaac could have used? The authors of vv. 15 and 18 responded in the affirmative. To explain why Isaac must re-excavate these reservoirs, they pointed to the Philistines, claiming that this population went out of their way to make the country inhospitable for Abraham's descendants by stopping up the holes he had dug.

If we have reason to believe that vv. 15 and 18 might be secondary, our next move should be to examine the three other places where Abraham appears in the account. The first place is a parenthetical note in v. 1 that invites the reader to compare Isaac's experience with that of his father: immediately after arriving in the Promised Land, Abraham had faced a famine and absconded to Egypt; there, out of fear for his own life, he duped the Egyptians into thinking that Sarah was his sister. That story, told in Genesis 12, is very similar to our own, and later we will consider what the similarity reveals about the origin of these accounts.

In two separate scenes, Yhwh appears to Isaac and reaffirms the promises made to his father (vv. 2–5 and vv. 24–25). The scenes are self-contained and interrupt the flow of the narrative; we can also remove them without inflicting damage to the story's structure. In the first, Yhwh tells Isaac 1) not to go down to Egypt, as Abraham had done when a famine broke out; 2) that he will bless Isaac; and 3) and that one day this land will belong to his descendants. In the second scene, Yhwh comes to Isaac in the night, introduces himself as the God of his father Abraham, and promises again to bless him. This revelation is supposed to have occured right before ("that very night") Abimelech visits Isaac, yet the description of Isaac building an altar and pitching his tent (v. 25) undermines the editorial intention.

By reporting these private revelations, later scribes introduced a new theological and didactic dimension to the story. They placed both episodes strategically before an important turn of events, which dramatically changes the way we interpret them: Isaac's success is due to Yhwh's protection, not the king's, and therefore after these revelations of promise and blessing, the reader has to wonder why the patriarch fails to act in confidence of divine providence. In other biblical texts, we can observe a similar editorial technique via prayers: their placement can either show what the protagonist is thinking or ascribe the events that unfold to the divine assistance that the protagonist requests.

WHERE ARE THE CHILDREN?

With all the focus on Isaac's revered father – his name is repeated eight times – it is easy to forget about his children. He has two of them, Jacob and Esau, and in the directly preceding chapter, we hear not only of their birth but also of their maturation into men, with Esau becoming "a skilled hunter and man of the field."

So where were these sons during the events recounted in our tale? Why did they not assist their father when he dug wells and faced hostility from the herders? During the lengthy tenure in Gerar, why would the kids never have paid a visit to their parents? Of course, if they had, they could have blown Isaac's cover and Abimelech would have known that Rebekah was his wife. But we would expect at least a brief statement explaining where they were at this time. Were they not members of Isaac's "great household"? Their omission is especially startling given the concluding announcement that Esau had married two Hittite women at the age of forty (v. 34).

It is possible that the story's earliest iterations did not mention Rebekah by name. If so, we could explain why the unnecessary reference to her name in v. 8, whereas in v. 7 the inhabitants of Gerar simply ask about Isaac's "wife." Moreover, in the surrounding accounts, Isaac is a passive figure, while Rebekah has the reins and orchestrates her family's future (see Chapter 22). Here, however, she is a sex object with neither agency nor voice, and she disappears after the first scene.

The addition of Abraham (and possibly Rebekah), coupled with the neglect of Jacob and Esau, suggests that our account constitutes an early building block that scribes used to construct an account of the nation's origins in Genesis. That account, what I call the Family Story, makes its points through personalities that it identifies as the nation's progenitors. However, our account, when read on its own, does not portray its protagonist as the father of Jacob and Esau. Likewise, when we bracket parts that appear to be supplementary, it does not present him as the son of Abraham and Sarah (or the husband of Rebekah).

The once widely accepted Documentary Hypothesis (also known as the "JEPD Theory") failed to resolve these problems, and in many ways exacerbated them. Thus, the theory assigns our story, in which Jacob and Esau are conspicuously absent, to the same source as the account of their birth and maturation.[3]

Searching for an alternative to the Documentary Hypothesis, a growing number of scholars locate the oldest portions of Genesis in legends of Jacob's life. These legends feature his wives and children (representing the later tribes of Israel) yet do not know about his relationship to Abraham, Isaac, and Esau; it was only at a later point that scribes began to connect these ancestral figures. What seem to be the earliest stories of Esau present him as Isaac's heir yet not as Abraham's grandson or Jacob's twin brother. Similarly, the oldest Abraham stories appear to have grown out of an earlier account related to a figure named Lot and the destruction of Sodom and Gomorrah, and these stories portray the patriarch not as the father of the nation but as a wealthy sheikh like Isaac.

Supporting this scholarly assessment, the figures of Abraham, Isaac, and Jacob usually show up separately in prophetic writings. Many of these texts are relatively old, and they do not presuppose that the three already had been combined into one family. Most often they designate the

[3] A new, and more compelling, version of this hypothesis, is known as the Neo-Documentary Hypothesis, which we touch on later in this chapter.

Northern kingdom as "(the House of) Jacob," but some refer to it as "(the House of) Isaac." For example, we read in the book of Amos:

> The shrines of Isaac shall be laid waste,
> and the sanctuaries of Israel reduced to ruins.
> Amos 7:9

> Do not prophesy against Israel,
> and do not preach against the House of Isaac.
> Amos 7:16

From such texts, it seems that Isaac and Jacob were competing identities for the Northern kingdom. The authors who created what I call the Family Story in Genesis did not opt for one over the other. Instead, they included both, transforming rival figures into father and son and aligning their stories into a continuous narrative.

And they did the same for Abraham and Sarah. The thread that connects what were once loose pearls is the promise of a great nation and a plot that follows the agony of an aged couple leading up to the birth of Isaac. It is doubtful, however, that Isaac was Abraham and Sarah's son before he was Jacob's father (and Rebekah's husband).

The combination of what were once separate stories created a richer and more complex narrative, albeit a confusing and occasionally contradictory one. In our story, Isaac has to dig the same wells that Abraham once dug, and give Beer-sheva its name after Abraham had already done so (see Genesis 21). Likewise, Isaac's ignoble act of passing off his wife as his sister is now to be understood as a pattern established by his father (see Genesis 12 and 20). Here, as often in Genesis, the apple does not fall far from the tree.

YHWH'S BLESSING

It would take a dissertation to treat the many dimensions of our account. Our aim, however, is to understand how scribes expanded and combined texts to form a larger narrative, and with this aim in mind, I want to explain the rationale for the remaining parts of my reconstruction on pages 255–257. In conclusion, I will outline several avenues of analysis for readers to pursue on their own.

We already discussed vv. 1–5, which connect Isaac to Abraham and attribute Isaac's success to Yhwh's blessing. If Isaac was an outsider in Gerar and faced conflict over water rights throughout the region, it is because the deity directs the patriarchs to reside in the Promised Land as "strangers," with the expectation that one day their descendants would take full possession of it. This is one of the many places where scribes used promises and private revelations to connect the Family Story to the Exodus-Conquest Account, which we study in the following chapters.

A gloss to v. 5 affirms the reason why Yhwh will one day award the land to Isaac's descendants: "because Abraham obeyed my voice, and kept my charge, my commandments, my statutes, and my laws." The statement introduces a highly developed concept of covenant, along with a legal lexicon, that we find in Deuteronomy. With a focus on obedience and reward, that concept is very different from the theology of promise and blessing that distinguishes the Family Story from the Exodus-Conquest Account. Here again we can observe scribes working to harmonize competing traditions.

According to my analysis, early iterations of the story began with the wife-sister episode in vv. 6–10. If the introduction in v. 1 were older, we would not expect the lengthy title ("King Abimelech of the Philistines") to be repeated in v. 8. A simple "Abimelech" would have sufficed, as in vv. 9–11, 16, and 26. The likely reason someone added v. 1 was to link the story to the wider narrative and explain how Isaac ended up in Gerar.

With respect to second half of the story, we observed how the notices about the Philistines stopping up the wells that Abraham had dug (vv. 15 and 18), as well as Yhwh's promise of blessing (vv. 24–25), preface the positive turn of events in the final episode. As for v. 12, this description of bountiful harvest is likely a supplement since we would otherwise expect v. 13 to be formulated simply as "he became rich and prospered." The use of "the man" here is highly unusual, but it makes sense when v. 12 is removed: "whoever touches *this man* or his wife" and "*the man* became rich." Isaac's prosperity in Gerar is presented here as an unintended product of the king's protection.

The addition of v. 12 identifies Isaac as a farmer rather than a herder as he is in the rest of the story. This expanded identity is in line with the new introduction in v. 1, which presents a famine as the reason for Isaac's residence in Gerar. Now, during a drought, Isaac not only sows seed but also reaps a hundredfold harvest. The following line explains the miracle: "Yhwh blessed him," and this statement points back to the promise of blessing revealed to Isaac in vv. 2–5.

Abimelech's affirmations of Yhwh's blessing in vv. 28–29 also appear to have been added at a later point. In keeping with ancient conventions of diplomacy, the basis for the proposed treaty is a record of good relations: "Let us ... make a covenant with you so that you will do us no harm, just as we have not touched you. We have done you nothing but good and have sent you away in peace." The added comments about Yhwh not only link Abimelech's goodwill back to the promise of blessing made the night before (vv. 24–25), but also transform the treaty from something transactional into a testimony to Yhwh's power by an outsider.

Finally, with respect to v. 22, there is a good reason why this reference to Rehoboth must be the result of a later redaction: Isaac has no cause to move on, as in the preceding two places, since the locals do not quarrel with him over this well. If this third time is a charm, why continue to Beer-sheva? That v. 22 is a late supplement explains its formulation: elsewhere Isaac's servants dig the wells; here he alone is the subject of the action. Moreover, in the other three cases, he simply names the place; here he also explains the name, declaring the fulfillment of the promise: "Now Yhwh has made room for us, and we shall be fruitful in the land." The addition of this verse provides a basis for Abimelech's later statement: "We see plainly that Yhwh has been with you."

In our account, we can thus study how scribes constructed a narrative of the nation's origins not only via genealogical relationships but also through an unfolding relationship with the national deity.

PARABLE AND PREJUDICE

The older account of Isaac and Abimelech is already a sophisticated specimen of storytelling, with its characters developing across the span of its three episodes: in the first, Isaac comes across as an egotistical coward; in the second, the herders of Gerar act aggressively while Isaac moves on to avoid conflict; and in the final episode, Abimelech takes the initiative to reconcile their differences.

The events are portrayed with a comic touch, poking fun at the audience's ancestor. Isaac is an anxious fellow. He is convinced that his wife is attractive, and that her appearance poses a threat to his life. The scene reveals a wide gap between reality and this man's perception of it. Its authors challenge their audience's inclination to assume, with their ancestor, that the denizens of Gerar would mistreat outsiders. It is Isaac who initially behaves in a morally questionable manner, and when denouncing his behavior, the foreign king also addresses the reader's prejudice. Notice also how Isaac in the final episode declaims how Abimelech had sent him away because he hates him, how Abimelech dismisses the allegation, and in conclusion how this ruler departs in a spirit of goodwill.

Elsewhere, the Bible portrays the Philistines as a pugnacious people, yet here their king pursues peace. A later supplement to the final scene goes a step further when it presents Abimelech affirming the impact of Yhwh's blessing on Isaac's life and citing it as the reason for wanting to make a treaty. The older account credits Isaac's wealth to this ruler's protection, even if Isaac acquired his protection through deceit. Only after Isaac establishes a record of avoiding strife and moving on, rather than insisting on his rights to the wells he digs, does the story reach a happy conclusion.

This account of conflict resolution dovetails with the political paradigm of peaceful coexistence promoted throughout the Family Story, and in coming chapters, we will compare that paradigm with the bellicose ethos that courses through the veins of the Exodus-Conquest Account. Readers could interpret this tale in relation to contemporaneous Philistines and the problems they posed – both before and after the downfall of the Northern and Southern kingdoms. (After the Assyrian onslaught, and then during the Persian period, the province of Ashdod became a major player in the region.) Similarly, they could identify the Philistines as the prototypical "Other" – analogous to the stereotypical "Indians" in Westerns – as they addressed relations with outsiders.

Beyond its larger paradigmatic purpose, the account stakes a historical-legal claim to land, even if those who are not its intended readers might take issue with its claim. The events that unfold run along the periphery of the later kingdoms of Israel and Judah, and like all borderlands, these places have hybrid identities and politically fraught histories. This is especially the case for Beer-sheva, which figures prominently throughout the Family Story. Thus, according to this reading strategy, the account "reminds" Isaac's descendants that they have a longstanding claim to this border town, and that its important well started producing water on the same day their ancestor ratified a treaty with the lord of the land.

What was once a purely political parable is now a chapter in an evolving relationship between Yhwh and his people. The reader learns that the nation's deity guided Isaac's fate as he had done for Abraham before him, and as he will do for Jacob and his descendants in the future. Just as the earlier iterations do not refer to Yhwh, they also contain nothing that links Isaac to the entire nation. Yet thanks to a series of supplements, the story now affirms that, with Yhwh's direct oversight, Isaac's seed will be as numerous as the stars of heaven. Likewise, whereas the story had originally asserted rights to Beer-sheva via an agreement with Abimelech, the divine promise in the new and improved versions preempts the pact: the descendants of Isaac have not only a historical-legal claim but also a divine entitlement. And the territory to which they are entitled is no longer solely Beer-sheva but "all these lands."

LOOSE THREADS AND LOOMING ISSUES

Instead of discrete sources (or documents) that a single compiler wove together at a late stage, our test case illustrates two basic ways biblical authors integrated and reworked their materials. The first way is rewriting: they created alternative versions that undermine or subvert an older account. And the second way is supplementing: they expanded an older account with lines that connect and harmonize it with the alternative versions. In the process of weaving together what were competing versions, they created repetitions (or "doublets") that often make for an incongruous narrative.

Any reconstruction is inevitably circular and always takes its point of departure from the study of related biblical texts. With only circumstantial evidence, we can never proceed with certainty. However, we can be more confident about a hypothesis when it provides a compelling solution to problems posed by multiple texts.

Our story contains several threads to the wider narrative of the Family Story, and the directions they take are fun to trace. In this final section, I isolate these threads, along with a few looming issues, as invitations to further study. Readers are encouraged to examine the texts and try their hand at the kind of analysis we have undertaken here.

Abraham and Abimelech – As noted earlier, the Abraham account presents its protagonist passing off Sarah as his sister just as Isaac does with Rebekah; it does so twice, and the depictions overlap with our story on multiple points. The first time is set in Egypt, immediately after we are introduced to him (Genesis 12). The second time features, strangely, the same antagonist (Abimelech) and the same place (Gerar), and in the following chapter, we read about a treaty with this figure, also at Beer-sheva, and also in connection with tensions around a water source (Genesis 20–21)!

The presence of these passages in the Family Story makes for a highly improbable and incongruous narrative (even with the many supplemental references to Abraham in the Isaac story). It does not make sense that the name of Beer-sheva is already forgotten one generation later, that Isaac makes a treaty with the same king there, and then gives the same name to the place yet with a different etymology.

Past research on the book of Genesis had broken down its contents into several running, and partially parallel, sources that a compiler combined into a single work (the Documentary Hypothesis). Thus, the first wife-sister episode with Abraham as well as the third one with Isaac is ascribed by this theory to J (the Yahwist/Jahwist), with the second episode with Abraham being attributed to E (the Elohist). While the theory solves some problems, it creates many new ones, so that over the past decades, most experts, especially those in Europe, have set it aside and begun to explore other options. Even so, a network of North American scholars who label themselves "Neo-Documentarians" are confident that this approach is still the most plausible one, and that the many problems it creates are a result of it not being executed with sufficient rigor. They also insist that the authors of the sources/documents did not know each other's work.

The issue may appear to be academic and inconsequential. However, this close, comparative reading is precisely the kind of engagement the book of Genesis invites by including parallel stories. For those who wish to dive into these colorful and rewarding texts, here are some questions to guide your study:

- What happens to Sarah in the first two episodes that does not happen to Rebekah in the third?
- How does the first Abraham episode treat the relationship between his actions and his wealth? How does it affect the larger portrait of the patriarch, especially in relation to the divine commission detailed in the preceding verses (Genesis 12:1–5)?
- Notice how the second Abraham episode in 20:1–18 continues in 21:22–34, and how the account of Isaac's birth and Ishmael's banishment in 21:1–21 severs the narrative into two parts. Is it plausible that all of chapters. 20–21 (including 21:1–21) are part of the same source? If not, what might have been a later scribe's intention inserting the material in 21:1–21?
- How is the depiction of Abimelech in the second episode similar to the third episode with Isaac? In what ways are they different?
- Is it plausible that these two episodes were composed independently of each other? Does one presuppose the other? Are they rival accounts?
- What does the presence of these three episodes in the Family Story reveal about not just the prehistory of this work but also its pedagogical purpose?

Jacob and Esau – The Family Story introduces Jacob and Esau in the chapter that precedes the one we examined here, and the chapters that follow it tell of a conflict that erupts between these twin brothers. The account consists of three parts: first Jacob robs Esau of his birthright and blessing; then he flees with the help of his mother Rebekah; finally, after becoming the head of a large household over the course of many years, he makes his way home and seeks reconciliation with his estranged twin.

According to a compelling theory, this account was composed around an older story of the patriarch working for a man named Laban, marrying his daughters, and becoming, like Isaac, the head of a large household (Genesis 29–31). The later account portrays Jacob's strife with his brother to explain why he is living in Laban's home in the older story.

Alongside that later account, a separate narrative thread offers a new reason for the years Jacob spends in Laban's home. Its authors drew directly on the notice of Esau's Hittite wives in the final lines of chapter 26: Rebekah fears that Jacob, her favorite son, would follow in Esau's steps and marry unsuitable women; she therefore urges her feeble husband to send Jacob away to their kin back in "the old country" of Syria where he has better chances of finding himself "a nice Jewish girl." (As part of this redaction, Laban is identified as Rebekah's brother.) So begins the tale of Jacob's tumultuous love life, torn to and fro between Laban's two daughters, Leah and Rachel.

The narrative thread that describes Rebekah's concern for her son is part of the Priestly Source, a late reformulation of the Family Story and the Exodus-Conquest Account (see discussion of Genesis 1 in Chapter 10). Whereas many scholars have long given up on the idea a Yahwist (J) and a Elohist (E), very few doubt the existence of the Priestly Source (P). In fact, Priestly texts are so easy to identify that many analyses begin by separating Priestly from non-Priestly passages and then proceed to investigate whether the non-Priestly parts pre-date or post-date the Priestly portions.

The reader can retrace these parallel accounts in 27:1–45 and 28:10 (the account of Jacob's conflict with Esau) and in 26:34–35, 27:46, and 28:1–9 (the retelling in the Priestly Source). When doing so, consider a range of issues that are treated variously in contemporary research:

- How does the depiction of Rebekah in these parallel accounts differ from chapter 26? What do these accounts have in common with the matchmaking tale in chapter 24? In what ways does Rebekah's newfound agency in these later texts resemble the depiction of other women in the Family Story (from Eve onwards)? What may have occasioned the increased attention to women and the pivotal roles they play? (For my own thoughts on this matter, see Part IV.) Finally, how does Rebekah become a linchpin connecting the Northern figure of Jacob and the Southern figure of Isaac?
- Does the Priestly account presuppose the earlier, non-Priestly account? Or could they have been composed without any knowledge of each other, as Neo-Documentarians now claim?
- How does the Priestly account portray Rebekah and Jacob in a more flattering light than in the non-Priestly account? Would the trickery in the earlier account have been troubling for its intended readers?

- How does the Priestly account reflect anxieties around intermarriage? In what ways is this anxiety reflected in writings from the post-exilic period? What might this anxiety mean for the origins and dating of the Priestly Source?

FURTHER READING

Exum, J. Cheryl, *Fragmented Women: Feminist (Sub)versions of Biblical Narratives*, Bloomsbury, 1993.

Frankel, David, "Isaac Before He Was Abraham's Son," *TheTorah.com*, 2020, www.thetorah.com/article/isaac-before-he-was-abrahams-son

Hayes, John H. and Holladay, Carl R., *Biblical Exegesis: A Beginner's Handbook*, 2nd ed., Westminster John Knox, 2007.

Jackson, Melissa A., *Comedy and Feminist Interpretation of the Hebrew Bible: A Subversive Collaboration*, Oxford University Press, 2012.

Keshet, Shula, "*Say You Are My Sister": Danger, Seduction, and the Foreign in Biblical Literature and Beyond*, Sheffield Phoenix, 2013.

Kratz, Reinhard G., *The Composition of the Narrative Books of the Old Testament*, Continuum, 2005.

Lemon, Joel M. and Richards, Kent Harold (eds.), *Method Matters*, Society of Biblical Literature, 2009.

Muller, Reinhard; Pakkala, Juha; and Romeny, Bas Ter Haar, *Evidence of Editing: Growth and Change of Texts in the Hebrew Bible*, Society of Biblical Literature, 2014.

Na'aman, Nadad, "The Isaac Story (Genesis 26) and the Land of Gerar," *Semitica* 61 (2019): 59–88.

Niditch, Susan, *Underdogs and Tricksters: A Prelude to Biblical Folklore*, Harper & Row, 1987.

Person Jr., Raymond F. and Rezetko, Robert, *Empirical Models Challenging Biblical Criticism*, SBL Press, 2016.

Rachmuth, Moshe S., "Observations on the Deeds of Isaac in Genesis 26," *Semitica* 63 (2022): 169–181.

Schneider, Tammi, *Mothers of Promise: Women in the Book of Genesis*, Baker, 2008.

Shectman, Sarah, "Israel's Matriarchs: Political Pawns or Powerbrokers?" in Mark G. Brett and Jakob Wöhrle (eds.), *The Politics of the Ancestors*, Mohr Siebeck, 2018.

Steck, Odil Hannes, *Old Testament Exegesis: A Guide to the Methodology*, Society of Biblical Literature, 1998.

17

Moses and Joshua

The People's History

Moses led his flock beyond the wilderness,
and came to Horeb, the mountain of God.
There the angel of Yhwh appeared to him
in a flame of fire out of the bush.
– Exodus 3:1–2

ONE DAY, WHILE TENDING THE FLOCKS of his father-in-law, Moses ventures "beyond the wilderness." Looming over this liminal space is the sacred mountain Horeb (an alternative name for Sinai). It is here that Yhwh, in the not-too-distant future, will make a covenant with the Israelites after liberating them from bondage in Egypt. And it is here that Yhwh, on this fateful day, calls Moses from a burning bush and sends him to the pharaoh "so that you may bring my people, the children of Israel, out of Egypt." This is the pivotal moment in myths when the hero learns of his mission. Yet instead of eagerly embracing his mission, Moses objects: "Who am I that I should go to the pharaoh and bring the children of Israel out of Egypt?" (Exodus 3:10–11).

When read its own terms, the protestation of inadequacy by a lowly shepherd makes perfect sense. But when read as part of the larger narrative, the question "Who am I?" comes as a surprise. The preceding chapter of Exodus describes how the pharaoh's daughter discovered the baby Moses in the Nile and adopted him as her own. The reader knows that as a "Prince of Egypt" Moses is uniquely qualified to negotiate with the pharaoh. There is no one better for the job than he. Augmenting the narrative dissonance, Moses says "go" to the pharaoh; the reader expects him to say "return," as he had already spent much of his life at the Egyptian court.

These and other incongruities suggest that we have here an older story that depicts Yhwh commissioning a humble herdsman from a burning bush in direct anticipation of the later events at Sinai.[1] Assuming that such is the case, what would have necessitated the composition of the preceding chapter in which this figure grows up at the Egyptian court?

The answer to this question bears directly on two rival accounts of the nation's origins. We have just explored how scribes created one account, the Family Story, by connecting the originally independent figures of Abraham, Isaac, and Jacob. We now turn our attention to a competing work, the Exodus-Conquest Account, that begins with the stories of Moses' birth and commission. In studying these stories, we will see how scribes created a composite history of Israel's pre-monarchic past (the "People's History") by combining two, originally separate, works.

THE BIRTH OF MOSES

From antiquity to modernity, Moses has inspired an array of fantastic legends. Yet who was he and where did he come from? The question is an ancient one, and the scribes who gave birth to the biblical story of Moses' life could not easily evade it. By examining their ingenious responses, which create a complex yet compelling character, we will witness how these scribes produced new texts and traditions by cleverly reinterpreting older ones.

The first chapter of Exodus sets the stage by describing the programs of extermination that the pharaoh pursues against "the Hebrews" (the name outsiders give Israelites in the Bible). First, he commands the Hebrew midwives to slay male infants at birth, and later he decrees that the babies be thrown into the Nile. The second chapter of Exodus depicts Moses' mother hiding the infant Moses (see the treatment of this text in the introduction to Chapter 2). The reader is supposed to interpret the second chapter in light of the first, so that Moses' mother is concealing him from the pharaoh's genocidal edict.

[1] The word for "bush" in Hebrew (*seneh*) is probably a play on the name "Sinai."

Yet here again, the narrative includes many details that resist a sequential reading. When Moses' mother hides the baby, we are told it was because "she saw that he was a good/beautiful." Nothing is said here about the pharaoh's decree to slay Hebrew boys. The narrator reveals that the infant was easy to identify as a Hebrew but fails to mention a special dispensation that exempted him from the evil edict. The only thing we are told is that pharaoh's daughter insisted on paying Moses' mother to be his nurse.

The second chapter also has its own internal logic. It responds to what must have been for many vexing questions posed by the older beginning in chapter three: Why does Israel's first leader have an Egyptian name? What is he doing out in the wilderness with his father-in-law's flocks while the Israelites are enslaved in Egypt? Was he even an Israelite? Chapter two removes any doubt that Moses was a full-fledged "Member of the Tribe." Not only that, it affirms that his parents belonged to the venerable Levitical clan.

In the clever tale spun by the authors of the second chapter, Moses was born to Israelite parents, yet was abandoned by his mother and later found by the pharaoh's daughter. The account suggests that the sexual relations between his parents were in some way illicit. It does not provide his father's name, as we would expect from biblical birth stories. Later we learn that the mother already has an older daughter. Instead of immediately abandoning the infant, she sees that "he was good/beautiful" and decides to keep him as long as she can.

Infant exposure is a recurring motif in the legends of great leaders. In fact, scholars have often suggested that the account of Moses' birth alludes specifically to the widely circulated Legend of Sargon the Great, copies of which were found in the Ashurbanipal Library:

> Sargon, the mighty king, king of Agade, am I.
> My mother was a changeling, my father I knew not.
> The brother(s) of my father loved the hills.
> My city is Azupiranu, which is situated on the banks of the Euphrates.
> My changeling mother conceived me, in secret she bore me.
> She set me in a basket of rushes, with bitumen she sealed my lid.
> She cast me into the river which rose not (over) me,

The river bore me up and carried me to Akki, the drawer of water.
Akki, the drawer of water lifted me out as he dipped his e[w]er.
Akki, the drawer of water, [took me] as his son (and) reared me.
Akki, the drawer of water, appointed me as his gardener,
While I was a gardener, Ishtar granted me (her) love,
And for four and [. . .] years I exercised kingship.[2]

Drawing on the same foundling motif from Sargon's birth-story, the authors of the biblical account tell, in fairytale fashion, how Moses' mother holds on to the special child for three months before eventually abandoning him in a basket of rushes pitched with bitumen (exactly as in Sargon's story). Later, the pharaoh's own daughter discovers him when she goes with her maidens to bathe in the Nile. Thanks to his sister's ingenious suggestion, Moses grows up in the home of his biological mother. It is only later that the Egyptian princess "makes him her son" and gives him the the name Moses (we are not told what his biological mother called him).

Moses was a popular name in ancient Egypt. It means "born of" or "child of," and was normally combined with the name of a deity, like Thutmose or Ahmose. The authors of our account, however, claimed that the name is actually Hebrew ("for I drew him out of the water"). How the Egyptian princess knew Hebrew goes unexplained. Implying that she discovered Moses when she was still a virgin, the narrator dispels any doubt that the pharaoh's daughter could be his natural mother. And although Moses later goes to live at the Egyptian court, he remains a Hebrew at heart and proves his undying solidarity when he slays an Egyptian.

The dramatic account of this murder explains how the adopted prince ends up as a shepherd far beyond Egypt's borders: one day after he was an adult, he roams beyond the palace and witnesses an Egyptian man beating one of his Hebrew brothers. Defending his kin, he kills the Egyptian bully and buries him in the sand. When the palace learns of his crime, he fears for his life and seeks refuge in a remote country. There he marries, starts a family, and earns his keep by tending to the flocks of

[2] Translation from Pritchard (ed.), *The Ancient Near East*, Vol. 1, pp. 85–86.

his father-in-law.[3] This is where the earlier introduction begins – the account in chapter three of Yhwh appearing to Moses while he is out in the wilderness. If our hero now no longer fears for his life after slaying an Egyptian, and if he protests that he is unworthy to speak to the pharaoh on his people's behalf, it is because, as the narrator explains, a long time had elapsed, and a new pharaoh was now on the throne.

GENESIS AND GENOCIDE

This is storytelling and character development at their finest, and Hollywood screenwriters have had a hard time improving on the biblical tale. But what do we really know about Moses' identity? The question is difficult to answer. If he only became a Levite at a later point, perhaps he was originally an Egyptian, as his name suggests and as supposed both by ancient historians (e.g., Manetho and Strabo) and modern authors (e.g., Sigmund Freud and Thomas Mann). Or, following more recent claims, he may have been a member of the Midianites, a nomadic people for whom his father-in-law served as priest. Whatever option one finds compelling, the story of his birth and beginnings in chapter two answers questions that arise from the older introduction in chapter three: yes, his name and origins may be obscure, but no one should doubt that he was a son of the people whom he led out of Egypt.

However, the new introduction in chapter two raised its own set of troubling issues: The nation's founding father was a foundling? His own mother abandoned him? His father's identity is unknown?

The birth account may have made Moses a full-fledged member of Israel, but it would have been disconcerting for many readers. To address these issues, scribes composed yet another episode, one that portrays the backstory to Moses' unbecoming beginnings.

This episode is found in the first chapter of Exodus, and it radically reinterprets everything that follows. Now the reason why Moses' mother hides him is because the pharaoh had decreed that all the male babies

[3] Notice the similarities in this composition-history to what we observed in Chapter 16 regarding Jacob's conflict with Esau: scribes appear to have composed the story of that conflict to explain why an older account presents the patriarch in Laban's home.

born to Hebrew women be thrown in the Nile. While Moses is deposited in the river, his mother had ingeniously subverted the king's command by placing him first in a basket; after all, the decree had said nothing about providing the children with life-rafts. Moreover, by describing the deceptive maneuvers practiced by the Hebrew midwives, the first chapter encourages the reader to interpret the actions of the women in the second chapter – Moses' mother, sister, and the pharaoh's daughter – also as deeds of daring defiance. What was once a light and delightful story is now a tale of tyrannical terror and valiant resistance.

The scribal skill on display in these first chapters of Exodus is stunning to be sure, but what motivated the authors was more than a concern with Moses' origins and his relationship to the people of Israel. The composition of chapter one not only introduces a more dramatic plot to the narrative but also cleverly connects that narrative to the Family Story in Genesis.

The story of Moses and the burning bush in chapter three, along with the first expansion that tells of his birth and flight in chapter two, introduces the Exodus-Conquest Account. This work, which Northern scribes likely composed in the years following the conquest of the kingdom of Israel, depicts the nation fleeing Egypt and conquering Canaan under the leadership of Moses and Joshua. The Exodus-Conquest Account does not describe how Israel became a people; rather, it simply presupposes their existence as an oppressed population in Egypt. As foreign slaves laboring for the pharaoh, they long for liberation and a land of their own. Once they are freed, they migrate to it collectively, at one point in time. When they set out for the Promised Land, they know nothing about it, not even how to get there. Instead of returning to their homeland, where their ancestors had once roamed, they are charting new territory. That this account originated among Northern scribes is clear from its depiction of the nation circumventing Judah and entering the Promised Land from the eastern side of the Jordan, at the border town of Jericho.

The Family Story in Genesis provides a competing account of the nation's origins. It too likely began as a work written by scribes from the Northern kingdom. But in comparison with the Exodus-Conquest Account, it imagines a more gradual genealogical evolution, beginning with a population that already lives in the Promised Land. Furthermore, like the Exodus-Conquest Account, it evolved as later generations (especially from the South) introduced new accents to it. Yet its primary purpose was to show how Israel's diverse population (eventually including Judah and the South) are all the descendants of one big family.

The oldest parts of the Family Story constructed political hierarchies within the Northern kingdom by depicting Jacob's love life. The father of the nation falls head over heels for Rachel and is betrothed to her first. He consummates his first marriage with Rachel's older sister Leah, but only because their father Laban hoodwinks him into marrying her. Jacob's affection also communicates political status: the core regions and tribes are portrayed as Rachel's children (or grandchildren), while those that the Northern kingdom subjugated later (e.g., in the Transjordan) are represented as the children of Leah or her and Rachel's handmaidens.

Later, scribes working in the kingdom of Judah adopted the Family Story and made it their own by heavily embellishing the narrative and adding other representative figures. Thus, these Southern scribes identified Laban (Rachel and Leah's father) as the brother of Rebekah, and via this matriarch, married originally unconnected Northern and Southern traditions. In the process, Jacob became the twin brother of Esau, ancestor of the Edomites that encroached on Judah's ancestral territories in the last years of the kingdom.

In the final stage, Southern scribes rounded out their work with the figure of Abraham. The oldest texts locate him as a sheikh living near Hebron, the first capital of the Southern kingdom, while later texts link him to the originally independent figure of Lot and make him the father of Ishmael and Isaac. As such, he serves as a unifying figure for a larger nation comprising both North and South, as well as an ancestral liaison to neighboring peoples.

WAR AND PEACE

The Family Story affirms that Israel is related to the surrounding populations by kinship, covenants, and long histories, and it promotes peaceful coexistence with Israel's historical enemies. The patriarchs ratify treaties with their neighbors, as Isaac does with the Philistine king Abimelech. Instead of taking the land through conquest, they purchase it. They rarely go to war, and when one of them does, it is to defend his Canaanite neighbors (Sodom and Gomorrah) from an assault by Mesopotamian kings.

This work presents a distinctive political model, one that stands in sharp contrast to the Exodus-Conquest Account. Whereas the patriarchs make peace with the inhabitants of Canaan, the Exodus-Conquest Account presents the newly liberated nation taking the country by force, destroying the kingdoms that occupied it, and giving no quarter to its inhabitants. When they do spare lives and enter into treaties, as in the case of Rahab and the Gibeonites, it is an exception to the rule (see Chapter 24).

The deep tension between these two political models – one ecumenical and conciliatory and other particularistic and militant – define the Pentateuch's character. In the Family Story, Egypt extends generous hospitality to Jacob's family when they migrate as refugees from famine-stricken Canaan. In glaring contrast, the Exodus-Conquest Account presents Egypt as a land of affliction from which a nation of former slaves flees. As a whole, the general animus toward outsiders in this work could not be more at odds with the vision of peace promoted in the Family Story.

These two works are deeply antithetical, but they share a basic, yet remarkable, feature: they imagine a national past in which their own monarchies play no role whatsoever.

The Family Story focuses attention on the genesis of a clan, and it treats issues of conflict and political relations via stories of representative, non-monarchic figures, such as Jacob and his wives. Kings appear in this work, but they are foreign rulers, as in the story of Isaac and Abimelech.

To portray a nation going to war without a king as their leader would have been a counterintuitive move for ancient West Asian scribes, but such is precisely what the Exodus-Conquest Account does. This work imagines Israel as people-in-arms that conquers the kings of Canaan and their professional armies. They engage in non-conventional warfare, without a human monarch at the helm. If anyone, it is Yhwh who is crowned king, and the narrative presents the nation celebrating his eternal rule after he triumphs over the pharaoh (see Exodus 15). The laws of Deuteronomy make the point more explicit: the nation may choose to appoint a king at some point, but only "after Yhwh, your God, has given you the land" (see Deuteronomy 17:14–20).

Thus, the Exodus-Conquest Account imagines a pivotal achievement in the nation's past (the conquest of its homeland) by completely erasing the role of the monarchy. This erasure is all the more remarkable when we recall (see Part I) that historically this achievement was in large part the work of the nation's later monarchs. Writing after the defeat of the Northern kingdom, its authors were convinced that Israel could still be Israel without a king of their own.

This Northern notion of peoplehood was a bold thought experiment, one that departed dramatically from conventional thinking. It did not gain purchase in Judah until the years directly prior to its conquest in 586 BCE and especially in the decades thereafter. At this time Southern scribes began not only to copy and embellish the Family Story and the Exodus-Conquest Account, but also to link these competing, parallel works in a single, linear, narrative history – what I call the "People's History."

The literary hinge on which the People's History hangs is found in the first chapter of Exodus. The passage begins by recounting how Jacob's family had gone down to Egypt during the days of Joseph and had grown into a large population in the land. Yet since that time, a new pharaoh had come to power "who did not know Joseph." The goodwill that Joseph and his family once enjoyed was a thing of the past. Far from favoring this people, the new pharaoh fears that "in the event of war, they would join our enemy, fight against us, and escape from the land" (Exodus 1:10). Perceiving Israel's numbers as a threat to Egypt's future, the pharaoh introduces programs of debilitating labor and genocide.

Therefore, by describing a radical regime change at the Egyptian court, the authors of the People's History could reconcile the positive image of Egypt in the Family Story with the negative image of Egypt in the Exodus-Conquest Account. The stories of the patriarchs and matriarchs are now to be understood as happening at a time long before the exodus. And when Israel leaves Egypt, they *return* to the land where their ancestors had once lived.

When reconciling the rival accounts, the authors of the People's History made numerous additions to their contents. For example, in the scene of the burning bush, Yhwh introduces himself to Moses for the first time as "the God of your father." A later author added an explicit connection to the Family Story in Genesis by adding to Yhwh's self-description an explicit reference to the patriarchs: "the God of Abraham, the God of Isaac, and the God of Jacob" (Exodus 3:6). Similarly, the Family Story has been expanded with passages that anticipate the nation's future stay in Egypt (e.g., in story of Abraham passing off Sarah as his sister in Genesis 12, discussed in the preceding chapter; see also Yhwh's explicit declaration in Genesis 15).

The first chapter of Exodus thus preserves the seams between what were originally two independent works, and this effort to create an extensive, composite, yet unified narrative is a remarkable achievement in the history of literature. While we do not witness anything like it in the cultures of the ancient Near East, it stands in direct continuity with the way scribes created the Family Story and the Exodus-Conquest Account by connecting stories of representative figures. In the preceding chapter, we studied this phenomenon in the Family Story; it remains to consider briefly how the Exodus-Conquest Account connects Moses to other figures.

CONNECTING THE DOTS: AARON AND JOSHUA

In Chapter 2 we noted that Miriam must have had her own story and been a venerated figure before she became identified with Moses' anonymous sister who intervened on his behalf in the dramatic tale of his nativity. Moses' other sibling is Aaron, the progenitor of a prominent priestly line ("sons of Aaron" or "Aaronides") from Jerusalem. This group figures prominently in the Priestly Source (see discussion in Chapters 10 and 16) and made their presence felt in the final forms of the Pentateuch.

After the conquest of the Southern kingdom in 586 BCE, the temple and priests replaced the palace and kings in Judean society, and it was at this time that the Aaronides began to assert their contributions throughout the Exodus-Conquest Account. Thus, in their reworked introduction, the deity sends Aaron to meet Moses in the wilderness soon after commissioning him to go to Egypt (see Exodus 4), and in the Priestly contributions to the following narrative, he and Moses often work together as a team.

After making their eponymous ancestor one the nation's leaders during its infancy, they went even further and made him a member of Moses' family. We can observe various stages in this genealogical grafting, with the first texts portraying Aaron as Miriam's brother and later texts identifying both as Moses' siblings. Thus, in Exodus 4:14, in response to Moses' protestations, Yhwh says: "Look, there is Aaron the Levite . . . he is now coming to meet you," which a later hand has likely reworked so that it now reads: "Aaron, your brother, the Levite."

The Levites had enjoyed special cultic privileges in North. After the fall of the Northern kingdom in 722 BCE, many were disenfranchised. Some would have migrated to the Southern kingdom, but there was only a limited place for them there, especially as many were pushing to centralize worship at Jerusalem. Their leading competitors were the Zadokites, a priestly clan that had served in Jerusalem for ages.

One way the Zadokites defended their privileges was tell about the special role their ancestor played in the formation of *the kingdom.* In the Palace History (the subject of the following chapter), King David chooses Zadok and his sons to be high priests because they had been loyal to him when he was fleeing for his life. In the Exodus-Conquest Account, the Levites and Aaronides countered these claims. Already early iterations of this work had identified Moses as a Levite, as we saw in our analysis of his birth-story. Thanks to their revisions of this work, the Aaronides could claim that their ancestor played a special role in the formation of *the nation,* long before David founded a state. Indeed, Aaron was Moses' direct brother, and instead of human king, it was Yhwh who chose him and his sons to occupy the most coveted, cultic roles.

In contrast to Aaron, the figure of Joshua was included in the earliest iterations of the Exodus-Conquest Account. This work consists of two basic parts, as its name suggests: on one side is Moses, who guides the nation during the exodus; on other side is Joshua, who replaces Moses after his death and guides the nation during the conquest of Canaan. If Joshua is a historical figure, we do not know when he would have lived.

He has a Yahwistic name (with the meaning "Yhwh saves"), and Yahwistic names did not become common until the mid-ninth and especially eighth century.

Even if Joshua is largely invented, some of the legends about him are older than others. In what appears to be the oldest, he is not Moses' successor but a warlord who commands his own private army in the central hill country. A federation of kings attacks the Gibeonites (a population from the central hill country), the Gibeonites call on Joshua for help, and Joshua "saves" them. In keeping with a pattern of military conquest attested from antiquity to the present, he ends up taking possession of a much larger territory and establishing his hegemony here. In the book of Samuel, Saul becomes king in this same religion by "saving" a besieged population, and this story of Joshua's salvific feats remembers him as a ruler from the central hill country.

When the authors of the Exodus-Conquest Account incorporated Joshua into their narrative, they made a dramatic change to his identity: instead of saving a population and becoming their king, he is now a prolific regicide, warring against, and later executing, a myriad of monarchs. In this new literary landscape, Canaan is home to formidable city-states, known by the names of the kings who rule them. They face an invasion not from other kings and professional fighting forces but from a recently liberated people-in-arms, with a non-king guiding them into battle. In contrast to the Canaanite kings who meet their demise in the Exodus-Conquest Account, the office that Joshua occupies is not hereditary: just as he is Moses' successor but not Moses' son, his authority is not bequeathed to his own descendants.

Instead of a local warlord who ruled in relatively recent times, Joshua is remembered in this work as one who left Egypt as part of the exodus generation. To connect him to the exodus narrative, the authors composed the well-known battle stories of Jericho and Ai, the two cities closest to the Jordan River that the Israelites cross when invading Canaan. These battle stories stand at the beginning of the book, which is directly preceded by the account in Deuteronomy of Moses dying on Mount Nebo as the nation prepares to cross the Jordan.

One of the thorniest problems for those who work on these texts is why Moses does not enter the Promised Land. Some biblical texts explain his death as the punishment for his sin: because he struck the rock against Yhwh's explicit directions, Yhwh condemned him to die outside the Promised Land. When Moses in Deuteronomy retells history from his own perspective, he claims that he begged Yhwh to be allowed to enter the land and blames the people for being turned down: "Yhwh was however angry with me because of what all of you did. He refused to listen to me, and said: 'That's enough! I don't want you asking me about this again!'" (Deuteronomy 3:26).

Still another, older explanation lurks below the text's surface that seems to draw on ancient traditions locating Moses' grave on (or near) Mount Nebo. Thanks to the Mesha Stele (see Chapters 5 and 15), we know that a Yhwh temple once existed at the town of Nebo, which would have been located in proximity to the mountain. The legend of Moses' death at this place, just as the older memories of Joshua saving the Gibeonites, has nothing to do with the story of Israel's escape from Egypt.

We cannot be sure what motivated the authors of the Exodus-Conquest to link Moses and Joshua. These writers could have easily just created a story from thin air. Yet instead of inventing their history, they discovered it by collecting and connecting earlier writings.

NATION AS NARRATION

The combination of competing accounts that we can study in these biblical texts relates to a fundamental problem facing national narratives: whose story should be the defining one? Thus, when writing a history of the United States, should one begin with the British colonists? What about the many communities that had lived on the land long before Europeans arrived on American shores? And how does a historical narrative do justice to the immigration of diverse populations over the following centuries and the many peoples that populated the continent before the arrival of Europeans? The issue is especially tangible at Thanksgiving, when the widest array of schoolchildren – from those who can trace their lineage to the first settlers, to those whose families entered at Ellis Island or crossed the nation's borders more recently – are expected to perform Pilgrim pageants and make the story their own.

In creating the People's History, our scribes did not opt for one or the other tradition; rather, they embraced both. Not only that, but they also fused them together to form a larger narrative. The Family Story of Genesis connects disparate clans to common ancestors, while the Exodus-Conquest Account tells how a group of freed slaves consolidated to form a nation and migrated to a new land, embracing many "fellow travelers" along the way. And while the Jacob traditions presents Israel's tribes as indigenous groups, the addition of Abraham and Sarah to the Family Story seeks to unite competing groups by declaring all to be descendants of this immigrant couple.

At an advanced stage in the formation of the People's History, scribes added instructions for applying the narrative to the pedagogical project that we studied in Part III. Thus, on the eve of the invasion, Joshua summons representatives of the nation's twelve tribes to carry stones across the Jordan and create from them a monument for future generations (see text quoted in Chapter 14).

Deuteronomy features some of the most developed applications of the narrative to nationhood. After delineating laws at length in the preceding thirteen chapters, Moses commands the Israelites to recite, word for word, a condensed form of the exodus story when they bring the land's first produce to Yhwh's sanctuary:

> When the priest takes the basket from your hand and sets it down before the altar of Yhwh your God, you shall make this response before Yhwh your God:
>
> "A wandering Aramean was my ancestor; he went down into Egypt and lived there as an alien, few in number, and there he became a great nation, mighty and populous. When the Egyptians treated us harshly and afflicted us, by imposing hard labor on us, we cried to Yhwh, the God of our ancestors. Yhwh heard our voice and saw our affliction, our toil, and our oppression. Yhwh brought us out of Egypt with a mighty hand and an outstretched arm, with a terrifying display of power, and with signs and wonders. Yhwh brought us into this place and gave us this land, a land flowing with milk and honey. So now I bring the first of the fruit of the ground that you, Yhwh, have given me."
>
> – Deuteronomy 26:4–9

Notice the use of the first-person singular in this recitation, such as "my ancestor," "I bring," and "you, Yhwh, have given me." Each member of the nation is to recite this narrative, to internalize and own it.[4]

We might judge such ritual affirmations to be historically naive. How could new members of the nation claim that their ancestors were part of the Aramean clan that suffered in Egypt before coming to the land?

Modern political theorists, from Ernest Renan to Homi Bhabha, emphasize the extent to which nations are acts of narration, and many today take for granted that national identities are not possible without narratives. Thus, most modern countries require civics tests during the naturalization of new citizens. However, for the scribes that produced our ancient texts, this use of narrative in the construction of a national identity was innovative. It was also aspirational: such individual recitations of the biblical story are not widely attested until centuries later.

Thanks to the efforts of the Jewish sages at the turn of the Common Era, the pedagogical project initiated by the biblical scribes persisted in new forms. As a testimony to the efforts of both the biblical scribes and the later sages, Jewish families for ages have come together each year at Passover to retell and reflect on the biblical narrative. Before they commence, they recite a command: "In every generation, all are obligated to regard themselves as if they personally left Egypt." And as they proceed, they are expected to embellish the narrative with new material, just as the scribes did in the process of creating it.

In the following chapter, we turn our attention to the Palace History, which differs from the People's History by being more statist in its orientation.

FURTHER READING

Assmann, Jan, *Moses the Egyptian*, Harvard University Press, 1998.

DeLapp, Nevada Levi, *Theophanic "Type-Scenes" in the Pentateuch: Visions of YHWH*, Bloomsbury, 2018.

[4] The first line about a wandering Aramean does not presuppose the Family Story; rabbinic interpretation, reflected in retellings for the Passover table, harmonizes this line with the texts from Genesis.

Farber, Zev, *Images of Joshua in the Bible and Their Reception*, De Gruyter, 2016.

Fischer, Irmtraud, "Rahel und Lea bauten ganz Israel auf," in Mark G. Brett and Jakob Wöhrle (eds.), *The Politics of the Ancestors*, Mohr Siebeck, 2018.

Frankel, David, "The Priestly Moses," *TheTorah.com*, 2015, www.thetorah.com/article/the-priestly-moses.

Germany, Stephen, *The Exodus-Conquest Narrative: The Composition of the Non-Priestly Narratives in Exodus-Joshua*, Mohr Siebeck, 2017.

Hunt, Alice, *Missing Priests: The Zadokites in Tradition and History*, T&T Clark, 2006.

Jeon, Jaeyoung, *The Call of Moses and the Exodus Story: A Redactional-Critical Study in Exodus 3–4 and 5–13*, Mohr Siebeck, 2013.

Leuchter, Mark and Farber, Zev, "Pre-Biblical Aaron, Miriam, and Moses," *TheTorah.com*, 2020, www.thetorah.com/article/pre-biblical-aaron-miriam-and-moses.

Pritchard, James B., *Ancient Near Eastern Texts Relating to the Old Testament*, 3rd ed., Princeton University Press, 1969.

Schmid, Konrad, *Genesis and the Moses Story: Israel's Dual Origins in the Hebrew Bible*, Eisenbrauns, 2010.

Shectman, Sarah, *Women in the Pentateuch: A Feminist and Source-Critical Analysis*, Sheffield Phoenix, 2009.

Tuchman, Shera Aranoff and Rapoport, Sandra E., *Moses' Women*, KTAV, 2008.

18

Hannah and Samuel

The Palace History

Where now is your king that he may save you in all your cities,
And your judges to whom you said, "Give me a king and princes"?
I gave you a king in my anger, and I took him away in my wrath.
– Hosea 13:10–11

HANNAH IS MARRIED TO MAN who has a second wife. She is also barren, and the second wife cruelly taunts her for it. Her husband, who loves her more than her rival, tries to comfort her: "Am I not more to you than ten sons?" Hannah does not agree, and she fervently prays for a child. Her plea is answered, a boy is born, and she names him Samuel (a name that plays on the deity "hearing" her entreaty). Celebrating her triumph, she intones a lengthy hymn, which begins:

My heart exults in Yhwh,
and my horn is exalted in Yhwh.
My mouth derides my enemies,
because I rejoice in your salvation.
– 1 Samuel 2:1

This song, which is echoed in Mary's Magnificat from the New Testament, extols Yhwh's power to bring down the mighty and raise the lowly. Yet in contrast to the Magnificat, it also concludes by praising the strength that Yhwh "will give his king," reflecting Hannah's premonition that her son will be closely involved in the rise of the nation's monarchy.

"The boy Samuel continued to grow both in stature and in favor with Yhwh and with the people" (1 Samuel 2:26). Eventually he becomes a judge and prophet. The only other figure who served in both roles is Deborah, and like her, Samuel rescues the nation from its enemies. Yet in contrast to Deborah, Samuel attempts to establish a dynasty by passing on his authority to his own progeny.

His sons turn out to be corrupt, and in response the nation's elders approach him and demand that he anoint a king to rule in their stead: "You are old, and your sons do not follow in your ways. Give us a king to govern us, like other nations!" The petition angers Samuel, and he goes to Yhwh for support. The response he receives, though, is not what he wanted: "Listen to the people's voice in all that they say to you. They have not rejected you, but they have rejected me from being king over them" (1 Samuel 8:5–7).

Their punishment will be the granting of their wish. As the account continues, Samuel anoints Saul and establishes the monarchy. Eventually, the throne is passed from Saul to David before it crumbles into two competing kingdoms: the Northern state of Israel and the Southern state of Judah. When is all is said and done, both have been conquered and their inhabitants exiled to foreign lands.

The story of Hannah and her son Samuel introduces the Palace History. In what follows, we explore how the Southern scribes responsible for this work presented a very different perspective of their ancestors' origins than the People's History that we studied in the preceding two chapters. Our treatment will also consider how later generations revised this work in the wake of the Judah's catastrophic defeat.

THE PEOPLE'S HISTORY VERSUS THE PALACE HISTORY

Part I devoted a lot of space to the Palace History, as it relates more directly than the People's History to the rise and fall of the Northern and Southern kingdoms. As readers will recall, the Palace History originated in the Southern kingdom, which survived the conquest of its Northern rival by some 130 years. In contrast to the People's History, this work makes the monarchy central to the nation's history.

The Palace History presents Israel as a people indigenous to the central hill country, the core territory of the later Northern and Southern kingdoms. The nation had long faced oppression: from the Philistines (to the west) and the Ammonites (to the east). The first sections of this work portray two royal figures, Saul and David, "saving" their people from these foes and, in the process, establishing a centralized state.

In contrast to the Palace History, the People's History began as the work of Northern scribes who reacted to this statist agenda by removing the monarchy from the most important periods in the nation's past. As it was expanded in each generation (and later by Southern scribes after Judah's defeat), this work maintained its focus on Israel as a people without a palace. There is a king, but it is Yhwh.

The Palace History has a clear agenda. Focusing on the political unification of two kingdoms under the Davidic dynasty in Jerusalem, its authors created a momentous, even if it short-lived, memory of a "United Monarchy." In this way, they identified the status quo – the existence of two kingdoms – as the tragic rupture of an earlier unity. This political division is the nation's "original sin."

By depicting David's dealings with such figures as Saul, Jonathan, Michal, Joab, and Absalom, the Palace History beckons the defeated population of the former Northern kingdom "back" to the dynasty that Yhwh had long ago chosen to rule his people. Only this royal line had divinely sanctioned authority over "all Israel," and by breaking away from Jerusalem, the Northern kingdom had broken faith with the nation's deity. Now that Assyria had deported these secessionist kings, populations of the North could finally return and embrace the divinely chosen dynasty ruling in the Southern capital (for more on this point, see Chapters 6 and 7).

The People's History goes much further. In the place of a political union forming a United Monarchy, it posits a national unity of one people. The book of Genesis traces the many regions and populations from both North and South to a single family, and its account of the exodus promotes a common kinship, even if it is not strictly genealogical as in Genesis. Later supplements expand the sense of kinship with a written pact (i.e., the covenant that Yhwh ratifies with the Israelites at Sinai), making it the foundation and framework for the nation's existence. If the "original sin" in the Palace History is a political division that results in two competing kingdoms, in the People's History it is when the Israelites breach the covenant by worshipping a golden calf. This was a dissolution of the direct bond between Yhwh and the nation. When Yhwh threatens to destroy the nation and replace it with another, Moses mediates on Israel's behalf and convinces Yhwh to restore a relationship with Israel (Exodus 32–34).

Instead of a pact between Yhwh and the entire nation, the Palace History features a divine promise to an individual ruler and his dynastic line – the so-called Davidic Covenant (2 Samuel 7; see Chapter 21). Older portions of the Palace History betray ignorance of the basic themes and characters of the People's History. Saul and David know nothing about Abraham and Sarah, Isaac and Rebekah, or Moses and Miriam. Later generations made dramatic changes to the Palace History, integrating themes from the People's History. Yet even with the editorial changes, it is easy to see how this work began at odds with the People's History, and the two must have been transmitted separately for generations before scribes brought them together to form a larger narrative.

THE PALACE HISTORY AS THE POINT OF DEPARTURE

The People's History consists, as we saw, of two parts: the Family Story of Genesis and the Exodus-Conquest Account. At the heart of the Family Story are traditions related to Isaac, Esau, and Jacob; they likely originated before the downfall of the Northern kingdom in 722 BCE but were clearly reworked – from both Northern and Southern perspectives – for centuries thereafter. Early additions to the Exodus-Conquest Account, which also began as a Northern product, appear to know, and respond directly to, the Palace History.[1] The authors of this account were likely reacting to propaganda from the royal court in Jerusalem, where some likely found employment after 722 BCE.

The Palace History calls the defeated population of the North to rally around the Davidic dynasty and acknowledge Jerusalem as the capital for "all Israel." Many parts disparage and denigrate the North. This work even gloats over this kingdom's destruction and deportation, presenting

[1] See, for example, my comments in the following chapter on the tension between Yhwh and monarchs "saving" the nation.

its fate as the inevitable outcome of its rulers' refusal to accept the dynasty and place that Yhwh had chosen to rule the nation.

Northerners would have undoubtedly viewed these messages as shameless, and callous, self-promotion by the Davidic dynasty, and thus the Palace History had an unintended effect: it provoked Northern scribes to compose a counter-narrative that portrays Israel becoming a nation, being liberated from bondage, and taking possession of its homeland long before any king – Davidic or otherwise – mounted the throne.

The first authors of the Exodus-Conquest Account may have been writing in response to earlier Northern monarchic accounts. The palace in Samaria had likely commissioned and collected tales of their royal ancestors saving the nation from foreign aggressors, such as we see in Saul story (1 Samuel 11). Whatever the case may be, the pro-Davidic writings of Southern scribes would have added fuel to the fire as Northern scribes were envisioning and embellishing a past during which Yhwh, not a human king, saved the nation from slavery and brought it to a new land.

In the final decades of the Southern kingdom, many could see the writing on the wall: Judah too would soon experience the same fate as its former Northern competitor. Having long insisted on Judean exceptionalism, Southern scribes were now more sympathetic with the principle that guided the work of Northern scribes after 722 BCE – that the monarchy does not connect the present to the past, and as a late development, this institution is not indispensable to Israel's identity.

When telling the story of Israel's origins, Northern scribes had consciously excluded the South. Thus, as noted in the preceding chapter, the newly liberated nation skirts the region of Judah when it migrates from Egypt, and it enters the Promised Land at Jericho, which lay at the southern border of the Northern kingdom. (Most scholars now agree that the book of Joshua did not originally report the conquest of the South.)

After the South experienced the defeat that its Northern competitor had suffered more than a century earlier, Southern scribes embraced the People's History and made space in it for Judah. Indeed, their new editions of this work assigned the South a preeminent place. Thus, a late passage in the Pentateuch presents the spies infiltrating the Promised Land from the South and discovering, in the Judean hill country, that "the land does indeed flow with milk and honey" (Numbers 13:27). That the nation does not immediately march up and take possession of the South, as the Judean hero Caleb recommends, and ends up entering the Promised Land from the Transjordan just north of Judah's border (as portrayed in the earlier Northern editions of the People's History) is declared to be an egregious sin against Yhwh.

PRESERVING THE PALACE HISTORY

This literary evolution prompts a basic question: as Southern scribes adopted the People's History and amplified it with their own traditions and representative figures, why did they not just jettison their own Palace History? After all, the perspectives of these two works are hardly compatible: one promotes the palace as the prime mover in the nation's past, while the other champions the cause of the people and rubs out any role for the monarchy.

The foregoing discussion points us to one of the most basic reasons: the reader cannot appreciate the nuances of these rival works without interpreting them in tandem. Over the centuries, Southerners came to see themselves as members of the people of Israel. As they did, the People's History became a prehistory and preamble to the older Palace History, with the People's History furnishing a framework for the most formative stories as well as collections of divinely revealed laws.[2]

The literary lopsidedness does a good job of obscuring the historical sequence. Traditional interpreters have usually read the Palace History as a sequel to, and commentary on, the Pentateuch (the first five books of the People's History). While this approach is at odds with the original historical sequence, it is in keeping with the later editorial intention: the narrative of the rise and fall of the two kingdoms demonstrates how the nation failed to live up to the potential that the Pentateuch envisions for it.

The duality of peoplehood and palace lies at the heart of the biblical story, with primacy given to the former. One must not give up hope that the nation will not always have to live in fear and that one day it would

[2] There are other key motivations to consider. Southern scribes insisted that Jerusalem had to be recognized as the nation's capital. Likewise, many of the psalms and prophetic writings hold out hope for the monarchy, assigning an important role to the Davidic dynasty in the nation's future.

"dwell in safety (see 1 Kings 4:25/5:5). But in the meantime, it had to learn to survive in an often-hostile world, with non-native kings ruling over them. It may no longer have a palace, but thanks to this new project of peoplehood, it now had something more essential and enduring.

Christian theologians often speak of the tension between "the already" and "the not yet," that is between the Kingdom of God inaugurated by the death and resurrection of Jesus Christ, and the full form of his divine rule that awaits his return. We can trace the roots of this tension to the duality of peoplehood and palace in Jewish scriptures: national liberation and native sovereignty are still options, but they are postponed to a future messianic age – and in the process, also redefined.

To take one example, Second Isaiah identifies the messianic ruler with the Persian ruler Cyrus, who liberates the exiles ("sets the captives free") and permits them to return to their homeland in the "new exodus" (see Isaiah 61). This liberation is very different from the first exodus: the Persian kings are still in control; the returning exiles do not reconquer their homeland; and a Davidic ruler does not mount the throne. The restoration of the political conditions that the nation once enjoyed is delayed, and this delay makes room for it to pursue a different path, following the roadmap for its future unfurled in the People's History.

These efforts to both postpone and redefine national liberation are closely connected to how the final authors of the Palace History subordinated their work to the People's History. In what follows, we examine two major editorial moves: 1) the humanizing of kingship, and 2) the framing of the nation's experience with the monarchy as just one, late chapter in a much longer story.

HUMAN, ALL TOO HUMAN

It is easy cast aspersions on the way rulers in the ancient world advertised success in word, image, and public performance. While we might be tempted to disparage their motives as egotistical and self-serving, we also need to recognize that to *be* a leader in the ancient world, one had to *behave* like one. By performing their role with self-assurance, sovereigns accrued the "symbolic capital" that is indispensable to effective rule. Without prestige and status, one can hardly develop the moral authority to influence group decisions, for good or ill. For any leader, but especially for an ancient monarch, a deficit of moral authority increases the chance of failure. And such failure is not in the interest of a community whose members need reliable leadership as they mobilize for collective action.

In their inscriptions and visual images, monarchs who ruled both great empires and small kingdoms portrayed themselves as immutable, stolid and stoic, fearless in the face of attack. Their courts made great efforts to evade the messy details of how they rose to power. Sometimes questions about their right to rule obliged them to acknowledge their disputed origins. But when doing so, they usually elided the less flattering facts by claiming that the deity had placed them on the throne.

Kings are ideally self-sufficient. Thus, the pharaohs of New Kingdom Egypt are portrayed advancing against Canaanite cities alone in their chariots, without drivers or weapons-bearers, and with the reins tied around their waists – a hazardous technique that was never actually practiced. A literary counterpart to this image of a larger-than-life, completely self-reliant ruler is the victory song of Ramses II (the so-called Kadesh Battle Poem). In it, the pharaoh begins: "No officer was with me, no charioteer / No soldier of the army, no shield bearer." He goes on to describe how everyone abandoned him and how he charged out alone to confront the enemy. After achieving extraordinary feats with the special assistance of his god Amun, both the enemy and his own army praise his name. Similarly, the Kushite ruler Piye/Piankhi (late eighth century) recounts how his troops declared their allegiance with a series of self-effacing statements:

It is your name that gives us power . . .
Your bread strengthens our bodies along the way.
Your beer quenches our thirst.
Your bravery gives us strength.
For everyone trembles at the mention of your name.
No army has success . . .
Who is thy equal therein?
Thou art a victorious king, achieving with his hands.[3]

[3] Translations of these Egyptian texts are adapted from J.H. Breasted, *Ancient Records of Egypt*, Kessinger, 2006.

Most societies in the ancient Near East viewed kingship as something divine, handed down from heaven at the beginning of time (see discussion of the Sumerian King's List in the following chapter). Possessing superhuman qualities, kings were created in the image of the gods.

This monarchic ideology is not foreign to biblical literature. For example, some of the psalms present the king as blameless, fighting alone, and benefitting from an exceptional union with the deity. Psalm 2 is a representative example:

> I will tell of the decree. Yhwh said to me:
> "You are my son –
> today I have given birth to you.
> Ask me, and I will make the nations your inheritance,
> the ends of the earth your possession.
> You will break them with a rod of iron,
> dash them to pieces like a potter's vessel."
> –Psalm 2:7–9

Research on this psalm and others like it have demonstrated their complexity and how they nuance earlier notions. (In Chapter 28, we will see how an early "messianic" edition of the Psalter made place for new versions that promote Torah-focused piety.) Yet even with their multiple layers and new frameworks, the Psalter celebrates the monarchy with an enthusiasm that has been muted in the Palace History.

Thanks to the edits and embellishments of later generations, the Palace History portrays even the nation's greatest kings as flawed and fallible figures. The first figures to wear the crown, Saul and David, are thoroughly human – indeed the most human of all biblical characters. By depicting the long, politically embarrassing, bloodstained paths they traverse on their way to the throne, the Palace History demystifies the monarchy, directly undercutting its pretensions of sacrality and self-sufficiency. Moreover, as the king often embodies hegemonic masculinity, these didactic tales also eliminate self-reliance as an essential element of manhood.

The scene of David single-handedly taking down the giant Goliath reminds us of the expressions of monarchic self-sufficiency that we witness from the reigns of Ramses and Piye. However, the final authors of the Palace History made many changes to the story, and in one of them, David proclaims to Goliath: "You come to me with sword and spear, but I come to you in the name of Yhwh" (1 Samuel 17:45). Likewise, these authors went to great lengths to attribute David's own name and fame to the work of others. They include both the women of Israel, who as the nation's memory-makers pave his way to the throne (see Chapter 23), and the nation's deity, who promises "to make your name great like the name of all the great ones on earth" (2 Samuel 7:9).

Notably, the tale of David's triumph over Goliath is positioned at the beginning of his career; the stories of the later years of his reign are much less complimentary. Indeed, they include perhaps one of most penetrating political exposés ever penned: a lengthy account in which David sends off "all Israel" to fight an illicit, imperialistic war, while he enjoys the comforts of the palace and sleeps with the wife of one of his foreign soldiers, whom he later has killed. The account concludes with the general of the army calling the vainglorious ruler to the battlefront at the final moment of victory so that he can take credit for the army's triumph (see Chapter 25).

Works of drama from early modernity scrutinize political affairs and institutions at a time before newspapers began to publish exposés. Thus, Shakespeare took the greatest rulers in the English imagination and revealed their all-too-human qualities. The authors of the Palace History did the same for their most celebrated monarchs, reworking older texts and composing new ones that provide behind-the-scenes glimpses of them in action. By detailing these rulers' ambitions and failures, they challenged older palace propaganda. In their account, venerated heroes like David bring security to the nation but also inflict unprecedented bloodshed on it. The scribes who created these memories were not denying the legitimacy or importance of the monarchy; their objective was rather to cut it down to size and subject it to scrutiny.[4]

[4] Whereas the Palace History paints an often-unflattering image of royal heroes and is not reluctant to declare that "the emperor has no clothes," the People's History goes much further, denying the monarchy any part in the most formative periods of the nation's past.

CONQUERED BY ONE'S OWN

We have seen now how authors of the Palace History revised their work in line with the People's History by reimagining kingship and ripping the rug out from under any pretension of sacrality or self-sufficiency. Let us now consider how some went a step further. By demarcating the monarchy as a discrete epoch in their narrative and adding new layers of reflection, these scribes embraced the point of departure for the People's History: the affirmation that the nation existed and thrived long before this institution was established and that it also could survive without it.

The Palace History originally argued for the Davidic dynasty as the point of unity for the entire nation, encompassing both North and South. As they reshaped the contours of this work, scribes placed speeches in the mouth of the prophet Samuel that present the monarchy as a sharp break from a long pre-monarchic past.

As we saw at the beginning of this chapter, Samuel's story begins with his mother Hannah celebrating the nation's deity as one who "gives strength to his king and exalts the horn of his anointed one" (1 Samuel 2:10). In keeping with this pro-monarchic stance, older parts of this story present Samuel as a "seer" who anoints Saul in keeping with Yhwh's wishes. As the stories of Saul and David were synthesized, Yhwh regrets this choice and instructs Samuel to anoint David in Saul's stead (see I Samuel 15–16). Samuel's remembered role as the nation's first kingmaker – one who assisted Yhwh in "bringing low and raising up," in the words of his mother's song – made him an ideal mouthpiece for later generations to voice their opposition not only to Saul, but, eventually, to the institution of the monarchy itself.

In the chapter preceding the nation's initial petition for a king, Yhwh intervenes in a battle with the Philistines, thundering from heaven and "confusing" the enemy (1 Samuel 7). This divine discombobulation of Israel's enemies is reported in the accounts of momentous, earlier battles in which Yhwh directly fights on Israel's behalf (see, e.g., Joshua 10:10), and it is not coincidental that the same action is portrayed at this pivotal point in the narrative. After the victory, Samuel erects a monument that he names *Ebenezer* or "Stone of Help," and he explains the name: "For thus far Yhwh has helped us." This monument marks a "place of memory" (*lieu de mémoire*), to borrow a concept from the French sociologist Pierre Nora: it exists not only on the geographical border to which the biblical account refers, but also on the narrative border that the biblical authors are delineating here.

Despite their success fighting directly under Yhwh's aegis, in the next chapter the people voice their desire for a king who "will march out at our head and fight our battles."[5] Yhwh recognizes that it implies a rejection of his role, yet he accedes to the nation's demands. Even so, he instructs Samuel to warn the nation about the dramatic societal changes it would undergo as it relinquished the deity's direct ("theocratic") rule in favor of human kingship:

> This will be manner of the king who will reign over you:
> He will take your sons to serve in his chariots, to be his horsemen, and to run before his chariots.
> He will appoint for himself commanders of thousands and commanders of fifties, and some to plow his ground and to reap his harvest, and to make his implements of war and the equipment of his chariots.
> He will take your daughters to be perfumers and cooks and bakers.
> He will take the best of your fields, vineyards, and olive orchards, and give them to his courtiers.
> He will take one-tenth of your grain, and of your vineyards, and give it to his officers and his courtiers.
> He will take your male and female slaves, and the best of your cattle and donkeys, and put them to his work.
> He will take one-tenth of your flocks.
> Indeed, all will be his slaves.
> In that day you will cry out because of your king, whom you have chosen for yourselves. But Yhwh will not answer you in that day.
> – 1 Samuel 8:11–18

This text parses out the *modus operandi* of ancient monarchies, which taxed property and conscripted bodies. The problem is not that the

[5] As noted in the opening to this chapter, the ostensible reason for this desire is the corruption among Samuel's sons whom he – flouting a charismatic, non-dynastic pattern of leadership – had appointed as his heirs.

centralized state will eventually fail to live up to its potential; no, the mere establishment of the monarchy, and the social transformation that it sets in motion, already inflicts suffering on the nation. Long before the onslaught of imperial armies, conquest and exile will begin already at home when their own kings seize their sons for their armies, their daughters for the royal household, and their lands, vineyards, and olive orchards to remunerate his administration. Private slaves will now have to work for the palace, and indeed all will be bondservants to the throne. Today the people desperately want a king "that we may be like the other nations," but when they get what they want, they will cry out to Yhwh.

Samuel's address links the birth of the monarchy closely to the formation of a professional fighting force that is armed with chariots.[6] The People's History, in contrast, assigns the task of defense to all members of the nation. Imagining a rich and formative past before the establishment of the monarchy, that work envisions what today we would call a militia or "citizen army," one that is voluntary and organized ad hoc on the eve of military conflict. Whereas Samuel describes the palace conscripting a standing army, the People's History portrays all able-bodied men mobilizing to fight as they repeatedly face foreign aggression in the wilderness and later when they conquer the Promised Land. (Those who dodge their duties are subjected to public censure.) This militia model is an indispensable feature of the new kingless nation envisioned in the People's History, and now in the Palace History, it is abandoned with the rise of the monarchy.

KINGSHIP AS A COMPROMISE

At the end of his career, Samuel follows the pattern of Moses and Joshua in delivering a farewell address to the nation in which he reviews events recounted in the preceding narrative.[7] The valediction recalls all the times that Yhwh had commissioned someone to "save" the nation from

[6] In keeping with Samuel's speech, chariots were indeed major catalysts of state-centralization in both the Northern and Southern kingdoms (see Chapter 5).

[7] Scholars have long identified these speeches as the work of the scribes who introduced new "Deuteronomistic" accents to an older narrative.

their oppressors. (Samuel is referring here to leaders in the book of Judges, which we treat in the following chapter.) However, when Israel saw the Ammonites coming against them, they inexplicably wanted a king. "You said to me, 'No, but a king shall reign over us,' when Yhwh your God was your king" (1 Samuel 12:12; see the quotation of Hosea at the beginning of this chapter).

Ultimately, Samuel's speech comes to terms with human kingship: "Be sure to fear Yhwh and serve him in truth with all your heart, for consider the great things he has done for you. But if you do wickedly, you will be swept away, you and your king" (1 Samuel 12:24–25). By emphasizing the discontinuity between divine rule and human kings, and by subordinating the monarchy to the nation ("you and your king"), Samuel strips away any pretensions of kings to represent the deity. Kingship is a purely human institution. It is not the ideal, but as a pragmatic political option, it is reluctantly accepted.

The institution of the monarchy poses a threat to the nation's direct, covenantal relationship with its deity, and if it is not essential to Israel's existence, it had to emerge at a particular point in time. In their efforts to deal with the downfall of their kingdoms, the scribes who redacted the Palace History created a discrete epoch that many introductions to the Bible designate the "Inauguration of the Monarchy." These texts are closely related to the book of Judges, and in the following chapter, we will see how that work, like Samuel's speeches, delimits the monarchy, creating an extended era in which non-kings governed the nation.

Historically, the monarchy was the point of departure for both Israel's and Judah's histories, not a radical change from a kingless past. However, the biblical authors relativized the role of the crown. What was once a glorious office – representing a coveted, and divinely sanctioned, role – is now little more than a concession to human foibles and nation's weakness. Moreover, the monarchy comprises a single chapter in the history of the nation, which had emerged and endured for many generations before it charted this new path.[8]

[8] The National Narrative, as a combination of the People's History and the Palace History (see the following chapter), presents the duration of monarchy as shorter than the

The Palace History's view of kingship and statehood – as a compromise with a stubborn and sinful nation – stands, then, in sharp contrast to the ancient, and widely unquestioned, ideology of monarchic statehood. It also runs counter to the views of European thinkers of modernity, such as the German philosopher Hegel who viewed the state as the crown and crest of human history. For the authors of the Palace History, the state has a pragmatic, political purpose to serve. It is a means to an end, and when it becomes an end in itself, it swallows the nation, leaving nothing in its wake: "So all Judah was exiled from its land" (2 Kings 25:21).

THE MONARCHIC MOMENT IN THE NATION'S HISTORY

In the post-destruction period, and especially as their communities began to establish themselves as provinces under foreign rule, the authors of the Palace History recognized that it would be imprudent to raise their communities' hopes in the imminent return of a messianic ruler and the establishment of a new kingdom. Yet instead of discarding their monarchic model, they heavily reworked and reinterpreted it, as we have seen.

The authors of the Palace History still believed that Yhwh had chosen Jerusalem to be his eternal dwelling place. Their account tells of David's conquest of Jerusalem and Solomon's construction of the temple there. These traditions were precious to Judean audiences, especially as Jerusalem competed with Samaria and its temple (see the discussion in Chapters 12–14).

The Palace History held out hope that eventually Yhwh would follow through with his promise to David. The account ends with a Davidic dynast enjoying the favor of the imperial court in Babylon (see the introduction to Chapter 19). Although the empire does not grant him the right to re-establish a kingdom in Judah, many readers would have found grounds for hope in the knowledge that the Davidic line had

people's past that precedes it. In 1 Kings 7:1, this is made explicit when it counts 480 years from the exodus until the building of the temple, a period longer than the duration of the kingdoms; the addition of the many generations from Abraham to the exodus makes the contrast even starker.

survived Babylonian conquest. It may not be any time soon, but perhaps one day Yhwh would raise up a messianic scion to rule over a united nation. This yearning reverberates throughout the Prophets and Psalms, which share with the Palace History a concern for the nation's survival under foreign rule.

In the following chapter, we examine how scribes synthesized the Palace History with the People's History to form the National Narrative, and what themes they chose used to construct continuities across their epic work.

FURTHER READING

Bodner, Keith and Johnson, Benjamin J. M. (eds.), *Characters and Characterization in the Book of Samuel*, T&T Clark, 2019.

Brisch, Nicole (ed.), *Religion and Power: Divine Kingship in the Ancient World and Beyond,* The Oriental Institute, 2012.

Edenburg, Cynthia, "A King Who Reads Torah: What Was Kingship Like in the ANE?," *TheTorah.com*, 2017, www.thetorah.com/article/a-king-who-reads-torah.

Halbertal, Moshe and Holmes, Stephen, *The Beginnings of Politics: Power in the Biblical Book of Samuel*, Princeton University Press, 2017.

Hamilton, Mark W., *A Kingdom for a Stage: Political and Theological Reflection in the Hebrew Bible*, Mohr Siebeck, 2018.

Joseph, Alison, *Portrait of the Kings: The Davidic Prototype in Deuteronomistic Poetics*, Fortress, 2015.

Kipfer, Sara and Hutton, Jeremy M. (eds.), *The Book of Samuel and Its Response to Monarchy*, Kohlhammer, 2021.

Steussy, Marti J., *Samuel and His God*, University of South Carolina Press, 2010.

Wagner-Durand, Elisabeth and Linke, Julia (eds.), *Tales of Royalty: Notions of Kingship in Visual and Textual Narration in the Ancient Near East*, De Gruyter, 2020.

Wilson, Ian D., *Kingship and Memory in Ancient Judah*, Oxford University Press, 2017.

19

Solomon and the Queen of Sheba

The National Narrative

When the Queen of Sheba witnessed Solomon's wisdom,
the house that he had built, the food of his table, the seating of his officials,
the attendance of his servants, their clothing, his cupbearers . . .
she was breathless.

– 1 Kings 10:4–5

IN ITS FIRST CHAPTERS, the book of Kings depicts Solomon's awe-inspiring reign. As it does, it pays special attention to his sumptuous table. More than the throne, the royal table was the place where ancient rulers displayed their success and exercised their sovereignty. During their daily repasts, they negotiated alliances, issued edicts, and performed rituals of kingship.

From her legendary kingdom far away in Arabia, the Queen of Sheba had heard of Solomon's achievements and wisdom. Wanting to test him with riddles, she embarks on a voyage to Jerusalem with a large retinue of servants and camels bearing precious items. Solomon welcomes her arrival, and during her visit they engage in lengthy discussions. Not only Solomon's insight but also his house, and especially his table and all that went along with it, impress her deeply. As she leaves, she showers her host with extravagant gifts: "Never again were spices donated in the amount that Queen Sheba gave King Solomon" (1 Kings 10:10).

From this point, it is all downhill. The reader is forced to watch as the sovereignty that David had established and the opulence that Solomon enjoyed are gradually forfeited to foreign powers. The final paragraphs of the book, and with it a larger narrative stretching back to the creation of the world, revisits the scene of royal feasting. Yet now the tables have turned: the host is a foreign ruler, and the hosted is David and Solomon's defeated descendant.

> King Evel-Merodach of Babylon, in the year that he began to reign, released King Jehoiachin of Judah from prison. He spoke kindly to him and gave him a seat above the other seats of the kings who were with him in Babylon. Thus Jehoiachin was permitted to put aside his prison clothes and dine for the remaining days of his life in the king's presence.
> – 2 Kings 25:27–30

This is a positive turn of events. The preceding paragraphs portray the devastation of Jerusalem and deportation of Judah's population. Now, however, a surviving member of the defeated Davidic dynasty is sitting higher than other vassals while he feasts in the presence of the Babylonian king.

Though this conclusion is hope-filled, the conditions it imagines for Judah's recovery are very different from the age of David and Solomon. Instead of occupying a throne of his own, the Judean monarch sits in a foreign palace, along with other conquered kings. Life goes on, but not as before. Instead of seeking glory on the battlefield, members of this defeated community must carve out a new existence while bearing the yoke of empires.

The present chapter treats the formation of the National Narrative, in which the table-turning epoch of the monarchy represents the final episode. We begin with the book of Judges, which serves as a bridge between the tumultuous monarchic epoch and a pre-monarchic past. We will then consider how the revisionist account in Chronicles erases this prehistory of peoplehood. Finally, we will examine how the authors of the National Narrative used various threads (such as the office of the prophet, the relationship with the national deity, and the Ark of the Covenant) to tie together its many chapters.

THE BOOK OF JUDGES AS A NARRATIVE BRIDGE

In the preceding chapters, we saw how the Family Story in Genesis was originally separate from the Exodus-Conquest Account that follows it.

These two works now form a single narrative; notice how Exodus 1:1 begins *in medias res* with "And these are the names of Israel's sons." When fusing these works to create what I call the "People's History," scribes were careful to preserve their very different emphases and perspectives. However, they had to address a glaring contradiction: whereas the Family Story in Genesis presents Egypt being extraordinarily hospitable to Joseph and his family, the Exodus-Conquest Account presents Egypt as a land of bondage. Our study of the introduction to Exodus (see Chapter 17) revealed how the authors of the People's History reconciled these polarized pictures of Egypt by reporting a regime change, with a new pharaoh in power who "did not know Joseph" (Exodus 1:8).

The subject of the present chapter is the grand National Narrative, which combines the People's History with the Palace History. The People's History ends on a high note, telling how Joshua and the people of Israel successfully conquered the Promised Land and settled there. The Palace History, however, begins in conditions of subjugation, with Israel struggling to achieve hegemony in their homeland, and Saul and David becoming kings as they vanquish the nation's foes.

The book of Judges constructs a narrative bridge between the People's History and the Palace History, and its architects adopted an editorial strategy similar to what we witnessed in the first chapter of Exodus. The book begins by reporting that a "new generation arose" (like the "new king" who "arises" in Exodus 2) after Joshua's death "who did not know Yhwh" (compare the new king in Exodus "who did not know Joseph"). The turning point initiates a downward spiral: Yhwh slowly brings an end to their streak of victories, allowing them to be assailed by foreign aggressors (Judges 2:10–19).

The National Narrative has competing climaxes: on one side, there is a divine liberation from a tyrannical ruler in Egypt, and on the other side, a monarchic liberation from the nation's foes in their homeland. As one can see in the graph on page 305, these competing climaxes are a result of the combination of the two, very different, histories that the authors of the National Narrative achieved through the book of Judges:

While Judges now connects rival accounts of the past, the oldest parts of the book appear to have been drafted as an addendum to the People's

Connecting Competing Accounts

Genesis	Exodus 1	Exodus 2-Joshua	Judges	Samuel-Kings
"The Family Story," which presents a positive image of Egypt.	A **narrative bridge** that tells how Israel now suffers in Egypt after "a new king arose who did not know Joseph." This chapter creates **"The People's History"** (Genesis–Joshua).	**"The Exodus-Conquest Account,"** which concludes with Israel in control of the Promised Land.	A **narrative bridge** that tells how the nation loses control of the Promised Land after a "new generation arose that did not know Yhwh." This book creates **"The National Narrative"** (Genesis–Kings).	**"The Palace History,"** which begins with the nation facing oppression from neighbors in the Promised Land.

History. The stories of Ehud, Deborah, and Gideon present tribes from Israel's core territory fighting together as a nation-in-arms and re-establishing the "rest" from wars that was first achieved during the days of Joshua. The Song of Deborah, as noted in Chapter 3, marks the end of Yhwh's divine reign, which began with his victory at the Red Sea and the Song of Miriam that commemorates it. Thereafter power-hungry males like Gideon and his son Abimelech appear on the scene and have the first dalliances with kingship.

These polemical parables warn the reader about the threat the monarchy poses for Israel's peoplehood. They grew over time and were supplemented with new ones. However, they did not coalesce into a self-standing book until Southern scribes, after the defeat of their kingdom, began to rework the People's History and combine it with Palace History. These same scribes added legends of their own Southern heroes as well as an appendix to the book that polemicizes against the contiguous region of Benjamin.

CASUS BELLI AND THE OFFICE OF JUDGES

The most basic service that kings provided, or at least claimed to provide, was military protection from neighboring enemies. The older Palace

History presents war as a natural political phenomenon and as an inescapable condition of Israel's existence in its land. Thus, when Saul becomes king, he defends a city that the Ammonites had attacked. The enemy ruler just marches up and besieges the town (1 Samuel 11).

The book of Judges demolishes this ideological foundation for the monarchy by identifying a deeper reason for the wars that their ancestors faced. In each episode, the narrator declares that "Israel again did what was evil in the sight of Yhwh," and the deity proceeds to punish the nation by allowing enemies to assault it. If Israel brought war upon itself by failing to follow Yhwh, then its decision to establish a monarchy was gratuitous. By persisting in covenantal faithfulness, it could have avoided military conflict and, consequently, the need for dynastic rule and centralized state. Leaving no room for confusion, the book's authors spelled out the principle at length in the prologue (Judges 2:11–23).

The Palace History presents Saul declaring after his first triumph that Yhwh "had brought salvation to Israel" (1 Samuel 11:13). Similarly, Abner, a former general of King Saul, persuades the nation's elders to accept David as king by appealing to Yhwh's promise to "save" Israel from its enemies through David (2 Samuel 3:18). These texts, and numerous others, affirm Yhwh's acts of saving his people, yet they still assign an indispensable role to the king as the instrument of salvation.

The People's History, in contrast, presents Yhwh saving the nation personally and directly from the Egyptians, without a king as his representative. As the authors of Judges expanded this narrative, they invented the non-monarchic office of "judge." This office performs the royal task of rescuing Israel from her enemies, but its incumbents do so without becoming kings or establishing institutions of centralized rule such as a professional army. When going to war, the ideal judges muster all the nations' members, who fight as "citizen soldiers" and thereafter resume their regular duties on their family estates. Because these leaders do not command a corps of professional fighters funded by taxation, their societies are not transformed by strong class divisions (see discussion of Samuel's first speech in the preceding chapter). And because war is a consequence of collective sin (rather than a natural, perennial phenomenon), it does not require a king and standing army.

As they constructed this past, the authors of Judges were not attempting to lay out a practicable plan for their people's future. Military conflict was not a situation that their communities could avoid simply by being faithful to Yhwh, just as the office of the judge was not a feasible political option. The making of this narrative must be appreciated as an intellectual (and historiographical) effort to imagine a national past without the palace.

The final chapters of Judges describe military conflict, yet now instead of facing foreign aggression, the tribes have turned against each other in civil war. The narrator repeatedly punctuates the episodes with a refrain: "in those days there was no king in Israel," which sometimes continues with "everyone did what was right in their own eyes." Since the book polemicizes at length against kingship, these statements in the final chapters have long posed a problem for interpreters. But there is an important reason why they appear only here, in the context of social injustice and internal conflict. Their presence affirms, implicitly, that the king's duty is not to accumulate political capital on the battlefield, as the honor-hungry heroes do throughout the book, but rather to defend the oppressed and establish justice in the land.[1]

NARRATIVE SUCCESSION IN JUDGES AND KINGS

In earlier chapters, we have seen how scribes consolidated a diverse political community by connecting the ancestors of various groups (e.g., the patriarchs and matriarchs, Moses, Miriam, Joshua, Aaron). The book of Judges does the same. It is easy to isolate independent stories of men and women who represent various regions, tribes, and clans.

We might compare Judges to nineteenth-century Italian and German historians who constructed narratives of their country's pre-unification periods by connecting independent histories of rival regions, kingdoms, duchies, and city-states. The difference is that the authors of Judges were not combining these histories in the service of an emerging nation-state.

[1] Similarly, the Deuteronomic code discharges the office of all military responsibilities, with his single duty being to make a copy of the Torah and "read it all the days of his life" (Deuteronomy 17:14–20).

On the contrary, they were working after the conquest of their kingdoms, and their objective was to consolidate vanquished, scattered communities as a nation without statehood.

Another feature that distinguishes Judges from European nationalist histories is that the biblical authors arranged their data in a linear narrative, with one judge for each period. Of course, modern histories of Germany and Italy would naturally include parallel narratives, in keeping with the multiplicity of competing powers before unification. Ancient historians, however, could permit themselves more liberties in their narratives. This was especially the case when treating events in their prehistory, as we can see in an important Mesopotamian source.

A major achievement of ancient Mesopotamian historiography, the Sumerian King List (SKL) was transmitted for two millennia and used by Babylonian kings to legitimate their reign. Thanks to archeological discoveries, it can be studied today in several variants. The SKL registers the names and reigns of Mesopotamian rulers, separating the mythical kings who ruled before the flood and those who reigned after it. As in the Bible, the antediluvian heroes enjoy fantastically long lifespans, and it is possible that the SKL was known to biblical scribes.

The SKL begins by identifying the institution of the monarchy as a divine inheritance: "After the kingship descended from heaven, the kingship was in Eridug. In Eridug, Alulim became king; he ruled for 28,800 years." As the SKL continues, it chronicles, one after the other, all the great kings and dynasties in Mesopotamia's history. Similar to the way the book of Judges constructs a sequential narrative from figures who may have been contemporaneous, the SKL aligns rulers in a succession even when they reigned simultaneously. An important study of this source draws attention to the political agenda that shaped it: "The author of [the SKL] worked . . . on the theory that Babylonia was and always had been a single kingdom. Within the country the capital could change from one city to another, but there was never more than one king at a time."[2] In the same way, the linear narrative of Judges assigns one judge to each generation.

[2] Thorkild Jacobsen, *The Sumerian King List*, University of Chicago, 1939, p. 139.

This Mesopotamian source shares structural features with not only Judges but also the biblical book of Kings. Before the Omride dynasty consolidated a state with its capital in Samaria, rival factions vied with each other for control (see Chapter 5). Although the scribes who produced the book of Kings aligned them into a succession, these pre-Omride kings would have reigned simultaneously from competing centers.

While the SKL resembles the succession of rulers in Judges and Kings, things look very different when we compare this source to the larger National Narrative. It would be as if scribes, working over centuries, took the SKL and added to it a much more extensive narrative of a *people*. This was not possible because the SKL commences at the beginning of time, before the flood, when kingship descended from heaven (as in the first line that was just quoted). Human history begins at this point; nothing precedes it.

Over the years, additions were made to the SKL as rulers sought to have their names recorded in these hallowed halls of history. But the changes did little to alter this work's basic structure and ideological profile. In contrast, the National Narrative owes its existence to circles who sought something beyond kingship. As they worked out their ideas on paper, they pushed back the monarchy to make space for stories of families, national liberation, a covenant with a transcendent power by which they became a political community, and non-monarchic figures who governed them long before their ancestors desired a monarchy "like the other nations" (1 Samuel 8:20).[3]

NARRATIVE AS NETWORK

Those who curated the National Narrative not only consolidated a diverse people by connecting rival traditions and groups, but also constructed continuities from their own time to a prehistoric past. These lines of narrative continuity include the office of the prophet, the deity in

[3] Moreover, the authors of Kings amplified the annals by adding older stories and creating new ones. In doing so, they used the chronicles as a framework for didactic tales relevant to the needs of a wider readership.

whose name these prophets speak, the Ark as the symbol of this deity's presence, and the covenant that the nation ends up breaking.

Let us begin here with the prophetic office. Prophets guide the nation long before kings. They warn the nation about the monarchy's pernicious influence on society. They call kings to account for the suffering they repeatedly inflict upon the nation. And last but not least, they survive the monarchy's demise.

Those who constructed this prophetic continuity went to great lengths to avoid identifying the nation's first leaders with kings. While the book of Deuteronomy likens Moses to a prophet, other biblical texts identify him as "Yhwh's servant," his "chosen one," "the man of God" (a prophetic epithet), and a "priest." As for Joshua, he may have been a king or local warlord in the central hill country. However, the biblical memories erase his monarchic features, depicting him as a regicide who executes a vast number of Canaanite kings as he leads a motley crew of migrants to their homeland and establishes a new non-monarchic political order. Whereas Joshua is a king-slayer, Moses stands opposite the pharaoh and other monarchs who rule Israel's enemies. The biblical memories have little if anything to say about the sons of these two leaders. Rather than establishing dynastic lines, what is important is all they achieved in their own lifetimes and for their people's future.

The leaders who follow Moses and Joshua include an array of non-kings, including judges, savior, and prophets. Samuel is depicted as both the last judge and a pivotal prophet. As we saw in the preceding chapter, his primary purpose is to counsel the nation through its transition from a pre-monarchic past to a centralized state. After him, the narrative assigns a righteous prophet to each generation.[4] The book of Ezra-Nehemiah is a sequel to this narrative, and it insistently denies a place to a native monarchy in Judean society. Yet at the same time, it ascribes a central leadership role to prophets: Haggai and Zechariah emerge on the scene and inspire the community, and its leaders, to rebuild their society and the temple.

[4] This depiction led later Jewish and Christian interpreters to assume that one of these prophets wrote each portion of the narrative.

When connecting the People's History and the Palace History, the authors of the National Narrative used not only the prophetic office but also sacred objects, such as the Ark of the Covenant. Built at Sinai, this icon and war palladium accompanies the nation as it migrates to the Promised Land, both at the center of their camp and in battle against their foes along the way. Later David brings it up to Jerusalem after he captures the city and prepares to build the temple (2 Samuel 6).

With this sacred object, scribes charted a path from Mount Sinai to Mount Zion. These two fixed points in the National Narrative correspond to two competing social circles, one that identified with the Torah and the study of texts, and the other that identified with the temple and priestly rituals. The Ark thread in the National Narrative ties them together by telling how Moses deposited the tablets of the Torah in the Ark, and then how later Solomon deposited the Ark containing these tablets in the temple (1 Kings 8).

The Ark represents the divine presence, and more than anything else, it is Yhwh who unifies the National Narrative. In writing the present book, I learned much from the works of Jack Miles and Ilana Pardes. Whereas the former reads the Bible as a biography of God, the latter reads it as a biography of Israel. My own approach blends the two, reading the Bible as the story of a relationship – a tumultuous love affair – between Yhwh and Israel.

A distinctive feature of the National Narrative and wider biblical corpus is the dynamic character of this relationship with Yhwh, who in contrast to Elohim (see discussion in Chapter 10), appears as a distinctively male deity. After creating the world, he is upset with the way things turn out and destroys it in the flood. Later, at the Tower of Babel, he scatters the earth's inhabitants and chooses to focus on one people. Fulfilling promises to their ancestors, he liberates his people from bondage in Egypt and covenants with them at Sinai. The rest of narrative portrays their rocky relationship and its ultimate rupture. As we will see in the next chapter, the prophetic writings pick up the narrative and push it forward, depicting the relationship as a love affair and often as an abusive relationship. While the rupture is portrayed as a breakup, the renewal inaugurates a marriage that is made to last.

Yhwh has a vibrant personality. This is not unusual: most ancient deities had distinctive temperaments. However, what provokes his pathos is not competition with other gods but the behavior of his people. Indeed, their actions preoccupy his attention to a degree like nothing we see in other texts from the ancient world. What the nation does in its collective life – oppressing the downtrodden or caring for the oppressed – determines his disposition between the two poles that define his personality: anger and compassion, justice and mercy.

Like all ancient deities, Yhwh's actions are not always predictable, and his presence is lethal. Thus, when someone tries to save the Ark from slipping off a cart, he is struck dead as if he had touched a high voltage wire (2 Samuel 6:6–7). Yet in contrast to other deities, what curbs Yhwh's caprice are the terms of the covenant, which are ratified at the nation's birth, inscribed in stone, and deposited in the Ark.

Without Yhwh and the covenant, there would be no National Narrative. Both define the contours of the biblical corpus, and in the coming chapters we will explore 1) how the covenant that constrains Yhwh's personality and pathos emerged from prophetic declarations of doom and 2) how it paved the way for the canonical demarcation of the Pentateuch from the Former Prophets (Joshua-Kings) that follow it.[5]

The authors of the National Narrative recognized that their communities would be stronger if they united as one people. This is a basic insight of networking: by joining forces, one has a better chance of success. Hence, these historians connected a wide spectrum of groups in their national project. Admittedly, in building their "narrative network," they eliminated texts and erased memories. Yet the National Narrative is remarkable for its complexity and diversity, and these qualities are the result of an ambitious effort to bring together a wide array of competing traditions.

[5] This continuity-principle is at work in other parts of the biblical corpus – from the story of the sacred vessels that connect various works, through the combination of originally separate figures (such Ezra and Nehemiah, Haggai and Zechariah), to the nationalization of legendary names (e.g., Daniel), to the anchoring of tales like Ruth in the time of the Judges and in the Davidic line. (In Part III, we will see also how Ecclesiastes and Proverbs to Solomon, and the Psalms to David.)

HISTORICAL REVISIONISM IN CHRONICLES AND THE PRIESTLY SOURCE

As so often throughout the biblical corpus, the National Narrative has a competitor, one that, while undoing its most important achievement, assists us in appreciating its aims. This work is the revisionist history of Chronicles, which dates to the late Persian or early Hellenistic period and which we began exploring in Part II.

We have witnessed how Northern scribes set something extraordinary in motion when, after the downfall of their kingdom, they drafted an account of the most pivotal events in their people's past. In this account, Yhwh works through non-kings (such as Miriam, Moses, and Joshua) to liberate his people from foreign bondage and bring them to their homeland. We have also examined how later generations combined this account with older materials related to the patriarchs and matriarchs (e.g., Abraham, Sarah, Isaac, Rebekah, Jacob), creating a prehistory of peoplehood that now precedes the palace.

The new history in Chronicles completely erases this formative past. It begins with Adam. Eve is not mentioned, and the following nine chapters consist of genealogies with the names of men. If women's names occasionally appear, it is because the authors needed to address issues in the genealogy of the (male) descendants.

When a narrative finally begins, the nation already has a king. In contrast to the Palace History, this figure, Saul, achieves nothing and is immediately replaced by David, whose story the authors have thoroughly whitewashed. Chronicles completely expunges everything about how this Judean hero pursued a path to power in Saul's family, how he formed the Southern kingdom by ripping territories from the state Saul creates, how he ordered the execution of the irreproachable Uriah after he had seized and impregnated his wife Bathsheba, how his son Amnon raped his sister Tamar, and how the nation thereafter faced a series of civil wars.

What occasioned Chronicles' revisionist account was a vision of unity, one in which North and South came together around the worship of Yhwh at the temple in Jerusalem. The Davidic dynasty has one and only one purpose to serve: to build, edify, and promote the temple and all that pertains to it, which explains why the book sweeps under the carpet all the crimes and dreadful deeds of the dynasty's founder. The massive surplus of materials in this late book describes David and his most praiseworthy successors taking measures to install the temple's personnel, provide for its sacrificial service, and organize national festivals in which the most remote regions of the nation take part. The work concludes with the throne being transferred to a foreign ruler, the Persian king Cyrus, who decrees the rebuilding of the temple with lines excerpted from the beginning of Ezra-Nehemiah.

In its revisionism, Chronicles resembles the Priestly Source, which originated as a separate retelling of the People's History. Similar to the way Chronicles omits unflattering features in its portrait of David, the authors of the Priestly Source erased many details they deemed unfavorable to their agenda. Thus, when Jacob flees to Laban, it is not because he fears for his life after stealing his brother's birthright, but because his parents fear that he might marry foreign women as his brother does (see Chapter 16). Those who drafted the Priestly Source and later integrated it in the Pentateuch clearly sought to promote the centrality of the Jerusalem temple. (At the center of the account is the tabernacle, which represents the temple's portable precursor.)

For the authors of Chronicles, such integration and supplementation did not suffice, and so they composed an alternative, more straightforward history that replaces Moses and Aaron with David and Solomon as the ones who establish a centralized cult for the nation. We saw in Chapter 12 how Chronicles is much more "pan-Israelite" than the Judah-centric work of Ezra-Nehemiah (which also dates to the late Persian or early Hellenistic period). Even so, its whitewashing of David's life is morally problematic.

TRUTH-TELLING AND MYTH-MAKING

Fictions are often what unite us as communities, as the philosopher and cultural theorist Kwame Anthony Appiah demonstrates in *The Lies That Bind.* What makes us human includes not only our ability to tell each other fables and imagine new futures but also, and especially, our proficiencies in reflecting together on our histories, even if these histories are more fabricated than factual. Of course, not all fictions are not equal. What is morally determinative is that we are honest about our pasts while at the same time finding ways—through stories, music, art, and film—to imagine unifying and liberating futures.[6]

Myths are crucial parts of healthy identities (both individual and collective), and the National Narrative achieves a successful balance between truth-telling and myth-making. Whereas the People's History constructs a mythic past that affirms the unity of the nation, the Palace History scrutinizes the dynasties that tentatively united but ultimately divided this nation. This second part goes all out in offering unflinching exposés of power-hungry monarchs and penetrating analyses of self-serving states.

The People's History provides a parade example of effective myth-making. Addressing a past that begins with the men who ruled over them, this foundational prehistory ends with Deborah, and is populated with women and strategies of survival. The book of Judges depicts a downward spiral from Deborah and a mythic past to the historic past in which men, monarchies, and machoism dominate, bringing destruction in their wake. The People's History takes its point of departure from this destruction and the trauma it inflicted. With its elaborate tales of family life and liberation, this part of the National Narrative has provided communities across the globe with powerful myths through which they have reimagined their identities [own pasts] and embarked on new collective futures.

The National Narrative is a truly remarkable phenomenon, especially for the world of ancient West Asia that, with few exceptions, took kingship for granted and viewed it as something sacred and primordial. This monumental achievement of historiography devotes a disproportionate amount space to a pre-monarchic past, and then it recounts, over a long

[6] Perhaps more than any other genre, children's literature excels in this effort, with its colorful illustrations of curiosity and compassion. Mistakes are made, however, when genres of myth and history are mixed.

stretch of chapters, how a nation makes a conscious decision to embrace the institution of the monarchy and the centralized statehood that it represents. In the following chapter, we examine how Judah's prophetic writings laid the groundwork for this new view of the state and its subordination to the nation.

FURTHER READING

Appiah, Kwame Anthony, *The Lies That Bind: Rethinking Identity*, Liveright, 2018.

Berner, Christoph and Harald Samuel (eds.), *Book-Seams in the Hexateuch I: The Literary Transitions between the Books of Genesis/Exodus and Joshua/Judges*, Mohr Siebeck, 2018.

Frolov, Serge, *Judges*, Eerdmans, 2013.

Janzen, David, *Chronicles and the Politics of Davidic Restoration: A Quiet Revolution*, T&T Clark, 2017.

Japhet, Sarah, *The Ideology of the Book of Chronicles and Its Place in Biblical Thought*, Eisenbrauns, 2009.

Kelle, Brad E. and Brent Strawn (eds.), *The Oxford Handbook of the Historical Books of the Hebrew Bible*, Oxford University Press, 2021.

Levenson, Jon D., *Sinai and Zion: An Entry into the Jewish Bible*, HarperOne, 1987.

Levin, Yigal, *The Chronicles of the Kings of Judah: 2 Chronicles 10–36*, Bloomsbury, 2017.

Marchesi, Gianni, "The Sumerian King List or the 'History' of Kingship in Early Mesopotamia," *The Ancient Near East Today*, IV.11, November 2016.

Milstein, Sara Jessica, *Tracking the Master Scribe: Revision through Introduction in Biblical and Mesopotamian Literature*, Oxford University Press, 2016.

Miles, Jack, *God: A Biography*, Vintage Books, 1995.

Pardes, Ilana, *The Biography of Ancient Israel: National Narratives in the Bible*, University of California Press, 2002.

Römer, Thomas, *The So-Called Deuteronomistic History: A Sociological, Historical and Literary Introduction*, T&T Clark, 2006.

20

Jonah and the Whale

The Prophets as Survival Literature

By decree of the king and his nobles:
Let human and beast be covered with sackcloth,
and let them call out mightily to God.
Let everyone turn from their evil ways,
and from the violence that is in their hands
–Jonah 3:8

ONE DAY YHWH COMMISSIONS A MAN named Jonah to go to Nineveh, capital of the despised Assyrian Empire. We do not know where he comes from or why he is chosen for the mission; all we know is what he is told: "Arise, go to Nineveh, the great city, and cry out against it, for their wickedness has risen up before me." Refusing to accept the assignment, Jonah goes to the local port, buys a ticket, and boards a ship headed in the opposite direction.

Familiar to many from Sunday School, this little book with a big message tells how the deity sent a mighty tempest that brings the ship and its multinational crew to the brink of destruction. Meanwhile Jonah goes below deck and dozes off. Bewildered by his behavior, the sailors wake him, and he instructs them to throw him to the sea to save the ship. When they reluctantly do so, the raging waters subside. In gratitude, the sailors sacrifice and make vows to Yhwh. Unbeknownst to them, a fish had swallowed Jonah and after three days spewed him onto dry land.

When Jonah finally reaches Nineveh and warns its inhabitants about their imminent destruction, the king orders everyone, including their animals, to cry out with all their might and to turn from their evil ways:

"Who knows? Maybe God will change his mind, relent, and turn from his fierce anger. And then we will not perish" (Jonah 3:9).

And such is what happens. Just as he had saved the storm-tossed ship, Yhwh shows mercy to the Assyrians so that disaster is averted. The tale ends with Jonah deeply vexed by the deity's change of mind. All along he had been reluctant to fulfill his commission because he knew that Yhwh is "gracious and compassionate, slow to anger and rich in mercy, and will repent from evil" (Jonah 4:2).

The droll account of a messenger who fears that his message will be heard presents a profound paradox: if the Assyrians had not begged for divine mercy, then they would not have been able, years later, to inflict suffering on Israel and Judah. Likewise, had Israel and Judah behaved like Nineveh and heeded the words of their prophets, they would have escaped the divine judgment that the Assyrians executed.

Repentance and mercy – many deem these to be the central teachings of the Bible's prophetic writings. While Jonah may support this impression, this book is an outlier, in both form and content. The prophets elsewhere announce that Yhwh had already resolved to punish his people. Indeed, he had determined to make an end of them, and there was no going back. All that remained for his messengers was to spell out the reasons for the dreadful decree.

In what follows, we will see that the first and primary purpose of the prophets was not to avert a future disaster, but to explain devastating trauma in the nation's past – the fall of the Northern and Southern kingdoms. The prophetic writings are works of theodicy: they provide elaborate justifications for the judgment that Yhwh had meted out to his people. These justifications laid the foundation for a powerful, new political theology of covenant. And as we shall see in the following, and final, chapter of Part III, this political theology transformed both the structure and character of the National Narrative.

PROPHETIC PERSONALITIES

The prophetic writings constitute literature in the fullest sense. Shaped for the reader and the pleasure of reading, they are also profoundly didactic. Older oracles are embedded in elaborate poetic discourses that have long inspired social activism. Some of these works include accounts of the prophets' lives, with their trials and tribulations mirroring both Yhwh's pathos and his people's plight. For example, the book of Jeremiah dwells at length on the burden of the prophet's commission: his battles with his peers, his imprisonment and trial, and his escape and sojourn in Egyptian exile. The experiences are portrayed with both dramatic sensibility and psychological poignancy.

When studying the origins of prophetic literature, scholars have long focused on the prophets' personalities, and today many persist in describing these figures as morally intuitive, inspired individuals who rise up against their societies – and especially the elites of these societies – with their penetrating social, political, and cultic critiques. Christian theologians often view their sermons and calls for "repentance" as predecessors to Jesus' teachings. When accounting for the transition from prophetic personality to prophetic book, many assume that "disciples" faithfully preserved the sacred, spoken words and symbolic actions of their teacher.

With roots in the Great Man Theory that shaped much of nineteenth-century historiography, this approach is not unique to biblical scholars who work on prophetic literature. As we saw in the first chapter of Part III, it has informed how many explain the existence of extensive narrative works, such as the writings of "the Yahwist" and "the Deuteronomist." If some today are searching for alternative explanations, it is because studies from the past several decades have drawn attention to literary subtleties and a scribal finesse that belie a simplistic stenographic scenario.

Yet there is a more basic problem with the conventional, personality-driven approach to prophetic writings, and it is one that scholars could have confronted long before the recent literary turn in research: In Israel and Judah there had always been injustices and the need for reform, just as much as in any other society. Things did not suddenly take a turn for the worse right before the demise of these two kingdoms. Why then are the earliest prophetic texts set in the time of their downfall and thereafter? Could the composition process not have begun earlier?

The Palace History refers frequently to prophets in the reigns of the first kings. Thus, the book of Kings features lengthy accounts of two prophets, Elijah and Elisha, from the reign of the Omrides (see

Chapters 5 and 6). But why do we not have any works called "Elijah" and "Elisha" like our books Isaiah and Jeremiah? Moreover, the book of Kings reports sundry activities of Elijah's and Elisha's followers (called "sons of the prophets"), recounting for example how they had to build a bigger place for themselves, how one of the followers lost the head from his ax in the Jordan River when felling trees to build the new place, and how Elisha threw a stick in the water to magically make the metal float. Charming. But it is also telling that we never hear of members of this community collecting oracles and composing texts.

What a prophet happened to have said on a particular occasion, to a specific group, and in response to a concrete problem, is hardly relevant to future generations. Which is why prophecies from the first centuries of the Northern and Southern kingdoms did not evolve into prophetic writings. And why should they have? There was not an existential crisis that would have catalyzed this corpus of didactic literature. (Thus, the Palace History portrays Elisha anointing a new king to replace the Omride dynasty, not proclaiming the downfall of the entire Northern kingdom.) However, oracles delivered closer to the time of defeat had a different potential. The words themselves were not fundamentally different from earlier exhortations, but now scribes could put them to new use as they came to terms with their collective trauma.

FROM SALVATION TO DAMNATION

Older materials that we can isolate in the prophetic corpus include oracles of deliverance (e.g., Isa 8:1–4), laments (e.g., Jer 4:7, 4:13, 4:19–21; 6:1, 6:22–23), polemics related to political and social corruption (e.g., Hos 6:7–9, Amos 3:12, 5:7; 6:2–6), and announcements of punishment for elites (e.g., Amos 3:13, 5:2, 5:3, 5:18–19, Micah 1:10–15, Zeph. 1:14–16). Some of the earliest texts prophesy punishment for the Northern kingdom. Israel's bane meant Judah's boon, and therefore, from the perspective of the South, these were not prophecies of judgment but promises of salvation.

Later generations augmented the older oracles so that Judah shares the fate of its Northern neighbor. Thus, in the context of the Syro-Ephraimite War (see Chapter 6), Isaiah 8:1–4 proclaims the conquest of Damascus and Samaria – the capitals of the Aramean and Northern kingdoms that had long been the biggest players in the Southern Levant. Isaiah delivers this oracle in support of Judah when the kingdom was facing a coalition between Israel and the Arameans. But a supplement in vv. 5–8 expands the judgment to include Judah itself:

And Yhwh spoke to me further, saying, . . .
"Then it will sweep on into Judah,
It will overflow and pass through,
It will reach even to the neck;
And the spread of its wings will fill the breadth of your land.

The earlier portion of this prophecy (in vv. 1–4) works within the system (promising peace for the Southern kingdom), and in this respect, Isaiah's words correspond to what we witness in other older oracles. Some of these sayings may have been recorded and deposited in palace and temple archives. But they would never have evolved into prophetic books if later generations had not made the pivotal move to interpret their declarations of doom in terms of a larger political demise, with the kingdom of Judah facing the same fate as its Northern rival.

The declarations of doom are often succinct, as when Amos announces on Yhwh's behalf: "The end has come for my people Israel; I will spare them no longer" (8:2). More often, though, they are lengthier and more elaborate, as in Jeremiah's description of a disaster that engulfs the entire land:

I looked at the land: it was unformed and void;
and at the sky: it had no light.
I looked at the mountains: they shook;
all the hills moved back and forth.
I looked, and there was no human being;
all the birds in the air had fled.
I looked, and the fertile fields were a desert;
all the land's cities were razed to the ground.
– Jeremiah 4:23–26

With its gut-wrenching impressions of "the day after," and its images of the ecological impact of an empire's military campaigns, this poem probably began as a public lament. It describes the undoing of creation (notice the similar language in the creation account of Genesis 1), and communities would have performed it in response to the catastrophe that had already engulfed them (see Chapter 9). However, in the book of Jeremiah, it functions as a vision of Judah's imminent downfall.

Without such specters of disaster and straightforward declarations that Yhwh was finished with his people, we would not have a body of prophetic writings in the Bible. And the reason is simple: pronouncements of unconditional judgment prompted a deeper question: Why? What have we done to deserve destruction? To justify the divine decree, the authors of our books augmented older oracles to show how the nation had long persisted in its ways, testing Yhwh's patience and provoking his wrath.

THE BIRTH OF A NEW ORDER

Pronouncements that Yhwh was finished with his people, and that there was no going back, not only provided the point of departure for the formation of the prophetic corpus but also laid the groundwork for a new political-theological order.

If the nation's relationship with Yhwh had now been rent asunder, as the prophetic writings proclaim, when, and how, did the two parties come together in the first place? In ancient West Asia, gods were tied by primordial bonds to their lands and to the inhabitants of those lands. Their alliances emerged naturally, in the twilight of history. The same goes for Yhwh and Israel. The Bible, however, lays out an elaborate account of the origins and history of their relationship, as we have seen in the preceding chapters of Part III.

For the kingdoms of Israel and Judah, like for all other ancient Levantine states, each member and institution was expected to do its part to maintain the natural and social order. The palace, the army, temples, priests, prophets, and not least the deity all worked together to keep the ship afloat. The system was designed to weather many storms. But what it could not cope with was unmitigated defeat and destruction.

Here we can appreciate the staggering scope of the biblical project. When foreign armies had conquered their kingdoms, scribes collaborated over time and space to fashion a new form of community that no army could undo. And the most groundbreaking step they took was to proclaim the rupture of the relationship between Yhwh and his people.

Everything we know from non-biblical sources about prophets and diviners are what we would call *system-immanent*: they worked within a widely shared and longstanding political-theological framework of monarchic statehood. The same can be said for references to prophets in archeological finds from ancient Israel and Judah; they are not essentially different from what we observe among their neighbors (see Lachish Letter 3 discussed in Chapter 14).

Likewise, biblical memories of the early years of the monarchy present prophets working within the system, reprimanding rulers or opposing particular dynasties but affirming (even if only implicitly) the status quo of statehood. In contrast, the biblical books of Amos, Hosea, Isaiah, Jeremiah, and so on are *system transcendent*. By pronouncing the end of Yhwh's relationship with his people, these writings declare the demise of statehood, along with its ancient ideological foundation.

Yes, deities throughout ancient West Asia could become angry with their peoples and punish them with warfare and exile. Such is what we find in the Mesha Stele from Moab (see Chapters 5 and 15). Gods could also abandon their peoples. Assyrian propaganda was especially fond of this idea: in numerous texts, we hear the deities of the defeated voluntarily joining the side of their people's opponents. In these cases, however, it is the conqueror who makes such claims. How the conquered explained their fate is difficult to say; we have very few texts from them.

Nowhere, though, do we find the kinds of messages of unconditional judgment, of doom and disaster, that pervade the Bible's prophetic corpus. In these writings, we witness the conquered themselves claiming that their deity had decreed their end, introducing an abrupt break in the nation's history.

Something completely new emerges after this rupture: history becomes relevant and important. The relationship between the nation and its deity is now said to have been established at a particular point in the past, in a formal way, and with written terms clearly defining the terms of the partnership. This is the pact that the people ratify with Yhwh after their exodus from Egypt, and its terms are found in the laws of the Pentateuch. These laws, and their covenantal framework, replaced the primordial, and unstated, rules that governed the existence of ancient kingdoms. And as we shall see in the next chapter, these laws are the sinew connecting muscle to bone in the National Narrative.

One of the foundational insights of modern biblical criticism is summed up in the Latin expression *lex post prophetas*, meaning that Pentateuchal law postdates the Prophets. Beginning in the nineteenth century, scholars perceived, based on analyses from various angles, that the earliest prophetic writings do not presuppose the Pentateuch and that the latter made itself felt in the prophetic corpus only at a later point. Thus Jeremiah calls Judeans to account for their transgressions, which include stealing, murdering, committing adultery, and swearing falsely (see Jeremiah 7:9). Traditional interpreters had long assumed that the prophet is quoting the Ten Commandments. However, it is more probable that this text (and others like it) informed the formation of laws in the Pentateuch, so that when one reads Jeremiah canonically, one is supposed to understand his words as referring to the Ten Commandments, even if only selectively and in the wrong order.

The prophetic writings address matters of theodicy inasmuch as they justify the wrath that Yhwh poured out on his people. As a new preface to the prophets, the Pentateuch serves this same purpose. Now instead of pointing to basic moral principles, the prophets sally forth as prosecutors, cataloguing direct infractions of the written contract that Yhwh made with the nation at the beginning of its history.[1] Of course, one did not need the Ten Commandments to know that robbery, murder, and adultery were wrong. Yet now a defeated nation should understand that it not only acted wickedly but had also breached a written

[1] The term often describing the prophets' prosecution is *riv*. Originally the term meant to "contend," but against the backdrop of covenantal law, it assumed the new meaning of "sue/indict." A similar compositional scenario is found in the account of Nehemiah's reforms in which he "contends" with the Judeans. Yet after the composition of chapter 10, his actions are to be understood as a legal prosecution of the community for failing to abide by their written pact; see Chapter 12.

arrangement. The contractual violation made them doubly culpable for their demise and Yhwh doubly just for his judgment.

RESPONSIBILITY AND HOPE

To explain their country's defeat in the First World War, many Germans embraced an antisemitic conspiracy theory according to which their country did not lose on the battlefield but had been betrayed by Jews and members of the Left.[2] However, in the aftermath to the Holocaust and atrocities of the Second World War, this stab-in-the-back myth (*Dolchstoßlegende*) made way for a different approach as politicians, writers, philosophers, and pastors began to confront their past with a courage to accept culpability. The intellectual movement sparked public debate around the theme of *Vergangenheitsbewältigung*, which can be translated roughly as "working through the past."

The writings and ideas that the debate stimulated are remarkably rich and have implications that extend far beyond German history. Recently European scholars have applied the concept of *Vergangenheitsbewältigung* to the study of biblical writings, especially those that emerged after Judah's catastrophic defeat in 586 BCE.

While many facets of this concept have direct relevance to the biblical project, one must be careful not to miss a key difference between the histories of Germany and Judah: Germans were working through their fascist past. In contrast, Judeans were searching for hope in the wake of disaster and devastation that had been inflicted upon them by foreign armies, but they did so by constructing a history of their own culpability. Indeed, the biblical writers created guilt where there was none. After all, the Babylonian Empire conquered Judah for political and strategic reasons, not because its inhabitants had abandoned Yhwh or had failed to care for the widow, orphan, and stranger, as biblical writings claim.

The prophetic corpus makes a basic assertion: the conquests of Israel and Judah were not just political events; rather, they were part of the punishment that Yhwh visited upon his people as stipulated in their

[2] This "stab-in-the-back myth" bears a striking resemblance to the "stolen-election myth" currently circulating in many countries today.

covenantal pact. That Assyria and Babylon had managed to worst their kingdoms is not because these imperial powers were militarily superior or that their own leaders had adopted a flawed political solution. If that were the case, there would not be much to learn – except perhaps for their military strategists and palace officials, who had long been exiled or executed. But if the reason for the destruction is the nation's covenant and conduct, then there are grounds for hope. A divine order underlies the ostensible chaos of geopolitical events, and their suffering had a deeper meaning and cause: the nation had forsaken Yhwh's explicit instructions.

This knowledge – that their ancestors' transgressions are the real reason for their present suffering – bolstered the will of the vanquished to carry on. Their kingdoms had fallen, but their deity had not. On the contrary, the political fate demonstrates their deity's power and the validity of the prophets' warnings. What the nation now needed to do was behave differently from past generations.[3]

As scribes shaped these prophetic survival strategies, they embraced Assyria's imperial propaganda and turned it on its head:

> O Assyria, the rod of my anger –
> the club in their hands is my fury!
> Against a godless[4] nation I send [the Assyrian king],
> and against the people of my wrath I command him,
> To take spoil and seize plunder,
> and to tread them down like the mire of the streets.
> Yet he does not mean to do so,
> neither does his heart think so;
> in his heart he intends to destroy,
> and to cut off nations not a few.
> – Isaiah 10:5–7

Yhwh was using the Assyrian army to destroy his own people. Instead of repudiating the empire's propaganda, prophetic writings made it the

[3] The consistent criticism hurled at ancestors, even at the "greatest generation" of the exodus, is not characteristic of conservative, patriarchal thinking, but it also cannot be identified easily with a revolutionary "monotheistic" break from a "pagan past."

[4] The word "godless" is a play on the word "Hebrew" in the original.

basis for envisioning the new covenantal-cosmic order that we study in the next chapter.

In many instances, the prophets offer their audience no opportunity for turning from their evil ways. The judgment is a decided matter, and the prophet's task is simply to declare that the end has come. This is the case, for example, in Isaiah:

> "Make the mind of this people dull,
> and stop their ears,
> and shut their eyes,
> so that they may not look with their eyes,
> and listen with their ears,
> and comprehend with their minds,
> and turn and be healed."
> Then I said, "How long, O Lord?" And he said:
> "Until cities lie waste without inhabitant,
> and houses without people,
> and the land is utterly desolate."
> – Isaiah 6:10–12

Isaiah's mission is not to bring about change, but to declare judgment and then to preserve the message for the day after: "Bind up this testimony and seal this teaching among my students/disciples" (Isaiah 8:16).[5] Such commands to write down the words of a prophecy, as a witness and testimony, recur throughout the prophetic corpus. The warnings and declarations of divine doom preserved in this corpus should testify to future generations: the destruction that Israel and Judah had endured was the work of none other than the nation's own deity. The fact of that destruction proved the veracity of the writings – both the Prophets and the Pentateuch – that foretold it.

SURVIVING TRAUMA

Being a survivor is about bearing witness to the past, not consigning it to oblivion. The testimony is painful for those living in a new age. It is easier

[5] On prophetic schools, see Chapter 26.

if it is forgotten. Yet new generations need to see their experiences as chapters in an ongoing story, even if that story is one of pain and suffering. Only by being honest about their past and confronting it with courage is it possible to chart a new and more sustainable future.

Primo Levi was an Italian-Jewish chemist and writer who lived through the death camps of Nazi Germany. His experience left him with a feeling that he described as remorse and guilt. As a way of dealing with the shame of his survival, he sat down and wrote. In time, he saw it as his duty to bear witness through his accounts to the lives of the many who did not survive. Those who escape destruction are obligated, Levi insisted, to remember it. Their job is to "testify" to future generations so that it is never forgotten.

This close relationship between survival and testimony is reflected in many works of art and literature. Thus Herman Melville told the story of *Moby Dick* from the perspective of a survivor: "Call me Ishmael." The novel concludes with Ishmael's providential rescue from a shipwreck. He recounts how sharks glided by "as if with padlocks on their mouths." And then: "A sail drew near, nearer, and picked me up at last. It was the devious-cruising Rachel, that in her retracing search after her missing children, only found another orphan." Ishmael is alluding here to the image of the bereaved matriarch Rachel in the book of Jeremiah:

> A voice was heard in Ramah,
> lamentation, and bitter weeping:
> Rachel is weeping for her children.
> She refuses to be comforted,
> because they are no more.
> –Jeremiah 31:15

As readers of Melville's novel, what Ilana Pardes calls "the Bible of American culture," we are privileged with a first-person account of trauma told by its lone survivor.[6] And this first-person account is presented explicitly as the testimony to that trauma.

[6] Ilana Pardes, *Melville's Bibles*, University of California Press, 2008.

Levi and Melville drew deeply, in both form and content, on the Hebrew Bible, which offered them a rich source for stories of survival and survivors: from Noah and his sons to Lot and his daughters, from Joseph to Jeremiah, from Job to Jonah.[7] But the Bible not only contains many of tales of destruction and the day after. The entire National Narrative, stretching from Genesis to Kings, is an extraordinarily sophisticated exemplar of the survival-literature genre.

Culminating in the destruction of the temple in Jerusalem and the rehabilitation of a Davidic dynast in Babylon, this account is narrated from the vantage point of the vanquished. Erecting an epic monument to defeat, its authors saw themselves as survivors. They testified to future generations that their national trauma was nothing other than divine judgment, in keeping with the covenantal terms their deity delineated at the beginning of their history.

The same can be said for much of the biblical corpus, not least the prophetic writings: they are both survivors and witnesses. They dealt with the death that overwhelmed Israel and Judah by transforming it into concrete evidence for the veracity and reliability of the words Yhwh spoke to "my servants, the prophets" (Jeremiah 44:4). As a result, these writings were preserved from the flames of destruction, and now they bear trustworthy testimony to future generations who would otherwise make the mistakes of their ancestors. The nation is culpable, and its only hope is that the relationship with Yhwh might be restored. But when it is restored, it will have to be established on a different foundation.

LOVE AND ABUSE

The primary purpose of the prophetic writings is, accordingly, to provide a witness and testimony. As works of theodicy, they describe the nation's transgressions in detail, both as a vindication of the divine decree and for the instruction of future generations. Moreover, as they addressed a suffering nation decimated by the ravages of war, they also introduced

[7] Both Levi and Melville regarded their projects (in part) as the making of a "new Bible." For Levi, see his *Survival in Auschwitz* (trans. Stuart Woolf), Orion, 1959, p. 72. For Melville, see the important work by Ilana Pardes cited in the preceding note.

the categories of culpability and responsibility – and therewith faith and hope.

In contrast to the National Narrative, which concludes with catastrophic defeat, the prophetic corpus has a Hollywood happy ending. Their devastating condemnations and gut-wrenching descriptions of disaster are consistently juxtaposed with promises of rebirth and renewal. Casting aside a tragic view of history, its authors discerned through the eyes of the prophets, and their penetrating critiques, a brighter day on the horizon – or in the lyrics of Yip Harburg, writing in 1939: "somewhere over the rainbow."

The onslaught of empires thoroughly dismantled the social structures and thinking that had long served as foundations for kingdoms of the Southern Levant such as Israel and Judah. Instead of accepting their fate, the scribes who shaped the prophetic corpus discovered a new way forward. By declaring that Yhwh had rejected his people, they reimagined the basis for their relationship going forward. This momentous move unleashed an outpouring of literary activity that reshaped not only the biblical narrative but also the personality of their national deity.

The personality is on display from the first chapters of Genesis, which portray the deity struggling with his creation in a series of trials and errors. Things do not go according to plan in the garden where the Creator forms the first human pair, and he drives them out. East of Eden, evil proliferates among both humans and animals. Fed up with his creation, the Creator decides to destroy it with a cosmic flood, saving only a few members of each species.

At the dawn of the new post-diluvian era, a mighty warrior builds a kingdom in the East, founding cities from which imperial powers would later consolidate and conquer the earth. There, in a region made rich by rivers, humans come together and achieve the earliest feats of civilization. Their ambition to build a megalopolis, one that reaches the heavens, proves to be an affront to the deity, and he thwarts the project by confusing their language and scattering them across the earth.

As the story continues, the divine plan spurns the material achievements of cities and civilizations in favor of a spiritual and political experiment of creating a people. This is where the narrative dramatically pivots to the promise: the deity decides to chart a new course, working through Abraham and Sarah to bring a people into existence. In this new covenantal order, what dictates the future are not the murky, mysterious machinations of gods in heaven, but the deeds of humans on earth.

History now becomes story, the tale of an ancient affair: Yhwh is the husband, Israel is his wife, and the covenant ratified at Sinai their marriage contract. If this tale counts as a love story, it is one that includes infidelity, spousal abuse, and unbridled violence. Hosea presents the restoration of this relationship after a divorce (i.e., national defeat). The couple reunites, and this reunion is accompanied by a change in Yhwh's heart. He declares his intention to take her to a place of solitude where she will respond favorably to his compassion:

> Therefore, I will now allure her,
> and bring her into the wilderness,
> and speak tenderly to her. . . .
> There she shall respond as in the days of her youth,
> as at the time when she came out of the land of Egypt.
> – Hosea 2:14–15

Imagined as Yhwh's wife, Israel had long called this deity *ba'al-i* ("My Lord," a play on the divine name Baal), but from now on, the prophet promises, she will call him *ish-i:* "My Man." As part of this new relationship, Yhwh will treat Israel with steadfast love and mercy, faithfulness and justice. And she will no longer live in fear of war and tribulation:

> I will make for you a covenant on that day,
> with the wild animals, the birds of the air,
> and the creeping things of the ground.
> I will abolish the bow, the sword, and war from the land;
> and I will make you lie down in safety.
> I will take you for my wife forever.
> I will take you for my wife in righteousness and in justice,
> in steadfast love, and in mercy.
> I will take you for my wife in faithfulness.
> And you shall know Yhwh.
> – Hosea 2:18–20

Here, and throughout the Prophets, the nation is depicted as "returning" to the early, innocent, happy days of its life with Yhwh. But those days are imagined. The nation's past establishes the norm for all that follows. And if that past is mythic, then the *return* to it is nothing less than the *beginning*. To use the language of Hosea, the divorce came first, and it prompted questions about the marriage that preceded it.

The biblical scribes detailed the prehistory of that relationship – in both the poetry of the Prophets and the prose of the Pentateuch. In this new political-theological order, both parties must do their part and abide by the terms of the covenant. Most often the nation is at fault, but not all the time. Thus, a variety of laments and psalms protest the divine decree, calling the deity to account and insisting that the punishment does not fit the crime.

A dogged determination to persevere in the face of overwhelming obstacles gave way to a revolutionary new way of thinking about the world and the peoples that inhabit it. We would not have a corpus of biblical writings had it not been for circles of counter-cultural thinkers who worked through their trauma by turning the focus to faithfulness – vis-à-vis both their deity and each other. In the following chapter, we explore the new covenantal order that emerged from this prophetic vision, and how the covenant transformed the character and structure of the National Narrative.

FURTHER READING

Boda, Mark J. and Wray Beal, Lissa M. (eds.), *Prophets, Prophecy, and Ancient Israelite Historiography, Eisenbrauns*, 2013.

Bolin, Thomas H., *Freedom beyond Forgiveness: The Book of Jonah Re-Examined*, Sheffield Academic Press, 1997.

Claassens, L. Juliana M., *Writing and Reading to Survive: Biblical and Contemporary Trauma Narratives in Conversation*, Sheffield Phoenix, 2020.

de Jong, Matthijs J., *Isaiah among the Ancient Near Eastern Prophets: A Comparative Study of the Earliest Stages of the Isaiah Tradition and the Neo-Assyrian Prophecies*, Brill, 2007.

Edelman, Diana V. and Zvi, Ehud Ben (eds.), *The Production of Prophecy: Constructing Prophecy and Prophets in Yehud*, Equinox, 2009.

Heller, Roy L., *The Characters of Elijah and Elisha and the Deuteronomic Evaluation of Prophecy: Miracles and Manipulation*, Bloomsbury, 2018.

Jacobs, Mignon R. and Person Jr., Raymond F. (eds.), *Israelite Prophecy and the Deuteronomistic History: Portrait, Reality, and the Formation of a History*, Society of Biblical Literature, 2013.

Kratz, Reinhard G., *The Prophets of Israel*, Eisenbrauns, 2015.

Nissinen, Martii, *Ancient Prophecy: Near Eastern, Biblical, and Greek Perspectives*, Oxford University Pres, 2017.

Pardes, Ilana, *Melville's Bibles*, University of California Press, 2008.

Radine, Jason, *The Book of Amos in Emergent Judah*, Mohr Siebeck, 2010.

Rom-Shiloni, Dalit, *Voices from the Ruins: Theodicy and the Fall of Jerusalem in the Hebrew Bible*, Eerdmans, 2021.

Seitz, Christopher R., *Prophecy and Hermeneutics: Toward a New Introduction to the Prophets*, Baker, 2007.

Sherwood, Yvonne, *A Biblical Text and Its Afterlives: The Survival of Jonah in Western Culture*, Cambridge University Press, 2000.

Weems, Renita J., *Battered Love: Marriage, Sex, and Violence in the Hebrew Prophets*, Fortress, 1995.

21

Yhwh and His People

Codes, Covenant, and Kinship

You have seen how I bore you on eagles' wings
and brought you to myself.
Now therefore if you obey my voice
and keep my covenant,
you shall be my treasured possession.
– Exodus 19:4–6

THE SCENE IS UNFORGETTABLE: fire and smoke shroud the mountain, the earth trembles, lightning flashes across the heavens, and a shofar blasts a blood-curdling cry. By performing purification rituals, the people had prepared themselves for this terrifying moment. Now they stand in rapt attention as the deity addresses them.

Yhwh speaks directly to the assembly, addressing all and each individually. He reminds them that he had liberated them from slavery in Egypt and brought them to this place. Having saved them in a majestic manner, he proposes henceforth to be their God and for them to be his people. If they accept the offer, they will have to follow his detailed, written instructions and laws, which bear on the way they relate not only to himself but also to each other. After Moses reads this "book of the covenant," the people respond: "All that Yhwh has spoken, we will do!" Ratifying the pact, Moses sprinkles sacrificial blood on the people and declares: "This is the blood of the covenant that Yhwh hereby makes with you concerning all these words!" (see Exodus 19 and 24).

This event is etched more deeply into biblical memory than any other. There, at the foot of Mount Sinai, a motley multitude of refugees became a nation, shedding the shackles of slavery and forming a fellowship that knits them to one another and to one deity at their center. This is a new social fabric, and what holds it together is a web of kinship, law, and love (*chesed*).

At the heart of the Palace History is a promise that Yhwh makes to David after he had settled in his palace and begun preparations for the building of the temple:

> When the time comes for you to die,
> I will raise up your descendant to succeed you,
> and I will establish his kingdom.
> He will build a house for my name,
> and I will make his dynasty permanent . . .
> Your house and your kingdom will stand before me for all time;
> your dynasty will be everlasting.
> – 2 Samuel 7:12–16

In times of crisis, the palace in Jerusalem would have appealed to this promise, and after Judah's defeat in 586 BCE, many awaited its fulfillment in the form of a re-established Davidic monarchy.

The preceding chapters of Part III have explored how a new generation of Southern scribes embraced the People's History and made it their own. Combining it with the Palace History, they declared that a pact Yhwh had made with the entire nation at Sinai is more foundational and determinative than the promise Yhwh made later to David and his dynastic line. When a native king on the throne was nothing but an aspiration for the distant future, the defeated could come together as a political community and live out the vision of the covenant they made with Yhwh when they first became a people in the wilderness. We also saw how the prophetic writings laid the foundation for this covenantal order.

Now, in this final chapter of Part III, we explore some of the most prominent features of what the Canadian philosopher Charles Taylor would call the Bible's "social imaginary."[1] Our concern pertains here to

[1] Taylor, *Modern Social Imaginaries.*

law and its covenantal framework, and in studying both, we will see how the Bible introduced a new understanding of jurisprudence, and how this understanding bears on a national consciousness of belonging and kinship.

LEGISLATED WISDOM IN DEUTERONOMY

The Omride kings who ruled the Northern kingdom in the ninth century had made Yhwh a point of unity for the Northern kingdom, just as the Moabite king Mesha seems to have used the deity Chemosh to consolidate the diverse realm of his kingdom. The authors of the earliest Exodus-Conquest Account drew directly on the Omride strategy, yet as they did, they removed the king from the picture and depicted a direct partnership between Yhwh and the people. Southern scribes not only copied and transmitted the Exodus-Conquest Account, but also amplified it, developing the Yhwh–people partnership in the realm of both narrative and law.

The assertion that establishes the trajectory for the new narrative is a simple yet powerful one: "Hear O Israel, Yhwh is our God, Yhwh is one." As noted in Chapter 6, this declaration from Deuteronomy (6:4) originally addressed historical conditions in which multiple deities bearing the name Yhwh inhabited rival holy places. The authors of Deuteronomy proclaimed that there is just *one Yhwh* – not a Yhwh of Samaria, a Yhwh of Jerusalem, a Yhwh of Bethel, a Yhwh of Arad, and so on. To unify both North and South under the name Israel, they realized that they first had to unify competing deities, each of whom laid claim to the name Yhwh.

Deuteronomy left a deep imprint on the entire National Narrative, serving as the lens through which all other biblical law codes are read. Its affirmation of "one Yhwh" served as the basis for thinking about a united people. But in contrast to the original vision of peoplehood, the new conception focused on one legitimate locus of sacrifice. The perspective from which scribes shaped this code is the centralization of all cultic and national life in "the place where Yhwh your God chose to make his name dwell" (Deuteronomy 12:11 *et passim*). Communities in the North claimed that the chosen place was Mount Gerizim, where their temple stood, and they could claim support in the references to Gerizim in Deuteronomy. Those in the South, however, insisted that this place was Jerusalem.[2]

Deuteronomy is suffused with a sense of kinship, and it spells out the implications for an ethos of solidarity. For example:

> You shall not watch your neighbor's ox or sheep straying away and ignore them. You must take them back to their owner. If the owner does not reside near you or you do not know who the owner is, you must bring it to your own house, and it shall remain with you until the owner claims it; then you must return it.
>
> You shall do the same with a neighbor's donkey, as well with a neighbor's garment, and with anything else that your neighbor loses and you find.
>
> You may not withhold your help. You shall not see your neighbor's donkey or ox fallen on the road and ignore it. You must help to lift it up. . . .
>
> If you come on a bird's nest, in any tree or on the ground, with fledglings or eggs, with the mother sitting on the fledglings or on the eggs, you shall not take the mother with the young. You may take the young, but be sure to let the mother go, so that it may go well with you and you may have a long life.
>
> – Deuteronomy 22:1–7

The final ordinance pertains to the preservation of natural resources. Elsewhere, the code strictly forbids the cutting down of trees, even of one's enemies, unless it served an indispensable purpose. The conventional tactic of siege warfare is presented as an unnecessary and immoral aggression against an innocent living thing: "Is the tree of the field a human who can retreat from you into a besieged city?" (20:20). As the authors compiled this impressive code, they took what were once wisdom teachings, such as this proverb about trees, and reformulated them as binding laws. What was once offered as advice to elites trained at court is now a written code that determines the future of the entire nation.

[2] The centralization of worship in Deuteronomy ignited a heated dispute between North and South familiar to readers of the New Testament (see, e.g., John 4).

COMPETING CODES

What is distinctive about biblical law is that multiple – and often contradictory – codes stand next to each other in single public document, and all are understood to be equally binding. The Deuteronomic Code may have left a deeper imprint on the National Narrative, but it is no more authoritative than the earlier Covenant Code and the later materials in the Priestly Source. The authors of the Pentateuch could have decided on one of the law codes, especially if their aim was to consolidate a nation. Likewise, we would expect new codes of law to have replaced earlier ones. But such is not the case. We witnessed how the biblical writings consolidate rival populations and regions by connecting their heroes and traditions in a single narrative. The Pentateuch does the same with its multiple codes, making them equally authoritative.

A collection of competing law codes is the antithesis of a dogmatic, unitary doctrine, and it represents an effort of compromise by which the scribes sought to surmount political and sectarian divisions. The Pentateuch's plurality of laws demands from its readers intensive study, comparison, and evaluation. Much is left to interpretation, and nothing is possible without careful reflection by critical readers.

While perhaps the most prominent of the biblical codes, Deuteronomy presupposes and updates laws that antedate it by at least a century. Found in Exodus 20–23, these laws, known as the Covenant Code, permit the worship of Yhwh in multiple places. They insist, however, that altars are to be built in the correct way:

> Make for me only an altar of earth and sacrifice on it your burnt offerings and your offerings of well-being, your sheep and your oxen. In every place where I cause my name to be remembered I will come to you and bless you.
>
> But if you make for me an altar of stone, do not build it of hewn stones; for if you use a chisel upon it you profane it.
>
> You shall not go up by steps to my altar, so that your nakedness may not be exposed on it.
>
> – Exodus 20:24–26

Notice how this early ordinance presupposes multiple sacred sites: "In *every place* where I cause my name to be remembered, I will come to you and bless you." The Deuteronomic Code draws on this ordinance yet centralizes the cult: there is only *one place* where Israel may worship Yhwh.

Although ancient, the Covenant Code contains statutes that are impressively progressive. Thus, the status of the father is no different from that of mother inasmuch as whoever strikes or curses either is subject to the same penalty. This code also introduces the first labor reforms, but in contrast to labor laws in contemporary democratic societies, it requires a rest day not only for human laborers but also the animals in one's employ:

> Six days you shall labor,
> but on the seventh day you shall cease,
> so that your ox and your donkey may have relief,
> and the son of your maidservant and the resident alien may be refreshed.
>
> – Exodus 23:12

Later laws link this statute to the Sabbath after this sacred day came to be celebrated weekly rather than as a full moon festival (see discussion in Chapter 10). Despite its many progressive elements, the Covenant Code has some deeply disturbing elements, such as leniency to the abuse of slaves (see Exodus 21:20–27).

The Pentateuch contains two other law codes. The first was transmitted in the Priestly Source, which originated less as a collection of laws than as a retelling of the first segments of the National Narrative. As already noted (see Chapters 10 and 16), the Priestly Source begins with the creation account of Genesis 1 and continues in small, easily identifiable sections that are juxtaposed with older materials. According to the most compelling theories, it concluded in Exodus 40, which depicts the building of the divine sanctuary (the tabernacle) and the cloud of the divine presence covering it.

For the priests of Jerusalem, the inauguration of the sacrificial system at Sinai was the most important thing to know about the past. The tabernacle offered these circles a way to highlight the role of the temple in the National Narrative. By depicting a portable sanctuary modeled on Jerusalem's temple, they could identify this temple and its cult as the culmination of history since the creation of the cosmos.

The Priestly Source is a thoroughly Judean product, with a clear social-religious agenda. Even so, it articulates a stunning, and highly sophisticated, view of the cosmos and Israel's place in it. Over time, both before and after the originally independent document was integrated into the National Narrative, it was expanded with legal materials (often related to sacrifices, purity, and ritual) as well as stories that describe laws being revealed ad hoc to the nation in the wilderness in response to issues that arise along the way.

HOLINESS AND LIBERTY

"Proclaim liberty throughout the land unto all the inhabitants thereof." This line is engraved on the American Liberty Bell. Its conspicuous crack represents for many the divisions within American society that counter the force of freedom. What few may realize is that the engraved line belongs to a body of biblical laws called the Holiness Code. Found in Leviticus 17–26, these laws bear the imprint of both the Priestly Source and the Deuteronomic Code, and they most likely originated in Judah.

The Holiness Code calls members of the nation to mimic Yhwh, according to the principle of *imitatio dei*: "Be you holy, for I am holy" (Leviticus 19:2). Just as Deuteronomy transforms a body of wisdom teachings for elites into a code of law for the nation, the Holiness Code transforms priestly rules of conduct into an ethical system governing all members of society (on this "open access" aspect, see Chapter 26). Detailed instructions culminate in general moral principles, all of which are grounded in Yhwh's special character. To cite an excerpt:

> When you reap the harvest of your land, you shall not reap to the very edges of your field, or gather the gleanings of your harvest.
> You shall not strip your vineyard bare, or gather the fallen grapes of your vineyard; you shall leave them for the poor and the alien: I am Yhwh your God.

> You shall not steal; you shall not deal falsely; and you shall not lie to one another. And you shall not swear falsely by my name, profaning the name of your God: I am Yhwh.
> You shall not defraud your neighbor; you shall not steal; and you shall not keep for yourself the wages of a laborer until morning.
> You shall not revile the deaf or put a stumbling block before the blind; you shall fear your God: I am Yhwh.
> You shall not render an unjust judgment; you shall not be partial to the poor or defer to the great: with justice you shall judge your neighbor.
> You shall not go about spreading slander among your people.
> You shall not do anything that endangers your neighbor's life: I am Yhwh.
> You shall not hate a fellow Israelite in your heart. Rebuke your neighbor frankly so you will not share in their guilt.
> You shall not seek revenge or bear a grudge against anyone among your people. Love your neighbor as yourself: I am Yhwh.
>
> – Leviticus 19:9–18

In contrast to Greek thinkers of their time, the authors of the Holiness Code set forth a notion of freedom that had little to do with the preservation of political autonomy or liberation from tyranny. Instead of freedom from external restraint, the biblical authors promoted what the political philosopher Isaiah Berlin called "positive liberty," a form of freedom that presupposes a just social order.[3] Leviticus demands its audience to liberate those who have lost their means of livelihood, to support those who might otherwise slide into irreversible servitude, to regulate business dealings to protect the vulnerable, and to prevent land from accumulating in the hands of the few.

Constraints on political *independence* prompted the authors of the Holiness Code to contemplate the reality of social *interdependence*. Freedom is to be proclaimed to all the land's inhabitants. The statement grows from the insight that a nation is only as strong as its weakest members. A society that fails to care for the socio-economic conditions of its members, and does not establish an equitable system of justice, cannot endure, let alone be free.

[3] Isaiah Berlin, *Four Essays on Liberty*, Oxford University Press, 1969, pp. 118–172.

The Holiness Code extends the sacred ordering of time to space. Not only are all humans and work animals to rest, but also the land. It must be let to lie fallow periodically so that it can regenerate its life-giving potential. Just as Yhwh planted the human in the garden to tend it, so he plants Israel in their homeland to care for it as his Holy Land. All members of the nation are to partake in the project and see themselves as divinely commissioned caretakers. This self-understanding makes (agricultural) labor noble rather than a drudgery imposed on humans (see Chapters 10 and 25).

REPLACING THE KING

Deuteronomy's law for the king begins by stipulating that he be one of "your kin" and that he not lift himself above other Israelites (Deut 17:14–15). But even more remarkable about both Deuteronomy and all the other biblical codes is that this is the *only* time they address the institution of the monarchy. And even this short section does not assign the king a role in governance. His only job is to study the law:

> When he has taken the throne of his kingdom, he shall write for himself a copy of this law on a scroll in the presence of the Levitical priests. It shall remain with him, and he shall read in it all the days of his life, so that he may learn to fear Yhwh his God, diligently observing all the words of this law and these statutes, neither exalting himself above other members of the community nor turning aside from the commandment, either to the right or to the left, so that he and his descendants may reign long over his kingdom in Israel.
>
> – Deuteronomy 17:18–20

Ancient kings were expected to not only be warriors and builders but also judges and adjudicators, establishing justice in the land. We hear often, in both biblical texts and letters from Mesopotamia, about plaintiffs seeking a hearing from the king when he was in the vicinity. A legal code, however, was not desirable, as it could restrict the king's liberty.

Figure 21.1 A stele on display at the Louvre in Paris depicting Hammurabi and the Babylonian sun god Shamash. Below are 4,130 lines of cuneiform text containing Hammurabi's "law code." Photo Jacob L. Wright.

We know of law collections from the ancient Mesopotamia. The most famous was compiled by the court of King Hammurabi (1810–*c.*1750 BCE). It was both inscribed on monuments and widely circulated on tablets. The first and most complete copy of this collection was found at Susa and now stands prominently in the Louvre. Over seven feet high, it depicts the king receiving special honors from the god Shamash (Figure 21.1). Below the image, scribes engraved the laws along with an extensive first-person narrative framework, which includes the lines:

> [T]hen Anu and Bel called by name me, Hammurabi, the exalted prince, who feared God, to bring about the rule of righteousness in the land, to destroy the wicked and the evil-doers; so that the strong should not harm the weak; so that I should rule over the black-headed people like Shamash, and enlighten the land, to further the well-being of mankind.[4]

[4] *The Code of Hammurabi*, trans. L.W. King, https://avalon.law.yale.edu/ancient/hamframe.asp.

As a monument to monarchic power and an emblem of statecraft, Hammurabi's laws do not represent a functioning legal code. They are not legally binding or meant to be used in the actual practice of adjudication.

The biblical laws, in contrast, are understood to be the direct revelation to the nation. By removing a human ruler from the picture, they are no longer about the performance of kingship and the display of power; rather, they represent the deity's charge to a nation, to be both studied and practiced. Here we can speak properly of a legal code. Indeed, a corpus of written codes represents Israel's ultimate authority, and infractions are nothing less than sin against the nation's God. This is a radical new concept of law, and its impact would be difficult to overstate.

The replacement of the king by the deity parallels the development of the biblical ethos of equality under the law as well as its concern to create and preserve the social-economic conditions for broad participation in the cultic and political life of the nation. The plight of individuals and communities forfeiting their spheres of agency – of small fish being swallowed by big fish – forms a scarlet thread running throughout law and narrative in the Bible.

In the context of Israel's and Judah's wars with the Assyrian and Babylonian empires, these new legal codes had a central role to play. At a time when the state was still intact and mobilizing for battle, it could strengthen national solidarity by various means such as restricting the power of the aristocracy. Yet at a time when the nation was defeated and dispersed, and a native king and army were no longer there to defend its territorial borders, the law could demarcate communal boundaries and, perhaps more importantly, provide a unifying political vision.

TREATY AND COVENANT

Scholars have long noted the striking parallels between the biblical covenant and the pledges that military powers imposed on their subjects. Instead of two individual rulers, the parties of the biblical covenant are the nation as a whole and its divine king. Israel has taken the place of the vassal king, and this valorization of the nation is matched by increased attention to the nature of the deity. Just as the state treaties conclude with a series of curses for the vassal if he fails to adhere to the stipulations, the covenantal laws conclude with curses if Israel fails to keep all the commandments (Leviticus 26 and Deuteronomy 28). The foremost stipulation of the state treaty is the requirement of absolute loyalty to the overlord, and in the biblical covenant, it is the first commandment: "You shall have no other gods beside me" (Exodus 20:3 and Deuteronomy 5:1).

The prologue to an international treaty from the late second millennium BCE describes how coalition attacked the king of Ugarit (an ancient port city in northern Syria) conquered his cities, deported their inhabitants, and devastated the land. The king then petitioned his Hittite overlord for help, who sent his troops to the rescue. Following this account of their past relations, the treaty text continues with a series of stipulations.

Many vassal treaties begin like this one, with historical prologues recounting how the suzerain saved the vassal from his enemies. In the same way, the memory of Yhwh redeeming Israel from their Egyptian oppressors loom large in biblical law: "Remember that you were a slave in Egypt and that Yhwh your God redeemed you from there; I therefore enjoin you to observe this commandment" (Deuteronomy 24:18, in reference to the rights of the stranger, orphan, and widow). Texts like these translate the experience of redemption from Egypt into an ethos for justice and law within Israelite society.

As many scholars today agree, the biblical notion of covenant emerged in direct response to Israel's and Judah's experience of political subjugation and defeat. However, the authors of the Pentateuch have concealed those origins. Indeed, texts like explicitly link the covenant not to defeat but to a great victory over the nation's first imperial oppressors.

> When your children ask you in time to come, "What is the meaning of the decrees and the statutes and the ordinances that Yhwh our God has commanded you?," then you shall say to your children:
>
> "We were Pharaoh's slaves in Egypt, but Yhwh brought us out of Egypt with a mighty hand. Yhwh displayed before our eyes great and awesome

> signs and wonders against Egypt, against Pharaoh and all his household. He brought us out from there in order to bring us in, to give us the land that he promised on oath to our ancestors. Yhwh commanded us to observe all these statutes, to fear Yhwh our God, for our lasting good, so as to keep us alive, as is now the case. If we diligently observe this entire commandment before Yhwh our God, as he has commanded us, it will be to our merit."
>
> – Deuteronomy 6:20–25

Here and in many other places, the authors of the Pentateuch took an instrument of imperial subjugation and reinvented it so that is now served the purposes of a new political project, one that could withstand the encroachment of imperial armies. Instead of being forced upon them, the nation enters this covenant freely and without coercion, recognizing that its stipulations are liberating and life-sustaining.

The biblical accounts of covenant-making consistently underscore the aspect of *choice*. By entering into the covenant, the nation of Israel makes a voluntary decision to abide by Yhwh's will as revealed in the laws, precepts, and statutes published in the Pentateuch. What distinguishes the Mosaic covenant is this volitional and conditional character. The nation chooses at a specific time and place to make Yhwh their God: "Choose this day whom you will serve. . .but for me and my house, we will serve Yhwh" (Joshua 24:15). Likewise, when the nation breaks the covenant, it will be punished with exile and destruction, as stipulated in the covenantal curses. Thus, Israel's existence as a people and their relationship to Yhwh was no longer to be taken for granted. When foreign armies exile them from their homeland, they should know that their suffering is in keeping with the terms of their covenant.

By making the relationship between Yhwh and Israel volitional, and the nation's future conditional, the biblical covenant abolished the status quo, as we saw in the preceding chapter. Yhwh is no longer part of the system; he transcends it. The partnership between Israel and Yhwh can no longer be understood as primordial, already existing from the shadows of time, as most ancient peoples thought of the partnerships with their gods. Rather, it was established voluntarily, at a discrete moment in the nation's history, and it could be terminated just as easily.

Thanks to this revolutionary new concept of covenant, Yhwh could now survive the destruction of his people, and that destruction could now be understood to be a consequence of the nation's collective behavior. What emerges in this new conception of covenant is a legal-rational cosmic order, with a written, public document determining the nation's fate and a transcendent deity governing history.

THE FIRST FORM OF SACRED SCRIPTURE

What happens to a narrative when it is expanded with divinely revealed law? The answer is that it becomes holy. It is no longer merely an account of the past, but a sacred, authoritative instruction for the present and future. What was once descriptive is now also prescriptive.

To understand the transformation of a narrative into sacred scripture, we have to start with the Covenant Code (Exodus 20–23). It may have been embedded into the Exodus-Conquest Account at a relatively early point. Its presence in this text made it more holy than the Family Story of Genesis, yet the combination of the two to form the People's History conferred a sacred status to the entire work. In comparison, the Palace History is profane; it is more of a political treatise than a sacred revelation. In creating the National Narrative, Southern scribes linked the profane Palace History to the sacred People's History, producing a synthesis of two very different types of writing.

While the National Narrative is a coherent whole, later generations (in the Persian and Hellenistic periods) found a way to isolate its most hallowed parts by drawing a division between we know call the Pentateuch, containing the first five books, and the Former Prophets (in the books of Joshua, Judges, Samuel, and Kings). Because the Pentateuch contains Yhwh's own words to the nation (i.e., Mosaic law), it constitutes sacred scripture or a holy book.

The new work has a new conclusion: an embellished version of the story of Moses' death. As Moses expires, so does the revelation of what's determinative for the nation's future. The motivation of those responsible for this division was to make adherence to the Pentateuch the precondition for crossing the Jordan and entering the Promised Land.

To thrive as a people, Israel would have to build a just and righteous society by carefully heeding the divine laws made known to them before they ever entered their homeland.

After telling how God buries Moses after his death, the Pentateuch culminates with the statement: "Never since has there arisen a prophet in Israel like Moses, whom Yhwh knew face to face" (Deuteronomy 34:10). By declaring Moses to be a prophet without equal, this epitaph subordinates all future revelation to the Pentateuch's authority. It also makes this work his memorial and legacy. As the nation's movable monument, it is both the touchstone of all new knowledge and a blueprint for the nation's future.

According to this new literary demarcation (corresponding to a later canonical division), the Former Prophets are to be interpreted as providing proof for the veracity of the truths set forth in the Pentateuch. Israel entered the Promised Land yet eventually abandoned Yhwh. In keeping with the covenant's stipulations, the nation was punished for its sins, conquered by foreign armies, and deported from its land. By studying the Pentateuch in relation to the rest of the National Narrative, communities should learn that its divine prescriptions still govern their future.

The inception of the covenant thus provided a major impetus for scribes to embellish the National Narrative. Older portions of those books had already combined disparate histories into a common story, giving divided communities a shared past and sense of kinship. But after being reworked, the narrative's overarching purpose is to demonstrate the validity of the covenant, culminating with the destruction of Jerusalem and the exile of Judah. By studying the nation's history in this narrative framework, the reader can see how, time and again, the nation's failure and infidelities brought the covenantal curses to fulfilment.

KINSHIP, LAW, AND STORY

Terms of kinship belong to the vernacular of ancient Near Eastern diplomacy. The partners to covenants called each other "brothers," and if a vassal made a treaty with a suzerain, he called him "father."

Thus, when a king in ancient Anatolia writes to his ally in Babylon in the late second millennium BCE, he refers to a history of both friendship and fraternity:

> When your father and I established close friendship and became brothers, we spoke thus: "We are brothers: We should be the enemy of one who is an enemy to anyone of us, a friend to the one who is a friend of anyone of us." [5]

Biblical texts apply this standard diplomatic parlance to their project of peoplehood (see discussion of Ruth in Chapter 24). The actors are not rulers and representatives of states but rather communities and individuals as members of a nation. Similar to the diplomatic kinship of international treaties, biblical kinship is not primarily genetic or ethnic but rather voluntary and consensual, formed by a body of shared laws and framed by a covenantal relationship.

In *Bridge of Spies*, James Donovan (played by Tom Hanks) is a famous lawyer called to defend Rudolf Abel, a man accused of spying against the United States. Everyone is convinced Abel's guilt. When Donovan's colleague insists that he makes the trial easy for the state, which lacked reliable evidence of Abel's wrongdoing, Donovan retorts: "You are Italian. I am Irish. But what makes us Americans? *It's the rule book.* And when we don't follow it, we are not Americans."

The National Narrative fosters kinship by portraying a people evolving from an extended family, with others joining them as "fellow travelers" along the way. However, kinship proves over time to be limited and inadequate. Families often quarrel. There needs to be ideals and a code to which one can appeal when adjudicating disputes, especially when the family comprises many clans, tribes, and communities. Hence the law. As an officially inscribed document to which all members of the nation formally subscribe, it represents a rallying point that simultaneously articulates the rules by which all must play.

National identities are shaped by shared experiences from which flow mutual obligations (see discussion of Renan's lecture "What is a Nation"

[5] For this text and similar ones, see Paul Kalluveettil, *Declaration and Covenant: A Comprehensive Review of Covenant Formulae from the Old Testament and the Ancient Near East*, Biblical Institute Press, 1982, pp. 99–103.

in Chapter 11). The law means little if it is not embedded in a meaningful story. Law is about the present and the future, while kinship is about the past. Kinship often involves no genealogical ties, but it is always suffused with a shared history, even if that history is imagined.

Stated simply, to be a people, communities must connect their sundry pasts, and especially stories about these pasts. As an ambitious project of peoplehood, the National Narrative embeds the nation's laws in a story of the deity's liberation of, and later pact, with slaves from Egypt. Understood as being ratified at the beginning of Israel's history, the biblical covenant places the nation's political contingencies in a new perspective. When Israel faces defeat, one can affirm Yhwh's transcendent presence and power by interpreting this political fate in relation to the covenant.

The National Narrative performs this interpretive task, and in doing so, it erects a massive memorial to the nation's collective trauma. Instead of being inscribed on stone, this monument is constructed on parchement and papyrus. This medium makes it malleable, permitting it to be edited and shaped from competing perspectives and factions. And because it is not anchored to a territory as many war monuments are, communities can carry it with them when they are exiled from their homeland.

FURTHER READING

Assmann, Jan, *The Invention of Religion: Faith and Covenant in the Book of Exodus*, Princeton University Press, 2018.

Barmash, Pamela, *The Laws of Hammurabi: At the Confluence of Royal and Scribal Tradition*, Oxford University Press, 2021.

Brett, Mark G., *Locations of God: Political Theology in the Hebrew Bible*, Oxford University Press, 2019.

Brett, Mark G., Political Trauma and Healing, Eerdmans, 2016.

Jackson, Bernard S., *Wisdom-Laws: A Study of the Mishpatim of Exodus 21:1–22:16*, Oxford University Press, 2006.

Levinson, Bernard M., *"The Right Chorale": Studies in Biblical Law and Interpretation*, Mohr Siebeck, 2008.

Mattison, Kevin, *Rewriting and Revision as Amendment in the Laws of Deuteronomy*, Mohr Siebeck, 2018.

Milstein, Sara J., *Making a Case: The Practical Roots of Biblical Law*, Oxford University Press, 2021.

Morrow, William S., *An Introduction to Biblical Law*, Eerdmans, 2017.

Nihan, Christophe, *From Priestly Torah to Pentateuch: A Study in the Composition of the Book of Leviticus*, Mohr Siebeck, 2007.

Rhyder, Julia, *Centralizing the Cult: The Holiness Legislation in Leviticus 17–26*, Mohr Siebeck, 2019.

Roth, Martha T., *Law Collections from Mesopotamia and Asia Minor*, 2nd ed., Scholars Press, 1997.

Stackert, Jeffrey, *Rewriting the Torah: Literary Revision in Deuteronomy and the Holiness Legislation*, Mohr Siebeck, 2007.

Taylor, Charles, *Modern Social Imaginaries*, Duke University Press, 2003.

Weeks, Noel, *Admonition and Curse: The Ancient Near Eastern Treaty/Covenant Form as a Problem in Inter-Cultural Relationships*, T&T Clark, 2004.

Part IV
A People of Protest

IN PART II, WE SAW HOW SEVERAL (rarely read) biblical books portray defeated communities rebuilding Jerusalem from the ruins of a former kingdom. In the same way, our scribes created a new narrative not from scratch, but by piecing together fragments from their pasts. That National Narrative, which we studied in Part III, evolved over the ages from smaller, originally independent pieces. Generations of anonymous scribes collected these pieces, embroidered them with new details, and wove them into an elaborate literary tapestry. Their work portrays the relationship between the two kingdoms, Israel and Judah, and their tragic ends. It not only blends their separate stories, but also sets them in relation to an earlier "United Monarchy." Yet its most significant achievement was to go beyond this political unity, telling the powerful story of a people who evolved from an extended family and existed for many generations before the emergence of the monarchy and the establishment of a centralized state.

What remains for us now in Part IV is to explore the new survival strategies the final generations of biblical writers implanted in their diverse corpus. The matters these circles addressed include the role of women in the life of the nation (Chapters 22 and 29), the need for a new non-martial masculinity (Chapter 23), the integration of newcomers to the national fold (Chapter 24), political martyrdom, procreation, and the afterlife (Chapter 25), as well as systems of transparency and accountability (Chapter 26). They created a "Songbook for the Nation" by collecting diverse psalms and laments (Chapter 27), and reshaped a body of elite courtly wisdom, making it accessible to the nation as a whole (Chapter 28). They also addressed questions of "the one and many," making space for egalitarian love as the sacred bedrock for the political community (Chapter 27).

In the end, these final generations of biblical writers made a surprising move: they incorporated books and texts that encourage their readers to challenge the teachings that they and their predecessors had developed over centuries (Chapter 27 and 29).These circles, who shaped the final form of the canon, were convinced that pushback and testing make a system more flexible and resilient. Only when their communities questioned and evaluated their teachings would they fully appreciate both their value and their limitations.

22

The Matriarch

Women and the Biblical Agenda

"Why should our father's name be erased from his clan
because he had no son?
We demand an estate among our father's brothers!"
– Numbers 27:4

THE FIVE DAUGHTERS OF THE RECENTLY DECEASED Zelophehad are standing at the entrance of the Tabernacle. This hallowed place was the deity's domicile, requiring the utmost respect and reverence. But instead of praying and worshipping there, these women are protesting.

As the newly liberated nation was preparing to conquer the Promised Land, Yhwh provided instructions for dividing the land among the nation's members. In keeping with a patrilineal system, these laws did not include women as potential heirs. Yet rather than resigning themselves to this fate, Zelophehad's daughters voice their dissent: "Why should our father's name be erased from his clan because he had no son?"

The desire to honor a deceased father would have inspired sympathy in male leaders and readers. Yet when framing their grievance from this perspective, the daughters are not obsequious. They do not beg; they insist: "We demand an estate among our father's brothers!"

Unable to determine the next step, Moses turns to the deity. In his response, Yhwh rules in favor of these five:

> It is right what Zelophehad's daughters are saying! You must certainly give them property as an inheritance among their father's relatives and give their father's inheritance to them!
>
> – Numbers 27:7

Not only does Yhwh side with the women; he also uses their plaint as an occasion to issue new inheritance ordinances that are binding for all:

> Say to the Israelites, "If a man dies and leaves no son, give his inheritance to his daughter. If he has no daughter, give his inheritance to his brothers. If he has no brothers, give his inheritance to his father's brothers. If his father had no brothers, give his inheritance to the nearest relative in his clan, that he may possess it. This is to be a statute of judgement to all the children of Israel, as Yhwh commanded Moses."
>
> – Numbers 27:5–8

This is a unique moment in the Bible. While all the laws of the Torah originate from Yhwh or Moses, here Yhwh issues a ruling in response to the remonstrations of community members – and they are all women. Together, these daughters not only guarantee their own financial future, but their protest also brings about a permanent, and significant, revamping of the law code, with consequences for the entire nation.

The book of Joshua reports that when the land was being divided after the conquest, Zelophehad's daughters appeared again and claimed their property. Yet now there is no mention of their intention to preserve their father's name, nor do their husbands play any role in laying claim to these estates.

The marriage of these women, secure in their prospects as future landowners, marks the conclusion of the wilderness journey. This episode might make a fitting ending to a Jane Austen novel. But then again, the five daughters of Mr. Bennett in *Pride and Prejudice* do not bring about a substantial amendment to inheritance law, as the five daughters of Zelophehad do. Where Austen portrays changes in her characters, the biblical story describes changes to the system.

What makes this episode all the more remarkable is that the names of Zelophehad's five daughters correspond to five geographical regions. The Bible mentions some of them, while others appear in materials discovered through excavations, such as the Samaria Ostraca (see Chapter 6). Thanks to this remarkable correlation, we can appreciate how biblical authors commemorated communities in their people's history by identifying their forebears as women who valiantly protested divine law and brought about legal reform for the entire nation.

If biblical writings are largely the work of male scribes, how are we to explain their considerable attention to the interventions and contributions of women? This question will occupy us throughout Part IV. We begin in the present chapter with a re-examination of the Family Story in the book of Genesis.

MORE THAN MOTHERS

Many readers suppose Yhwh punishes Adam in the Garden of Eden because he "listened to the voice of [his] wife," yet this oft-quoted line misrepresents the text. Yhwh punishes Adam not for listening to Eve's voice, but because he fails to heed the instructions that Yhwh directly communicated to him. Thus, when Adam attempts to pass responsibility off to Eve ("it was she who"), Yhwh rejects the excuse: "Have *you* eaten of the tree about which I commanded *you*, '*You* shall not eat of it'?" (Genesis 3:11).

From Genesis and Exodus to Proverbs and Esther, listening to women is, more often than not, a good idea. In a variety of roles, women prove to be a crucial source of moral, political, and legal transformation. As in the case with Zelophehad's daughters, they challenge the status quo and contradict expectations. Indeed, without their strategic interventions, Israel never would have become a people in the first place.

Throughout the National Narrative, women introduce the major epochs and their central themes:

- Eve at beginning of an existence east of Eden;
- Sarah and Hagar at the genesis of the nation;
- Midwives and Miriam at the beginning of the exodus;
- Rahab at the start the conquest of Canaan;
- Achsah at the period of Judges;
- Hannah at the birth of the Monarchy;
- Bathsheba and Abishag at "the beginning of the end."

Indeed, women figure prominently across the entire biblical corpus: from the matriarchs who create the nation to Esther who saves it; from Israel as Yhwh's wife in the prophets to Jerusalem as "Daughter Zion" in

Lamentations; from the wise mother in the book of Proverbs to the assertive lover in the Song of Songs.

Moreover, the roles women play in these texts are diverse. Societies at war tend to reduce womanhood to motherhood. Thus, Teddy Roosevelt once compared the woman who "shirks her duty to bear children" to the man who "fears to do his duty in battle." In delivering that famous speech, the American president was participating in a long-established patriarchal discourse that juxtaposes the birthing-beds of women with the battlefields of men. While some biblical texts buy into this gender bifurcation, as a whole they assign men a greater part in the quotidian affairs of the family while expanding women's roles far beyond childbearing. Biblical women play a pivotal part in many military victories; they are expected to be present at public assemblies; they are extolled for taking individual initiative; and many exert considerable political influence.

Just as the National Narrative consistently pays tribute to the key contributions that women make alongside those of their male counterparts, it makes the home, not the war camp, the center stage of collective life. It also de-genders the domestic domain so that it is no longer a place principally for women. And with regard to combat zones, it expands this space to include the conventional confines of women, as when Jael invites an enemy general into her tent and slays him while he sleeps (see Chapter 24).

In many accounts, the strength that women display directly impugns the character of the male protagonists. Thus, Miriam exudes confidence, while Moses harbors deep doubts about his abilities to confront the pharaoh and lead his people to freedom (see Chapters 2 and 17). After the exodus, a group of male spies instills fear in the nation and dissuades them from invading Canaan. Their cowardice stands opposite Rahab's courage. This woman risks her life to hide a later generation of spies, and when she does, she boldly declares her faith in Israel's future and Yhwh's power (see Chapter 24).

The biblical authors sketched in these and other episodes less than flattering images of their male heroes. Yet when they lampooned them, they were not seeking to destabilize the social order, with no alternative in sight. Their intention was rather to introduce their (male) audience to a new way of being in the world.

SARAH

The Family Story translates the nation's collective experiences into stories of its ancestors, with their lives foreshadowing the fate of their descendants. The nation's earliest ancestors, Abraham and Sarah, are an aged couple who make their way to Canaan to pursue the promise of becoming parents. Once they get settled in their new home, Abraham begins complaining that he is childless. Sarah, however, takes action to solve the problem and relinquishes her childbearing role to her Egyptian maid Hagar, who gives birth to an heir (Ishmael). Eventually, the new mother gains confidence and treats her mistress with contempt. In response, Sarah harasses Hagar and causes her to run away (Genesis 16).

Modern readers understandably wish that Sarah would respond more generously to the enslaved Egyptian and her torturous plight. But ancient readers would have appreciated a basic point: why should the matriarch, in sacrificing one of her roles, have had to forfeit her honor and authority? Next to Abraham, Sarah was the head of the household, and she was convinced that she had an important role to play in the unfolding of the promise.

When Yhwh renews his pledge to Abraham, he gives both him and Sarah new names, and speaks directly about Sarah's contribution: "I will bless her, and she shall give rise to nations; kings of peoples shall come from her" (Genesis 17:16). This promise resembles the one that Yhwh had made to Abraham, yet now the man of faith falls on his face laughing incredulously. He urges Yhwh to fulfill the plan through the son whom he had with Hagar, an option that the deity resoundingly rejects.

Abraham had thought that all that matters is his paternity.[1] Twice he was willing to give up Sarah to foreign kings as he sought to save his own skin. The reader watches as he, at an agonizing pace, comes to realize that the divine promise cannot be fulfilled without Sarah. His seed is necessary, but not sufficient. His sons are not equally heirs of the covenant; only the one born to Sarah will bear the promise. Her role as the co-creator of the nation is critical, and the reader figures this out long before Abraham.

[1] Abraham initially attempts to make his servant Eliezer his adopted heir until he learns that only his own seed would bear the promise.

The matriarch's strength is evident again when she must defend her position a second time from the encroachment of her younger rival. Anticipating death yet unsure about Isaac's future, she takes steps to secure his place as heir, commanding Abraham to send away Hagar and her son. When Abraham balks at these orders, Yhwh instructs him: "Whatever Sarah tells you, do as she says" (Genesis 21:12). From the vantage point of the intended audience, the maternal maneuvering of this aged matriarch on her child's behalf made possible their own existence.

Throughout Genesis, the Family Story affirms a basic principle: it is proper that a mother contends for her child, just as one should be devoted to the welfare of his or her people. Buttressing this point, the authors awarded Hagar and her son, for whom she had endured much grief and suffering, a story of promise and redemption that parallels Israel's narrative.

REBEKAH, RACHEL, AND LEAH

The child of promise, Isaac, turns out to be a passive figure, and the Family Story does not have much to say about his life (see Chapter 16). We learn much more about his wife Rebekah, who, just as other matriarchs in the account, guides her husband's hand at decisive moments.

At the beginning, Rebekah is barren, like Sarah before her. However, in contrast to Abraham, Isaac entreats Yhwh on her behalf, and she conceives. From that point on, the patriarch fades into the background.

Rebekah is pregnant with twins, and they fight in her womb. Not knowing what is going on within her, she goes to a medium to "inquire of Yhwh" (on divination practices, see Chapter 26). Whereas Yhwh hears her husband, he goes further and responds to Rebekah with an oracle describing the future of two peoples who live within her:

> Two nations are in your womb,
> Two separate peoples shall issue from your body;
> One people shall be mightier than the other,
> And the older shall serve the younger.
>
> – Genesis 25:23

This secret knowledge, which Rebekah does not disclose to Isaac, drives her actions as the story unfolds. Defying the status quo that assigns the birthright to the eldest (Esau), she works behind the scenes to undermine her husband's plans and therewith an established patrilineal system. We watch as she devises a clever plan to dupe the aged Isaac into conferring firstborn privileges upon the younger son (Jacob), whose actions she directs at every step of the way. The reader is on her side, knowing that the child for whom she fights, and whose future she orchestrates, is none other than their national ancestor.

Jacob will later end up being tricked into marrying two women, Leah and Rachel, and theirs is a story of sibling rivalry. Whereas rivalries between brothers in the Bible (e.g., Jacob and Esau) are violent and often result in death, the sisters' competition yields new life. These wives choreograph the impregnation when they decide who will have Jacob for the night. Such stories make birth about more than biology.

Longing for Jacob's love, Leah produces many children, and the names she gives them express her yearning for her husband's affection. On the other hand, Rachel can count on Jacob's devotion, but she is unable to conceive. After resorting to various measures, she finally bears two sons of her own. However, she does not survive the birth of the second (Genesis 35). Except for Samson's story perhaps, this account is the closest the Bible comes to commemorating heroic death. Yet here it is a woman who dies; her death is involuntary, and most importantly, it results in the birth of a child. (On the repudiation of heroic, substitutionary death in the Hebrew Bible, see Chapter 25.)

The four matriarchs – Sarah, Rebecca, Rachel, and Leah – are not only bearers of children and thus mothers of the nation, but are also lauded for the ways they, like Hagar, define their children's destinies and thereby shape their people's collective future. It is their acuity, judgment, and sheer gumption that bring the divine promises to fulfillment. The book of Ruth pays tribute to Rachel and Leah as those "who together built the house of Israel."

Throughout the Family Story, mothers are more than mere vessels of male heirs. While men supply the seed, women create and nurture the children, and then determine their direction and destiny. As such, they are partners with the divine, a partnership that already Eve recognizes after the birth of her first son: "I created a man with Yhwh."

Let us consider one more episode from the Family Story that illustrates these points better than any other (Genesis 38). It depicts a woman, who had been stripped of her rights, resorting to unconventional methods to regain her place in society. In so doing, she becomes the ancestress of the nation's most distinguished lineage.

TAMAR

Judah, son of Jacob and the eponymous ancestor of the tribe/kingdom Judah, had three sons. His firstborn was married to a woman named Tamar. Yet he had behaved wickedly and was killed by an act of God, leaving Tamar as both a widow and childless. As such, her future was uncertain: widows without children were the most vulnerable members of ancient societies.

The institution of levirate marriage was designed to deal with this situation. It required that a brother of a deceased man impregnate his childless widow, with the offspring of their union counted as the heir of the deceased. In keeping with these expectations, Judah commands his second son to sleep with Tamar. But the son refuses to produce offspring for his dead brother, and every time he sleeps with Tamar, he spills his semen on the ground. (This man's name is Onan, from which we derive our term "onanism.") For this wicked behavior, Yhwh kills him too.

After the death of his second son, Judah is unwilling to risk the life of his third. He therefore sends Tamar back to her father's house, claiming that his only remaining son is too young and that she would receive him as soon as he comes of age. Yet Judah has no intention of keeping his promise, and Tamar is left to languish in limbo.

With such unscrupulous men in her life, Tamar could have easily given up. But instead, she resolves to do whatever it takes to get the job done. Concealing her identity with a veil, she places herself on the path that Judah will travel on the way to the annual flock-shearing festivities. In a festive mood, Judah mistakes her for a sex worker and solicits her services. However, he does not have a sheep from his flock with which he could pay. Thus, at Tamar's demand, he relinquishes his seal and staff (emblems of his identity and authority comparable to a driver's license and ring or watch) as guarantees until she received payment.

What is so significant about this detail? Tamar needs a child, but Judah's sons refuse to do what is required of them. Hence, she goes right for the patriarch himself. She knows that she faces social scorn, if not also death, once the pregnancy becomes public. However, with Judah's seal and staff, she could prove that Judah had slept with her and thereby re-establish her honor in society. And that is exactly what happens. Tamar handles the situation in the most diplomatic fashion, allowing the patriarch to save face. In the end, things work out even better than planned: Judah publicly confirms her righteousness, and the birth of twins signals divine approval.

This tale of "a harlot on the roadside" was told to raise eyebrows. As an underdog who resorts to unorthodox means, Tamar is a hero in the biblical imagination. To adapt a line from the Jewish ethicist Rachel Adler, this account exposes patriarchy with its pants off. It reveals Judah's shortcomings, while commending Tamar's character. What motivates her actions is an unrelenting concern for own future, and as the story shows, her concerns as a widowed woman bear directly on the future of many others: had it not been for her daring act, doing what was necessary to survive in a patriarchal system, the tribe of Judah would have died out and there would have been no King David (see Ruth 4).[2]

RECONCEIVING GENDER ROLES

The project of creating a nation is, as these stories show, both a collaborative and a competitive effort, and the ones who sustain it are first and foremost women. J. Cheryl Exum notes the striking paradox that characterizes biblical literature: "Whereas the important events in Israelite tradition are experienced by men, they are often set in motion and determined by women."

The Bible makes infertility an agonistic struggle for men, rather than solely the fault of women. When Sarah hears the divine promise that her

[2] Tamar is also the first woman in the New Testament, holding an honored place in the genealogy of Jesus; see Matthew 1:3.

aged husband would make a child with her, she laughs to herself, "How will I still have pleasure [in bed] when my husband is an old man?" (Genesis 18:12). Similarly, Rachel demands that Jacob make children with her, implying that he must be impotent. With his manhood offended, Jacob angrily insults the woman he loves: "Am I in the place of God? He has withheld from you the fruit of the womb!" (Genesis 30:2).

The theme of the barren wife calls attention to the crucial role of women. It also demonstrates husbands' loyalty to their wives despite their barrenness. When Rebekah struggles with her infertility, Isaac prays for her. Jacob's love for Rachel is independent of her procreative role.

As we saw in Chapter 18, the Palace History begins with the story of a man who, like Jacob, has two wives. One had given him children, yet the other, Hannah, was barren. The mother torments Hannah for failing to produce a child, but the husband favors Hannah and comforts her as she struggles with barrenness: "Why are you sad? Am I not more to you than ten sons?" Hannah wants more than her husband and refuses to be comforted. She eventually conceives and bears a son – none other than Samuel, the kingmaker. And it is Hannah, not her husband, who determines the boy's future: she brings him to the temple, separating him from his father. There, in the service of the high priest, he becomes a leader of the nation, bringing down the mighty and raising up the downtrodden, in keeping with the vision that his mother had expressed in her majestic prayer that inaugurates the monarchy.

The choice to place household stories at the beginning of a nation's narratives is a bold statement that power resides in the inner workings of the family. In the Family Story, the home is where the heart is, and the nation's collective future is repeatedly decided here. In this realm, women have great influence and wield it with finesse – even when their societies fail to grant them formal authority.

All readers could relate to these tales of family life, and their inclusion in the biblical corpus ensured that it would continue to speak to many for millennia to come. In the following chapter, we explore how other narratives expand the influence of women beyond the home while revamping the roles men play.

FURTHER READING

Adelman, Rachel E., *The Female Ruse: Women's Deception and Divine Sanction in the Hebrew Bible*, Sheffield Phoenix, 2015.

Crowder, Stephanie Buckhanon, *When Momma Speaks: The Bible and Motherhood from a Womanist Perspective*, Westminster John Knox, 2016.

Davison, Lisa Wilson, *More Than a Womb: Childfree Women in the Hebrew Bible as Agents of the Holy*, Cascade, 2021.

Demsky, Aaron, "The Daughters of Zelophehad: A Historical-Geographical Approach," *TheTorah.com*, 2019, www.thetorah.com/article/the-daughters-of-zelophehad-a-historical-geographical-approach.

Exum, J. Cheryl, "'Mother in Israel': A Familiar Figure Reconsidered," in Letty M. Russell (ed.), *Feminist Interpretation of the Bible*, Presbyterian Publishing, 1985.

Hutner, Jan Lisa, *Tevye's Daughters*, FF2 Media, 2014 (see sections 5 and 6 on Jane Austen and the biblical account of Zelophehad's daughters).

Junior, Nyasha, *Reimagining Hagar: Blackness and Bible*, Oxford University Press, 2019.

Kozlova, Ekaterina E., *Maternal Grief in the Hebrew Bible*, Oxford University Press, 2017.

Matskevich, Karalina, *Construction of Gender and Identity in Genesis: The Subject and the Other*, T&T Clark, 2020.

McKinlay, Judith E., *Troubling Women and Land: Reading Biblical Texts in Aotearoa New Zealand*, Sheffield Phoenix, 2014.

Menn, Esther Marie, *Judah and Tamar (Genesis 38) in Ancient Jewish Exegesis: Studies in Literary Form and Hermeneutics*, Brill, 1997.

Moss, Candida R., and Baden, Joel S., *Reconceiving Infertility: Biblical Perspectives on Procreation and Childlessness*, Princeton University Press, 2015.

Schneider, Tammi J., *Sarah: Mother of Nations*, Continuum, 2004.

Shectman, Sarah, *Women in the Pentateuch: A Feminist and Source-Critical Analysis*, Sheffield Phoenix, 2009.

23

The Hero

Redefining Gender Roles

They gave him seventy pieces of silver
from the temple of Baal-Berith,
and Abimelek used it to hire reckless scoundrels,
who became his followers.
–Judges 9:4

ON THE HORIZON, BILLOWS OF SMOKE could be seen rising from the neighboring town of Shechem. In his quest to become king, an abhorrent figure named Abimelek had set it ablaze, killing almost one thousand of its inhabitants. Now he had besieged and captured the town of Thebez. The inhabitants knew they too faced death at the hands of this scoundrel, and with no help in sight, they have taken refuge on the roof of a fortified tower.

In this quivering crowd is a woman with a millstone, the object with which many women spent their days grinding grain for their family. Had she brought it with her in the hope that she would live to see another day? Did she happen to find it on the roof of the tower? Whatever the case may be, when the miscreant monarch approaches the tower with the intention of burning it to the ground, she realizes that the stone tool could serve a different purpose. Taking careful aim, she hurls the object so that it lands squarely on the assailant's head, cracking his skull.

Knowing that he will soon die, the malefactor commands his attendant to give him the *coup de grâce* so that he would not suffer what he deemed to be the greatest disgrace – dying at the hands of woman:

Draw your sword and finish me off,
so it won't be said about me,
"A woman killed him."
–Judges 9:54

In this oft overlooked tale, a lone, unnamed, and otherwise inconspicuous woman saves her people from an arriviste on his way to becoming Israel's first king. Despite his protestations, he is remembered not for what he achieved, but how he died. The millstone of "a certain woman" (in Hebrew: "one woman") represents the daily grind of average folks, and it overpowers his sword as an instrument of state terror.

The philosopher and psychoanalyst Jonathan Lear writes in *Radical Hope* about the blind spot in human societies: our inability to conceive of our own devastation. He considers how the Crow nation (Apsáalooke) of North America lost their traditional life of nomadic hunting, along with "the conditions that allowed for warrior glory and the spiritual context that endorsed just such a life." The catastrophe provoked "a deeply upsetting (in the literal sense of that term) and weirdly enigmatic, practical question: what does it any longer mean to be Crow?"[1]

As in the Native American context, the conquest of the Northern and Southern kingdoms of Israel and Judah resulted in the loss of a life that had long revolved around martial prowess and battlefield honor. Yet instead of tossing in the towel, the biblical scribes, like the Crow, fashioned a new identity and crafted a new culture with very different ideals of heroism. They recognized the positive potential of ambition and quests for honor among their members, but they now channeled that competitive energy to the needs of their defeated communities.

The new heroes who populate the nation's imagined past range from mothers and fathers struggling to create families, to builders and teachers devoting their energy to the edification and education of their communities. As all go about their daily lives, they display courage while resourcefully making do with what little they have. Thus, the unnamed

[1] Lear, *Radical Hope*, p. 28.

woman of Thebez takes the instrument with which she mills grain and wields it as a weapon to eliminate a monstrous monarch. She embodies a new cultural ethos in which diurnal duty and domestic life are exalted, and the heroes of old meet ignoble deaths.

This post-defeat national culture still has a place for heroes like David who bring down giants with pluck and confidence. However, as the present chapter will demonstrate, the biblical scribes heavily reshaped the warrior legends they inherited. They also did not assign them pride of place at the beginning of the National Narrative, opting instead for tales of domestic life.

THE IMPORTANCE OF FORGETTING

Without memory, there is no identity, and as our identities evolve and change, we supplement and sometimes replace old memories with new ones. The same goes for our political identities: new nations need new pasts. The biblical scribes not only created a "prehistory of peoplehood" for their conquered communities (as we saw in Part III), but also reinvented their heroes.

Consider the character of Jacob. The Family Story in Genesis paints him as the consummate trickster. When his father-in-law Laban does everything to handicap his endeavors, he repeatedly resorts to schemes and prospers. Earlier, with the help of his mother Rebekah, he pulled the wool over his father's eyes and purloined the firstborn blessings from his elder twin Esau, as we saw in the preceding chapter.

The story of these brothers is a study of opposites. "Esau was a skillful hunter and a man of the field, while Jacob was a mild man, one who dwells in tents" (Genesis 25:27). The contrast between the fraternal twins is on full display in the final scene of their rapprochement. The two men had lived for years with unresolved tension and outright hostility. During this time, Esau had become a mighty warrior, while Jacob has become the father of large clan. Knowing that Esau has long wanted to kill him, Jacob advances cautiously behind his women and children. His brother, however, stands staunchly with his large force of armed men. The pivotal scene identifies the nation's eponymous ancestor not with warriors and weapons, but with women and children.

As they crafted their ancestor's character, the authors of the Family Story consciously forgot competing memories, and in the process, eliminated traits that he once shared with his bellicose brother. Echoes of the other, more militant, figure can still be heard in unexpected places. Thus, on his deathbed Jacob gives his son Joseph a "portion" of the land (a play on the name of the town Shechem) that he claims to have "captured from the Amorites with my sword and my bow."

These fragmented memories of Jacob as a pugnacious patriarch, who seizes Shechem with his weapons, clash with the later, more embellished, ones in which Jacob seeks a peaceful coexistence with these same neighbors. One of the most stirring accounts in the Family Story describes how the prince of Shechem rapes Jacob's daughter Dinah. Her brothers retaliate by wiping out the town's inhabitants. In keeping with his non-confrontational and cunning character, Jacob does not commend his sons for defending the honor of their sister; instead, he sharply denounces their violent conduct:

> You have brought trouble on me by making me odious to the inhabitants of the land, the Canaanites and the Perizzites. My numbers are few. If they gather themselves against me and attack me, I shall be destroyed – both I and my household.
>
> – Genesis 34:30

Jacob here is not the fearless fighter who succeeds with sword and bow, but the underdog survivor who learns, through painful trial and error, how to save his skin and succeed. As an underdog in a world of warriors, his success is measured above all by the formidable family he fathers.

In *Recovered Roots*, Yael Zerubavel shows how early Zionists consciously sought to reshape Jewish memory. The Rabbis had sublimated many memories of statehood (e.g., the Maccabees, Masada, and the Bar Kokhba rebellion) as they fashioned a new identity in response to defeat and exile. (Later, as conditions were more propitious for statehood, Zionists recovered these roots.) What is important for our purposes is how the biblical scribes, as the Rabbis' predecessors, were already engaged in this activity of sublimation when they, in an ambitious act of redaction, constructed new archetypes and set aside memories they deemed deleterious to their new post-destruction identity.

THE CRITIQUE OF MACHOISM IN THE BOOK OF JUDGES

Representing an advanced stage in the evolution of the National Narrative, the book of Judges displays many features of the new post-destruction identity. As we saw in Chapter 19, this work serves as a literary bridge between two older parts of the National Narrative. On the one side, there is the people who escaped bondage, and on the other, there is the kingdom that protects the people yet also ends up oppressing them. The point is underscored in the account of Solomon's reign, which depicts this ruler subjecting the nation to the same corvée labor they performed in Egypt. The authors of Judges expanded older traditions to show how the pendulum swung from one side to the other. As a prelude to the monarchy that emerges in the centuries thereafter, these parables of statehood prompt the reader to ask: how did these early generations of male leaders establish a precedent for the behavior of the nation's later kings?

Judges features a diverse range of voices. While its authors allowed these voices to be heard in their original accent and cadence, they combined them in a symphonic arrangement with a somber tonality. The overarching theme to the work is the trauma men wreak on others in their quest for power and the barometer that women's lives provide for the nation's well-being.

Of the book's twenty-one chapters, thirteen include stories about women. The first woman is Achsah. As the nation lays claim to the Promised Land, her father, Caleb, offers her as a trophy wife for the warrior who will capture a key city. But contrary to expectations, Achsah proves to be one in control. As soon as she is married, she persuades her husband to request a gift from her father. Her husband, however, fails to get the job done. So she seizes the reins, both literally and metaphorically, and goes forth to confront her father: "Give me a present, for you have given me away as Negev-land [dry land]. Give me now springs of water." Her father concedes and endows her (not her husband) with two important water sources. Thanks to her assertiveness, her clan possessed resources that were crucial to their survival in the arid region of the south.

Achsah's story appears twice in the Bible, and its repetition here at the beginning of Judges establishes the benchmark for the episodes that follow. The next women in the narrative are Deborah and Jael. A respected prophet who unites the nation, Deborah initiates a successful campaign against the Canaanites. She stands next to Jael, an outsider who defies her husband and delivers the final blow to the enemy. When the leader of Israel's troops had demanded that Deborah accompany him into battle, she both warned him that he would not achieve glory and prophesied Jael's valor: "For Yhwh will deliver [the enemy general] into the hand of a woman." (For more on Jael, see the following chapter.)

Deborah is uniquely unsullied and is a paragon of national leadership. In contrast, her successor Gideon is a coward, and women are conspicuously absent from his story. He seems originally to have been a formidable warrior, yet the authors of Judges, similar to what we observed for Jacob in Genesis, buried these memories by composing an extensive introduction that portrays him as an apprehensive and unlikely leader. He summons the courage to fight only after receiving many divine signs assuring him of success.

When the nation wishes to make Gideon its king after his victory, he formally declines the offer and insists, "I shall not rule over you, nor shall my son rule over you. It is Yhwh who rules over you!" His later behavior, however, belies his objection. His son is none other than Abimelek, the violent king from the beginning story of this chapter. Abimelek's name means "my father is king," and if Gideon only flirted with monarchic aspirations, his son fully embraced it.

A DOWNWARD SPIRAL

By the time the woman of Thebez crushes Abimelek's skull, men have begun to run amok in society. From this point on, Israel's women will go unnamed – a sign of their depreciated value and the general decline of society. In this new era, male leaders fail to restrain their thirst for power that slaughters women and ultimately strangles the nation.

Jephthah follows Gideon and Abimelek in the narrative, and he exemplifies the martial and megalomaniac mentality that begins to take hold. His unnamed daughter is one of the few damsels in distress in the Bible. Yet in her case, no one comes to the rescue. To make matters worse, the killer is her own father.

Jephthah does not have a son to carry on his name. Since the unnamed daughter is his "only one," he is anxious to make a name for himself on the battlefield. Willing to do anything for triumph, he makes a vow to Yhwh that he will sacrifice the first member of his house to receive him and celebrate his triumphant return. This was a traditional role for women. Thus Miriam guides the women of the nation in a celebration of Yhwh after the battle at the Red Sea (Exodus 15:20–21), and later the women of Israel come out to sing David's praises after he slays Goliath (1 Samuel 18:6–7). Jephthah would therefore expect either his wife or daughter to be the one who welcomes him back from the battlefield. Yet when his daughter goes forth, with timbrels and dance, to acclaim him as victor, all this scoundrel can say is: "Oh my daughter, you have brought me low!"

His daughter insists that he follow through with the despicable vow, yet she also requests two months to wander the hills with her friends "bewailing her virginity." The narrator reports that it became a custom that every year "the daughters of Israel would go out and commemorate the daughter of Jephthah the Gileadite." The festival these women created honors her courage; meanwhile, what preserves Jephthah's memory is an account that pillories his thirst for power.

Jephthah is succeeded by Samson, another man with dubious judgment, especially in relation to women. The story of his mother, an unnamed woman, provides the lens for his life. She is barren yet does not seem particularly perturbed about it. A divine messenger appears to her and announces she will give birth to a son with a unique destiny. When she reports the meeting to her husband, Manoah, he promptly begs Yhwh to send the messenger again. The messenger returns, yet again he appears only to his wife. When Manoah asks for information, the angel replies curtly that he already instructed his wife.

The comical scene reveals the unnamed wife to be astute and discerning in contrast to her obtuse husband. Their son Samson embodies a masculinity that relies on brute force. Although he is unusually clever, he depends on superhuman strength to decimate the Philistines. His fatal flaw is his longing to be loved, which causes him to divulge his secrets – including the key to his strength – to (Philistine) women.

The book's final chapters paint an ever-widening cycle of violence. It begins with the vicious treatment of an unnamed concubine, initiated by her own husband, a Levite priest. After suffering abuse at home, the concubine returns to her father. The Levite goes to retrieve her, and as the two are on their way home, they seek lodging in the town of Gibeon, an important place in the nation's history. There, against ancient conventions of hospitality, they have to wait around until they are finally offered a place for the night.

The inhabitants of the town turn out to be reprobates. They pound on the host's door, demanding that he hand over the Levite so that they may "know" him. To save themselves, the men of the house cast the concubine to the mob. A gang rape that lasts the entire night leaves the woman unconscious at the doorstep at daybreak. "Get up," the Levite orders her, "we are going." When the woman does not respond, he loads her on her donkey and continues on his journey. Was she dead at this point? The reader does not know, and this uncertainty makes the following actions even more odious: when he arrives home, he proceeds to carve her up into twelve pieces. He then sends the pieces of her corpse throughout the land, summoning the nation to punish the crime that the town of Gibeon had committed.

The narrator exposes the hypocrisy and culpability of this loathsome Levite, placing it on par with the perpetrators of the rape. Violence against one unnamed woman implicates the entire society. As the degeneracy engulfs the entire nation in the book's final chapters, tens of thousands are dead, and six hundred virgin women are abducted to provide wives for warriors.

The book thus depicts the dismantling of the body politic via the violence that men perpetrate on women's bodies. It begins with women as heroes who save the day, and it ends with them as victims who suffer unspeakably from the nation's own leaders. Throughout the narrative, women serve as canaries in the coal mine: when they are strong and enjoy agency, the nation is thriving, but when they are reduced to silence and violated, the reader knows that, to adapt a line from *Hamlet*, there is something rotten in the state of Israel.

THE WOMEN IN DAVID'S LIFE

Let us now turn our attention to the Palace History in which David plays the leading role. The scribes responsible for the final contours of his life story use four women – Michal, Abigail, Bathsheba, and Abishag – to demarcate four phases in his life. David may have achieved great things, but without women, his fame, and life, would not have endured long. It is women who sing his praises, comparing his feats to those of the king, and these songs "make a name" for David that becomes known even among the enemy Philistines.

At the beginning of the narrative, the power-hungry upstart yearns to be part of the royal family, and Saul's daughter Michal is his ticket. Like her brother Jonathan, Michal loves David and seeks to protect him from her father's wrath. But whereas Jonathan proves to be naive, underestimating their father's murderous intent, Michal correctly diagnoses Saul's obsession and enables David's escape.

A defining moment in David's career is his encounter with Abigail. Intent on assassinating her wealthy husband for his ingratitude, David is literally stopped in his tracks by this woman. Yes, Abigail is pretty, but the narrator notes her intelligence before her appearance (1 Samuel 25:3). When she meets David, she delivers a speech (the longest by any woman in the Bible) that paints David's glorious future and urges him not to tarnish it with foolhardy decisions. Thanks to her sagacity, David recognizes that bloodshed would be the wrong political move. He marries her soon after her husband dies, and with this wealthy, beautiful, and wise woman on his side, he goes on to become king of Judah and Israel.

Bathsheba begins as a passive sex object whom David beds at will after he had reached the summit of his career (see introduction to Chapter 25). By the end of David's life, however, she is in control. Solomon, her son, is the youngest of David's male descendants. The odds are stacked against him as heir to the throne, but Bathsheba fights for him, collaborating with the prophet Nathan to ensure that he is enthroned – without civil war or bloodshed.

In preparing to approach the feeble king on his deathbed, who is now lying with a young woman named Abishag, the prophet Nathan instructs Bathsheba what to say. He plans to come after her and second her words. He also proposes that she rhetorically ask if David had promised to give his throne to her son Solomon. Yet Bathsheba does not follow Nathan's instructions. Instead, she tells the senile David that long ago he had chosen her son to be his heir (1 Kings 1:17). Her more assertive approach renders superfluous Nathan's obsequious speech. She is like

David's great-grandmother Ruth who, rather than merely heeding instructions, follows her own intuitions and instincts.

Other women in David's story act to prevent wanton bloodshed, and one of them deserves special attention. Her advice is pivotal in the account of a revolt against David is reign, yet she is often overlooked. She is referred to as a "Wise Woman." Her name is not provided, suggesting that she is a paradigm of female sages that provided guidance to their societies.

Joab, David's general, had pursued a rebel leader to a fortified town named Abel on Israel's northern border. As soon as he and his soldiers arrive, they begin to breach the walls:

> Joab's forces were battering the wall to break it down.
> Then a Wise Woman called from the city, "Listen! Listen! Tell Joab, 'Come here, I want to speak to you.'"
> He came near her; and the woman said, "Are you Joab?"
> He answered, "I am."
> Then she said to him, "Listen to the words of your servant."
> He answered, "I am listening."
>
> – 2 Samuel 20:15–17

Notice how this woman acts with self-assurance and authority. It is all business, and her confidence captures the commander's attention. She begins by establishing the city's good reputation and her own credentials as a peacemaker, but then quickly turns to accusing him of destructive behavior:

> Then she said, "They used to say in the old days,
> 'Let them inquire at Abel and so the matter will be settled.'
> I am one of those who are peaceable and faithful in Israel.
> You seek to destroy a city and mother in Israel.
> Why will you swallow up the heritage of Yhwh?"
>
> – 2 Samuel 20:18–19

Here is a negotiator who knows how to argue persuasively. Joab hastens to excuse himself, and after deferentially explaining his position, he makes a request:

> Joab answered, "Far be it from me, far be it, that I should swallow up or destroy!

> That is not the case. A man has lifted up his hand against King David. Give him up, and I will withdraw from the city."
> The woman said to Joab, "His head shall be thrown over the wall to you."
> – 2 Samuel 20:20–21

This unnamed woman is so confident of her status that she agrees to Joab's terms even before consulting with the townspeople. Although the rebel must have had allies in the town, they are no match for the persuasiveness of this woman's "wise plan" (2 Samuel 20:22). Thanks to it, the rebel is quickly beheaded, David maintains his rule, and a border town is spared gratuitous destruction.

EVALUATING THE EVIDENCE

The Bible's law codes miss many opportunities to expand women's spheres of influence, subjecting them to men's control. (See the exception to this rule in the accounts of Zelophehad's daughters discussed in the preceding chapter.) The Bible's prose narratives, however, rarely depict women as passive. Instead, they portray them repeatedly using ingenuity to transform society and undercut those in authority.

In these texts, most women do not exercise the formal authority, yet they do wield real power. And that power is often more effective than authority. For example, the book of Esther portrays a young Jewish woman, whom an eccentric king with unlimited authority had taken as his queen, wining and dining those in control and in the process overturning a genocidal decree issued against her people. In Chapter 29 we consider how Esther's story captures the heart of the biblical project of peoplehood better than any other book in the Bible.

Why are there such stories about women? And why so many of them? One answer pertains to the writers and the readers themselves. Power without recognized authority happens to be the position that they and their communities find themselves in a world under imperial rule. As such, stories about women reflect their readers' existential concerns. The way these biblical women maneuver in relation to men is precisely what these communities must do to survive under foreign rule. The men who wrote the Bible thus found women to be "good to think with," to borrow an expression from the anthropologist Claude Lévi-Strauss. In their effort to imagine news ways of coping with defeat, they discovered that their vanquished communities had a lot to learn from women's ways of being in the world.

But there is also a real demographic concern that explains why the Bible contains so many stories about women. The scribes who shaped this corpus seemed to have realized that with their communities being clear underdogs, they could not afford to confine women to the shadows. They, therefore, told stories of women to teach their male readers that women had long played critical roles in their nation's history and have a critical role to play in its future.

When Israel and Judah were thriving kingdoms, elite and noble women were conventionally restricted to domestic spaces and guarded carefully. But now that Israel and Judah had been defeated and reduced to smaller, struggling societies, they could not survive by excluding half of their population from participation in public life. The earlier status quo had to be abolished.

The biblical truth is profoundly pragmatic. It is about keeping the boat afloat and mobilizing all hands. It is not about what is eternally and ideally true for the gods, as Plato and other philosophers conceived it. The scribes who shaped the biblical corpus were concerned with what sustains life and can work under less-than-ideal conditions. And what did not work in an age of foreign rule was a macho-martial culture that imperiled the nation's future and prohibited half of the population from taking part in public life. Instead of being like Samson's simple-minded father, men needed to listen to the voice of women, just as women needed to play a more central role in public life.

The new counter-culture that scribes in the post-destruction period promoted was crucial to their strategies for surviving under imperial rule. The direct approach of duking it out with enemy and defending national honor promised only to inflict more grief and suffering on their communities. The male members of the nation needed to relinquish their individualist, bootstrap mentality and learn the ways of their female forebears – from collaboration and compromise to subterfuge and stratagem.

As a whole, the Bible assigns primacy to families and introduces many measures to ensure that nothing undermines their futures. This concern explains why the Pentateuch does something that is seemingly contradictory. On the one hand, it includes many stories that celebrate and strengthen the roles of women in the family, while sidelining and even outright maligning males. On the other hand, it preserves a patriarchal order, and instead of abolishing it, makes exceptions, as in the account of Zelophehad's daughters with which we began Chapter 22.

Another passage from the Pentateuch addresses, at length, the issue of women's vows (Numbers 30). Instead of ruling that women's vows have no validity whatsoever, these laws provide detailed instructions for the circumstances in which the head of the household (father or husband) has a right to annul the vow of women in that household. Why do these laws treat this issue so seriously? Because the vows of women had great power and potentially posed threats to the family's integrity and their property, as when a mother, like Hannah, vows to give her son to the temple (see Chapters 18 and 22).

Now one may have wished that the biblical authors had simply jettisoned the patriarchal-patrilineal system and created something completely different in its stead. But once again their concern was that their communities flourish in the face of cultural devastation, and they deemed strong, long-enduring families crucial to this objective. As they turned their focus on the family, they worked hard to curb the enthusiasm of their macho readers.

Envisioning an alternative to the patriarchal order is a feat that remained for Jewish biblical scholars and feminists who, more than two millennia later, have taken inspiration from, and worked in continuity with, the work of their biblical forbears.[2] To put things into perspective for those who hastily condemn the biblical authors, assuming that they were just sitting around looking for opportunities to make life more difficult for their women, we need to remember that these folks were writing three thousand years ago. If the task of abolishing the patriarchy was so easy, why are we still struggling to undo it today?

[2] Two notable examples of this work are Carol Meyers' *Discovering Eve* from 1988 and twenty years later Eskenazi and Weiss's monumental project *The Torah: A Women's Commentary* (2008).

FURTHER READING

Brenner-Idan, Athalya, *The Israelite Woman: Social Role and Literary Type in Biblical Narrative*, 2nd ed., Bloomsbury, 2015.

Brenner, Athalya and Yee, Gale A. (eds.), *Joshua and Judges*, Fortress, 2013.

Creangă, Ovidiu (ed.), *Hebrew Masculinities Anew*, Sheffield Phoenix, 2019.

Edinburg, Cynthia, *Dismembering the Whole: Composition and Purpose of Judges 19–21*, SBL Press, 2016.

Eskenazi, Tamara Cohn and Weiss, Andrea L. (eds.), *The Torah: A Women's Commentary*, URJ Press, 2008.

Lear, Jonathan, *Radical Hope: Ethics in the Face of Cultural Devastation*, Harvard University Press, 2006.

Melanchthon, Monica Jyotsna and Whitaker, Robyn J. (eds.), *Terror in the Bible: Rhetoric, Gender, and Violence*, SBL Press, 2021.

Meyers, Carol, *Discovering Eve: Ancient Israelite Women in Context*, Oxford University Press, 1988.

Murphy, Kelly J., *Rewriting Masculinity: Gideon, Men, and Might*, Oxford University Press, 2019.

Newsom, Carol A., Ringe, Sharon H., and Lapsley, Jacqueline E. (eds.), *The Women's Bible Commentary*, Westminster John Knox, 2012.

Stone, Kenneth A., *Sex, Honor and Power in the Deuteronomistic History*, Sheffield Academic Press, 1996.

Wright, Jacob L., *David, King of Israel, and Caleb in Biblical Memory*, Cambridge University Press, 2014.

Zakovitch, Yair, *Jacob: Unexpected Patriarch*, Yale University Press, 2012.

Zerubavel, Yael, *Recovered Roots: Collective Memory and the Making Israeli National Tradition*, University of Chicago Press, 1995.

24

The Other

Tales of War, Outsiders, and Allegiance

Only Rahab the harlot, and all who are with her in her house, shall live, because she hid the messengers we sent.

– Joshua 6:17

THIS WAS THE TIME they had long been waiting for. The nation had finally crossed the Jordan and stepped foot in the Promised Land. It was not yet in their possession, and many battles lay ahead. They were also marching with a disturbing directive from the deity to wipe out all the Canaanites – no exceptions.

Jericho is the first place they attack, and as they are about to storm the city, Joshua reminds the people that they are to destroy every living thing. Yet now he makes an exception: no one is to lay a hand on "Rahab the prostitute" and her entire household. Why would the nation's commander defy Yhwh's explicit orders?

Just days before, two Israelite spies had entered Rahab's house while they were on an espionage mission. When the king of Jericho learned of their arrival, he demanded that she deliver them into his custody. Yet instead of complying with his demands, she put her life in danger by concealing the spies on the roof of her home and blatantly lying to the king's officers. Later when she sent the spies away in safety, she revealed to them her confidence in Yhwh and made them swear that they would rescue her and her entire family during the impending invasion. Now that the city had fallen to Israel, Joshua follows through with the promise. To conclude, the narrator reports: "Her family has lived in Israel ever since. For she hid the messengers whom Joshua sent to spy out Jericho" (Joshua 6:25).

In Part III, we explored how the covenant cultivated a sense of kinship uniting rival clans and competing regions. All families and individuals were equal under a single, written, divine law code, with allegiance owed first and foremost to the nation and its deity, not to one's clan, city, guild, and so on. But what about outsiders, minorities on the margins of society, those who did not have a long history with the nation, or groups that sought to maintain their distinctiveness? How did the biblical authors address the issues of belonging and collective identity that they presented? And why did these writers address it most often through stories of war and military conflict? In what follows, we answer these questions by briefly considering four cases: Rahab and the Gibeonites, Jael and the Kenites, the tribes of the Transjordan, and Ruth and the Moabites.

HOLY WAR

War permeates the pages of the Bible. We would expect biblical writers to remember the major battles and wars in their people's history, but how are we to explain not only their preoccupation with the subject but also their embellishment of older war stories and invention of battles that their ancestors never fought?

Some scholars account for the pervading presence of military conflict in the biblical corpus on the assumption that ancient Israel and Judah were bellicose societies. Others point to notions of "Holy War" that were supposedly prevalent in a "primitive" or "tribal" society.

These explanations are problematic for multiple reasons. Most importantly, they fail to appreciate how the Bible is a project of peoplehood, and for a political community, war constitutes the ultimate threat. Floods, drought, disease, and other natural catastrophes afflict regions, with little regard to political borders; wars target communities, nations, and states. For this reason, peoples commonly construct their identities via memories of military conflicts.

Wars are so decisive for communities because they are moments when all their members are expected to come together and assist each other. After the cessation of conflict, they often look back at their common experiences and commemorate those who contributed in both ordinary and extraordinary ways. They also draw attention to those who shirked their duties. By engaging in this political activity of "war commemoration," they call into question a group's loyalty or, alternatively, provide proof that a disputed group had earned a place of honor in the halls of their history.

War commemoration, like all political activities, is contentious. Populations on the margins of society – women, religious or ethnic minorities, LGBTQ, and other marginalized groups – confront "collective amnesia" by calling attention to their own service and sacrifice on behalf of the larger community. In this way, they lay claim to public honors and political rights. Such battles over memory make and mold the nation's identity.

In two earlier books, I demonstrate how this same activity of war commemoration produced much of the biblical narrative.[1] Scribes from both North and South forged a new national identity via memories of war, both real and imagined. Their texts portray how representative members of contested groups made crucial wartime contributions on the behalf of the nation, either fighting in its ranks or demonstrating courage as civilians. With the help of these memories, one affirmed that a group belongs or deserves a place of prominence in society. Conversely, by claiming that an individual or group shirked their wartime duty or failed to assist the nation at a time of crisis, one raised questions about their membership or the special privileges they enjoyed.

Typical monarchic inscriptions from ancient West Asia focus on the deeds of a king or a dynasty; they have little, if anything, to say about other groups that contributed to the war effort. In contrast, biblical war commemoration is a more horizontal in perspective: the nation and the wide array of groups that comprise it figure prominently in the memories of major wars and battles that had been waged in the past.

Why then does war loom so large in biblical writings? It is because the authors of these texts were addressing issues of belonging and status within an emerging national community that they called "Israel." In what follows we see how this approach helps us appreciate a wide array of biblical texts.

[1] Wright, *War, Memory and National Identity*; Wright, *King of Israel, and Caleb in Biblical Memory*.

RAHAB AND THE GIBEONITES

Rahab's story provides a poignant parable of wartime contributions and belonging. By contributing to Israel's war effort, risking her life, and betraying her own city, she procures protection for her clan. As a Canaanite, a woman, and a sex worker, she moves from the margins of one society to the center of another by taking part in its war effort. The biblical authors mark the social transition in concrete spatial terms. They position Rahab's house in the wall of Jericho, where she, with the help of a scarlet cord, could signal her place to passersby. When the wall falls, she moves from the margins of this Canaanite city to "the midst of Israel."

We should not reckon with the existence of a clan of "Rahabites" who took pride in this heroic tale of an eponymous ancestor. Rahab is, rather, a generic outsider. Indeed, she is the paragon of "the Other." Similar to a mercenary soldier, her affection as a prostitute is for purchase. But in the biblical account, she demonstrates undivided allegiance – not to a man, but to a nation.

Today many view Rahab as a *collaboratrice* who joins forces with a colonial power that takes possession of her people's land. Just as she sells her body, she is unfaithful to her own community. In comparing her to Pocahontas, one misses that Israel historically was not a colonizing power, nor is being depicted in the biblical account as such. On the contrary, the biblical authors were writing from the perspective of the colonized. As they constructed a new identity after being subjugated by imperial powers, they worked not only to delineate the nation's boundaries, but also to open the gates to others who earnestly wanted to be part of their new political project.

Rahab's story stands at the beginning of the account of Canaan's conquest in the book of Joshua. In composing her story, the book's authors were addressing the question of integrating outsiders in the national fold, yet they treated these socially sensitive matters indirectly: Rahab is a safe character insofar as she is a generic Canaanite and is not linked genealogically to a specific community.

Rahab's declarations about the power of Israel's deity and her negotiations with the spies are reported at length. Why so? Displays of loyalty are of limited value if they do not culminate in legally binding obligations. Such pledges constitute the foundation of political community and citizenship. If Rahab, as a paradigmatic outsider, is to be included, she needs not only to prove her loyalty through her actions but also to interpret them with her words:

> I know that Yhwh has given you the land. The dread of you has fallen on us, and all the inhabitants of the land melt in fear before you. For we have heard how Yhwh dried up the water of the Red Sea before you when you came out of Egypt . . . As soon as we heard it, our hearts melted, and there was no courage left in any of us because of you. Yhwh your God is indeed God in heaven above and on earth below! Now then, since I have dealt kindly with you, swear to me by Yhwh that you in turn will deal kindly with my family. Give me a sign of good faith that you will spare my father and mother, my brothers and sisters, and all who belong to them, and deliver our lives from death.
>
> – Joshua 2:9–13

Throughout biblical writings, Yhwh is the core of Israel's identity as a nation. The symbols of this deity correspond in many ways to the flags, insignias, and national emblems of modern nation-states. These emblems originated as secularized incarnations of deities and religious symbols, even if modern thinkers have often deified the state. As such, Rahab's statements may be compared to the testimonies and oaths of loyalty required for naturalization in modern nation-states.

The new ideal of the nation envisioned in the biblical corpus is not the same as modern secular democracies. Biblical texts honor a transcendent deity around whom various communities can unite as a people. However, this does not mean that the peoplehood they promote has more in common with an assembly of religious believers than with a political community. As we saw in our discussions of the covenant in Part III, the reason the biblical authors placed a deity at the center of the nation's identity was to rise above political divisions and warring factions.

Rahab's story illustrates how a non-Israelite secures protection and privileges via a contractual guarantee. It also demonstrates the possibility of "breaking the rules" for someone who stands in undivided solidarity with the nation and who proves her loyalty when push comes to shove.

At the center of the book of Joshua are a couple of chapters that treat the case of the Gibeon, a revered cultic place that Judah's kings had long patronized. While the earliest part of their story treats the place favorably, a later preface to the account (Joshua 9) tells how its population duped Israel into making a pact with them. Like Rahab, the Gibeonites secure a place "in the midst of Israel." Both they and Rahab deliver speeches that acknowledge the power of Israel's God. Yet Rahab not only speaks, but also acts and does so honorably. Her brave deeds merit the special treatment she and her family receive. Conversely, when all the kings of Canaan assemble to make war on Israel, the Gibeonites do not rally to the side of Israel. Their only deed is an elaborate act of deception with which they manage to save themselves. The Rahab story thus provides a template for evaluating the societal privileges that others, like the Gibeonites, had long enjoyed.

JAEL AND THE KENITES

The Kenites are a population group mentioned only in a handful of biblical texts, and we know precious little about them. They appear to have been tent-dwelling nomads famous for sheepherding and metalworking. In many ways, they resemble the Bedouins who continue to inhabit the periphery of the modern state of Israel and maintain a distinctive way of life. As outsiders, they presented the same issues of belonging and status (or "citizenship" and "rights") that minorities and marginal groups have posed throughout history.

The biblical authors addressed these issues by commemorating the part they played in Israel's history. The Exodus-Conquest Account identifies Moses' father-in-law as a Kenite. He serves as a scout for Israel, bringing them safely through the wilderness. For his solidarity and service, the nation awards him a portion of the Promised Land.

In the book of Judges, the Kenites appear again when Deborah leads the nation in battle with the Canaanites. During the conflict, one of the Kenite clans joins forces with the Canaanites. After Israel vanquishes the Canaanite force, Sisera, the Canaanite commander, manages to escape with his life. He flees to the camp of this Kenite clan and there enjoys gracious hospitality from its chieftain's wife, Jael. What Sisera does not know is that Jael had repudiated her husband's political affiliations and remained loyal to Israel. Thus Sisera gullibly drinks the warm milk she offers him and drifts off to sleep, confident that he is safe from all harm. At the first opportunity, Jael stealthily reaches for a hammer and drives a tent peg into his temple (Judges 4:17–21; 5:24–27).

In this way, the biblical writers attribute the greatest martial feat in a contest with the Canaanites to a daring Kenite woman. Going against her husband's politics, Jael makes a memorable contribution to Israel's war effort, even if she must do so from her domestic confines. And when she fights, she wields weapons that mark her ethnic identity: milk, a tent peg, and a hammer – corresponding to the Kenite activities of herding, nomadism, and metalworking.

The tale of Jael's heroism appears to be a late addition to the battle account in Judges. If so, why would someone have wanted to add the episode to the memory of a victory over the Canaanites? As I argue elsewhere, the motivation would have been the same one that inspired many war monuments for minorities, such as the Shaw Memorial on Boston's Beacon Hill that commemorates the service of African American soldiers in the Civil War. These monuments send a message to their audience that marginal groups deserve honor, respect, and civil rights.

THE AVANT-GARDE FROM THE TRANSJORDAN

In the Bible, war commemoration not only provided a narrative framework for negotiating belonging and status vis-à-vis others, but was also an important means by which a national identity emerged in the first place. Thus, by reporting how the inhabitants of a peripheral territory contributed to major war efforts and battles, biblical writings affirmed their membership among the people of Israel.

The Bible devotes an entire book to the history of the conquest, and that book, Joshua, begins with the crossing of the Jordan from the east and the subjugation of the land that extends from the Jordan to the Mediterranean Sea. Yet what about the communities who affiliated with Israel yet lived in territories east of the Jordan? Were they not full-fledged members of the nation? This issue elicited a dynamic exchange throughout the biblical corpus.

The book of Numbers depicts the tribes of Israel preparing to cross the Jordan and conquer the Promised Land. At one point, the leaders of two of Israel's twelve tribes, Reuben and Gad, approach Moses with a petition: they had noticed that the Transjordan provided ideal grazing grounds for their cattle, and they wished to settle there. Their petition incenses Moses and he proceeds to harangue them at length. Yet after hearing that they are willing to cross the Jordan and fight for their Israelite kin, he accedes to their request (Numbers 32).

When Reuben and Gad render military service on behalf of the nation, they do so voluntarily. They do not need to be coerced with threats of corporal punishment or harsh penalties that kings and officers wielded when conscripting soldiers. Not only do these two tribes offer armed service to their Israelite kin, but they also promise to lead the way into battle by placing themselves in the most dangerous position on the battlefield: "But as for us, we will march as shock-troops in the *forefront* of the Israelites until we have brought them to their place" (Numbers 32:17). The vanguard battalion (or "avant-garde") conventionally consists of the most skilled, fearless, determined, and loyal of all units of an army.

The book of Genesis presents key Transjordanian towns (Mahanaim, Penuel, and Succoth) as places where the patriarch Jacob roamed. There he built houses for himself and his cattle, encountered Yhwh, and underwent a name change to Israel. Yet many texts present a very different image of the Transjordan. Thus, in the book of Judges, the warrior Gideon is leading Israel's armies in pursuit of the enemy armies (the Midianites). Once he crosses the Jordan, he implores the towns of Succoth and Penuel to provide bread for the soldiers:

> "Give my troops some bread; they are worn out, and I am still pursuing the kings of Midian." But the officials said, "Do you already have the kings in your possession? Why should we give bread to your troops?"
>
> – Judges 8:5–6

These towns, where Jacob once sojourned, refuse to feed hungry soldiers who are fighting on Israel's behalf. Consequently, they are later subjected to harsh sanctions: after returning triumphantly from his campaign, Gideon tramples the town elders with briars, kills the men of both places, and tears down one of their towers. Thus, while the Jacob traditions confer honor on these towns, the Gideon account raises questions about their loyalty.

The most impressive biblical war monument is the Song of Deborah (discussed in Chapters 3 and 23), and it indicts Transjordanian tribes for failing to participate in a major war effort:

> Among the clans of Reuben,
> there were great searchings of heart.
> *Why did you sit/settle* among the sheepfolds,
> to hear the piping for the flocks?
> Among the clans of Reuben,
> there were great searchings of heart.
> Gilead dwelt beyond the Jordan.
> –Judges 5:15–16

These lines, which belong to a section of the Song that commemorates the individual tribes that participated or failed to do so, recall the episode from Numbers just discussed. In that episode, Moses indicts the two tribes by asking: "Will your brothers go to war while *you sit/settle here*?" (Numbers 32:6). Deborah uses the same verb to indict these tribes for failing to participate in her war effort. Whereas she and Moses pose similar questions, the earlier exchange with Moses allows the two tribes to affirm at length their commitment to their Israelite "brothers." And when they do, they demonstrate their allegiance by taking the most dangerous position in the ranks of the nation's armies.

In these texts, we witness a back and forth between groups that had very different views on central issues facing the nation. Such "polyphony," or plurality of voices, characterizes the entire span of the biblical corpus. In this regard, biblical literature resembles, and anticipates, the open exchange that produces rival war memories in democratic societies. As such, it stands out sharply from the much more "monophonic" quality of texts typically produced by palaces and communities monopolized by a single power.

RUTH'S LOYALTY

In times when Israel no longer possessed a native army to fight wars, stories of wars and military conflict provided a powerful literary framework in which they could demarcate the contours of Israel and define the status of its members. However, they sometimes addressed these questions by drafting accounts that conspicuously remove war from the picture. In Part II, we saw how building activities replaced battles as the public activities in which individuals and groups living after military defeat demonstrated their belonging. Texts like Nehemiah's memoir pay tribute to post-exilic building donors in the same way that other biblical texts honor contributions to war efforts from the monarchic period.

Consider the book of Ruth. It was likely composed at about the same time as Ezra-Nehemiah (in the late Persian or early Hellenistic period), yet it is set in the days of the judges who govern the nation before the monarchy. Whereas the book of Judges describes battles and wars on every page, the book of Ruth never refers to military conflict. Instead, it tells about a famine and how a Judean family escaped it by migrating to the neighboring country of Moab. There, their two sons married Moabite women, one of whom is named Ruth. Eventually all the men of the family die, leaving the aged Naomi with her two Moabite daughters-in-law. After the death of her husband and sons, Naomi makes her way back to Judah.

The first scene culminates with Naomi at the border urging the wives of her deceased sons to turn back to their homeland of Moab. The two women are reluctant to part paths. Eventually, the first one kisses Naomi goodbye and departs. Ruth, however, "clings" to Naomi and declares:

Do not urge me to leave you,
to turn back and not follow you.
For wherever you go, I will go.
Wherever you lodge, I will lodge.
Your people shall be my people.
Your god, my god.
Where you die, I will die,
and there I will be buried.
Thus and more may Yhwh do to me
if anything but death parts me from you.
– Ruth 1:16–18

When the kings of Israel urge the kings of Judah to go to war with them against their enemies, the Judean kings respond with similar words: "I am as you are. My people are as your people. My horses are your horses" (see, e.g., 1 Kings 22:4). Such declarations play on the double meaning of "people," which in Hebrew, as in many other languages, can describe not only population or subjects but also army/troops. When Ruth uses the language of these kings forming an alliance for a war effort, she is doing something more profound, pledging to join the people of her mother-in-law.

Notice Ruth's reference to Yhwh. She does not claim that there is only one god. On the contrary, each people have their god, and in becoming a member of Naomi's people, she affirms her willingness to make Naomi's god her own.

But her statement is about much more than a deity. Religious reverence, even if it is exclusive to Yhwh, did not suffice for the biblical authors. One needed to follow the example of Ruth (and Rahab) by making a resolute and unswerving commitment to throw her/his/their lot in with the nation.

Ruth is a "fellow traveler," like the Kenites and their ancestor who accompanies Israel to the Promised Land. Attaching herself to Naomi, Ruth's journey leads back to the borders of Judah, where she eventually marries another Judean man (Boaz) and gives birth to the ancestor of none other than King David.

What makes Ruth's story especially memorable is the way it directs attention away from rulers and diplomacy to more modest matters – the quotidian struggles of widows, the poor, and non-natives. It demonstrates how personal relationships, built on generosity and loving-kindness (*chesed*), not only bring about the birth of Judah's most celebrated monarch but also, and more importantly, promote the well-being of a people. The book's culminating blessing commemorates this Moabite woman in the company of the nation's matriarchs Rachel and Leah, who "together built the house of Israel" (see Chapter 22).

LAWS OF LOVE

The story of Ruth directly challenges Pentateuchal law. According to Deuteronomy, Ammonites and Moabites do not qualify for membership in the nation:

No Ammonite or Moabite shall be admitted into the assembly of Yhwh.
To the tenth generation, none of their descendants
shall ever be admitted into the congregation of Yhwh.
You must not seek their peace and prosperity through all the ages to come. ...
You must not hate an Edomite, for he is your brother.
Their children, beginning in the third generation, may enter the assembly of Yhwh.

– Deuteronomy 23:3–8

The book of Ezra-Nehemiah reveals that some circles in the post-exilic period appealed explicitly to this law to ostracize members of their community. The culprits had married persons identified as Ammonites and Moabites. Ruth's story, which emerged at the same time as Ezra-Nehemiah, offers a counter view: yes, foreign marriages may pose a problem, but not when those partners are determined, like Ruth, to become a full-fledged member of the community. (Because of her commitment to Israel, she did not have to give up her identity as "the Moabite," as the book consistently calls her.)

In stark contrast to its position on Moabites and Ammonites, the quoted passage from Deuteronomy forbids hatred of Edomites. Many biblical texts vilify this people, claiming, for example, that they contributed to Judah's suffering at the hands of the Babylonians. Deuteronomy undercuts the anti-Edomite stance. It joins important parts of the Family Story in Genesis that depict Esau, the Edomites' ancestor, as none other than Jacob's twin. That Family Story begins by portraying the enmity that grows between them, and it concludes with a dramatic scene in which the two overcome years of hostility, embracing each other in tears.

Throughout history, projects of nation-making have often been xenophobic, ethnocentric, and intolerant. To thwart these "nationalistic" tendencies, the biblical corpus contains not only powerful stories like the ones we have studied in this chapter, but also laws requiring nothing less than love for non-natives who take up residence in the country:

When an immigrant resides with you in your land,
you must not oppress him.
The immigrant who resides with you
is to be treated like a native citizen.

You must love him as yourself,
for you too were once immigrants in the land of Egypt.
I am Yhwh, your God.
– Leviticus 19:33–34

FURTHER READING

Conway, Colleen M., *Sex and Slaughter in the Tent of Jael: A Cultural History of a Biblical Story*, Oxford University Press, 2017.

Eskenazi, Tamara Cohn and Frymer-Kensky, Tikva, *Ruth: JPS Bible Commentary*, Jewish Publication Society, 2011.

Frolov, Serge, *Judges* (The Forms of Old Testament Literature), Eerdmans, 2013.

Graybill, Rhiannon and Huber, Lynn R., *The Bible, Gender, and Sexuality: Critical Readings*, T&T Clark, 2020.

Leveen, Adriane B., *Memory and Tradition in the Book of Numbers*, Cambridge University Press, 2008.

Powell, Stephanie Day, *Narrative Desire and the Book of Ruth*, Bloomsbury, 2018.

Rowlett, Lori L., *Joshua and the Rhetoric of Violence: A New Historicist Analysis*, Sheffield Academic Press, 1996.

Schipper, Jeremy, *Ruth: A New Translation with Introduction and Commentary*, Yale University Press, 2015.

Smith, Mark S., *Poetic Heroes: Literary Commemorations of Warriors and Warrior Culture in the Early Biblical World*, Eerdmans, 2014.

Southwood, Katherine E. and Halvorson-Taylor, Martien A. (eds.), *Women and Exilic Identity in the Hebrew Bible*, Bloomsbury, 2018.

Tamber-Rosenau, Caryn, *Women in Drag: Gender and Performance in the Hebrew Bible and Early Jewish Literature*, Gorgias, 2018.

Taylor, Marion Ann and de Groot, Christiana (eds.), *Women of War, Women of Woe: Joshua and Judges through the Eyes of Nineteenth-Century Female Biblical Interpreters*, Eerdmans, 2016.

Toczyski, Andrzej, *The "Geometrics" of the Rahab Story: A Multi-dimensional Analysis of Joshua 2*, Bloomsbury, 2018.

Wright, Jacob L., *David, King of Israel, and Caleb in Biblical Memory*, Cambridge University Press, 2014.

Wright, Jacob L., *War, Memory, and National Identity in the Hebrew Bible*, Cambridge University Press, 2020.

25

The Soldier

Sacrificial Death and Eternal Life

In the spring of the year,
the time when kings go out to battle,
David sent out Joab with his officers and all Israel with him . . .
But David remained at Jerusalem.
– 2 Samuel 11:1

IT ALL BEGINS WITH AN AFTERNOON DALLIANCE. King David lays eyes on a bathing beauty named Bathsheba. She happens to be the wife of Uriah – one of his top soldiers who was both a non-native (a Hittite) and serving on the front lines. But that does not stop the king: "He sent messengers, and they took her. She came to him, and he slept with her" (2 Samuel 11:4). As fate would have it, Bathsheba, who had been bathing after her menstrual cycle, becomes pregnant after the illicit liaison.

The deed was despicable enough, yet the real crime is in the cover-up. David summons Uriah from the battlefield. His intention was to wine and dine his Hittite soldier in the hope that he would go home, sleep with his wife, and then assume that the child was his own. This devious scheme precipitates a series of decisions that brings the king to the brink of ruin.

A drunk Uriah turns out to be more patriotic and pious than a sober David. The Hittite warrior explains why he could not comply with the king's demands and seek pleasure at home:

The Ark, Israel, and Judah are all dwelling in tents.
My lord Joab [the general] and the servants of my lord are camping in the field.

> Should I then go to my home, to eat and drink and to sleep with my wife?
> By your very life, I cannot do such a thing!
> – 2 Samuel 11:11

The exemplary dedication to the nation – by a soldier of foreign origins, no less – must have angered David. Yet now with his reputation on the line, he manages to exercise a bit of self-constraint and conceal his anger: "Stay here today, and I will send you back tomorrow." We know that when Uriah returns, it will be to meet his orchestrated demise. Following orders, David's general assigns the soldier a place opposite the most experienced enemy combatants, where he falls in the line of duty.

The account of David and Bathsheba is often understood to be a morality tale about adultery and murder, but it is much more. As a paragon of biblical prose, the account unpacks a penetrating critique of monarchic power that not only rapes but kills its subjects. Its authors take aim at a state that sustains itself with sacrificial deaths on the altar of imperial ambition.

An important clue that helps us to discern the Bible's political agenda is its attitude toward martial valor and martyrdom. In both modern and ancient societies, veneration of fallen soldiers occupy a central place in public rituals (e.g., memorial days) and public spaces (e.g., cemeteries and monuments). Since states must often demand of their subjects a readiness to die, it is not surprising that many cultures elevate sacrifice on the battlefield to the highest civic virtue. In this chapter, we explore a wide range of biblical and non-biblical texts that relate to battlefield death and procreation. The two may seem like an odd combination, but together, they offer a powerful perspective on a distinctive ethos that informs the biblical project of peoplehood.

MAKING A NAME

In the world of ancient West Asia, it was imperative for families to have at least one son. The male heir played a critical role in caring for his aged parents, providing them with a proper burial, tending to their graves, and paying tribute to their names in ritual performance. That a daughter usually did not perform this function is because she legally belonged to her husband's household and was expected to assist him in caring for his parents. As the heir, the son inherited not only the paraphernalia for the rites but also a long genealogical tradition, which was to be learned and passed on.

The biblical scholar Jon D. Levenson notes that the failure to produce a male child is "the functional equivalent to death as we think of it."[1] This point is expressed by a "wise woman" who petitions King David to save the life of her one remaining son. His execution would "extinguish the only coal left to me, leaving my husband without a name and survivor on the earth" (2 Samuel 14:7). The reference to "name" in this woman's statement refers to the son who perpetuated the family line.

One could "make a name" not only by producing male heirs but also by doing something extraordinary, such as feats in combat. In the words of Egyptian pharaoh Ramses II (d. 1213 BCE):

> Does a man not act to be acclaimed in his town when he returns as one brave before his lord?
> A name made in battle is truly good; a man is ever respected for valor.[2]

When facing death on the battlefield, soldiers often console themselves with the knowledge that they are dying brave, heroic deaths. This martial mentality is not confined to modernity. We find it, for example, in a dispatch that an Assyrian commander sent to the king (Ashurbanipal, d. 627 BCE), lamenting the straits in which he and his troops found themselves. Since the enemy far outnumbered them, they knew they would fall in action. Yet his men assured themselves: "If we die, we will do so with an excellent name."

Noble death figures prominently in many heroic traditions. In *The War that Killed Achilles*, the classicist Caroline Alexander shows how the Greek hero in Homer's *Iliad* must choose between a heroic life that is short and glorious, or a long and obscure existence in his Greek homeland. Like the ancient myths of Achilles, the 5,000-year-old Gilgamesh tradition from Mesopotamia promotes this ethos, with its accompanying

[1] Levenson, *Resurrection and the Restoration of Israel*, pp. 114–115.

[2] For a discussion of all the ancient texts cited in this chapter, see Wright, "Making a Name for Oneself."

ideal of a valiant and tragic death. The hero Gilgamesh goes off in battle against a monster confident that "if I should fall in battle, I will have nonetheless made my name to stand." To die peaceably was not fitting for a formidable warrior:

> Then Enkidu called to Gilgamesh, "My friend, the great goddess cursed me and I must die in shame. I shall not die like a man fallen in battle; I feared to fall, but happy is the man who falls in the battle, for I must die in shame."

The Gilgamesh traditions, like those of Homer, provide models of heroism to which their audiences should aspire. Ancient rulers realized that their troops, especially those who lacked sons, would perform their service more fearlessly if they could rest assured of royal honors should they die in the line of duty. Thus, when King Ammi-saduqa of Babylon (sixteenth century BCE) made offerings to the dead, those whom he encouraged to imbibe the offerings were not only his (real and fictive) royal ancestors but also every soldier who "fell in the service of his lord [the king]." These fallen warriors belong to the category of those "who have no one to provide and care for them" in their death. The Babylonian ruler took upon himself the ritual role traditionally assigned to a son, allotting his soldiers a place of special recognition when performing the commemoration ceremonies for the royal family.

SACRIFICIAL DEATH

In the form of cemeteries, monuments, parades, anthems, and national holidays, the commemoration of fallen warriors has endured as one of the chief expressions of statehood from antiquity to the present. In *The Invention of Athens,* the classicist Nicole Loraux studies the genre of funeral orations that were delivered each year in ancient Athens to celebrate the war dead. Her work demonstrates how the commemoration of citizen casualties became an occasion to articulate values to which all Athenians should aspire. Chief among these values was the willingness to lay down one's life for the polis.

The most famous funeral oration is the one Pericles, according to Thucydides, delivered after the first year of the Peloponnesian War in

432 BCE (which corresponds to final year of Nehemiah's activities in Jerusalem). The speech saluted Athens as the city for which many citizens gave their all:

> So died these men as became Athenians. You, their survivors, must determine to have as unfaltering a resolution in the field ... For this offering of their lives made in common by them all, they received ... that noblest of shrines wherein their glory is laid up to be eternally remembered.[3]

By celebrating citizens who had selflessly died for Athens, and by urging the living to "resolve that these dead shall not have died in vain," the speech of the Athenian statesman provided a pattern for many others (e.g., Abraham Lincoln's "Gettysburg Address").

The commemoration of heroic sacrifice and substitutionary death is found in writings that were omitted from the Jewish (Masoretic) canon. The best example is 1 Maccabees, which tells of the establishment of a powerful Judean kingdom in the second century BCE. In one passage, the enemy marches with a massive army against Jerusalem, inciting most of the Judean forces to flee in fear. Even though they are now far outnumbered, Judas Maccabees commands the remaining soldiers to advance. Fearing death, they attempt to dissuade their commander: "We lack the strength – let us save our lives now." Rebuking their hesitation, Judas urges them to die an honorable death: "Far be it from us to do such a thing as to flee from them. If our time has come, let us die bravely for our kin and leave no cause to question our honor!" (1 Maccabees 9:10). Sure enough, his army is vanquished, with Judas falling in battle. At his funeral, the nation eulogizes his bravery and willingness to put his life on the line: "How the mighty have fallen, the savior of Israel!" (1 Maccabees 9:21).

The attitude toward heroic death in 1 Maccabees – the book features several other episodes of martial martyrdom – matches what we observed for Mesopotamia and Greece, and it is just what we would expect for any state, ancient or modern. That sacrificial death ensures everlasting life is a concept central also to religious traditions, not least Christianity. Not

[3] Translation by Richard Crawley (1866).

only is the crucifixion of Jesus Christ salvific and even substitutionary, but throughout history, it has also often provided a model for others (including soldiers) to emulate. In addition to earning an honored name among their survivors, martyrs should die in confidence knowing that they will inherit eternal life.

A SURPRISING TWIST

Now what about the Hebrew Bible? The varied writings in this corpus affirms the importance and benefits of military security and territorial sovereignty. They extol valor, on the battlefield and beyond. Yet they also orient readers to a different model of heroism. The biblical project was ultimately about creating a new national culture under conditions of foreign rule, and in the process of creating this new culture, its authors rewrote their battle stories with a surprising twist: no one dies.

Consider the case of Joshua. More than any other biblical book, this one is preoccupied with wars, portraying the campaigns in which the nation conquers the Promised Land. But in all its stories of wars and battles, the only casualties are those who perish as *punishment* for misconduct; no one falls heroically in battle. One would expect Joshua, on the eve of invasion, to exhort the nation not to shirk their duties and be willing to die a noble death, but such scenes are conspicuously absent. This work also could have included at least one prominent scene in which the nation pauses to bury the dead and pay tribute to their sacrifice. Yet we find nothing of the sort.

The following book of Judges, which depicts the nation's moral decline after the age of conquest, includes many deaths. One of the most famous scenes depicts Samson dying with the Philistines as he brings the roof down on their party (Judges 16:23–31). His death, however, is not an ideal to be emulated; like most of his lifetime deeds, it is a sign of things gone wrong. The authors placed his story not at the beginning of the book, next to ideal figures such as Deborah and Jael, but at the end, in the company of denigrated and despicable antiheroes.

With respect to David, the authors of the Palace History did not have a problem with him achieving fame through martial feats, yet they left no room for name-making through heroic death. Thus, when Saul suffers a fatal blow in his battle with the Philistines, he, like Abimelech from the book of Judges (see Chapter 16), petitions his arms-bearer to finish him off (1 Samuel 31:4–6). When David hears of his death, he utters a lament similar to that of Achilles and Gilgamesh. Yet one cannot miss the deep disparity between these traditions. David does not praise Saul for bravely sacrificing his life for the nation's survival. The death is shameful, without any redeeming value: "Tell it not in Gath, nor proclaim it on the streets of Ashkelon" (2 Samuel 1:20).

The turning point in David's life revolves around another battlefield death, that of Uriah the Hittite and his comrades, with which we began this chapter. The authors painted that scene in an unusual manner. It is the only one in the entire Bible in which a victory incurs casualties. Yet this victory is of a very different sort from Joshua's triumphs: it is in the service of a state that has set its sights on the territory of its neighbors. The king sends others to die in his quest to conquer, while he relaxes in the comforts of the palace and forces himself on the wife of a formidable Hittite warrior serving faithfully in Israel's army. The penetrating critique of royal misconduct that the authors of Samuel planted at the center of their book communicates a monumental message: a monarch's thirst for triumph devours the lives of the nation's most devoted members.

Dulce et decorum est pro patria mori – "Tis sweet and beautiful to die for the fatherland." Some variation of this line from the Latin Odes of Horace appears in the histories of most peoples, such as in the speech Nathan Hale delivered at his execution during the American Revolutionary War: "I only regret that I have but one life to lose for my country." Such sentiments of martial martyrdom are expressed symbolically by one of the most impressive war monuments: the Arc de Triomphe standing at the center of Paris. Lying underneath this majestic memorial of military grandeur is the "Tomb to the Unknown Soldier." The edifice affirms the bloody truth that statehood requires triumph, and triumph requires sacrificial death.

BEYOND THE GRAVE

We search in vain for a biblical text that glorifies battlefield death, and this astonishing absence speaks volumes about the ethos and concerns of this corpus. As biblical authors articulated their philosophy of peoplehood, they repudiated the statist ideology of martial martyrdom and its accompanying death-cult. Closely tied to this decisive disavowal is their denial of a blissful existence beyond the grave. The eternal life that they envisioned is to be sought in one's descendants and daily deeds. As a whole, the Bible echoes the response that the German playwright Berthold Brecht wrote during the First World War against Horace's famous line: "Tis sweeter and more and beautiful *to live* for one's country!"

Relative to many other bodies of literature, including the New Testament, the Hebrew Bible does not devote much space to activities in heaven. Nor does it have a positive view toward the afterlife; the focus of attention is almost entirely on the activities of individuals, families, and communities during their days on earth. Repeatedly we hear that there is nothing beyond the grave. When the Assyrian armies are besieging Jerusalem, Hezekiah prays:

For Sheol [Hades] cannot thank you.
Death cannot praise you.
Those who go down to the pit cannot hope
for your faithfulness.
It is the living, the living, who give thanks to you,
as I do today.
A father tells his children
about your faithfulness.
– Isaiah 38:18–19

Why does Hezekiah not hold out a hope beyond the grave? Many assume that he would not *yet* have known about it, but that assumption is unfounded. Cultures in Mesopotamia, Egypt, and the Levant had already produced elaborate conceptions of the afterlife, and archeologists encounter their many dimensions. One does not need to visit Egypt's Valley of the Kings to witness the remains of civilizations that devoted much of their energies a postmortem existence. Much of it can be found in the many tombs from ancient Israel and Judah that contain rich evidence of rituals for feeding the dead.

Since their societies seem to have been concerned with postmortem existence, we would expect the biblical authors to devote considerable space to it. But they do not. When Pentateuchal laws occasionally treat rituals related to mourning the dead, they do so only to tell their audience what one *must not do.* For example:

> You are children of Yhwh, your God: You shall not cut yourselves, nor make baldness between your eyes for the dead. For you are a holy people unto Yhwh your God, and Yhwh has chosen you to be his treasure out all the peoples on the face of the earth.
>
> – Deuteronomy 14:1–2 (see also Leviticus 19:28)

Admittedly, the Bible often mentions tombs of the nation's ancestors, but it has nothing to say about the afterlife of those interred in them. One of the few occasions in which the deceased appear is when the matriarch Rachel raises a heart-rending cry from her tomb in Ramah: "She refused to be comforted for her children, because they were no more" (Jeremiah 31:15; see the discussion of *Moby Dick* in Chapter 20). Highlighted here is not the cherished ancestor's existence after death, but the *non-existence* of the children she mourns.

The scribes who curated the biblical corpus clearly did not want make space for some form of heavenly afterlife. For them, future life and "resurrection" were to be sought in a revived community after its death in defeat – one with families finding their ultimate happiness in the enjoyment of the good, God-given earth that had been created to endure for eternity.

THE POWER OF PROGENY

"Be fruitful and multiply." This is the deity's opening directive to humans, issued in the first chapter of Genesis, and then again, no less than three times, after the flood. Contrast this mandate for humanity with Atrahasis, the most popular flood story from Babylon. It presents the gods decreeing a deluge precisely because humans were being too fruitful and multiplying too much. Genesis tells a version of this story, but what causes the flood, according to it, is an ethical, not an ontological, problem: the evil actions of the earth's inhabitants. Procreation is, in contrast, entirely in keeping with the divine will. Whereas Atrahasis presents conflict between humans and the gods, Genesis imagines an original harmony with the Creator, who *commands* humans to multiply.

The making of children is in the interest not only of individual families but also of a people, especially a small and conquered people. The National Narrative begins by depicting the growth of families and family life. Although Abraham proves to be a successful warrior in Genesis 14, he complains to God in Genesis 15 about being childless; nothing else seems to matter. In the story of Jacob, the patriarch and his huge household stand over against his bellicose brother Esau with his four hundred warriors (Genesis 32–33). Jacob's claim to fame is his family.

The power of progeny is illustrated in a host of other texts. Recall, for example, how in the first chapter of Exodus, the Egyptian king oppresses the Hebrews out of fear that, in the event of war, they may "increase and join our enemies and fight against us" (Exodus 1:10). His final solution is to command the Hebrew midwives to destroy the male infants. But the midwives fail to implement these genocidal orders. When the king calls them to account for their actions, they describe the Hebrew women as so full of life or "lively" (a double entendre with the Hebrew expression for "wild animals") that they bear children on their own, without needing the midwives' assistance (see Chapters 2 and 17).

As we saw in the preceding chapter, the late book of Ruth tells about the time of the Judges, yet in contrast to the book of Judges, this story portrays neither war nor warriors. Its main characters are women, and the male protagonist, Boaz, is a "Man of Valor/Might" – an ancient title of warrior nobility that refers now to *social virtue*, not *military prowess* (on the "Woman of Valor/Might" in Proverbs, see Chapter 27). When the community blesses Boaz on his marriage with Ruth, they encourage him to act heroically: "May you do a mighty deed of valor in Ephrathah and make a name in Bethlehem" (Ruth 4:11). The mighty deed of valor and the making of a name refer here to marriage and procreation.

The Bible pursues its agenda not only through grand narratives and tender stories, but also in the form of prescriptive law:

> Then the officials shall address the troops, saying,
> "Has anyone built a new house but not dedicated it?
> He should go back to his house,
> or he might die in the battle and another dedicate it . . .

> Has anyone become engaged to a woman but not yet married her?
> He should go back to his house,
> or he might die in the battle and another marry her."
> – Deuteronomy 20:5–7

The excerpt from Deuteronomy requires a draft deferral for soldiers who had not yet established a family. A furlough for the purpose of procreation might have served the interests of the state. But these laws do not offer practical guidelines for military organization so much as set forth a social ethos (pertaining to the ideal "citizen army") and the concrete legal consequences that flow from it. The concerns of the nation, and the families that constitute it, take precedence over the state and its drive for expansion and triumph. These concerns explain why this code transfers the crown's military role to spontaneously appointed generals and commands the king to spend his days copying and studying its contents (see Chapter 18).

Throughout history, procreation in preparation for war has often been officially fostered through state incentives. While state-sponsored fertility and reproductive politics deserve consideration when evaluating biblical "natalism," the absence in the Bible of any glorification of heroic death, which figures so prominently in the public culture of states (both ancient and modern), suggests that rather than statehood, it was the *loss* of statehood and conditions of defeat that best explain the primacy the Bible assigns to procreation.

THE BIBLICAL AGENDA

With military triumph in sight, Pericles delivered his famous funeral oration paying tribute to the fallen in the war with Persia and beckoning the citizens of Athens to keep up the fight. In contrast, the Bible emerged when defeat was on the horizon.

Pericles in Athens stands opposite Jeremiah in Jerusalem. With imperial armies besieging the city, the prophet admonished his audience to "bend your necks to the yoke of Babylon so that you may live!" The book that bears his name assigns much of the responsibility for the catastrophe in 586 BCE to a political faction in Jerusalem who insisted on resisting any foreign encroachment on Judean sovereignty. What the resistance achieved, the book argues, was only the destruction of the temple and the forfeiture of the right to dwell in their homeland.

The biblical scribes fought a perennial battle with recalcitrant politics. Many groups in ancient Israel and Judah were willing to pay the highest price to resist the encroachment of imperial armies and the loss of territory. They preferred liberty and death to defeat and survival.

Freedom often comes at the highest price. In the words of the Patrick Henry spoken on the eve of the American Revolutionary War (1775): "Give me liberty, or give me death!" Most national landscapes are dotted with monuments and burial grounds that call to remembrance the bravery of those who fell in battle. Such honor of citizen sacrifice is necessary and right, but the biblical authors were after something different. By including memories of heroic death, they would have bolstered the willingness of radicals to offer up their lives in acts of resistance to imperial rule.

Given the limitations of a small nation, destined to remain on the sidelines in the world's great military contests, violent resistance would have only impeded reconstruction under new political realities. Which explains why the Bible promotes such survival skills as solidarity, shrewdness, and a willingness to compromise – and why it repudiates machismo, a bootstrap mentality, and martyrdom. The vision of redemption in the Hebrew Bible (in contrast to the New Testament) is for the here and now. Its hope is both terrestrial and collective: the jubilation of wedding parties, the grinding of millstones, children playing in the streets, and all living long lives:

> Old men and women will again sit in the streets of Jerusalem,
> each bearing a staff because of age.
> And the city's streets will be filled with boys and girls –
> all will be playing in her streets.
> – Zechariah 8:4–5

FURTHER READING

Ackerman, Susan, *When Heroes Love: The Ambiguity of Eros in the Stories of Gilgamesh and David*, Columbia University Press, 2005.

Alexander, Caroline, *The War that Killed Achilles: The True Story of Homer's Iliad and the Trojan War*, Viking, 2009.

Brichto, Herbert Chanan, "Kin, Cult, Land and Afterlife: A Biblical Complex," *Hebrew Union College Annual* 44 (1973): 1–54.

Feldman, Yael, *Glory and Agony: Isaac's Sacrifice and National Narrative*, Stanford University Press, 2010.

Frymer-Kensky, Tikva, "The Atrahasis Epic and Its Significance for Our Understanding of Genesis 1–9," *The Biblical Archaeologist* 40 (1977): 147–155.

Hays, Christopher B., *A Covenant with Death: Death in the Iron Age II and Its Rhetorical Uses in Proto-Isaiah*, Eerdmans, 2015.

Henning, Meghan, "No Heaven or Hell, Only She'ol," *TheTorah.com*, 2021, https://thetorah.com/article/no-heaven-or-hell-only-sheol.

Levenson, Jon D., *Resurrection and the Restoration of Israel: The Ultimate Victory of the God of Life*, Yale University Press, 2006.

Loraux, Nicole, *The Invention of Athens: The Funeral Oration in the Classical City*, Harvard University Press, 1986.

Suriano, Matthew, "Sheol, the Tomb, and the Problem of Postmortem Existence," *Journal of Hebrew Scriptures* 16 (2016): 1–31.

Wright, Jacob L., "Making a Name for Oneself: Martial Valor, Heroic Death, and Procreation in the Hebrew Bible," *Journal for the Study of the Old Testament* 36 (2011): 131–162.

Zsengellér, József and Xeravits, Géza G. (eds.), *The Book of Maccabees: History, Theology, Ideology*, Brill, 2007.

26

The Prophet and the Priest

Open Access, Public Transparency, and Separation of Powers

My people are destroyed for lack of knowledge.
Because you have rejected knowledge,
I will reject you from being my priests.
– Hosea 4:6

THE JUDEAN KINGDOM IS IN ITS FINAL THROES, and Jehoiakim is on the throne. His father, Josiah, is famous for finding a copy of the Torah and instituting religious reforms. In his son's reign, however, Judah had become a vassal to Babylon, and now it was looking to Egypt for the right moment to break free. In doing so, the palace has to contend with major obstacles, and one of them is a prophet: Jeremiah. He is loudly protesting the state's policies as they pertain to both international and internal relations.

Our account begins with the scribe Baruch memorializing Jeremiah's prophecies in a scroll. The prophet then instructs him to take the document and read it to the inhabitants of Judah. "It may be that they will present their supplication before Yhwh, and everyone will turn from his evil way. For great is the anger and fury that Yhwh has pronounced against this people" (Jeremiah 36:7).

Concerned to make the scroll available to as many as possible, Baruch goes to the temple when the inhabitants of Judah's cities were coming to Jerusalem for a public fast day. After he reads the scroll in public, a smaller circle of scribes and officials instructs Baruch and Jeremiah to lie low and hide the scroll.

It is wintertime, and when members of the royal cabinet bring the scroll to the court, the king is sitting before a fire and has his scribe read it to him and the princes who were present. As they proceed, he uses a scribe's scalpel to slice off columns, casting them piece by piece in the flames. When they had read and burned the entire document, Jehoiakim orders his men to arrest Jeremiah and Baruch.

It would be difficult to imagine a more graphic illustration of state censorship. On the eve of destruction, a monarch warms himself by burning a book – not because he lacks fuel for his fire, but because its contents challenge his rule and political agenda. The only reason we still have Jeremiah's prophecies, this legend claims, is because Jeremiah and Baruch were in hiding and able to produce a new scroll, which they concealed from the court.[1]

Knowledge is power, and throughout history rulers have gone to great lengths to control the flow of information. Sociologists and historians study this phenomenon under the rubric of *Wissensmonopol*, a German term that means "monopoly of knowledge." Modern democratic societies recognize the importance of transparency, freedom of information, and open access. Likewise, the scribes who shaped the biblical corpus knew how crucial it was to check the power of the crown and communal authorities. In the present chapter we consider how they applied the principle of transparency to the knowledge that was the special preserve of palace, prophet, and priest.

KNOWLEDGE, POWER, AND DIVINATION

The most critical knowledge in the ancient world was information that the gods possessed, and palaces invested substantial resources to study natural phenomena that could divulge that knowledge. Many today may have difficulty relating to diviners and prophets who by scrutinizing the livers of sheep, gazing at the stars, and speaking on the behalf of a deity, directly influenced the governance of a state. But the system would not have existed if many did not deem it indispensable to their decision-making process.

1 The book's authors reveal that they were aware that the work evolved over time when they state that "many additional words were added to it" (Jeremiah 36:32).

Deities governed the monarch's welfare, and the palace needed to know their will before embarking on a military campaign, undertaking a building project, or initiating any other kind of important activity. Consequently, royal courts spared no effort in their attempt to harness the power of prophets and diviners. Because these specialists could discern destinies and the will of deities, they possessed inside knowledge that was vital to the state's future. And because they could also use this knowledge to challenge the regime, kings and queens kept them close – or at least closely monitored their activities.

For ancient West Asia, we must distinguish prophets from diviners, as they belonged to very different classes. Prophets had little if any contact with the throne, many were women, and most were considered to be mad. As votaries, they served as the mouthpiece of the deity, often in an enraptured state. Diviners, on the other hand, were usually men. Consisting of educated experts who studied the stars, animal entrails, and other natural phenomena, they were of a higher social status than the illiterate classes of seers, dreamers, and ecstatics whom we call "prophets."

In the Neo-Assyrian Empire, diviners belonged to an official class of "scholars" (*ummani*). Although they served in the palace and enjoyed many honors, rulers could not always be confident of their allegiance. Therefore, the throne kept them in close reach, rewarded them with gifts, and hosted them frequently at the royal table. They were required to take oaths, swearing to divulge their knowledge solely to the throne. The throne also closely guarded their research, storing it under lock and key in their royal libraries.

The social location of prophets was much different from that of diviners. Most performed in public spaces. Because they did not serve at the court, their oracles had an independent authority and a greater potential for dissidence. Thus, in the reign of Esarhaddon (681–669 BCE), we hear of a certain "slave girl" on the outskirts of a provincial town who proclaims the downfall of the king and his dynasty: "This is the word of the god Nusku: The kingship is for Sasî. I will destroy the name and seed of Sennacherib [Esarhaddon's father]!"[2] The one who writes to

[2] For references to the ancient texts cited in the following pages (as well as a treatment of others like them), see Wright, "Prolegomena."

inform Esarhaddon urges him to take immediate action and annihilate the conspirators who stand behind this prophecy. In sending the warning, the official does precisely what he swore to do when he took oaths of allegiance to the throne:

> If you hear any evil, improper, ugly word which is not seemly nor good from the mouth of a prophet, an ecstatic, an inquirer of oracles, or from the mouth of any human being at all, you shall not conceal it but come and report it to Ashurbanipal, the great crown prince designate, son of Esarhaddon, king of Assyria.

Political turmoil and civil war plagued Esarhaddon's succession. Reflecting the public disquiet, he and his son Ashurbanipal repeatedly claimed in their inscriptions to have received prophetic messages – as well as dreams from various sources – confirming that the gods supported their reigns.

During the official ceremonies of the Assyrian Empire, only prophets who could be trusted to deliver favorable oracles were invited to perform at state ceremonies. A typical prophetic oration for these occasions included the proclamation: "Hear O Assyrians! The king has vanquished his enemy. Your king has put his enemy under his foot."[3] These performances assisted the crown prince in neutralizing potential opposition.

While prophets posed a greater threat than diviners, kings strove to foster good relations with them too. In the kingdom of Mari from the early second millennium BCE, prophets received gifts that included garments, donkeys, rings, and bronze lances. Yet on the most basic level, the palace knew that the best way to maintain good relations with these potential menaces was to heed their messages and attend to the temples of the deities for whom they spoke.

Thus, a Mari letter from *c.*1770 BCE presents the god Adad, through his prophet Abiya, demanding that the king not only hear the pleas of the oppressed and judge their cases fairly but also pay heed to Adad's

[3] The proclamation resembles the structure of the *Shema Yisrael* from Deuteronomy, but the content is very different: "Hear O Israel! Yhwh is our God. Yhwh is one" (Deuteronomy 6:4).

oracles: "[I]f you go off to war, never do so without consulting an oracle. When I become manifest in my oracle, go to war. If it does not happen, do not go out of the city gate." Similarly, the widely circulated and heavily redacted Cuthean Legend of Naram-Sin depicts this ruler, who was known for his great conquests from the late third millennium BCE, suffering massive defeats. The cause of the catastrophe is his arrogant self-reliance. Instead of heeding divine oracles, he relies on his own strength:

> What lion (ever) inquired of those who read livers?
> What wolf (ever) consulted a dream-interpreter?
> I will go like a brigand according to my own inclination.
> I will cast aside the oracle of the god(s).
> I will be in control myself.[4]

Throwing caution to the wind, he meets an unsuccessful end and is only saved from complete ruination once he learns to act in accordance with the gods as revealed through divination. As one of the earliest "mirror for princes," the legend has a didactic purpose, warning future rulers against hubris: even if they are as valorous as the great Naram-Sin, they will fail when they do not pay careful attention to the divine word revealed in the research of mantic professionals.

PROPHETS FROM ISRAEL AND JUDAH

Throughout the biblical books of Samuel and Kings, we find similar points about the necessity of rulers "inquiring of Yhwh" before going to battle. Thus, whereas Saul fails to consult the deity properly, David not only does so but also closely heeds the oracles.

The memories of the kingdoms of Israel and Judah in the National Narrative feature a wide range of mantic professionals, including diviners and prophets. Many were not on the palace payroll, working instead at temples and sacred sites. The prophet Samuel, for example, resides at a "high place" where cultic activities were conducted, and it is there that he

[4] See discussion in Wright, "Human, All Too Human," pp. 67–68.

receives Saul and anoints him king (1 Samuel 9–10). Later Saul visits a medium, "the Witch of Endor," who lives far away (1 Samuel 28).

Both diviners and prophets were often paid for their services. Thus, when Saul visits Samuel, it is because the family donkeys had wandered off and he wanted to hire a "man of God" to help him find them. (What he plans to pay for this service – before his anointing as king distracts him from his mission – was just a ¼ shekel of silver; see 1 Samuel 9.) In the book of Kings, we hear of bands of prophets living in seclusion and offering their services to a wide range of clients. The leader of one of these bands, Elisha, helps a poor widow in a time of scarcity or after the tragic death of boy; the only remuneration he accepts, though, is room and board (2 Kings 4).

Prophets and diviners served a diverse clientele, yet kings were their best-paying patrons. The courts in Samaria, Jerusalem, and elsewhere in the Southern Levant engaged in elaborate gift-giving in their efforts to attract diviners and prophets to their courts. There they could keep them under close surveillance and exploit them for their own interests. Those who remained on the periphery, or declined a palace position, were a source of great concern.

For example, when King Jeroboam attempts to bring a prophet under his control by imploring him to eat at his table and offering him a gift, the prophet responds: "If you give me half your kingdom, I will not accompany you" (1 Kings 13:8). A respected non-Israelite seer named Balaam responds similarly when the Moabite king, on the eve of Israel's conquest of Canaan, offers him generous divination fees if he comes from afar and pronounces a curse on Israel (Numbers 22).

Because royal patronage was highly desirable, most diviners and prophets sought to ingratiate themselves with the court. The accounts of David's and Solomon's reigns identify prophets who served in official capacities next to army commanders, secretaries, and priests, and throughout the books of Kings and Jeremiah we hear repeatedly about prophets who surrounded the king.

Even if many biblical authors approved of the close relationship between prophets and kings, they were ultimately wary of it and went to great length to establish a separation of powers. Thus, instead of instructing the king on how to rout the enemy, the prophets frequently pronounce judgment on throne. When David seizes Bathsheba and has her husband killed, the prophet Nathan boldly stands before the king and – in one of the Bible's most stirring scenes – proclaims, "You are the guilty one!" (1 Samuel 12; see Chapter 25). Those who promise peace and security for their royal patrons are "false prophets," sycophants oblivious to impending doom. The ideal prophet in the Bible stands at a distance to the throne and is often isolated from society. Thus, in the reign of the wicked rulers Ahab and Jezebel, a multitude of Baal-prophets eat daily at the royal table; meanwhile, Yhwh's prophet Elijah camps out in solitude by a wadi in the desert, where he relies on ravens to feed him (see 1 Kings 17).[5]

In another passage from the Palace History, the kings of Israel and Judah prepare for battle by participating in the prophets' pre-battle performance. The divine messengers deliver oracles of favor to the kings: "Go up to the city of Ramoth and triumph! Yhwh will give it into the hand of the king!" One of the diviners dons horns of iron and announces, "Thus says Yhwh: 'With these shall you gore the Arameans until they are destroyed!'" In this crowd, there is a solitary dissident, Micaiah. Prophesying defeat, he fails to comply with his orders to deliver a favorable oracle, as all the others had done. When called to account for his crimes against the state, he describes his vision in which Yhwh puts a lying spirit in the mouth of all the royal prophets (1 Kings 22).

FROM PALACE TO PEOPLE

Among the letters found from the final years of the Judean kingdom, one refers to an oracle ("Take heed!") that a prophet delivered on the eve of the Babylonian invasion (see Chapter 14). In stark contrast to the actual prophecies from the kingdoms of Israel, Judah, and their neighbors, the prophetic literature of the Bible is much lengthier. It was written, as argued in Chapter 21, for the instruction of a community living after defeat. For that reason, it rarely addresses day-to-day concerns

[5] According to later rabbinic legend, these birds brought bread to Elijah from the king's table so that the prophet could both benefit from the palace yet not succumb to its influence.

for a ruler's success, and it often brazenly challenges the conventional means by which states legitimated their authority. Instead of preserving this literature, the palace would have been eager to eradicate it, and one of the finest illustrations of how the palace censored prophets is the story of Jeremiah and the Judean king recounted in the introduction to this chapter.

"My people are destroyed for lack of knowledge." This line from Hosea (4:6) conveys a core principle for the biblical authors: the nation's strength depends upon all its members being educated in its history, laws, lore, and wisdom – that is, "knowing Yhwh/God." A fundamental feature of the biblical agenda is broad participation in public life, and the biblical prophecies address first and foremost not the palace but the people.

Historically, however, very few if any ancient Near Eastern prophets (including those from Israel and Judah) either delivered their messages to an entire nation or condemned the crown's actions. The Esarhaddon collection from Nineveh consists mostly of oracles of peace and reconciliation for the king, with direct implications for the struggle with his enemies. To cite a typical example:

Esarhaddon, king of the lands, fear not!
What is the wind that has attacked you,
whose wings I have not broken?
Like ripe apples your enemies will continually roll before your feet.
I am the great Lady, I am Ishtar of Arbela,
who throws your enemies before your feet.
Have I spoken to you any words that you could not rely upon?
I am Ishtar of Arbela, I will flay your enemies and deliver them up to you.
I am Ishtar of Arbela, I go before you and behind you. Fear not.[6]

Here Ishtar affirms through the mouth of the prophet that she protects the king and fights for him. "Fear not" is a common prophetic expression (the antithesis of "Take heed!"). It appears frequently in the Bible as an admonition to the king in response to military threats (see Isaiah 7:4 or 37:6), but more often, it is addressed to the entire nation: "O my people who dwell in Zion, do not fear Assyria, who beats you with a rod and

[6] Nissinen, *Prophets and Prophecy*, pp. 102–103.

wields his staff over you as did the Egyptians" (Isaiah 10:24). This shift from palace to people coincides with the Bible's solicitude for the nation as a whole rather than a particular ruler or institution: "Give ear, all you inhabitants of the land!" (Joel 1:2).

Closely related to the wider scope of biblical prophecies is their preoccupation with doom and destruction, as we saw in Chapter 20. Condemnations of the king's reign are absent in the Esarhaddon collections, and one must look far and wide for non-biblical prophecies that accuse the king of any wrong deed. Occasionally an oracle demands from the king greater attention to the feeding of a god or the words of his prophets. However, biblical prophecies proclaim the imminent demise of the state. When assigning blame, they most often point their finger at the king, his court, as well as "lying prophets" who perform in the palace and temple. These court prophets, who promise peace and security for their royal patrons, are opponents of the divine order: "They have treated the wound of my people carelessly, saying, 'Peace, peace,' when there is no peace" (Jeremiah 6:14).

FROM STATE ARCHIVES TO DIDACTIC LITERATURE

In a widely transmitted Mesopotamian text called the Marduk Prophecy, the deity claims that instead of being deported (in the form of his sacred image) from Babylon by conquering enemies, he left on his own accord. This theology resembles the ways biblical prophetic literature attributes defeat to the deity's decision to abandon his land. Yet the text also illustrates two distinctive features of the biblical tradition: the context of its transmission and its larger, national scope.

Marduk declares that one day a great king would arise, restore his temple Sagila, and, by crushing his enemies, create the political conditions that permit him to return. The identity of this prophesied king is uncertain. Originally it probably referred to Nebuchadnezzar I (1124–1103 BCE), and it resembles other texts describing how, prior to the rule of this king, Marduk had allowed Elamites to ravage Babylonia. We know of this prophecy thanks to three Neo-Assyrian copies, two of which were found in the Ashurbanipal Library in

Nineveh. Their presence in the palace archive suggests that the prophecy was transmitted for centuries along with other oracles and records of divination that Ashurbanipal (and probably earlier kings) collected and appropriated.[7]

In contrast, prophetic writings from the Bible are filled with promises of a future great Davidic ruler (e.g., Isaiah 11), but most often these promises are just one piece of a larger prophecy relating to the rebirth of a *people* (e.g., Jeremiah 33:14–26). Thus, Amos promises the reestablishment of "the fallen booth of David" in terms of a restoration of "my people Israel" who will rebuild their cities, plant their own vineyards, and till their own gardens (Amos 9:11-15. Similarly, Second Isaiah presents the enduring loyalty promised to David as being fulfilled in the future flourishing of a war-torn people (Isaiah 55).

The broader audience of these writings is closely tied to their genre, size, and transmission. Their authors did not merely index individual oracles according to date or theme, as we witness in Mesopotamia among scholars working in the palace. Instead, they used older materials to create something entirely new: sophisticated works of literature, books designed to be read by and to larger communities. These works are thoroughly didactic. By studying them, communities learn from the sins of past generations and reflect on the foundations of communal life.

The book of Jeremiah spans the career of the prophet, while Hosea's personal experience mirrors the collective fate of the nation. This intimate bond between prophet and people is distinctive and differs drastically from the catalogues of oracles stored in the palace. As "state secrets," those oracles were revealed *sub rosa*, safeguarded under lock and key in a royal library, off limits to anyone beyond the king and a small, select group of officials and scholars who had sworn allegiance to him.

Because those palace texts were never reworked into literature for a reading community, they were eventually lost. That we know about them

[7] See Wright, "Commemoration of Defeat," pp. 446–447.

today is not because communities from a defeated kingdom copied and transmitted them. The reason is rather that conquering armies set the palaces ablaze. With these infernos, foreign forces unintentionally baked the clay tablets into stone so that they did not disintegrate for the millennia they lay buried in the earth.

Why did these texts end up being preserved in this manner? The simple reason is that no one thought to salvage records of oracles addressed to a vanquished dynasty. The Ashurbanipal Library is the product of a state intent on monopolizing divine knowledge. Scholars working at the court guarded it from everyone beyond the king and an inner circle that had sworn loyalty to him. It is no wonder then that this body of classified knowledge was forgotten after Nineveh's downfall.

If prophetic writings survived the flames that destroyed Jerusalem, it is because scribes modified, rescripted, and expanded them to address newly emerging communities. They were not locked away in royal archives. As they were studied and amplified, they evolved into a massive portion of the biblical canon. The corpus in turn prompted the composition of countless commentaries, such as those discovered among the Dead Sea Scrolls. And for two millennia, they have continued to be studied by a wide array of communities and social movements.

A KINGDOM OF PRIESTS

The principle of public transparency and open access has shaped not only the formation of the prophetic writings and the Pentateuch's laws but also the publication of what were originally the priests' privileged materials.

As an aristocratic caste, priests enjoyed many special prerogatives. Their authority grew when imperial powers conquered their societies, since temples often served as conduits of imperial benefaction. The book of Ezra-Nehemiah presents the Persian kings not only decreeing that the Judeans rebuild their temple but also showering this institution and its personnel with generous gifts and tax exemptions.

Because priests could make rulings on a wide array of matters pertaining both to personal and public life, they exerted considerable influence.

Reflections of their political pull – including their personal alliances with Judah's enemies and their frequent financial corruption – are found in many post-exilic writings.

As to be expected, priests were jealous of their status and protected it through various means. The first and most basic way they did this was to make descent the criterion for membership in the guild: only those who were born to priests could serve as priests. The second way was by safeguarding their trade secrets. Priestly knowledge, which touched on some of most important matters of communal life, was transmitted exclusively among members of the hereditary guild. This special, secret knowledge qualified them as the ultimate authorities on many issues.

In its present form, the Pentateuch consists of lengthy descriptions of cultic activities, along with rules and instructions that had formerly been restricted to priestly circles. These texts treat – in considerable detail – matters that today are the purview of physicians, such as quarantines for diseases, plagues, and physical afflictions. Thus, a lengthy chapter (Leviticus 13) consists entirely of technical instructions for priests who diagnose and evaluate skin diseases (frequently, although falsely, identified as "leprosy"). Such manuals were originally composed for exclusive use by priests and temple personnel. However, biblical scribes divulged and reworked their contents so that others could evaluate their rulings, especially as these rulings were often politically motivated and had direct ramifications for participation in public life.

As the Bible's premier public document, the Pentateuch grants non-priests access to what was once restricted and esoteric knowledge. Now non-priests could study the deity's directions for sacrifices and offerings: what each class of individual and group were to offer on various occasions, what portions the priests were allowed to take from offerings, how they were to distribute the portions among themselves, and so on. With access to laws and regulations pertaining a wide range of issues (from unintentional sins to matters of impurity), lay leaders could identify fraudulence, wrongdoing, venality, and extortion in the priests' ranks, and subject their performance and rulings to public scrutiny.

Thanks to these ambitious editorial moves, the Pentateuch punctures the bubble of priestly privilege. Prerogative becomes duty. It is no longer a matter of what the priests *get to do* but rather what they *have to do*. They are to perform their tasks on behalf of the nation, and they must neither shirk their duties nor bend them according to political influence.

The Pentateuch's authors not only published what was once shielded from the public eye, but also amplified it for the instruction and edification of a new nation. In keeping with their project of creating a didactic corpus for the entire nation, they made priestly knowledge available and relevant to the wider community. All could now learn about the will of the nation's deity by studying the divine knowledge preserved in these sacred writings. Moreover, this study could serve as a substitute for sacrifice when the temple and altar were no longer standing, as in rabbinic times, or when the authority and qualifications of the high priest was in doubt, as in the days of Nehemiah (see Chapter 12).

A HOLY NATION

While the priests retained ultimate authority in a wide range of matters, the Pentateuch applies the model of their sacredness and separation to the entire nation. A prominent line in Leviticus reads: "You shall be my holy ones, because I, Yhwh, am holy, and have separated you from other people, that you should be mine" (Leviticus 20:26). Just as the priests are distinguished from other members of Israel, so is Israel, as Yhwh's chosen people, separate from other peoples. At Sinai, the deity asserts that "all the earth belongs to me," and if Israel keeps the terms of his covenant, it will be his own "kingdom of priests and a holy nation" (Exodus 19:15–16).

In the biblical corpus, nationhood is a state of mind – a kingdom of not only collective consciousness but also collective conscience. It exists to the extent that its members honor the holiness of their God, know the narratives of their national past, and then choose to make the divinely revealed, covenantal laws the constitution of their corporate life. In Part II, we saw how these writers, in keeping with their notion of nationhood as both a volitional and a voluntary enterprise, introduced a new pedagogical program. Education was not to be another means by which elites distinguish themselves from lower social classes; instead, it should mark off Israel corporately as a people from others. The Pentateuch uses the paradigm of priesthood in the same way. As members of "a kingdom of priests and a holy nation," all must adhere to a strict code, with regulations ranging from what one eats, what fabrics are mixed, and the fringes on one's garments.

What might have motivated the Pentateuch's authors to make these surprising moves, applying a model of priestly holiness to the nation as a whole?

Most communities demarcate their identity with the help of various kinds of conventions and behaviors. If the identity markers delineated in the Bible are unusually wide-ranging and developed, it is because this corpus emerged largely after the destruction of the Northern and Southern kingdoms, which had long defined Israel's and Judah's borders. What gave the new nation its identity in the post-destruction period were no longer physical borders but rather practice and performance. Action replaced location.

Given the precariousness of their people's existence after being conquered by foreign armies, the scribes who produced the Pentateuch adopted these extraordinarily strict regulations to serve as identity markers for their communities. They wanted their new nation to view itself as an assembly of Yhwh's priests, which meant not only special obligations to follow but also a sacred and sublime calling to fulfill.

Building on this treatment of public transparency and open access, we consider in the following chapter how the book of Proverbs "democratizes" wisdom and how the Psalter revamps older hymns, laments, and temple liturgies to produce a new songbook for the nation. We will also see how two closely related books, Job and Ecclesiastes, push the pedagogical program forward by validating protest, doubt, and even outright skepticism.

FURTHER READING

Gordon, Robert P. and Barstad, Hans M. (eds.), *"Thus Speaks Ishtar of Arbela": Prophecy in Israel, Assyria, and Egypt in the Neo-Assyrian Period*, *Eisenbrauns*, 2013.

Hamori, Esther J., *Women's Divination in Biblical Literature: Prophecy, Necromancy, and Other Arts of Knowledge*, Yale University Press, 2015.

Himmelfarb, Martha, *A Kingdom of Priests: Ancestry and Merit in Ancient Judaism*, University of Pennsylvania Press, 2006.

Knohl, Israel, *The Divine Symphony: The Bible's Many Voices*, Jewish Publication Society, 2003.

Leuchter, Mark and Hutton, Jeremy M. (eds.), *Levites and Priests in Biblical History and Tradition*, Society of Biblical Literature, 2011.

Moore, James D., *Literary Depictions of the Scribal Profession in the Story of Ahiqar and Jeremiah 36*, De Gruyter, 2021.

Nissinen, Martti, *Prophets and Prophecy in the Ancient Near East*, SBL Press, 2019.

Pongratz-Leisten, Beate, *Religion and Ideology in Assyria*, De Gruyter, 2015.

Sharp, Carolyn J., *Prophecy and Ideology in Jeremiah: Struggles for Authority in the Deutero-Jeremianic Prose*, T&T Clark, 2003.

Stökl, Jonathan and Carvalho, Corrine L. (eds.), *Prophets Male and Female: Gender and Prophecy in the Hebrew Bible, the Eastern Mediterranean, and the Ancient Near East*, Society of Biblical Literature, 2013.

Stökl, Jonathan, *Prophecy in the Ancient Near East: A Philological and Sociological Comparison*, Brill, 2012.

Wright, Jacob L., "The Commemoration of Defeat and the Formation of a Nation the Hebrew Bible," *Prooftexts* 29 (2009): 433–473.

Wright, Jacob L., "'Human, All Too Human': Royal Name-making in Wartime," in Yigal Levin and Amnon Shapira (eds.), *War and Peace in Jewish Tradition: From the Ancient World to the Present*, Routledge, 2011.

Wright, Jacob L., "Prolegomena to the Study of Biblical Prophetic Literature," in Thomas Römer and Jean-Marie Durand (eds.), *Comment devient-on prophète?*, Vandenhoeck & Ruprecht, 2013.

27

The Sage

Job, Proverbs, and Ecclesiastes

> There was once a man in the land of Utz whose name was Job.
> This man was blameless and upright, fearing God and shunning evil.
> – Job 1:1

So begins a biblical book whose forty-two chapters launch an assault on the Bible's most fundamental teachings. The work begins with Yhwh and "the Accuser" (Hebrew: *haSatan*) making a wager. The test was simple: would the man Job remain faithful if Yhwh took everything from him, including his children and his health? What begins as a trial of one person's righteousness spirals into a raw and unrelenting evaluation of divine justice. Unlike the prophets, this work does not point the accusing finger at the palace or even the people. Instead, it indicts the deity. The spectacular speeches of Job, his friends, and finally Yhwh move toward an obscure conclusion. With no clear resolution, the reader is compelled to listen to its orations and make a judgment about their merit.

We are now positioned to appreciate a most surprising turn in the biblical corpus. After establishing an alternative covenantal order that places culpability on the nation for its collective fate, this body of writings makes space for voices that destabilize that order, subverting it with nuanced and eloquently formulated discourses of doubt. Thus, in the thought experiment that is the book of Job, a man is sentenced to suffer in a cruel scheme to see if he would "sin with his lips." When he levels relentless attacks and counterattacks at biblical teachings, his pious friends are quick to call him out. However, the book itself not only welcomes but even champions the protagonist's rhetorical onslaught.

How are we to explain this unexpected move? Why would the scribes who shaped this corpus set forth a coherent concept of covenant in its first two parts (the Pentateuch and the Prophets) and then call into question that same concept in the third and final section (the Writings)? Before addressing this conundrum, we must first learn a bit about biblical "wisdom."

PROVERBS AND PARENTS

Proverbs appear in some of the earliest written remains from West Asia and North Africa. More than 5,000 years ago, the Sumerians coined and collected popular wisdom sayings, and from Egypt to Mesopotamia, proverbs were a central part of the scribal curriculum. By learning aphorisms and maxims, and copying them in daily exercises, young men from the upper classes cultivated not only courtly *savoir faire* but also probity and sound judgment:

> Tell a lie and then tell the truth: it will be considered a lie.[1]
>
> A good name is to be chosen over great riches,
> And loving favor more than silver and gold.
> – Proverbs 22:1

Proverbs were also once essential components of American school curricula. Thus, *The New England Primer* (first published in 1678 and reissued often) combined proverbs with acrostic exercises that introduce the alphabet to school children:

> A = In **Adam's** fall, we sinned all.
> B = Heaven to find, the **Bible** mind.[2]

Many of *The New England Primer's* proverbs refer to biblical stories, and their purpose was to implant a distinctive (Protestant) morality and civic virtue in their young audiences. The theology of these works is not always consistent with the biblical text. (For example, the book of Genesis does

[1] See the *Electronic Corpus of Sumerian Literature*, Proverb 2.71 (128): https://etcsl.orinst.ox.ac.uk/proverbs/t.6.1.02.html.

[2] From the 1777 edition, available at www.sacred-texts.com/chr/nep/1777/index.htm.

not make Adam responsible for the "fall" of all humankind.) Nevertheless, the use of biblical writings to inculcate morality and virtue broadly – and among members of a fledgling nation – stands in continuity with the origins of these same writings.

As so often throughout the Bible, the book of Proverbs combines earlier and competing collections: ten speeches and three poems in chapters 1–10; a different compendium in chapters 10–22; "Words of the Wise" in 22:17–24:34, materials attributed to King Hezekiah in chapters 25–29; "Words of Agur" in chapter 30; and "Words of King Lemuel" from his mother in chapter 31. (The book has a sevenfold structure, marked by superscripts; compare the "seven pillars" of wisdom in 9:1.) Many of these parts may have originated at a time when the kingdom of Judah was still thriving. Yet the bulk of the book coalesced during the post-destruction period, as part of the larger pedagogical project that we discussed in Part II. By collecting and reshaping older works of instruction, scribes enabled broader access to what was once the preserve of the palace and a privileged few. The result of their efforts is a corpus of wisdom for the entire nation, one that is an essential part of the biblical curriculum.[3]

If the book of Proverbs continued to take shape in the Hellenistic period, one might assume that its authors conceived it for the instruction and moral formation of young aristocrats in Judean society. However, instead of focusing on elites, the book democratizes wisdom, making it available to all who wish to be wise. Its publication grows out of the insight that a people can be resilient and flourish only when all its members behave wisely, act nobly, and treat each other with honor and deference. By identifying its author as King Solomon, the book's superscript (1:1) makes these proverbs the secret to this ruler's success, especially now that the power and prosperity of his legendary reign were unattainable.

Proverbs imagines wisdom as a woman who calls out from the mountaintops, on roadsides, in waystations, and at the city's gates. Not only is she a prized commodity to acquire, but she will also exalt the wise person and crown the one who seeks her.

[3] See the discussion in Chapter 14 of the late addition in Deuteronomy 4:5–8.

The beginning of wisdom is this: Get wisdom,
and whatever else you get, get insight.
Prize her highly, and she will exalt you;
she will honor you if you embrace her.
She will place on your head a fair garland;
she will bestow on you a beautiful crown."
Hear, my child, and accept my words,
that the years of your life may be many.
– Proverbs 4:7–10

One way to trace the development of this book is via its repeated question: "What's the beginning of wisdom?" In older portions, it is first and foremost the will to acquire it, as one would seek a beautiful, noble woman (as in the portion of Provers 4 just quoted). Some of these early sections speak of God more generally. In contrast, later additions link wisdom not merely to "God-fearing" conduct, but to reverence specifically for Yhwh. For example:

The fear of Yhwh is the beginning of wisdom,
but fools despise wisdom and instruction.
– Proverbs 1:7

In most cases, it is easy to identify the references to Yhwh as editorial supplements. Thus, notice how the italicized lines, speaking of both Yhwh and "the righteous," stick out in their context:

One who is slothful in his work
is close kin to a destroyer.
The name of Yhwh is a strong tower;
the righteous run into it and are safe.
The wealth of the rich is their strong city;
in their imagination it is like a high wall.
– Proverbs 18:9–11

In the final stages of the book's composition-history, wisdom is identified with the Torah (see Proverbs 28:4, 7, 9, 29:18; cf. "torah" = teaching in 1:8, 3:1, 4:2, 6:20, 13:14, 31:26), and this identification has made itself felt in both the Pentateuch (e.g., Deuteronomy 4) and the Psalter (e.g., Psalms 1, 19, 119). A prosperous life requires education and instruction

(Proverbs 1:3), and thus wisdom is naturally allied with the most important collection of the nation's teachings.

Proverbs charges parents with transmitting wisdom across generations, instructing their children with the very words that their parents once taught. Originally, the language of father and son related to teacher and student, but in the new editions, the father is the actual parent. Moreover, his role is now juxtaposed with that of the mother, who figures prominently throughout the book.

> My child, keep your father's commandment,
> and do not forsake your mother's teaching.
> Bind them upon your heart always;
> tie them around your neck.
> – Proverbs 6:20

The term "teaching" (*torah*) is noteworthy here. When it appears in the Pentateuch, it is usually translated as "law," and the principal dispensers of this special knowledge are the deity, Moses, and priests. Proverbs, however, brings teaching/*torah* to home and hearth, with the mother as a primary source. The emphasis on the home is woven into Proverbs' persistent claim that choosing the right wife is crucial to a man's success.

The Proverbs of Ahiqar is a non-biblical Aramaic work that was internationally circulated at this time and, as noted in Chapter 13, was read among Judeans in the Persian colony of Elephantine. Many of the proverbs resemble those in the biblical book, yet Ahiqar makes no mention of women. Likewise, Egyptian proverbs are suffused with suspicion about women and their contributions to society. The biblical book of Proverbs has its share of dangerous female figures, but this work also assigns women a leading role in the acquisition of wisdom.

Having begun with a young man's relation to his parental home, the book ends with an encomium to a strong woman. The poem enumerates this paragon's qualities by means of an alphabetical acrostic, similar to what we witnessed in *The New England Primer*. The catalogue of her accomplishments includes children who honor her. However, it measures her worth not by her procreative and maternal abilities, but by her business savvy and administrative skill. She successfully manages a thriving household, and provides for her family and staff, even as her generosity benefits the needy in her community.[4]

The poem begins: "Who shall find a 'Woman of Might/Valor'? She is far more precious than jewels" (Proverbs 31:10). We might think that such a woman is a rare phenomenon, hard to find. But rarity is not the point; rather, the poet is comparing her worth to gems.

The expression 'Woman of Might/Valor' (see also Proverbs 12:4), is an adaptation of 'Man of Might/Valor,' a traditional title of distinction for warriors and noblemen who occupy positions of honor in society (see Chapter 25 on Boaz). In the directly preceding passage, King Lemuel recounts the discourse his mother taught him, which includes the exhortation "Do not give your might/valor to women" (Proverbs 31:3). In contrast to that teaching, this poem praises the woman for the might/valor that she and other women already possess:

> Strength and dignity are her clothing,
> and she grins at the future.
> She opens her mouth in wisdom,
> and the teaching/torah of generosity (*chesed*) is on her tongue.
> – Proverbs 31:26

> Many women have done deeds of might/valor,
> but you surpass them all.
> – Proverbs 31:29

By using such language, and by bringing her priceless life into the limelight, this culmination to the book honors her contributions next to that of both warriors and scholars, and thereby participates in the creation of the new post-defeat culture that we have been exploring in Part IV.

ECCLESIASTES: REPAIRING THE TRADITION

Ecclesiastes is a strange biblical book. The first line ascribes its contents to a "son of David, king in Jerusalem," and perhaps we are to identify him

[4] This text has taken many turns in its reception history, being long loved, recently rejected, and now regularly redeemed as a portrait of a woman's authority, self-reliance, and communal significance; see Maier, "Good and Evil Women in Proverbs and Job," pp. 81–82.

as the wise and wealthy Solomon. Its Hebrew name, Kohelet, resembles the word for "congregation" (*kahal*); similarly, the title Ecclesiastes derives from the Greek word for "assembly" (*ecclesia*). While both suggest a sage who teaches an assembly or preaches to a congregation, his message undermines the Bible's mainstream teachings with its unrelenting skepticism.

Ecclesiastes is a work of wisdom, and it features many sapient precepts (including its share of misogyny; see 7:26–28). But whereas certitude and answers fill the pages of Proverbs, Ecclesiastes meditates on life's big questions, beginning with a most basic one: "Why do I spend my days in toil and labor?" The book makes its readers witnesses to an extended, and exasperating, quest. Kohelet, as its implied author, looks at the world and reaches conclusions about life. His dialectic approach quickly discerns the limits of what he deduces, and he presses on, persistently, to a better resolution. Yet each discovery is frustratingly subverted in his search.

Having parsed out every piece of the puzzle that life poses, Kohelet finally turns to wisdom:

> Then I considered all that my hands had done,
> and the toil I had spent in doing it.
> And again, all was a vapor and a chasing after wind,
> and there was nothing to be gained under the sun.
> So I turned to consider wisdom and madness and folly . . .
> Then I saw that wisdom excels folly as light excels darkness,
> but fools walk in darkness.
> – Ecclesiastes 2:11–13

One assumes that by this point, the quest has finally reached a conclusion. But then we learn that also wisdom is, alas, of limited value:

> Then I said to myself, "What happens to the fool will happen to me also.
> Why then have I sought to be so wise?"
> And I said to myself that this also is vanity.
> For there is no enduring remembrance of the wise or of fools,
> seeing that in the days to come all will have been long forgotten.
> How can the wise die just like fools?

So I hated life,
because what is done under the sun was grievous to me.
All is a vapor and a chasing after wind.
– Ecclesiastes 2:15–17

Ecclesiastes is emotional rollercoaster. What troubles the sage is that nothing endures, justice is not discernible, and death proves to be the ultimate equalizer. What, then, is the point of living or of acting justly? Wisdom itself, he discovers, is not an answer, as it fails to guarantee either prosperity or life.

What is the answer to life's riddle? Perhaps there is none. Perhaps it is all about the quest. The closest we come to a resolution is when Kohelet – returning to his dialectical point of departure (see the extended discourse in 1:12–3:22) – exhorts his readers to enjoy the simple pleasures of daily life:

Let your garments always be white,
and your head never lack ointment.
Enjoy life with the woman whom you love
all the days of your vaporous life that are given you under the sun.
Because that is your portion in life
and in the labors in which you toil under the sun.
Whatever your hand finds to do, do with your might!
For there is no discourse, thought, knowledge, or wisdom in the hereafter [Sheol].
– Ecclesiastes 9:8–10

This passage parallels Siduri's speech in the (much older) Gilgamesh Epic:

Let your clothes be clean.
Let your head be washed; in water you may bathe.
Look down at the little one who holds your hand.
Let a wife ever be festive in your lap.
This is the lot (of humans).
– Meissner-Millard Tablet, iii.1–13[5]

Since our time is short and little lies beyond the grave, we must enjoy our days under the sun. This is our "portion." The Psalter repeatedly

[5] See Anderson, *A Time to Mourn*, pp. 74–82.

identifies God as one's "portion." In Ecclesiastes, it lies nowhere else than in the enjoyment of life with the one you love. Here Ecclesiastes overlaps with the Gilgamesh Epic. Yet where Gilgamesh includes a "little one," Ecclesiastes features labor.[6]

With Ecclesiastes, we have traveled far from the realm of confidence in which the authors of Proverbs dwell. This skeptic sage cannot affirm what others teach, namely that doing good and being wise paves a path to success and security. None of Kohelet's core claims echo the exhortations of Moses or the admonitions of the prophets; in fact, Israel is never mentioned, nor is Yhwh's name. Instead, this book celebrates a freethinker who ventures beyond established boundaries. Its hero is one who ponders existence with brutal honesty, questions conventional wisdom, and persists in a search for meaning. A concluding remark praises his achievement, his commitment to truth, and his contributions as a teacher of "the people."

> Koheleth was a sage, but he also taught knowledge to the people. He pondered, analyzed, and corrected/repaired many proverbs. Koheleth sought to discover delightful sayings/things, and to record integrity and words of truth.
>
> – Ecclesiastes 12:9–10

If Ecclesiastes breaks the mold with its skepticism, why was it included in the biblical corpus? One answer is to be found in a note that someone added to the end of book:

> When all is said and done, the end of the matter is this: fear God and keep his commandments. This is all there is for humans. God will bring every act to judgment, everything that is hidden, whether it is good or evil.
>
> – Ecclesiastes 12:13–14

This final summation seeks to subvert Kohelet's entire disquisition, affirming a system of divine justice that the sage had valiantly called into question. But the editor's effort was hardly successful: Kohelet's doubts still loom large, and readers through the ages have rightly taken them

[6] See Chapter 10 where we note how a leading myth from Mesopotamia denigrates labor, identifying it as a detestable drudgery that the rest-loving gods created humans to bear as their slaves. The Gilgamesh Epic was later expanded with a story of the flood that shares this sentiment.

seriously. Moreover, this work stands next to others in a section of the canon (the Writings) that challenges the system. In what follows, we consider finally the case of Job – a man who after losing everything, engages in combat with his creator.

JOB: THE HEROIC ANTAGONIST

Kohelet is a cool-headed old man who is sated with life's pleasures and wonders if there is any deeper meaning to it all. Job, in contrast, is one who loses it all at his prime and is left to lie on an ash heap, scraping his rotting skin with potsherds. His wife urges him to curse God and die. Yet instead of resigning himself to his fate, he emerges as an intrepid fighter who unabashedly calls the deity to account for his suffering.

Doubt descends to unprecedented depths in this lengthy work. Its forty-two chapters interrogate divine justice not only persistently (as in Ecclesiastes) but also vehemently. Questions shoot forth in rapid fire: Why do I suffer? Why do others suffer even when they are righteous? And why do the wicked prosper? What will you, God, do to account for your injustice and redeem yourself?

Stripped of family and fortune, and plagued with a skin disease, Job is patient at first. His friends try to console him in his misery by reminding him of familiar teachings: no human is perfect, God is just, and the world is ultimately in good order. Job should examine himself. Surely he has done something to deserve his fate:

> Think now, when have the innocent ever perished?
> Or where were the upright cut off?
> As I have seen, those who plow iniquity, and sow trouble, reap the same.
> – Job 4:7–8

The friends' counsel – that if he repents, all will be well – infuriates Job, and he erupts in a flood of accusations against the divine order, railing against the harm done to him and to the world at large:

> It is all one [the same].
> Therefore I say:
> [God] destroys both the blameless and the wicked.

When disaster brings sudden death,
he mocks at the calamity of the innocent.
The earth is given into the hand of the wicked.
he covers the eyes of its judges.
If it is not he, who then is it?
–Job 9:22–24

Never doubting the deity's presence and power, Job demands an explanation for his own suffering, and for the suffering of the innocent everywhere, as he boldly catalogues the wrongs he witnesses in the world. What began as a test for him becomes a trial for his creator. The audience is invited to watch this bout between a lone righteous man and the sovereign of the universe.

Some thirty-five chapters after Job lifts his voice in seething remonstration, the deity finally responds. The answers, though, do not really correspond to the questions. Instead, Yhwh hurls challenging questions back at Job, demanding him to man-up and fight: "Gird your loins and answer me!" (Job 38:3).

Like the patriarch Jacob struggling with a stranger in the night and having his name changed to Israel thereafter, Job rises now as a prize fighter in the final round. Battling for what is left of his existence, he musters strength from his opponent's energy. But the valiant words he utters are opaque, and translators differ widely in the way they render them. A leading one, from the King James Version, reads:

I know that you can do everything,
and that no thought is withheld from you.
Who is he that hides counsel without knowledge?
Therefore have I uttered that I understood not,
things too wonderful for me, which I knew not.
Hear, I beseech you, and I will speak:
I will demand of you, and declare unto me.
I had heard of you by the hearing of the ear,
but now my eye sees you.
Therefore I despise myself,
and repent in dust and ashes.
–Job 42:2–6

Another translation, from the Jewish Publication Society, renders the final two lines differently:

Therefore I recant and relent,
being but dust and ashes.

Stephen Mitchell notes that the word that others translate as "repent" or "relent" means "comfort" throughout the book. He therefore offers this translation:

Therefore I will be quiet,
comforted that I am dust and ashes.[7]

After valiantly fighting against divine injustice for so many chapters, Job's final retort is unexpected. But what is he actually saying? Perhaps this is a final underhand jab at the Creator: I'm glad that I'm just dust and ashes (i.e. human), and not one who does this to the ones he created from dust and turns into ashes (see 2:8 and Genesis 2:7).[8] Whatever the case may be, Job thus takes comfort in his creatureliness while leaving unresolved questions about the nature of God's moral standing as sovereign of the universe.

The deity's final words are even more unexpected. Far from objecting to Job's impudence, he chastises the three others for spouting off conventional tropes from biblical theology:

My wrath is kindled against you
and against your two friends.
For you have not spoken of me what is right,
as my servant Job has.
Now therefore take seven bulls and seven rams,
and go to my servant Job,
and offer up for yourselves a burnt offering.
My servant Job shall pray for you.
I will accept his prayer
not to deal with you according to your folly.
For you have not spoken of me what is right,
as my servant Job has done.
–Job 42:7–8

[7] Mitchell, *Into the Whirlwind*, pp. 87–88. [8] Travis, *From Job to the Shoah*, pp. 36–54.

While Job's friends are said to have spoken folly, Job's discourses are commended – even though they indict the deity and repeatedly deny some of the Bible's most of foundational teachings.[9]

The conclusion leaves the audience uncertain as to outcome of this face-off between Yhwh and Job, yet one thing is clear: Job's courage to challenge divine justice, with both rage and defiance, meets with divine approval. His searing protests, which span most of this lengthy book, are more acceptable to the deity than the praise of divine justice that the friends piously rehearse.

A PEOPLE OF PROTEST

Job and Ecclesiastes persistently contest a precept from the pages of the Pentateuch, the Prophets, and Proverbs – that good deeds secure good fortunes. What, then, are these books doing in the Bible?

Perhaps their inclusion intends to communicate something about limits of the new covenantal order, namely that there is a difference between the collective and the individual experience. The promise of reward for righteousness applies only on the collective, systemic level, yet does not work for the individual. A society that perpetrates injustice against its own members will inevitably fall; however, just as wicked individuals often get away with murder, the sinless often suffer.

While such may be the larger lesson, there is another point that is possibly even more paramount. A strong current of skepticism and protest courses through the Bible, and it appears especially in the Writings (the third and final section of the canon). As some of the latest books the canon, they force their readers into a challenging dialogue with earlier works. They defend the reader's right to argue – with the text, with the tradition, and even with the deity. In so doing, they validate, and give voice to, those who struggle with the perennial problem of theodicy that arose from the new covenantal order. In the older

[9] The antagonistic character of Job's speeches and Yhwh's final approbation for his words are all the more remarkable given that book goes to great lengths to depict Job as one concerned with language and not "sinning with his lips." He goes so far as to offer sacrifices for his sons and daughters for any possible blasphemy they may have spoken silently while partying for days on end (Job 1:4–5).

order, Yhwh was much more limited in sovereignty and sphere of influence, and he did not promise a nation that it would succeed if it followed his written instructions.

Now if one has the right to argue with the deity and with divine revelation, then one should be emboldened to challenge even the highest political powers. Indeed, these works train their audience to interrogate the status quo and to challenge institutions and systems. For that matter, all biblical books contain contradictions that undermine their overall message, requiring the reader to ponder the problems and take a personal stance.

Through both dialogues and disputation, and in protest as much as in assent, the Bible embodies a model of cohesion that does not depend on uniformity. The answers are not provided in the clearcut and tidy forms of faith-confessions that members should espouse without questioning. The new national identity that emerged in the post-defeat period was a volitional and voluntarist one. Rather than being coerced by the crown through its conquests and creeds, it was inspired by questions and fostered through conversations.

The biblical scribes built questioning into the system. Taking doubt and skepticism seriously, they urged readers to assess the evidence for themselves. Instead of swallowing dogmatic assertions whole, their communities needed to feel free to evaluate – collectively and individually – the new covenantal order. Only then would one fully appreciate both its merits and its limitations.

Pushback and questioning make a system more flexible and resilient, and this intuition clearly informed the inclusion of a couple of other controversial books – the Song of Songs and Esther – next to the more familiar piety of the Psalms. In the final chapters that follow, we explore how these three very different works lay out important new directions and dimensions for the biblical project.

FURTHER READING

Anderson, Gary, *A Time to Mourn, A Time to Dance: The Expression of Grief and Joy in Israelite Religion*, Pennsylvania State Press, 1991.

Bolin, Thomas M., *Ecclesiastes and the Riddle of Authorship*, Routledge, 2017.

Bundvad, Mette, *Time in the Book of Ecclesiastes*, Oxford University Press, 2015.

Clifford, Richard J., *Wisdom Literature in Mesopotamia and Israel*, Society of Biblical Literature, 2007.

Dell, Katharine J., *The Book of Proverbs in Social and Theological Context*, Cambridge University Press, 2006.

Fox, Michael V., *Ecclesiastes: The Traditional Hebrew Text with the New JPS Translation*, Jewish Publication Society, 2004.

Greenstein, Edward L., *Job: A New Translation*, Yale University Press, 2019.

Maier, Christl, "Good and Evil Women in Proverbs and Job," in Christl M. Maier and Nuria Calduch-Benages (eds.), *The Writings and Later Wisdom Books*, SBL Press, 2014.

Mitchell, Stephen, *Into the Whirlwind*, Doubleday, 1979.

Morrow, William S., *Protest against God: The Eclipse of a Biblical Tradition*, Sheffield Phoenix, 2006.

Newsom, Carol A., *The Book of Job: A Contest of Moral Imaginations*, Oxford University Press, 2003.

Schipper, Bernd U., *Proverbs 1–15 (Hermeneia)*, Fortress, 2019.

Stewart, Anne W., *Poetic Ethics in Proverbs: Wisdom Literature and the Shaping of the Moral Self*, Cambridge University Press, 2016.

Travis, Reuven, *From Job to the Shoah: A Story of Dust and Ashes*, Wipf & Stock, 2013.

28

The Poet

The Song of Songs and Psalms

I am a rose of Sharon,
a lily of the valleys.
As a lily among thorns,
so is my love among the daughters.
As an apricot tree among the trees of the forest
is my beloved among the sons.
– Song of Songs 2:1–3

The Song of Songs, otherwise known as Canticles or the Song of Solomon, is a most unusual biblical book. What does this duet of two young lovers, who sensually shower each other with affection and adoration, have to do with the Bible's overarching purpose?

The work begins with one who describes herself as both black and beautiful:

Let him kiss me with the kisses of his mouth,
for your love is better than wine . . .
Your anointing oils are fragrant,
your name is perfume poured out;
therefore the maidens love you . . .
I am black and beautiful,
O daughters of Jerusalem,
as the tents of Kedar,
as the curtains of Solomon.
– Song of Songs 1:2–3, 5

Although her lover will speak and praise her beauty throughout the collection, it is her voice that we hear most often. Euphoric, enraptured, and often outright ecstatic, her words cause readers to blush as they move briskly from memories of a shared past to fantasies of future intimacy, from unreserved expressions of erotic desire to sensible counsel for her companions:

With great delight I sat in his shadow,
and his fruit was sweet to my taste.
He brought me to the banqueting house,
and his intention toward me was love.
Sustain me with raisins,
refresh me with apples,
for I am faint with love.
O that his left hand were under my head
and that his right hand embraced me!
I charge you, O daughters of Jerusalem,
by the gazelles or the hinds of the field:
do not stir up or awaken love until it is ready!
The voice of my beloved! Look, he comes,
leaping upon the mountains,
bounding over the hills.
– Song of Songs 2:3–8

How are we to account for the presence of such words in an anthology of sacred scripture? What does a collection of poems that celebrates physical pleasure and sexuality – and does so so colorfully – have to do with the Bible's larger purpose?

We saw how the biblical scribes created a new culture in which name-making is achieved through progeny more than martial, heroic performance. Given this shift from the battlefield to the bedroom, one might surmise that this poetry's purpose is to serve as a prelude to procreation.

Such a reading is, however, difficult to defend. The Song of Songs pays tribute, with full-frontal imagery, to a kind of "free love" that culminates neither in marriage nor in the birth of offspring, but in the immediate intimacy and erotic exchanges between two bodies. Both this book's images and its agenda are "Not Suitable for Children." Although readers over the ages had had trouble fathoming it, physical desire here is not merely the means to a more pragmatic, procreative end; it is an end in itself.

Why then is this paean to physical desire included in the Bible? What makes it "the Song of (all) Songs"? And how does it relate to a more familiar work of biblical poetry, the Psalms?

THE HOLY OF HOLIES

Our questions are not new. When someone in the second century CE challenged the propriety of the Song as sacred scripture, Rabbi Akiva not only defended its inclusion but attributed to it a *non plus ultra* status: "All scripture is holy, but Song of Songs is the Holy of Holies."[1] For two millennia, Jewish and Christian interpreters have claimed such elevated sanctity for the Song. They have read it as an allegory of love between God and Israel, or Christ and the Church, or as a journey of the soul to God. In the sixteenth century, the Song inspired Saint John of the Cross to write his famous *Dark Night of the Soul*.

From the perspective of our study, we will see that Rabbi Akiva may have been right: the Song of Songs is the Holy of Holies. Yet whereas the Jewish sage saw it as an allegory for the love between Israel and her God, what makes the Song perhaps the holiest of all books is its spirited salute to hallowed *human* love.

The Song imagines a world in which the beloved's body is sacred, and the space of physical intimacy sacrosanct. Such love is just as personal as it is political. Without shared spaces of one-on-one engagement, a people is bereft of the bonds that hold it together through thick and thin. Without partnerships between two, it is not realistic to expect a community of thousands to survive let alone thrive.

Such love is the "key to the kingdom," and it offers the first clue to the Song's inclusion in a corpus of national literature: when two come together in mutual desire, something new blossoms, and when couples come together as a collective people, something monumental emerges. But without couples, there can be no communities. Without friendship, trust, and intimacy between two, the bonds connecting three, or four, or four thousand, are easily severed.

[1] Mishnah Yadayim 3:5.

The synergy of the lovers' union reverberates throughout society and nature. Just as the "daughters of Jerusalem" join the gazelles and deer of the field, the man describes his lover's body with scapes of their homeland:

How beautiful you are, my love,
how very beautiful!
Your eyes are doves
behind your veil.
Your hair is like a flock of goats,
moving down the slopes of Gilead.
Your teeth are like a flock of shorn ewes
that have come up from the washing,
all of which bear twins,
and not one among them is bereaved.
Your lips are like a crimson thread,
and your mouth is lovely.
Your cheeks are like halves of a pomegranate
behind your veil.
Your neck is like the tower of David,
built in courses;
on it hang a thousand bucklers,
all of them shields of warriors.
Your two breasts are like two fawns,
twins of a gazelle,
that feed among the lilies.
– Song of Songs 4:1–5

Happy coupling is not only the precondition for community; it also creates it – not through marriage and family so much as through a new lease on life. When two individuals find themselves and fall in love, they cannot help but see the world through new eyes. They embrace nature, others around them, and their collective pasts.

POETRY'S POWER

The Bible devotes a lot of space to interpersonal relations. In addition to its lengthy legal codes and collections of proverbs, it tells stories and teaches love of neighbor through parables of peoplehood. Laws, narratives, and sermons address a wide range of social, economic, political, and religious behaviors, but poetry does something different.

Describing the work of Wendell Berry, the theologian and ecologist Jenny Howell observes how poetry is "an interaction of words and deeds that are particular and connected to place." The poet "invites the reader into a local conversation in a way that demands a response of action." This conversation is open-ended:

> [T]he voice of the poet herself is only one voice among many. The outcome of the poem cannot be controlled or contained, but rather makes space for a certain futurity or potentiality to reside within it. Only time, and the response lived out in time, can reveal the truth of a poem.[2]

The same can be said for the Song of Songs. It models a dialogic imagination in the interactions between two lovers and in their relations to those around them. It shows, not tells, how people prosper in mutuality. Time has also revealed its revolutionary "truth," with its images of two equal partners rankling generations of patriarchal readers.

By making a place for the Song, some seem to have recognized the pedagogical value of love poetry – its ability to cultivate virtue in ways that other genres cannot. In the Song, each partner enlarges the potential of the other, each invites the other to unfold. He urges her to rise; she awakens him. In their ability to acclaim and nurture each other, the lovers model an I–Thou encounter that is foundational for a thriving community.

Love here is both passionate and tender. It does not consume; it inspires. It causes the human world to flourish, to bloom and blossom, just as the natural world unfolds as a canopy for the couple's self-exploration. Shunning both the asceticism and the libertinism that often accompany revolutionary ideals, the Song pairs tenderness with sensuality – both bread and roses. To adapt a line from political activist and writer Emma Goldman, this revolution makes time for dancing.

[2] Howell, "The Dialogical Imagination of Wendell Berry."

AN ALTERNATIVE TO ABRAHAM

The poets Channa and Ariel Bloch describe the Song as "the sexual awakening of a young woman and her lover."[3] Its poetry revels in a form of human relationship in which reciprocity and joy reign supreme. The woman recalls how her partner invites her to rise up:

My darling spoke and said to me:
"Rise up, my friend! My beauty, come away!
See, the winter has passed,
The rain is finished and gone,
The flowers are appearing in the countryside,
The time has come when the cooing of doves
can be heard in the land.
The fig trees are forming their fruit,
And the grapevines in bloom give off their perfume.
Rise up, my friend! My beauty, come away!"
– Song of Songs 2:10–13

The usual translations obscure the full force of the invitation when they render the words *lechi lach* in the first and final lines as "come away." Such a sense implies no more than a call to escape confines, to come and roam the countryside on a rendezvous. Both moves are indeed embedded in this verse, but the language of the Song is more specific and more momentous: "Go forth." The reader cannot help but hear here an echo the words Yhwh speaks to Abraham in Genesis. It is the charge that launches the aged patriarch and his wife Sarah on their fateful journey, quoted in Chapter 1 of this book:

Go forth (*lech lecha*) from your country and from your kindred and your father's house,
to the land that I will show you,
and I will make of you a great nation,
and I will bless you, and make your name great,
so that you will be a blessing.
– Genesis 12:2

[3] Bloch and Bloch, *The Song of Songs*, p. 3.

The woman from the Song and Abraham from Genesis are a study in contrasts. When Yhwh promises a great nation and name, the patriarch assumes that he is all that matters. Without a son of his own, he attempts to adopt his servant Eliezer as his heir and urges the deity to fulfill the promise through him. When that does not work, he resorts to impregnating Hagar, Sarah's slave. Along the way, he passes off Sarah to others, fearing for his own survival. The reader watches as this man gradually grasps an obvious point: when Yhwh promises him that he would father a people, he should assume that his partner has a crucial role to play (see discussion in Chapter 22).

This story, like many others in the Bible, challenges its male readers to check their sense of self-sufficiency and to recognize that the only way forward is through partnership and collaboration. Now, on the other side of history, it is a young woman who, dwelling behind a wall, is urged to go forth and blossom. Her face is to be seen and her voice heard:

> O my dove, in the clefts of the rock,
> in the covert of the cliff,
> let me see your face,
> let me hear your voice;
> for your voice is sweet,
> and your face is lovely.
> – Song of Songs 2:14

PARADISE REGAINED

The story of Abraham and Sarah has the birth of children at its center. In contrast, the Song rhapsodizes about a love that is not procreational. As such, it takes us back to the Garden of Eden, when Yhwh declares: "It is not good for the human to be alone. I will therefore make a companion this one needs" (Genesis 2:18). He then puts this non-binary human to sleep and, from one side of this paramount creature, creates what in Hebrew is called *ezer k'negdo*, literally "a help that is meet for this one" (the English term "helpmeet/helpmate" derives from this expression). Here, in the first chapters of Genesis, the Bible takes aim at any construction of the self that is not fundamentally collaborative. It also lays out the most basic principle of human partnerships, one that has nothing to do with progeny.

The Song of Songs celebrates the construction of this collaborative self and the kind of partnership that is essential to human flourishing. In an influential study of sexuality in the Bible, Phyllis Trible highlights the ways in which the Song evokes images of Eden, with lovers harmoniously inhabiting nature.[4] Just as Yhwh starts over by creating a new nation through Abraham and Sarah, couples have the capacity, according to this poetry, to recreate the primordial garden in a post-edenic world – in places where wars, defeat, and death persist. What makes this re-creation possible is the overpowering force of love:

For love is as fierce as death;
its desire unyielding as the grave.
It burns like a blazing fire,
like a flame of Yah [Yhwh].
Roaring waters cannot extinguish love,
no flood can sweep it away.
– Song of Songs 8:6

The book of Deuteronomy understands love as covenantal loyalty and responsibility, qualities that define the nation's bond with its God in the face of imperial subjugation (Deuteronomy 6:5). Leviticus translates love into proper care and respect for others: the neighbor and the stranger, the orphan and the widow (Leviticus 19). In the Song, love defies death itself.

Many insist that the Song is more universal and less connected to Israel's particularity than other biblical writings. Yet the Song is ascribed to none other than King Solomon, who reigned at the height of the nation's might and glory, and its verses repeatedly refer to important people and places in the National Narrative. The couple locates their love on the landscape of a larger story.

According to one of the most common orderings of the Jewish canon, the Song follows the book of Job. The latter, as we saw in the preceding

[4] Trible, *God and the Rhetoric of Sexuality*, p. 139.

chapter, raises questions about divine justice as it gives voice to an individual who loses everything. The biblical scholar Tamara Cohn Eskenazi draws attention to the dialogue between this book and the Song of Songs. Taking her cue from Carl Jung's controversial work, *Answer to Job*, she examines the thematic development that this canonical arrangement implies.

For Jung, the New Testament provides the answer to the theological, ethical, and psychological challenges that Job raises and that are embodied in this man's personal story of loss and suffering. For Eskenazi, the sequence in the Jewish canon suggests that the Song is the most immediate and the ultimate answer to Job. This poetry is a "first response" in the face of earth-shattering trauma and bodily suffering – of both Job and the defeated communities that told his story.[5] Yet rather than grand theological reflections or communal resolutions, the Song responds to loss and pain with a love "as fierce as death." In the place of Jung's celestial triumphalism, here there is a turning to the other in their terrestrial beauty and human vulnerability.

PSALMS IN THE MAKING

If the Bible is a pedagogical project, a textbook for a new project of peoplehood, as proposed in Part II, we can appreciate why it includes not only wisdom literature but also poetry, like the Song of Songs, that affirms the primacy of love between individual members of the nation. Yet why include an extensive anthology of hymns, petitions, and laments such as we find in the Psalter? What didactic purpose does this collection serve?

The Psalter includes 150 individual psalms and a wide variety of genres, including lamentations, hymns of thanksgiving, paeans of triumph, wisdom poems, pilgrim songs, blessings, and imprecations. The individual psalms originated in different times and places. Despite the superscriptions that frequently mention David, most scholars agree that none are the work of this historical figure.

[5] Eskenazi, "Song of Songs as an 'Answer' to Clines's Book on Job."

Within the Psalter, we can isolate smaller anthologies, such as the Asaph and Korah collections (named after cult singers and officials), the "Yhwh-is-King" psalms, the Hallel collection, and the Songs of Ascent. Compilers appear to have drawn on these and other anthologies to create early editions, such as the "Elohistic Psalter" (Psalms 42–83). Over time, these editions were joined and expanded to create a larger "Messianic Psalter" (Psalms 2–89). This expanded edition begins and ends with the divine promise to the anointed king and Davidic dynasty. As a response to Judah's defeat, it expresses a hope for a re-establishment of the monarchy and has much in common with the Palace History in Samuel-Kings.

The Psalter familiar to most readers represents a reworking of this older edition: first in 1–119 and then in 1–150, the version found in most Bibles today. The new editions promote a piety focused on the Torah and the temple, respectively. Psalm 1 introduces these larger editions by praising those who delight in the Torah of Yhwh and who meditate on it day and night:

> Happy is the one who does not follow the advice of the wicked,
> or take the path that sinners tread,
> or sit in the seat of scoffers.
> His delight is in the Torah of Yhwh,
> and on Yhwh's law he meditates day and night.
> He is like a tree planted by streams of water,
> which yields its fruit in its season,
> and its leaves do not wither.
> Whatever he does prospers.
>
> – Psalm 1:1–3

This language closely resembles what we encounter in the first chapter of the book of Joshua. There Yhwh promises Joshua, as the commander of Israel's armies, that he will prosper if he mediates day and night on the Torah:

> Only be strong and very courageous,
> being careful to act in accordance with all the Torah
> that my servant Moses commanded you.

> Do not turn from it to the right hand or to the left,
> so that you may be successful wherever you go.
> This Scroll of the Torah shall not depart out of your mouth.
> you shall meditate on it day and night,
> so that you may be careful to act in accordance
> with all that is written in it.
> For then you shall make your way prosperous,
> and then you shall be successful.
>
> –Joshua 1:7–9

In reshaping both the older Messianic Psalter, with its militant accent, and an older version of the book of Joshua, which celebrates battlefield bravery, later scribes introduced a dramatic shift from martial valor to meditation. True strength comes from deep and sustained engagement with the Torah. Thus, Psalm 2, as the introduction to the older Messianic Psalter, focuses on the king, who with the help of the deity, conquers his enemies and takes possession of their territories. The new preface in Psalm 1 shifts attention from kings and war to all members of the community who devote themselves to the study of the Torah.

If David is the implied author of this book, he has metamorphosed from a triumphant warrior to one who meditates day and night on Yhwh's instruction. In the same way, Joshua 1 makes the success of the nation's war hero depend on his study of, and faithfulness to, the Torah. Joshua's task was to conquer the land, but what charge remained for the nation after it lost all that Joshua and his generation achieved? The first and abiding duty (especially in an age when the command to conquer no longer applies) was the study of all that Yhwh revealed to the nation through Moses.

These editorial moves grow in significance when we consider how they demarcate the three divisions of the Hebrew Bible. While Joshua 1 introduces the second section of the Bible (Nevi'im or "Prophets"), Psalm 1 introduces the third and final section (Ketuvim or "Writings"). Both introductions orient the reader to the first section of the canon, the Torah or "Pentateuch."

In this way, the entire Hebrew Bible is structured to underscore the Torah's unmatched importance as the foundation for the nation's collective future. The signposts in Joshua 1 and Psalm 1, planted by late editors, establish the Pentateuch as both the written repository for studying the divine will and the point of departure for interpreting the Prophets. (On the significance of this canonical ordering, see Chapters 20 and 21.) Together, they promote a shift from warrior to student, and from combat to cognition.

A SONGBOOK FOR THE NATION

The Psalter as we have it today is divided into five books, and this arrangement conveys a great deal. Just as Moses gave the nation five books of the Torah, so David gave the nation the five books of the Psalms. While the Torah is revealed to the nation, the Psalms may be understood as the voices of the nation responding to this revelation, responses that include not only praise but also petition and protest.

As noted in Chapter 21, an important step in the consolidation of a new nation was the combination of disparate and rival law codes in the Pentateuch. A similar scenario applies to the Psalter. Instead of transmitting materials from one group or place, the Judean scribes who created this work collected poetry from diverse traditions.

The Psalter not only grew as new psalms were added to it, but the individual psalms also evolved over time. Scribes expunged elements deemed deleterious, "nationalized" the work by adding the name Israel throughout, and reoriented praises from various gods to Yhwh as the nation's transcendent point of unity. They also arranged the chapters to juxtapose the individual's plight with the collective experience of their people. Finally, they prefaced many with superscriptions that anchor the book in the nation's narrative.

As they worked, they synthesized subject matter, moods, and motifs across the span of the book similar to the way a studio producer blends themes from separate tracks on a music album. However, they were careful not to homogenize the contents and collapse the differences of the individual units. Mirroring a model of communal diversity, each psalm has a distinct voice while simultaneously being in dialogue with those that surround it.

Both the orientation and the culmination highlight the special significance of Jerusalem and the temple. In keeping with the pattern of "open access" that shaped the Bible as a whole, the Psalter makes priestly liturgies available to a wider public. This production is not merely a compendium of songs and laments for liturgical use, or prayers for personal edification, but also a songbook for the nation.

We may compare this pedagogical purpose to *The American Song Book* published in 1917 or *The National Song Book* published in Great Britain in 1905. Both collections, and their counterparts in other countries, were conceived for use in schools. Educators were convinced that music should be an essential component of the curriculum – that nations need music and that education should include immersion in the poetry of one's people. In contemporary American and British schools, such national songbooks have been widely abandoned. But for many countries across the globe, music and dance are not only indispensable expressions and celebrations of their national identities, but also central to their educational curricula.

Recent research shows how the psalms are intended to function in moral formation. The psalms not only train readers to adopt various postures toward the deity, which include, as we shall see, protest and remonstration, but in keeping with the principle *imitatio Dei* (see Chapter 10), they also train readers to adapt their consciousness and conduct to the deity's behaviors and concerns, which include showing loving kindness, loathing evil, pursuing righteousness, and caring for the poor.

PRAISE AND PROTEST

The Psalms are often reduced to the *hallelujah* (a transliterated word from Hebrew meaning "praise Yhwh"). Praise has, to be sure, a prominent presence in the Psalter, but in the Christian tradition, it has often been the focus, with little attention paid to the posture of protest that this book promotes. Listen to Psalm 44, which begins by acknowledging the deity's redemptive power:

> We have heard with our ears, O God,
> our ancestors have told us,

what deeds you performed in their days,
in the days of old:
you with your own hand drove out the nations,
but them you planted;
you afflicted the peoples,
but them you set free.
– Psalm 44:1–2

For the community making its voice heard in this psalm, the deity's redemptive actions are only hearsay, not a present reality. The nation's loyalty proved to be of no avail:

In God we have boasted continually,
and we will give thanks to your name forever. Selah.
Yet you have rejected us and abased us,
and have not gone out with our armies.
You made us turn back from the foe,
and our enemies have gotten spoil.
You have made us like sheep for slaughter,
and have scattered us among the nations.
You have sold your people for a trifle,
demanding no high price for them.
– Psalm 44:8–12

According to Bible's covenantal theology, collective suffering is the result of the nation's sin. If Israel fails to practice justice toward each other and abide by the divine commandments, then Yhwh will punish his people by failing to provide them protection. But here the nation insists it has done nothing to merit this punishment. It is rather Yhwh who has failed to keep up his end of the agreement:

All this has come upon us,
yet we have not forgotten you,
or been false to your covenant.
Our heart has not turned back,
nor have our steps departed from your way."
– Psalm 44:17–18

The final outcry demands the deity to act:

Because of you we are being killed all day long,
and accounted as sheep for the slaughter.
Rouse yourself!
Why do you sleep, O Yhwh?
Awake, do not cast us off forever!
Why do you hide your face?
Why do you forget our affliction and oppression?
– Psalm 44:22–24

In reciting texts such as this one, a defeated and distressed community boldly calls Yhwh literally to wake up from his slumber and address its collective trauma.

The legacy of the Psalms is as consequential for its cries of protests as for its more familiar words of comfort and praise. Without such models of complaint and challenge, many would be reticent to take on the deity, especially using such brazen words and in such an unabashed manner.

These prayers embolden protest of not only heavenly authority, but of political powers on earth as well. Indeed, a religious tradition that prohibits protest vis-à-vis the deity will hardly foster courageous resistance to lesser powers. In an essay on "The Costly Loss of Lament," the Old Testament scholar Walter Brueggemann points out that Protestant communities often have been uncomfortable with the biblical lament tradition. By eliminating it from liturgy and personal piety, worshippers also eliminated a scriptural foundation for political protest.

We saw in Chapter 9 how the five poems from Lamentations provided the defeated community of Judah with a set of scripts for both grieving and grievances, and how the performance of these scripts cultivates a people of protest. Adding its own scripts to this repertoire of remonstrance, the five books of Psalms champion the cause of those who challenge the deity.

FURTHER READING

Bloch, Ariel and Bloch, Chana, *Song of Songs: A New Translation with an Introduction and Commentary*, University of California Press, 1995.

Blumenthal, David, *Facing an Abusing God*, Westminster John Knox, 1993.

Buster, Aubrey, *Remembering the Story of Israel: Historical Summaries and Memory Formation in Second Temple Judaism*, Cambridge University Press, 2022.

Brueggemann, Walter, "The Costly Loss of Lament," *Journal for the Study of the Old Testament* 36 (1986): 57–71.

Carr, David, *The Erotic Word: Sexuality, Spirituality, and the Bible*, Oxford University Press, 2003.

Eskenazi, Tamara Cohn, "Song of Songs as an 'Answer' to Clines's Book on Job," in J. Cheryl Exum and H.G.M. Williamson (eds.), *Reading from Right to Left*, T&T Clark, 2003.

Exum, J. Cheryl, *Song of Songs*, Westminster John Knox, 2005.

Flint, Peter W. and Miller, Patrick D. (eds.), *The Book of Psalms: Composition and Reception*, Brill, 2005.

Fox, Michael V., *The Song of Songs and Ancient Egyptian Love Songs*, University of Wisconsin Press, 1985.

Howell, Jenny, "The Dialogical Imagination of Wendell Berry," *Integrite*, 2011.

James, Elaine T., *Landscapes of the Song of Songs: Poetry and Place*, Oxford University Press, 2017.

Janowski, Bernd, *Arguing with God: A Theological Anthropology of the Psalms*, Westminster John Knox, 2013.

Jung, C.G., *Answer to Job*, 2nd ed., Princeton University Press, 2010.

Landy, Francis, "The Song of Songs and the Garden of Eden," *Journal of Biblical Literature* 98 (1979): 513–528.

Mandolfo, Carleen, *God in the Dock: Dialogic Tension in the Psalms of Lament*, Sheffield Academic Press, 2003.

Trible, Phyllis, *God and the Rhetoric of Sexuality*, Fortress, 1978.

Willgren, David, *The Formation of the "Book" of Psalms*, Mohr Siebeck, 2016.

29

The Queen

Peoplehood without Piety

For how can I bear to see the calamity
that is coming on my people?
Or how can I bear to see
the destruction of my kindred?
– Esther 8:6

Our final story is set at the court in Susa, the winter capital of the enormous Persian Empire reaching from India to Ethiopia. There young women are participating in an empire-wide beauty pageant. They have a year to get ready, and then the king will choose one of the candidates to be his queen.

The book of Esther has a fairytale quality, similar to that of *One Thousand and One Nights.* But for all its lightness and many farcical features, the story it tells is gravely serious. It depicts a twisted world, one in which an imperial power abuses women and its subjects for its own pleasure. Its protagonist cleverly orchestrates a dramatic reversal of misfortune, and in doing so, she models survival strategies for the book's readers.

Surprisingly, these strategies have nothing to do with the deity, the covenant, the land, the temple, confession of sin, and so on. Compensating for these omissions, early generations of readers inserted prayers and passages that bring the story into line with more mainstream biblical piety. However, this more theologically conventional version is not the one transmitted in the Hebrew ("Masoretic") canon.

The exclusion is counterintuitive, but as we shall see, the preference for the older, "godless" version helps us understand and appreciate –

perhaps more than any other book – the worldview of the circles who composed, curated, and canonized the biblical corpus.

REFUSING TO SUBMIT

The story begins with the expulsion of an earlier queen. The Persian king had been feasting for six months, and at the culmination to these celebrations, he decided to parade his beautiful wife Vashti before all his guests wearing her royal diadem. Yet Vashti refused to comply with his wishes, and her response embarrassed and enraged him.

When he consults with his seven sages, he is warned about the implications of the queen's conduct:

> Not only has Queen Vashti done wrong to the king, but also to all the officials and all the peoples who are in all the provinces of King Ahasuerus. For the queen's behavior will be made known to all women, causing them to look with contempt on their husbands. They will say, "King Ahasuerus commanded Queen Vashti to be brought before him, and she did not come." This very day the noble ladies of Persia and Media who have heard of the queen's behavior will rebel against the king's officials, and there will be no end of contempt and wrath! – Esther 1:16–19

Fearing that Vashti's insubordination would set a precedent for the behavior of wives throughout the empire, the sages advise the king to depose Vashti and give her position to someone more suitable. "When the decree made by the king is proclaimed throughout all his kingdom, vast as it is, all women will give honor to their husbands, high and low alike" (Esther 1:20). The king accepts the proposal and organizes a contest to find a replacement.

The winner is a strikingly beautiful, Jewish woman named Esther. She succeeds, however, not because of her appearance but because she had managed to obtain kindness from a eunuch named Hegai, who served in the palace as "Keeper of the Women." We are not told how she won his favor, yet as a result, she was promoted in the pool of candidates and eventually carried the day.

As Esther later prepares to take Vashti's place as queen, her uncle Mordecai urges her to conceal the identity of her people. Why the secrecy? The narrator does not provide a reason. All we know at this point is that Esther's parents had died, and that Mordecai is a Jewish man living with fellow exiles in Mesopotamia.

Eventually things go awry, and it happens when, once again, an individual refuses to submit. The king had promoted a villainous, narcissistic figure named Haman to the highest rank in his government. Those under him were demonstrating deference by bowing down and doing obeisance. However, one man fails to fall in line, and it is none other than Mordecai.

Why does Uncle Morty refuse to bow to the Persian Pajandram? The reason he offers – that he is a Jew – does not make sense. Nowhere does Jewish law prohibit genuflecting to authorities. Obeisance to idols and foreign gods is, of course, prohibited, but Haman was not expecting the lower ranking officials to worship him. And if for some reason Mordecai felt that what the other officials were doing was beyond the bounds of his personal piety, he could have explained his situation to Haman and paid homage to him in another form.

The nation's existence had long depended on a political flexibility that often required bowing down to superiors. Recall, for example, how the earliest artistic rendering of an Israelite portrays a Northern king (or his emissary) kissing the feet of the Assyrian king (see Chapter 6). What motivates Mordecai's refusal to bow is the same kind of pride and political obstinacy that other biblical texts repudiate. For example, during Babylon's siege of Jerusalem, Jeremiah had rebuked the men of Judah for refusing to compromise. He urged them to "bend your necks to the yoke of Babylon and live!" (Jeremiah 27:12). In the days of Jeremiah, Judah's collective recalcitrance results in conquest and deportation; in the days of Esther, just one man's non-compliance brings all those who survived that conquest and deportation to the brink of annihilation.

Insulted by Mordecai, Haman develops a genocidal plan and approaches the king with a petition:

> There is a people scattered and dispersed among all the other peoples in the provinces of your realm. Their laws are different from those of any other people, and they do not obey the king's laws. It is not in Your

> Majesty's interest to tolerate them. If it please Your Majesty, let an edict be drawn for their destruction, and I will personally pay ten thousand talents of silver to the stewards for deposit in the royal treasury. – Esther 3:8-9

Persuaded by Haman's petition, the king issues a decree that everyone should be ready by a certain day to "destroy, massacre, and exterminate all the Jews, young and old, children and women, and to plunder their possessions."

As soon as Mordecai learns of the edict, he implores his niece, who is now the queen, to intervene. Fearing for her life, Esther refuses to act. He then sends a second message reminding her that she may die anyway. "Who knows? Perhaps you have landed in royalty for such a time as this" (Esther 4:14). Eventually Esther decides to take action, and in the span of time between Mordecai's second message and her response, she undergoes a transformation from object to agent.

Before the budding heroine makes her first move, she solicits the solidarity of her people; their unity will embolden her to act on their behalf. Having long followed orders, she is now the one who issues them. Esther commands Mordecai to assemble all Jews living in the capital and have them fast on her behalf for three days. Thereafter she would go to the king, even though such a move is contrary to the law requiring everyone – including the queen – to have first received an audience from the king. "If I perish, I perish" (Esther 4:16).

As the story continues, Esther proceeds cautiously but courageously, devising an elaborate plan and executing it effectively. As she brings about a reversal of fortune for her people, Haman is hung on the gallows he had built for Mordecai, while Mordecai, the man whose ill-advised actions brought his people to the brink of extermination, is awarded a place of honor, second only to the king.

DISPERSED YET UNITED

On the one hand, Esther is a comedy, one that satirizes imperial power by portraying a mercurial monarch pulled to and fro by those who surround him. On the other hand, it is a sobering parable that depicts pernicious and lethal xenophobia haunting the halls of imperial power.

The book links Esther's story to Purim, a festival still celebrated by Jews across the globe. Whereas other biblical festivals are commanded from on high, Purim evolves from below – and from far and wide. In the book, the *community* collectively create this holiday, and because it is uniquely theirs, it has special significance.

The Jews are described as a united people while simultaneously scattered throughout the empire. In these conditions of diaspora, it is difficult to maintain cohesion and unity, to "stay on the same page." Such would not be the case if everyone were living in the same territory, such as the land of Judah. This book thus depicts "the paradox of diaspora identity: to be *dispersed* and *one* simultaneously."[1]

The book also illustrates the dangers of diaspora, and perhaps its readers should recognize the urgency of returning to the security of their homeland and re-establishing a kingdom of their own. Yet if the book's authors wished to communicate this point, they could have conveyed it in various ways. They present Judah (and Benjamin) as a country whence one comes, not whither one returns.

Now if a kingdom with a native ruler is not an option in this new imperial age, we would expect Jewish communities to call on Yhwh for help. Not surprisingly writings from this period highlight personal piety. They also portray at length, and in diverse ways, how the nation's deity providentially directs world history, both to punish and to protect his people.

The best example of this post-exilic piety is the book of Daniel. The posture that it and similar writings promote is "political quietism" – communities focusing on their own internal affairs and leaving governance to their God and the imperial powers that he guides. But in Esther, quietism, or any calm acceptance of things as they are, is not an option. The Jews are about to be annihilated, and instead of intervening in the nick of time, God is nowhere to be found. As such, the book stands in stark contrast to Daniel's depiction of Jewish young men openly practicing their piety, defying imperial decrees, marching intrepidly to martyrdom, and then receiving a miraculous intervention from their deity (first in a fiery furnace and then in a den of lions).

[1] Beal, *The Book of Hiding*, p. 55.

Esther offers a counterpoint to these writings, and it does so by posing a basic question: is it possible to live as a Jew without residing in the homeland, praying to the nation's deity, and living according to the commandments? The answer it offers is a resounding yes.

It is not as if the authors are secularists or uninterested in theological matters. Rather they have consciously created a God-sized void in their story, a void that the protagonists do not pray to be filled. God remains hidden throughout the book, and the authors went to great lengths to keep it that way.

DIFFERENCE AND DIPLOMACY

Esther is one of first writings to speak of Jews, rather than Judeans. Notice that Mordecai comes from the tribe of Benjamin, and as such, we would expect the authors to call him "Mordecai the Benjaminite." However, he and the community to which he belongs are consistently called *yehudim*, which must mean here not "Judean" in the territorial sense but "Jew" in the ethnic sense. In line with a long development that we can trace to the earliest Northern writings, Jews are now no longer those who live in Judah but those who, dispersed throughout the world, behave Jewishly. As we have seen, Judah had long lived in the shadow of the Northern kingdom of Israel, but now their name is applied to all inhabitants of the nation.

Haman does not imagine destroying Judah, Mordecai's ancestral homeland, but Jewish communities throughout the empire. When letters and decrees are dispatched, they are translated into 127 different languages, implying that Jews inhabit every province from India to Ethiopia.

And others know who they are. When the tide finally turns in the Jews' favor, many peoples of the provinces adopt Jewish identity markers (literally, they "Judaized," Esther 8:17). However, in keeping with the book's sophisticated strategy, it never says what these markers are.

This work has a minimalistic approach to Jewish identity. Yes, Jews have distinctive laws and customs, but we are left wondering what these laws and customs are. What unites far-flung communities in this story is their "otherness." Their laws and customs are simply different from those of other peoples. They have not assimilated, and their distinctiveness elicits hate. All are consigned to death because of the mistake of one man, "Mordecai the Jew."

As a people apart, the Jews are easy to identify and therefore vulnerable to hostility. The solution is not for them to give up their otherness and fit in. During Purim, both then and now, Jews celebrate that they managed to survive crisis and upheaval. They made it through another year without having to renounce their non-conformist ways. Purim and the story of Esther both honor the freedom to be different and recognize the antipathy that this difference often elicits.

To be different in a world that does not value difference, one needs diplomacy, and this book depicts its lead character with a savvy that saves her people. Esther seems to have this quality at the beginning when she manages to win the favor of Hegai, who promotes her over her competitors in the palace. But now the stakes are much higher, and she is reluctant to overplay her hand. When she eventually decides to act, she devises a shrewd strategy, inviting the king and Haman to a series of banquets. While they are drinking wine, she waits for the king to grant her a wish and then responds in the most diplomatic manner:

> If I have won your favor, O king,
> and if it pleases the king,
> let my life be given me – that is my petition,
> and the lives of my people – that is my request.
> For we have been sold, I and my people,
> to be destroyed, to be killed, and to be annihilated.
> If we had been sold merely as slaves, men and women,
> I would have held my peace.
> For this adversary is not even worthy of the king's trouble.
> – Esther 7:3–7

Notice how her entreaty, which she frames in exquisite poetic form, appeals to the king's fondness for her and refers to her people only in the second instance. Moreover, she never says who her people are and insists that she would not have inconvenienced the king were the situation not life-threatening. To clinch her case, she makes a point of not identifying the culprit by name.

When immediately thereafter the king learns that the offender is none other than Haman, who was at the time enjoying honors at the royal table, he rises in wrath and retreats to the palace garden.

Meanwhile Haman tarries behind, begging Esther that she spare his life. By the time the king returns to the banquet hall, Haman had thrown himself on the couch where Esther was reclining. The king exclaims: "Will he even assault the queen in my presence, in my own house?"

What follows is the reversal of fortune on which the story depends and which the carnivalesque festival of Purim celebrates:

> As the words left the mouth of the king, they covered Haman's face. Then Harbona, one of the eunuchs in attendance on the king, said, "Look, the very gallows that Haman has prepared for Mordecai, whose word saved the king, stands at Haman's house, fifty cubits high." And the king said, "Hang him on that." So they hung Haman on the gallows that he had prepared for Mordecai. Then the anger of the king abated. – Esther 7:9–10

In this new imperial context, Jewish otherness is perilous. This is a world in which the king on the throne is not one of their own and is easily susceptible to nefarious influence. Diaspora without diplomacy is dangerous. For every Mordecai, one needs an Esther – leaders who infiltrate the inner recesses of power and, with cool-headed efficiency, repair damage done by male egos.

ESTHER AS THE ARCHETYPE

At the beginning of the book, both Esther and her community are passive, seemingly helpless in the face of Haman's deadly decree. Yet as the story unfolds, both evolve into active agents, ones who take control of their individual and corporate lives.

With confined agency both at home and abroad, Jewish communities had much in common with Esther. In his study of this book, Aaron Koller suggests: "It was with the female that the Jews of the Diaspora likely identified. The female may be taken as a symbol of the less powerful and less confrontational, but potentially more subversive and more effective in resisting."[2]

Laffey's suggestion supports what we have seen throughout Part IV. Biblical writings hold up women as identification figures and role models

[2] Koller, *Esther in Ancient Jewish Thought*, p. 77.

for their readers, and one of the reasons they do is that both women as a gender and Judeans/Jews as a nationality were in weaker social positions. They therefore needed to adopt more cunning means if they wished to achieve their goals. With the loss of political autonomy, the received models of martial valor, mirrored in Mordecai's defiance, had to give way to alternatives.

Closely aligned with this alternative identity is a different morality – that of the outsider, underdog, trickster, and "wily woman." Conventional codes of honor, more often than not, protect the powerful, and the biblical writings show how an alternative approach was crucial to their people's survival in an age of foreign rule.

Not only is Esther an archetype for a new Jewish identity, but she also communicates women's empowerment. As such, her book joins other late works that celebrate the contributions of women. To reiterate a point from Chapters 22 and 23, if many biblical writings highlight women's roles, it is because their authors realized that their participation in public life was desperately needed. Facing new challenges, Jewish communities could not afford to exclude half of their population.

It is noteworthy that Esther's story begins with Vashti spurning the drunk king's request to parade herself before his male guests. Here and throughout the story, the authors lampoon the male ego, which compensates for its insecurity and fragility with fits of wrath and rage. The king and his sages are convinced that Vashti's insubordination would bring down their imperial order, with wives from all classes refusing to obey their husbands. Their imperial rule rests on intimidation and domination.

The authors could have found a different way to introduce their protagonist, but they included this scene as a foil for a young woman who matures into a courageous agent of change. In charting Esther's passage from powerlessness to a position of authority, this book moves women from the bedroom to the boardroom. It authors take pride in imagining that the exceptional beauty of one of their own had the capacity to secure her a place on the throne of the Persian Empire. But in their account, it is her other qualities that carry the day.

Esther's initial reluctance and hesitation are crucial to her success. We like our heroes bold. We want them to leap into action like Superman or Wonder Woman, wholeheartedly embracing the cause. We want them to take a stand and not back down. We want them to march out fearlessly against the enemy, as when the young David takes up his sling against the giant Goliath. That is why the defiant Vashti often gets more cheers from modern readers than the diffident Esther.

Vashti's actions are courageous and commendable, but they are not canny or calculated and therefore bring about no lasting change. She is banished, and wives throughout the empire suffer because of her insubordination. Likewise, when Mordecai stands up to power, his macho obstinacy unleashes vindictive recriminations and a genocidal decree. In this book, what succeeds is Esther's circumspection.

As part of her punishment, Vashti forfeits her privileged place, yet she does not face execution. Esther, in contrast, cannot afford to be so brazen. She works within a system that had long been chauvinist and had recently become xenophobic and genocidal. The success of her plan communicates a political point: Jewish communities might long for more hospitable conditions and a world in which they do not have live in fear. But in the meantime, one must survive, and that means behaving like Esther, not Mordecai and not Vashti.

THE MOST BIBLICAL BOOK

Like other biblical books, Esther affirms the primacy of peoplehood, but in contrast to others, it reduces peoplehood to the essentials. By jettisoning theology, religious observance, life in the homeland, and many other principles that other biblical writings promote, its authors made room for a broader community.

Portraying peoplehood in its purest form, Esther might be the most biblical book. Throughout the ages, Jewish communities have devoted more commentary to it than any other work outside the Pentateuch. In keeping with the book's minimalist approach to Jewish identity, the rabbis of late antiquity declared that a Jew is none other than one who shows up each year at Purim for the reading of Esther, which they call "the Scroll."

Even if Esther does not champion the content of other biblical books, it promotes their larger vision. The book illustrates principles that permeate the biblical corpus, including fasting and feasting, shared laws, public reading of texts, women in leadership, repudiation of machismo, joining forces across borders, gift-giving, and feeding the poor (see Esther 9:24). Defending these strategies, Esther demonstrates their viability and potency even when they are not accompanied by a concomitant attachment to God, land, and covenant. The book may even be understood as a parallel program to the one laid out in the Pentateuch. The one promoted by Esther is certainly more modest in its ritual and legal expectations, yet it pursues the same agenda of uniting a people in the absence of native sovereignty.

The book's audience is a community with a power deficit living in an inhospitable, and often outright hostile, world. Its authors recognized that being different is not something that one can always conceal. However, they were convinced that by behaving shrewdly and showing solidarity, their communities could carry on.

In this new age of foreign imperial rule, there is no David to deliver a blow to the nation's adversaries, and the nation cannot wait for another Moses to liberate it through miraculous interventions. The world now is much more perilous. God's face is hidden. Things can easily go awry. The lots are not always cast to the nation's advantage.

This book depicts the doom of the defiant, when standing up to antagonists only brings more suffering. Whereas Exodus portrays the departure from these precarious conditions and the creation of something new, Esther urges its readers to come to terms with the world as it is. Even so, it builds on the achievement of Exodus, demonstrating the power of peoplehood even when deprived of the divine deliverance that gave rise to it.

FURTHER READING

Beal, Timothy K., *The Book of Hiding: Gender, Ethnicity, Annihilation, and Esther*, Routledge, 1997.

Berlin, Adele, *Esther: The Traditional Hebrew Text with the New JPS Translation*, Jewish Publication Society, 2001.

Fox, Michael V., *Character and Ideology in the Book of Esther*, Eerdmans, 1991.

Hancock, Rebecca S., *Esther and the Politics of Negotiation: Public and Private Spaces and the Figure of the Female Royal Counselor*, Fortress, 2013.

Koller, Aaron, *Esther in Ancient Jewish Thought*, Cambridge University Press, 2014.

Laffey, Alice L., *An Introduction to the Old Testament: A Feminist Perspective,* Fortress, 1988.

Macchi, Jean-Daniel, *Esther* (International Exegetical Commentary on the Old Testament), Kohlhammer, 2019.

Mapfeka, Tsaurayi Kudakwashe, *Esther in Diaspora: Toward an Alternative Interpretive Framework*, Brill, 2019.

Miller, Tricia, *Three Versions of Esther: Their Relationship to Anti-Semitic and Feminist Critique of the Story*, Peeters, 2014.

Southwood, Katherine E. and Halvorson-Taylor, Martien A. (eds.), *Women and Exilic Identity in the Hebrew Bible*, Bloomsbury, 2018.

Stone, Meredith J., *Empire and Gender in LXX Esther*, SBL Press, 2018.

Yarden, Ophir, "Jewish Not Judean: The Diaspora in the Book of Esther," *TheTorah.com*, 2022, www.thetorah.com/article/jewish-not-judean-the-diaspora-in-the-book-of-esther.

30

Conclusions

Nations, Nationalism, and New Bibles

SPEAKING AT A EUROPEAN ACADEMIC CONFERENCE, the American biblical scholar Bernard Levinson pointed out that cuneiform literature from ancient West Asia contains, in isolation, "almost all the individual phenomena that we associate with the Bible," including textual stabilization, a textual curriculum, memorization and study of texts, and texts acting as forms of acculturation. The literary genres are also for the most part the same, with their legal collections, theophany texts, prophetic utterances, rituals, omens, laments, hymns, prayers, and proverb collections. Moreover, our analyses of these texts reveal similar scribal techniques, such as superscriptions, acrostics, annotation, and colophons. Yet there is, according to Levinson, a crucial difference between biblical and cuneiform literature:

> [I]n the ancient Near East, none of this material ever came together to form anything like a scripture, either with its distinctive textual features, like the dense weave of inter-textual connections that hold the separate parts together, let alone with its distinctive ideological features, such as the truth claims it mounts, the extraordinary demands for adherence it requires from its audience to uphold the demands it seeks to place upon them, or the polemics it makes opposing competing ideologies.[1]

Levinson goes on to point out how the Bible is unique in the ancient world for bringing together different and rival collections of law; integrating ritual, criminal, and civil matters; and embedding them in a larger narrative. The organization of the entire biblical corpus rejects

[1] Levinson, "The Development of the Jewish Bible," p. 387.

not only historical verisimilitude but also generic consistency (i.e., books are not grouped according to literary genre). For the past two centuries, the field of academic biblical scholarship has occupied itself in the composition history of this diverse, didactic, counterintuitive corpus. In doing so, however, it has neglected an issue of wide-ranging intellectual significance: "The remarkable issue is not *how* the Bible developed but *that* it developed altogether."[2]

The Bible is indeed an astounding achievement. Nowhere else in the ancient world do we witness a people's effort – and such an elaborate and collaborative effort at that – first to document and depict their own defeat, and then to use this narrative history as a framework for rethinking every facet of their existence.

Our point of departure has been the *why*. While we devoted significant space to the *who*, the *what*, the *when*, and the *where*, we did not stop there. Our larger concern has been the Bible's raison d'être, its why and wherefore.

If this issue of "intentionality" is not one that my colleagues in biblical studies have often addressed, it is because many work on an assumption that the Bible's contents represent essentially a cross-section of "ancient Israel's library" (albeit edited from a Judean and Jerusalemite perspective). In keeping with this assumption, many seasoned scholars still confuse the biblical depiction with the historical reality, as if our texts reflect common ways of thinking and behaving in ancient Israel and Judah.

Our study charted a different path. We began by surveying the histories of the Northern kingdom of Israel and the Southern kingdom of Judah. As we saw in Part I, these states were located not at the centers of ancient civilization (in Mesopotamia and Egypt), but on a land-bridge that connected these centers. They and their neighbors in the region lived in the superpowers' shadows, and they were acutely aware of their precarious position in world affairs. In contrast, the imperial powers that emerged in Mesopotamia and Egypt had long taken their preeminent positions for granted, and when they fell, they did so precipitously, leaving few survivors to preserve their legacies.

[2] Ibid.

It makes sense that places of power and privilege, like Nineveh and Babylon, did not launch projects of peoplehood in response to their downfall. But many other smaller kingdoms were conquered. Why then was it scribes from Israel and Judah who took the extraordinary steps of not only admitting defeat but also commemorating it and making it the foundation for such an innovative project of peoplehood?

As we learned in Parts II and III, defeat is a necessary condition for the making of the Bible, but it is not a sufficient condition. In addition to defeat, our explanation pointed to *division*. Without the special relationship between two kingdoms, there would be no Bible. North and South had long been divided, and they had repeatedly come to blows in long civil wars.

What first ignited the biblical project was a vision that the populations of these two rival states could be one people. Working for the royal court in Jerusalem, Judean scribes imagined a "United Monarchy" that later split into two competing kingdoms. This was above all an affirmation of political unity. Yet even if it was statist in its agenda, this older work inspired others – especially members of the recently conquered Northern kingdom – to think in terms of a nation that transcends the borders of its kingdoms. Diminishing the role of the throne, these circles composed counter-narratives, portraying a large family evolving into a diverse nation and existing for many generations before the establishment of the monarchy. After the downfall of the Southern kingdom, the counter-narratives were joined to the older account of Israel's monarchies. The combined work grew to its present epic proportions as it was supplemented with law codes and didactic stories that address all aspects of what it means to be a people, and what a people needs to prosper.

By demonstrating the limits of native sovereignty, the programs of destruction and deportation pursued by the world's first empires provoked the vanquished to re-evaluate received wisdom and to conceive new ways of belonging. Across the four parts of our study, we saw that the generations of scribes who curated the biblical corpus were profoundly political in their orientation. Their aim was not to transform Israel from a people into a religious sect after the kingdom's downfall. On the contrary, these scribes sought to construct a robust and resilient *national* identity ("peoplehood") capable of withstanding military defeat and the encroachment of expansionist powers. Their effort is the earliest, and still one of most breathtaking, of its kind, and throughout history, political communities have often imagined themselves as peoples and nations by looking to biblical Israel.

Rather than a conventional polarity of nation versus religious community, what we witness in the formation of the biblical corpus is the groundbreaking discovery of a distinction that we take for granted today – namely, between nation and state. The decisive step that these scribes took was to bracket an era of the monarchy, presenting it as a turning point in their people's history. In the framework of an extensive prose narrative, these ancient intellectuals sought to demonstrate how Israel became a people long before it established a kingdom. Although their narrative runs counter to what we know about Israel's political evolution, they wanted their audience to understand that – via a national narrative and the laws embedded in it – a vanquished, exiled, and divided population can come together as a people even when imperial domination prohibited political independence.

The scribes who engaged in this effort were convinced that their communities would survive conquest and colonization when they had not only a spiritual vision but also a material incentive to take an active part in public life. Instead of abandoning world affairs and political engagement, the biblical scribes worked to unify them as members of a new nation. As they reimagined Israel's corporate identity, these scribes asked themselves what it means to be a people. Their responses to this foundational question – formulated in the widest array of genres: law, narrative, songs, laments, prophecies, wisdom, and love poetry – charted important new territory in political philosophy.

That Israel and Judah produced a Bible is not because an early form monotheism or unique intuitions permeated these societies. The reason is rather that generations of anonymous, counter-cultural thinkers pushed against the status quo and sought real, pragmatic truth that could sustain their communities in a world governed by foreign powers.

In grappling with the consequences of defeat, these thinkers resorted to something no army could conquer: language and the power of the written word. Their efforts in collecting, editing, and expanding texts resulted in an exceptionally rich corpus of literature, which attracted communities of readers and formed them into one people. The Bible's model of peoplehood embraces diversity, an ideal exemplified in the weaving together of competing traditions and texts. Although this corpus is heavily redacted, it does not speak with a single voice. Instead of one view, its authors set forth a shared text.

The scribes who contributed to this project were seeking to fashion an unprecedented corporate identity capable of consolidating and mobilizing a subjugated, dispersed nation, and the writings they produced have inspired populations across the globe to form robust and resilient communities. Thinkers and activists have found in the Hebrew Bible alternatives to the status quo – political identities that assign power to the people as a whole, rather than to monarchies, aristocracies, corporations, state and ecclesial institutions. Likewise, the Bible has consistently been at the center of literacy initiatives, while others have learned from the Bible the role of canons of common literature in fostering a collective national conscious.

As a Jew teaching in a Christian seminary, I work with students in learning how to bring the Hebrew Bible to bear not only on their work in the parish but also on their engagement in the public sphere. Many of our students are troubled by the growing scourge of Christian nationalism, both in the United States and across the globe. To confront the challenge it poses, and to counter its simplistic use and cynical abuse of biblical texts, we are committed to studying and communicating the Hebrew Bible's grand vision for a nation — one founded not on military might and ethnic purity, but on education and love for one's neighbor.

To help students dissociate the term "nation" from its associations with "nationalism," I assign several readings that provoke deep reflection on the nature of political community. These include Kwame Anthony Appiah's *The Ethics of Identity*, Martha C. Nussbaum's *For Love of Country?*, and Jill Lepore's *This America: The Case for the Nation.* These works lay out, succinctly and brilliantly, the deep chasm separating patriotism from nationalism. It is a big jump from love for, and solidarity with, the citizens of your country, to a chauvinistic, jingoistic sense of superiority that is deeply suspicious of newcomers and outsiders.

Like patriotism, and in sharp contrast to nationalism, the Bible's notion of peoplehood is about members of a political community coming together to make positive contributions for the wider world and for the future of our globe. To borrow language from Jill Lepore, nationalism is about *who we are not*, while peoplehood is about *who we are*. One feeds on insecurity, fear, and hate. The other grows out of love, openness toward the other, and hope for the future.

We might deem the biblical model of peoplehood to be a far cry from an equitable, egalitarian social-political order. If the nation is required to worship a single deity at a single place and in a precise manner, where is there room for the most basic religious freedoms?

Needless to say, the biblical writers were after something different from the concerns of modern secular democracies. However, by appealing to a shared past, kinship, written laws, and a single deity, the scribes who produced our texts were not seeking, first and foremost, to *eliminate* communities from the national fold. Their project was more about inclusion than exclusion. Similarly, the later process of canonization was more about the collection and incorporation of texts representing competing traditions and communities, even if it also meant the omission of that which was deemed to be deleterious to a sustainable national identity.

This book has explored how biblical texts construct bonds of filiation that hold together competing communities, and we have much to learn from the authors of these texts. They realized that law without a story was ineffective. Thus, the command to "love your neighbor as yourself" is followed throughout the narrative by stories that answer the question, "Who is my neighbor?" Likewise, the command to "love the stranger" is embedded in a larger narrative that portrays Israel's origins as a group of refugees who make their way to a new land after escaping bondage; this story of liberation lays the foundation for the law.

The promulgation of law can provoke deep resentment if it does not draw on shared experiences. This is the job of storytelling. Nations need narration, and perhaps the biggest challenge faced by political communities is finding a way for our members to tell their stories – a way that, by being both honest and inclusive, has the capacity to engender a real sense of kinship and solicitude for our neighbor's welfare. If there is anything that the history of ancient Israel and its neighbors can teach us, it is that without such a narrative, we are destined to perish.

The Hebrew Bible models a robust and persistent engagement around issues of belonging. Though often wielded in contemporary political debates as if it were a static authority, this corpus is characterized by lively exchanges from competing perspectives and across generations. Our study has laid bare the textured fabric of these exchanges, with scribes skillfully weaving new materials into the narrative tapestry they inherited from earlier generations.

Is the biblical model of peoplehood adaptable to the exigencies of modern secular democracies? Perhaps not. But the task at hand is to find new ways of bolstering a sense of kinship, as the biblical authors did in their time. Both then and now, the most powerful means of creating community is to tell stories. At this moment of populistic upheaval – fomented by cynical, corrupt leaders who deem themselves to be above the law – we need narratives that reflect the diversity of our communities, temper the hostility that often characterizes national discourses, and offer tangible reasons why we should cultivate affection for our laws. As we create these narratives, perhaps we will discover a unifying force under whose aegis we will be able to face an otherwise frightening future.

Our countries face ever-widening rifts between political persuasions, religions, ethnic groups, regions, generations, and classes. Building on insights from Steven Prothero's project of *The American Bible* and Rogers M. Smith's *Stories of Peoplehood*, perhaps what we need are new bibles – collections of narratives, laws, wisdom, poetry, and songs like the Hebrew Bible that inspire citizens to engage in a deep conversation about what it means to be a people.

Today there is widespread opposition to the notion of canons and national narratives, as they have historically tended to be discriminatory and prejudicial. But canons need not be closed, just as a narrative need not be simple, linear, or singular. The advantage they afford is that they stimulate a debate that not only has deeper historical dimensions but also can appeal to a common set of texts. To be effective, these new bibles must approximate the richness, complexity, and diversity of the Bible. They must follow the ancient scribes not only in collecting and canonizing our disparate, and often competing, traditions, but also in publishing them in accessible new media. Above all, these new bibles must stimulate reflection on what it means to be a people and inspire a sense of kinship, devotion to justice, and love for neighbor.

But what about the future of the Bible itself? Throughout its history, it has traditionally been interpreted by those for whom it is sacred scripture and thus authoritative and normative. That history is one of the reasons why most of us today would be reticent to grant it a place in the public square. To be sure, the biblical writings historically have informed many of our national identities and continue to make themselves felt in our public discourse through private – and often uneducated and intolerant – channels.

Going forward, the Bible can continue to shape our public cultures if we are willing to assign it a new role. It cannot be taken as normative. But it can be mined for wisdom – wisdom that bears directly on questions of corporate life, common welfare, and collective survival.

In her courses for the past three decades at the University of Chicago, Martha Nussbaum has demonstrated the indispensable philosophical value of reading classical Greek literature, even when we do not believe that Zeus lives on Mount Olympus. Likewise, we would not deny that *Moby Dick* reveals deep truths about the human condition just because Ahab never actually captained a ship called *Pequod*. The same goes for the Bible. Even as agnostics and atheists, we can appreciate the political truths preserved on its pages.

The promise for the Bible's new role is great. Its original purpose was to create an alternative form of political community, one that could weather the most devastating crises. As such, it holds invaluable insights for us as we strive to build more just and resilient societies.

FURTHER READING

Appiah, Kwame Anthony, *The Ethics of Identity*, Princeton University Press, 2007.

Lepore, Jill, *These Truths: A History of the United States*, Norton, 2019.

Lepore, Jill, *This America: The Case for the Nation*, Liveright, 2019.

Nussbaum, Martha C., *For Love of Country? Debating the Limits of Patriotism*, Beacon Press, 1996.

Levinson, Bernard, "The Development of the Jewish Bible," in Karin Finsterbusch and Armin Lange (eds.), *What is Bible?*, Peeters, 2012.

Prothero, Stephen, *The American Bible: How Our Words, Unite, Divide, and Define a Nation*, Harper One, 2012.

Smith, Rogers M., *Stories of Peoplehood: The Politics and Morals of Political Membership*, Cambridge University Press, 2003.

Subject Index

In lieu of a glossary, a simple definition of technical terms is usually provided the first time they appear in the text.

Scholars Cited

Biblical References